Mobile Virtual Work

J. H. Erik Andriessen · Matti Vartiainen
(Editors)

Mobile Virtual Work

A New Paradigm?

With 60 Figures and 26 Tables

 Springer

Professor J. H. Erik Andriessen
Delft University of Technology
Department of Work and Organisational Psychology
Jaffalaan 5
2628 Delft
The Netherlands
j.h.t.h.andriessen@tbm.tudelft.nl

Professor Matti Vartiainen
Helsinki University of Technology
Laboratory of Work Psychology and Leadership
P.O. Box 5500
02015 TKK Espoo
Finland
matti.vartiainen@tkk.fi

ISBN-10   3-540-28364-1 Springer Berlin Heidelberg New York
ISBN-13   978-3-540-28364-5 Springer Berlin Heidelberg New York

Cataloging-in-Publication Data
Library of Congress Control Number: 2005932315

Springer is a part of Springer Science+Business Media

springeronline.com

© Springer Berlin · Heidelberg 2006
Printed in Germany

Hardcover-Design: Erich Kirchner, Heidelberg

SPIN 11541707   42/3153-5 4 3 2 1 0 – Printed on acid-free paper

Preface

Dear Reader

This is a book about mobile virtual work. It aims at clarifying the basic concepts and showing present practices and future challenges. The roots of the book are in the collaboration of few European practitioners and researchers, who met each other under the umbrella of the Swedish SALTSA programme (see next page) in January 2002 in Stockholm. The group was first called 'ICT, Mobility and Work Organisation' but redefined itself quickly as 'Mobile Virtual Cooperative Work' group. The change of the name reflects the development of reasoning in the group. We could not find much material on mobile work, certainly not systematic studies, although a growing interest in mobile technologies and services could be found. Practices of telework and virtual organizations were better known, but we were convinced that the combination with mobile work was something different and new. Our main target became to understand what it was all about.

The next step was an expert meeting in October 2004 at Rånäs Castle again in Sweden. A wider group of experts was invited to present their views on mobile virtual work and ideas about book chapters from different perspectives of working life. Some of the expertise could be found through the network of the AMI@Work family created by the New Working Environments unit of the European Commission's Information Society Directorate-General. Also close collaboration was developed with the related MOSAIC program.

Today, much more is known about mobile work systems as can be seen in the following chapters. There are now many other researchers and practitioners in this field. Mobile business models are being developed, bringing along human, organizational and societal challenges.

With this book we realise our intention to present a 'state of the art' collection of knowledge on this subject. We very much hope that you will find the discussion about present day reality and future challenges of mobile virtual work as exciting as we do. It is possibly a new paradigm.

Erik Andriessen   Matti Vartiainen
Delft, The Netherlands   Helsinki, Finland

SALTSA

A Joint Programme for Working Life Research in Europe

SALTSA is a programme for research on European working life run in close co-operation by the National Institute for Working Life in Sweden and the Swedish Confederation of Trade Unions (LO), the Swedish Confederation of Professional Employess (TCO) and the Swedish Confederation of Professional Associations (SACO).

The aim of SALTSA is to generate applicable research results of high academic standard and practical relevance. Research is carried out in areas like labour market and employment, labour law, work organisation and health and safety.

http://www.arbetslivsinstitutet.se/saltsa

JOINT PROGRAMME
FOR WORKING LIFE RESEARCH IN EUROPE
The National Institute for Working Life and The Swedish Trade Unions in Co-operation

Contents

Part 1

Concepts and Prevalence

1 Emerging Mobile Virtual Work

Erik Andriessen[1] and Matti Vartiainen[2]

[1]Faculty of Technology, Policy and Management, Delft University of Technology, The Netherlands
[2]Laboratory of Work Psychology and Leadership, Helsinki University of Technology, Finland

1.1 Fundamental changes and driving forces

Something new is happening in the nature of organisations and the role of employees, a change that may be indicated by the concept of 'Mobile and Virtual Work (MVW)'. This type of work is already a reality in different business areas with mobile customer services, such as sales, logistics, maintenance, and professional services like consulting or health care. These developments do not only take place in the commercial world, but also in public and non-profit sectors.

A number of driving forces let us expect that this type of work is rapidly gaining momentum in working life worldwide. Some of the driving forces are related to reducing costs and increasing economical outcomes. Others grow out of the needs and preferences of employees. The driving forces form an interwoven set of relationships. They can be clustered into a) societal forces including technology and b) organisational and individual choices.

A driving force is the competition in the markets and new business practices, e.g. a globalised business is not possible with a local organisation. Ongoing globalisation of markets and businesses leads to higher mobility requirements and widely distributed international cooperation. Customers of a product and talents needed to create a product or a service are globally dispersed. Products and services are getting more and more complex and are, to an increasing extent, being based on knowledge from different domains and disciplines. This means that they require growing efforts to bring together and combine multiple expertises and competences in order to create specific customer solutions. Customer orientation as a strategic business perspective requires higher efforts in exploring customer needs, in shaping and streamlining products and services according to these needs, and in providing comprehensive after sales services for maintaining their effectiveness.

Technology is a driving force or at least an important enabler. Technological changes, particularly the developments in mobile and wireless information and communication technologies (ICT), create possibilities to work in any place and time. This driver is closely related to the business driver, because of economical benefits it potentially implies. The European Information Technology Observatory (2004) forecasts that although many mobile applications and services are still in their infancy, the demand of technology and services will grow, because of the following reasons: the number of mobile employees is to increase in Europe sharply in the coming years, the number and features of hand-held equipments increase as well, wireless LAN spreads, Bluetooth replaces cables, 3G is implemented, and operators develop their assortment, when broadband networks are widely implemented. Mobile technology opens a new perspective to products, services, work and organisation by increasing possibilities to select more freely the place of working, and by allowing higher mobility than "wired" technologies. Salesmen, auditors, consultants, patrolling police, truck drivers, ambulance staff, on-site customer service and repair and maintenance groups are some of the most common examples of physically mobile workers using mobile technologies and services. Many other professions have a strong mobile element as their job content.

A driving force may even be a new strategic thought or a theoretical construct, e.g. an idea of developing a virtual community to increase mutual learning and creativity may start the design of new technology to support it, and later create new business opportunities. When Marshall McLuhan forecasted the "global village" in the 1960s, he was, in fact, speaking of the dispersed, virtual workplace.

The role and significance of people and their needs and habits cannot be underestimated. Needs and benefits of citizens – customers in the case of companies – are in the end a decisive factor in the implementation of both mobile technologies and forms of organisations.

These drivers constitute some of the major forces in this arena. In the following chapters more specific factors are discussed (see e.g. the chapters of Gareis and of Schaffers in this volume) The market side together with the technological changes stimulate the demand side, i.e. what needs to be done and how. Demographic and social changes influence the supply side, i.e. the kind of workers that are available. The impacts of the major changing forces on the world of work are mediated by inter-organisational structures and strategies; and the interaction between all these forces takes place in a larger political-economic-societal context.

Altogether, the implications of these rather general and lasting trends for work requirements sum up to increased shares of MVW in business and work processes. The direct consequence of this all is to be found in the growth of distributed work processes, network organisations, physical mobility of workers and intensive interaction through various ICT tools. The development of mobile virtual work can, therefore, be highly attractive, both for companies who in this way can become more flexible, effective and innovative, and for those employees who prefer dynamic work environments or a more flexible integration of work and private life.

At the same time, we see indications of more fundamental and sometimes negative developments. The possibilities for professional development and learning of employees who do not meet colleagues face-to-face may be limited. Working in a dispersed and mobile manner requires new skills and competences both from employees and leaders. The social cohesion (social capital) in organisations may face large gaps when workers are not only geographically distributed, but also have less fixed contractual relations with companies. The management of work may become quite difficult when intellectual and social capital is threatened by new organisational arrangements. On the other hand, new technologies make the monitoring and control of employees often much easier, even from afar.

This requires a new deal between employers and employees. And wellbeing may suffer from work under high time pressure without social support. If one works at varying places new social and emotional requirements are needed. The balance of work and family life may be shaken, because work is brought to home. There are also some signs of the increasing digital divide not only between continents and countries but also inside countries. For example, statistics show that big companies have better resources than small- and medium-sized companies to invest on new technologies. One of the main reasons not to implement wireless and mobile technologies and to increase working outside the main office is the issue of security. The weaknesses in the security of transferring information and confidential knowledge in the Internet are real challenges, which slow down the development of e-business models.

Summarising, it appears that the trends toward mobile and virtual work processes are central in a wider process. A process, in which organisations become less integrated, both geographically and in terms of employment, and a process, in which people may become more independent but possibly also isolated both socially and contractually. It is a trend toward less bureaucracy and more interaction in terms of communities. But the new possibilities can bring risks, and short-term effectiveness may conflict with long-term sustainability. Before organisations become too optimistic about the alleged virtues of mobile and virtual work processes they may consider whether this development is really essential for their business or not. What is needed is the design and implementation of high-performance work processes. By high-performance we mean processes that are effective and sustainable at the same time: They are effective in that production and innovation are according to intentions, with controlled effort; and they are sustainable in that they regenerate rather than consume individual and social resources needed and used in work.

In our view, this implies an integrated socio-technical approach. Information and communication technology is the instrument and medium through which MVW is enabled, but not determined. In contrast, we consider the forms and requirements of the task and of the social interaction of the workers collaborating in MVW as shaping the actual work process and determine the performance and quality of the business they are designed for. Consequently, computer technology has to meet work-oriented social requirements in order to be a support rather than a hindrance for work, while, at the same time, the functionality of the networked ICT systems impose specific action requirements on the collaborating workers.

1.2 What is Mobile Virtual Work?

Is there a difference between MVW and the traditional concept of telework? The chapters of Gareis and Helle will show that there is quite some overlap. But the term telework is often associated to home-based telework and is strongly related to an individual's preference to do the work on another place than the traditional office. The concepts of mobile and virtual are, however, to be associated with the work content and with a change in organisational processes, which makes mobile and virtual work necessary.

The definition of Mobile Virtual Work and related terms is taken up in several of the following chapters (see particularly the chapter by Vartiainen). As will become clear, one has to distinguish between mobile workers, mobile work and mobile technology. Mobile workers are employees that work at and move between different work places. The concept of mobile work has two meanings, i.e. in a stricter sense the documents and tasks that move, either physically or digitally, but in a wider sense it is also used to refer to the work of mobile worker. The concept of mobile technology is also used in two different ways. It may refer both to portable ICT tools (e.g. laptops) and to all the tools and infrastructures (e.g. the Internet) that support mobile workers and work.

The term mobile is often associated with individuals, although of course a team can be mobile to a certain degree in the sense that all or some of its members are sometimes physically mobile during their work.

Virtual is a concept that is used in various frameworks, such as virtual working space and virtual group or organisation. Virtual space is an Internet-based or intranet-based electronic working environment, in which documents, messages and images and even representations of people, i.e. avatars, are stored, exchanged, retrieved and worked. Virtual spaces are used for communication and collaboration.

The 'virtual group' concept signifies that a number of persons are to a certain extent dispersed in space, sometimes in time, and that a substantial part of their communication is through the media. The concept of virtual organisation may be understood in the same way. In fact, being virtual is a matter of degree. A virtual group or a virtual organisation is not so much a pure form as a continuum for describing a range of relationships along the dimensions of space, time, culture and organisational boundary. Relative to the traditional organisation, relationships in the virtual organisation are more geographically distributed, more asynchronous, more multicultural, and more likely to extent outside the firm. There is, however, also literature that considers a virtual organisation as a network of legally independent companies that acts as one organisation vis a vis a client. Thus, virtual organisations can be classified into levels of networks, companies, projects, teams and dyads.

Apart from space, time and ICT use, other dimensions are sometimes also parts of an author's concept of virtuality, such as the diversity of members, e.g. different cultural background and language, and the looseness of contractual binding of the members (see also the chapter by Vartiainen). Mobility is a feature closely related to the use of different spaces and tools for communication and collaboration. However, for many authors in this book these aspects are not considered and discussed in their analysis.

The focus on mobile virtual work implies that we are generally interested in settings were physically distributed and mobile people interact through digital infrastructures and mobile tools to perform their tasks in an organisational context that has a mobility oriented structure and culture. Strictly speaking this definition may also apply to the traditional physician that calls his assistant by telephone, while being at a patient's home. The phenomenon of mobile virtual work becomes, however, only interesting and challenging when dealing with new forms of mobility and when dealing with new forms of technological support, in the framework of flexible work arrangements, and network organisations.

1.3 Objectives and general design of a research program

This book is the result of two forums: a SALTSA[1] workgroup on Mobile Collaborative Virtual Work (MCVW), which started its work in January 2002, and a workshop of experts held in autumn 2004.

The overall aim of the SALTSA work group has been to analyse conditions for and to help create competitive and sustainable MCVW processes in various business areas that have growing economic weight, such as health care, professional services, sales, and maintenance. To this end, existing practices of mobile computer-mediated work have been analysed and evaluated with respect to effectiveness and sustainability and new business opportunities based on MVW processes have been explored. The objective of this work is to contribute to the understanding and the improvement of MVW processes. The concept of mobile virtual work and its context may have been defined as in the above sections, but this does not mean that we know all about it. On the contrary, it still appears to be an elusive phenomenon. Apart from the question "*What is it?*" many other questions have to be answered, such as: "*Why is it?*", "*What are the consequences?*", "*How to organise and manage it?*" and "*How to design it?*".

This book is also a result of a workshop dedicated to try to find up-to-date answers to these questions. In the workshop, European experts were brought together in fields that are related to mobile virtual work. In the workshop, they presented and discussed the developments as to questions such as the following:

- What *scenarios* can be formulated concerning expected future mobile virtual work settings?
- What are the *ergonomic* aspects that are relevant in designing effective tools supporting MVW?
- What are the potential *effects* of MVW *on well-being, stress* and *social relations* of workers? How can mobile work be organized, managed and supported in order to avoid these and other negative effects for employees?

---

[1] SALTSA stands for the joint program for working life research in Europe. SALTSA is a joint undertaking by the three Swedish confederations of employees - LO, TCO, SACO - and the National Institute for Working Life. The purpose of the program is the collaboration on problem-oriented working life research in Europe.

- What is the *role of mobile technologies and services* in supporting MVW? Which are the main trends in the evolution of mobile technologies and services?
- What are the implications of MVW for *coordination and control*?
- How to foster *knowledge sharing* and *organisational learning* in an MVW environment?
- What new *business models* are emerging in companies using MVW? What are, in the different models, the perceived benefits and the strategic implications of MVW?
- How to *assess* the usefulness and implications of the introduction of MVW and supporting tools and technologies?
- Which are the *contractual issues and employment solutions* related to the use of MVW?

1.4 The contributions to this book

This book aims at answering the above-mentioned questions. In all, the book consists of sixteen chapters, which illustrate the topic from different perspectives. The chapters are organised into three sections: first, concepts are defined and the prevalence of mobile virtual work in Europe, including the relevant European legislation, is shown; secondly, mobility and virtuality in many work settings are described and analysed from different perspectives; third, organisational strategies to meet the mobile challenge are discussed.

After the general introduction showing the challenges of mobile virtual work, Matti Vartiainen in his chapter '*Mobile virtual work – concepts, outcomes and challenges*' studies mobility as a quality of a work system consisting of a subject using tools to process objects of work in a working context. Manifestations of mobility in these different elements are described. Mobile virtual work as distributed collaborative work is also discussed. Some impacts and outcomes of MVW are identified.

Karsten Gareis, Stefan Lilischkis and Alexander Mentrup explore in their '*Mapping the mobile eWorkforce in Europe*' the prevalence and key characteristics of mobile workers and mobile eWorkers, based on several large scale surveys in Europe. The findings also show the reality of mobile eWork in Europe today.

Minna Helle's '*New forms of work in labour law*' evaluates mobile and virtual work as new forms of work organisations from the perspective of (European) labour law. The article discusses the legal implications and status of mobile and virtual workers under the legal framework.

Mark Perry and Jackie Brodie in their article '*Virtually connected, practically mobile*' tackle the question: what is the work of mobile workers? They point to the phenomenon of 'mobilisation work', which means that much activities of mobile and virtual workers is actually spend on finding each other and keeping contact, instead of on the primary work task itself. They also show how mobile workers mix their mobility with their work, home and social lives.

John Wilson in his '*Collaboration in mobile virtual work: a human factors view*' writes about the necessity to understand the nature of collaboration and teamwork and how to organise it before beginning to implement future information and communication technologies. Several cases are described showing various aspects of mobile virtual collaborative work.

Ludger Schmidt and Holger Luczak in their '*Model-based design of mobile work systems*' present, firstly, dimensions of mobile work against the background of the classical fields of industrial engineering and ergonomics. Then, a model is introduced that aims at shaping and supporting the design of mobile working systems in a human-centred and task-oriented way. Its application is demonstrated by exemplary research questions, which have been developed in a real world case study.

Niklas Johansson, Torbjörn Lind and Bengt Sandblad in their chapter on '*Usability in IT systems for mobile work*' discuss usability aspects of mobile IT support systems, and also report on parts of their findings from a large survey performed in Sweden in 2004. In this survey, user's opinions concerning usefulness in a broad sense are evaluated. The article continues with a discussion regarding methods for design of mobile work support systems.

Marion Wiethoff, Thierry Meulenbroek, Hans Stavleu and Rogier van Boxtel in their chapter '*Participative Design for Home Care Nursing*' present an approach for participative concept development in the field of health care. Through this approach the needs for ICT-support for elderly, chronically ill patients and their mobile practitioners are made visible and concrete applications are developed. In the chapter, textural and pictorial scenarios are presented to illustrate the approach.

Peter Richter, Jelka Meyer and Fanny Sommer provide in '*Well-being and stress in mobile and virtual work*', first, an overview about terms and theories of the modern mental work load research. Next, investigations on mental strain and well-being in the context of mobile virtual work are described. Here, the main emphasis is put on the design of tasks, motivation and collaboration in virtual teams as well as the role of operational uncertainty. Finally resources for mobile virtual work are presented and discussed.

Veli-Pekka Niitamo describes in his '*Building scenarios for a globally distributed corporation*', how a scenario was built in Nokia for shortening the product creation process by exploiting better the network of co-located sites in different time zones and by utilizing optimally the available competencies of different sites. It has had direct implications to the workplace design, i.e. design of work process and work environment needed for increasing productivity. For the purpose, a global team of mobile work developers was established.

Robert Verburg and colleagues Stefanie Testa, Ursula Hyrkkänen and Niklas Johansson collected and analysed four comparative case studies from MVW settings in Italy, Finland, the Netherlands and Sweden. The descriptions and analysis are presented in the chapter '*Case descriptions of mobile Virtual Work in practice.* The cases describe conditions for the implementation of mobile technologies to support mobile work in different contexts.

The chapter by Mariano Corso, Antonella Martini and Luisa Pellegrini, '*Knowledge sharing in mobile work environments*', builds its evidence from a survey and three case studies. The chapter explores the relations between dispersed workers activities, knowledge management tools and worker satisfaction. This chapter explores the emerging approaches that companies use to manage knowledge in MVW environments. It provides evidence that business performance and people satisfaction depend on the fit between the type of work processes (more or less routine) and type of knowledge management strategy.

Sven Lindmark, Mats Magnusson and Filippo Renga in their chapter '*Factors influencing the diffusion of new mobile services*' investigate enablers and disablers of the development and diffusion of services for mobile work. Based on case studies of companies developing services for mobile work, the writers identify and analyze factors influencing the development and diffusion of such services.

Hans Schaffers, Liz Carver, Torsten Brodt, Terrence Fernando and Robert Slagter explore in '*Mobile workplaces and innovative business practice*' perspectives for using mobile technologies in three industrial sectors, i.e. aerospace, automotive and construction. Challenges and success factors are identified for mobile workplace innovation, and human, organisational and technical issues are discussed in the transformation to innovative mobile and networked workplace settings.

In the concluding chapter '*Mobile virtual work, what have we learned?*', Matti Vartiainen and Erik Andriessen bring together the findings and discussions of the previous chapters. Conclusions are integrated, a typology of MVW settings is developed and a research agenda for the future is presented.

One of the strong points of this book appears to be that many chapters include descriptions and analysis of concrete MVW cases. Since systematic empirical analysis of existing Mobile Virtual Work settings is very rarely found in the literature, it is now possible to go beyond assumptions and speculations. This makes it also possible to discuss the main implications of the present developments in mobile virtual work in terms of scenarios and roadmaps.

References

European Information Technology Observatory (2004)

2 Mobile Virtual Work – Concepts, Outcomes and Challenges

Matti Vartiainen

Laboratory of Work Psychology and Leadership, Helsinki University of Technology, Finland

2.1 Emergence of new concepts

Working life and organisations are changing rapidly. The worlds of work and technology are full of new concepts fighting for a living space. The variety of concepts and their concurrence are an understandable outcome of the recent developments in working life, which inevitably result in confusion and sometimes chaos in the minds of both laymen and experts. A consolation is the consciousness that it usually takes several years to reach a widely accepted definition of a joint object when some new thing or idea is invented. People coming from different disciplines identify the same new phenomenon at the same time and from different perspectives. It takes time to compare and match visions and agree on them. Business people are interested in 'mobility scenarios' and 'mobility roadmaps' in order to create 'e-Business models' and ways of doing business electronically. Their headache is the management of partnerships in network organisations while trying to find and create new business opportunities. Technologists are interested in the development of new technologies and want to create mobile collaborative 'virtual working spaces'. Sociologists and social scientists write about the 'network society' and 'eWork' and aim at understanding and describing developmental trends in societies and defining new types of jobs, such as 'flexiwork', 'telework', and 'mobile work'. Organisational scientists try to figure out how 'company networks' and 'virtual organisations' function, and how they should be managed. Managers and human resources people want to learn how to lead 'virtual organisations' and 'distributed teams', in spite of disturbances in their internal and external processes and relationships. Social psychologists explore intragroup processes in dispersed teams and psychologists and cognitive scientists the functioning of the 'distributed mind' in order to understand the purpose of communicative actions and the emergence of telepresence and awareness. There are additional concepts around, such as 'distributed work', 'multi-local work', 'virtual work', 'micromobility', 'campus mobility', 'multi-site employees', 'multimobility', 'total mobility', etc. In all, it is clear that some conceptual clarifications are needed just to guarantee the quality of discussion. The purpose of this chapter is to provide a coherent picture of the concepts of 'mobile' and 'virtual' work and how they are related to each other. Additionally, the definitions are operationalised in order to analyse and describe mobile and virtual work systems. Some challenges and impacts of mobile virtual work are also presented.

2.2 What is mobile?

The concepts of 'mobile' and 'mobile work' are ambiguous from the perspectives of working life, organisations, and employees. 'Mobile' and 'Mobility' have a strong link to wireless technologies. Most often 'mobile work' is related to the possibility of a person moving and executing tasks anywhere and at any time, with the help of wired and wireless technologies and in a flexible manner, i.e. regarding his or her physical mobility. 'Mobile', in this case, is defined as a quality of an individual who moves to and from different places and works in them and, while travelling, uses information and communication technologies as tools. However, studying 'mobility' on the level of an individual is not enough: more levels, components, and viewpoints are needed to understand the complexity of mobile work as a goal-oriented activity.

In this chapter, 'mobility' is studied as an aspect of an activity system consisting of a subject[1] using tools to process objects of work in a working context (Fig. 2.1). Activity systems in working contexts are goal- and interest-driven entities, which aim at fulfilling given or self-set tasks and assignments. Work is realised through purposeful actions.

Subjects, as actors, are social and cultural entities such as individuals, pairs, groups, organisations, and networks. They use both concrete and mental tools to work on their objects in their respective environment, which can be characterised by its complexity. The objects of work are manifested as self-set and given assignments, tasks, and goals related to them. In addition to goals, the driving force can be an interest without any exact goal, but one which does, however, create joint actions. Because of the systemic nature of work and working, 'mobility' is preliminarily de-

---

[1] It is underlined that although 'subject' is used in singular, it refers to both individual and collective actors that share their interest, goals and volitions.

fined as an aspect of an activity system. The tripartite entity 'subject-tool-object' is the basic functional unit of mobile work, which is carried out as actions in different working contexts or spaces. In the following sections, 'mobility', as a feature of a work system, is studied from the viewpoints of the working context ('space-time setting'), subjects, tools, and objects of work.

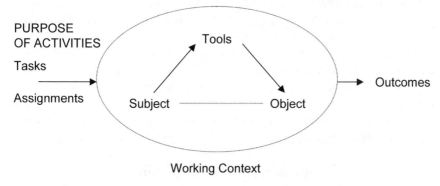

Fig. 2.1. 'Mobile work' as a work system and its elements (based on Vygotsky 1962, Leont'ev 1978, Engeström 1987)

2.2.1 Mobile spaces and places as working contexts

Work is always carried out in some space. The concept of 'ba' (Nonaka et al. 2000) is useful for differentiating various spaces in use for mobile workers. *Ba* refers to a shared context in which knowledge is shared, created, and utilised by those who interact and communicate there. *Ba* does not just mean a physical space, but a specific time and space that integrates layers of spaces. *Ba* unifies the *physical space*, such as an office space, the *virtual space*, such as e-mail, and the *mental or social space*, such as common experiences, ideas, and ideals shared by people with common goals as a working context. Today's working life, and the contexts of individuals and groups, are combinations of physical, virtual, social, and cultural working environments (Fig. 2.2).

Physical places. A subject's mobility is typically related to changing physical places. The physical environments that employees use for working are divided into five categories: home, the main workplace ('Office'), moving places, e.g. cars, trains, planes, and ships, a customer's or partners' premises ('other workplaces'), and hotels, cafés etc. ('third workplaces').

The use of physical places can be described with different indicators, such as their distance from each other (near – far), their number (one –

many), and the frequency with which they change (seldom – often). The indicators are then used in modelling various types of mobile work units. A physical place itself can move, for example, a car, a train, or an aeroplane. This type of working in many places is sometimes called multi-location work (Lilischkis 2003).

A *virtual place* refers to an electronic working environment or virtual working space. The internet and intranet provide a platform for working places for both simple, e.g. e-mail, and complex communication tools, e.g. collaborative working environments.

The combinations of physical and virtual workplaces can be described as a 'workscape' (Harrison et al. 2004). The term 'workscape' refers to the "layers of where we work", i.e. the constellation of 1) real and virtual work settings, i.e. furniture + IT, within 2) particular spaces, i.e. meeting rooms, project areas, cafés etc, that are, again, 3) located in a specific environment, i.e. office building, city district, street, home, airport, bus etc.

REALISING PURPOSES OF ACTIVITIES
Tasks and assignments are carried out as practical and communicative actions
IN enabling and disabling spaces
PHYSICAL SPACES
which are settings, arenas and environments at home, in the main workplace ('Office'), moving places (e.g. cars, trains, planes, ships), other places (e.g. partners', clients' and suppliers' premises), and third places (e.g. hotels, cafés, congress venues)
VIRTUAL SPACES
which are connections (e.g. Internet, intranet, extranet, wlan, broadband), devices (e.g. laptop, mobile devices) and applications and services (e.g. e-mail, calenders, access to databases) enabling communication and collaboration
MENTAL AND SOCIAL SPACES
which are shared common experiences, ideas and ideals based on human interaction and collaboration

Fig. 2.2. Work activities are carried out in physical, virtual, and mental/social spaces

Mental/social place refers to cognitive constructs, thoughts, beliefs, ideas, and mental states that employees share. Creating and forming joint mental spaces requires communication and collaboration, for example, exchanging ideas in face-to-face or virtual dialogues.

2.2.2 Mobile subject

The mobility of a subject takes place in two formats, physical motion and virtual movement from place to place in a net, and often as a combination of the two.

A subject's physical mobility = an actor moves (travels) from place to place and works in different locations and on the way from one location to another.

A subject's virtual mobility = an actor works on the object of work in virtual working spaces by communicating and collaborating with the help of information and communication technologies. Mentally, i.e. cognitively and emotionally, (s)he moves from place to place. For example, workers in call centres and collaborative 3D design are virtually mobile. A subject itself may be physically stationary and may work on the object of work in a working space. A paradox is that the development of mobile and wireless technologies simultaneously makes stationary, fixed-place working requiring no physical mobility easier and easier.

A subject's physical and virtual mobility = an actor moves physically from place to place and uses information and communication technologies in a virtual working space.

This book deals mainly with those types of physically mobile subjects using virtual spaces. Work today is mostly a combination of physical and virtual movement when a physically mobile employee collaborates with his or her distributed team members by using communication and collaboration tools and services. In fact, the use of technologies adds a new second-degree feature to the physical movement ("a moving employee moves in a net").

2.2.3 Mobile tools

Mobile devices, applications, and services are mentioned in many chapters of this book. Without doubt, mobile technologies are one of the main drivers of mobile work. Next, a difference in principle between mobile and wireless technologies is emphasised (Fig. 2.3).

Mobile technology as a tool = mobile wireless (or, in fact, less-wired) technology allows a person to communicate and collaborate flexibly at any time and in any place. Mobile technology provides essential tools for physically mobile employees or groups. Mobile tools are not only devices but also applications and services. A physically mobile employee also benefits from wired technologies in the places (s)he visits and works in. Mobile and wireless technologies are not, however, equivalent (Hayes and

Kuchinskas 2003). 'Mobile' is the ability to easily carry a computing or connectivity device from location to location. 'Wireless' is the ability to connect to remote servers so as to access information and applications over a wireless network. Not all wireless devices are mobile, e.g. stationary devices in the office that are connected by Bluetooth or infrared, and not all mobile devices are wireless; sometimes a worker just needs to carry information or applications with him on the job, but does not need to connect remotely to servers. Other workers may need to connect to remote servers only a few times a day or once a week.

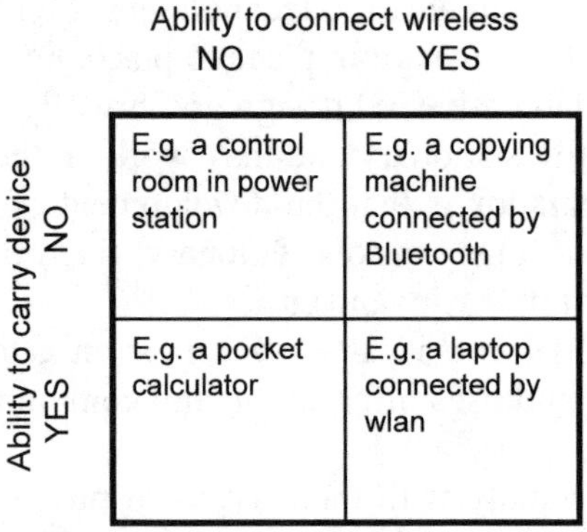

	Ability to connect wireless	
	NO	YES
Ability to carry device NO	E.g. a control room in power station	E.g. a copying machine connected by Bluetooth
Ability to carry device YES	E.g. a pocket calculator	E.g. a laptop connected by wlan

Fig. 2.3. The relationships of mobile devices and wireless connections

2.2.4 Mobile object of work

Mobile object of work = the object of work moves or is transported from one place to another in physical (material) form or is transformed in electronic (immaterial, digitalised, virtual) form. A traditional material object of work is some raw material, a commodity, or a product that is transported for reworking or consumption in another place. Reworking usually takes place in a consecutive manner. An immaterial, virtual object of work is, for instance, a drawing or a document that is transferred digitally in a net from one virtual place to another or that is reworked synchronously in a virtual working space by team members.

2.2.5 Mobility in organisations and business models

Instead of individually acting persons, key actors in mobile and virtual organisations are pairs and groups of employees, who communicate and collaborate from afar, using mainly information and communication technologies. The fact that organisations and networks of them consist of these units complicates the definition and practices of mobile work. The complexity of tasks and assignments usually increases and contextual complexity grows. The increasing number of acting subjects multiplies the aspects of the work system. The degree of physical mobility varies: one of a pair moves a lot, while another stays in a fixed place; one of the teams in an organisation may work more in a mobile manner than the others. The quality and use of tools for communication and collaboration vary, as do the objects of work in groups and large organisational units. In addition, the increased number of actors brings with it a variety of social relationships, which increases the complexity of job-related communication.

Mobile business models aim at providing an integrated view of the benefits of physical mobility and use of mobile, wireless technologies from the viewpoint of companies. They provide models of how to realise a way of action in which physical and virtual mobility are utilised. The business models concentrate on providing new ways to benefit from wireless connections and mobile devices and services by redefining standard work processes and by increasing the ability to transfer information quickly to employees, wherever and whenever. In principle physical and virtual mobility provide employees with the possibility of being near customers and, at the same time, accessing joint enterprise resources, e.g. data, guidelines, and work orders, from afar and while moving. In order to work, employees need a wireless network, devices, applications, and support. For example, Capgemini[2], which provides consulting, technology, and outsourcing services, defines mobility to its customers as "creating business value through mobile devices and wireless technology, by enabling communication, information access and business transactions". In mobile business models, mobility uses the capabilities of wireless networks to connect computers, Personal Digital Assistants (PDA), telephones, cars, and household appliances. Some like to talk about real-time enterprise, a business that eliminates the time lag in receiving critical information and acting on it (Hayes and Kuchinskas 2003).

---

[2] http://www.capgemini.com/technology/ mobility/

2.3 What is virtual?

The concept of 'Virtuality' has connotations of the 'imaginary', as well as the 'designed' or 'engineered' (Oravec 1996). The term 'virtual' originates from the Latin word 'virtus', which basically means 'proficiency, manliness' (Scholtz 1994, see Franke 2000), an intimate personal quality of goodness and power. The term defines an attribute of a thing, which does not really exist but has the possibility of existing. 'Potential' is equivalent to one of the meanings of 'virtual', as Cooper et al. (2002) note. A mobile virtual team would, according to this sense of the term, be one that was not (yet) fully realised: almost a team, with the possibility of becoming a team. In this meaning, the term 'virtual' does not fit well with dispersed organisations, which actually exist to a great degree. Lipnack and Stamps (2000) add two other contemporary meanings for virtual: 'not the same in actual fact' but 'in essence', 'almost like', and virtual as in 'virtual reality'. They consider the 'almost like' definition, as in "they act virtually like a team", to be on target. There are similarities, but also differences, between co-located and dispersed teams. In fact, it is a challenge to research to find out to what extent the structures, processes, dynamics, and outcomes of co-located small groups and other forms of organisations appear in virtual form. 'Virtual reality' can anyhow be used to denote a space for the communication and work of dispersed teams.

In the meaning of dispersedness, virtual organisations have a very real existence. The term 'Virtual Organisation' dates back to two sources. One source is the groupware technologies of the '80s (Baecker 1993, Oravec 1996), which made working while apart possible by providing support tools for group members' collaboration and communication. Another source is the early vision of the virtual corporation (Davidow and Malone 1992, Byrne 1993), which provided a model for networks of enterprises to operate in a global context. Davidow and Malone remarked: "the Virtual Corporation will ... for the first time tie all of these diverse innovations, i.e. just-in-time supply, work teams, flexible manufacturing, reusable engineering, worker empowerment, organisational streamlining, computer-aided design, total quality, mass customisation, etc, together into a single cohesive vision of the corporation in the twenty-first century." Multi-site, multi-organisational, and dynamic organisations began to appear in the 1970s (Snow et al. 1999). In the middle of the '90s, the first empirical studies were carried out with the aim of understanding the nature of virtual organisations and related concepts such as 'telework' (e.g. Jackson and van der Wielen 1996).

The tentative definition of a dispersed virtual organisation is the following one: it consists of employees or teams working apart but towards a joint goal, mainly collaborating via information and communication technologies (ICT). In a fully virtual organisation, all the communication and collaboration takes place through ICT in the mental and virtual workspaces. Virtual teams are groups of people who work interdependently but with a shared purpose across space and time, using technology to communicate and collaborate (Lipnack and Stamps 2000). As companies expand globally, face increasing time compression in product development, and use more foreign-based subcontracting labour (Peters 1992, Stewart 1994), virtual work groups may provide flexibility, responsiveness, lower costs, improved resource utilisation, and stress reduction as a result of not having to travel long hours to the office (Hanhike 2004, Pratt 2003).

2.4 What is Telework?

"Today it takes an act of courage to suggest that our biggest factories and office towers may, within our lifetimes, stand half-empty, reduced to use as ghostly warehouses or converted into living space. Yet this is precisely what the new mode of production makes possible: a return to cottage industry on a new, higher, electronic basis, and with it a new emphasis on the home as the centre of society." (Toffler 1980).

The discussion of *telework* has a long history and has continued for almost thirty years (Pekkola 2002). Traditionally, telework provides the viewpoint of an individual working apart at a location other than an employer's office or plant. In telework, many of the central dimensions of virtual work meet each other: working remotely in a different place and at a different time than others in a workplace and using information and communication technologies to interact with others and to work. Why not then use 'telework', 'teleteam', or 'teleorganisation' instead of 'virtual work', 'virtual team', or 'virtual organisation'? One reason might be that the concept of 'telework' has provided a basis on which to study virtual dispersed work as individual jobs in the context of a society and an organisation. Another reason is that the term 'telework' has long been associated exclusively with work performed solely at home. The core unit of analysis has been either a teleworker or his societal position.

Telework is sometimes mixed with mobile work. Working afar from the main workplace does not, however, imply moving. Toffler's vision of future work 25 years ago only partly describes the present situation in working life, which is more mobile and virtual work than telework performed only at home.

2.5 Forms of physical and virtual mobility

Next, mobile virtual work is described as a form of eWork. The prevalence of mobile eWork in Europe is further elaborated in the chapter by Gareis, Lilischkis, and Mentrup in this volume.

2.5.1 Emergence of eWork

Statistical data on employees in Europe show the increased prevalence of new types of work and organisations (Lilischkis 2003, Lilischkis and Meyer 2003). Most of the available data concerns the use of information and communication technologies (ICT) as tools in eWork, which is defined as "work practices making use of information and communication technologies to increase efficiency, flexibility (in time and place), and sustainability of resource use" (Collaboration@Work). e-Work has been subdivided into three types.

1. *Home-based telework* is the most widely recognised type of eWork. Home-based teleworkers are those who (ECATT 2000):

- "work from home (instead of commuting to a central workplace) for at least one full working day per week
- use a personal computer in the course of their work
- use telecommunication links (phone/fax/e-mail) to communicate with their colleagues/supervisor while working at home
- are either in salaried employment or self-employed, in which case their main working place is on the contractor's premises"

In the ECATT study, a threshold of at least one full day per working week spent at home or at the contractors' premises was used to distinguish teleworkers from those who occasionally bring work home. Several categories of telework are listed. The majority of teleworkers divide their time between home and the office, and they are called "alternating teleworkers". Individuals who spend more than 90% of their working time at home are called "permanent teleworkers". "Supplementary teleworkers" are those who spend less than one full day teleworking from home per week. They are also called "occasional teleworkers", to distinguish them from regular teleworkers.

2. *Self-employed teleworkers in SOHOs* (Small Office Home Office) are those (ECATT 2000):

- "who are self-employed or effectively self-employed (e.g. persons employed by their own company or employed by an organisation they have considerable managing power over),
- whose main place of work is at home or who claim not to have a main place of work,
- who use advanced ICT for communicating with clients and/or (other) business partners."

The critical difference between teleworkers in SOHOs and home-based teleworkers is their work market position as self-employed. They are private entrepreneurs, for example, consultants working and communicating with their contractors, partners and clients by way of new technologies.

3. *Mobile workers* have been defined in two related ways:

- "mobile teleworkers are those who work at least 10 hours per week away from home and from their main place of work, e.g. on business trips, in the field, travelling, or on customers' premises, and use online computer connections when doing so." (ECATT 2000)
- "in the last four weeks, have you spent any of your working time away from your home and from your main place of work, e.g. on business trips, in the field, travelling or on a customer's premises?" (SIBIS 2002)

The former definition pays attention to three characteristics of work: the duration of work, its place, and the use of ICT as a tool, i.e. it meets the criteria of physical and virtual mobility. The latter, on the other hand, underlines physical mobility, i.e. only time and place. All three are acceptable criteria but possibly not enough to cover the rich contents of mobile virtual work. This topic is elaborated more in the section of this chapter entitled 'Mobile Work in Distributed Organisations'.

'At least 10 hours per week' and 'in the last four weeks' are criteria as good as any time-related criteria. Their roughness and ambiguity are, however, striking. The length of time usage as a criterion is just a contract: even one hour of work on the move adds a feature of physical mobility to any work. The definition of places as 'non-home' and 'non-main-place-of-work' is satisfactory but leaves open what the other places of physical and virtual mobility are in practice. Using online computer connections is a satisfactory criterion as well, though it does not show the mode of communication and collaboration.

The latter definition is supposed to produce higher numbers of mobile employees than the former one, in the sense of physical mobility. According to Lilischkis (2003) 'multi-location work' could also be used in this context.

Who are the home-based and self-employed teleworkers and the mobile employees? As early as 1980 Toffler (1980) mentioned as teleworkers such people as "... salesmen and saleswomen who work by phone or visit, and only occasionally touch base at the office; architects and designers; a burgeoning pool of specialised consultants in many industries; large numbers of human-service workers like therapists or psychologists; music teachers and language instructors; art dealers, investment counsellors, insurance agents, lawyers, and academic researchers, and many other categories of white-collar, technical, and professional people." Toffler did not foresee mobile virtual employees, but they seem to be drawn from the same groups of people. Probably a salesperson is the most obvious candidate for physically mobile work and as a user of wireless mobile technologies and applications. Salespeople are out in the field, meeting with customers, and working in airports and cars. The other groups of people at the head of the mobile virtual workforce are maintenance engineers, repair technicians, and delivery drivers (see case descriptions in this book).

In all, this book concentrates on physically mobile employees using increasingly mobile information and communications technologies (ICT) for communication and collaboration, i.e. physically and virtually mobile employees.

2.5.2 Types of physically mobile employees

Lilischkis (2003) presents the following five types of physically mobile work based solely on alternating locations of individuals:

- *"On-site movers"* work on a certain site but have to move around on that site or back and forth for certain purposes. Examples are farmers harvesting their land with a tractor, security agents walking around and watching sites, material drivers in manufacturing companies, and hospital doctors visiting patients.
- *"Yo-yos"* occasionally work away from a fixed location. Examples are work on business trips, e.g. taking part in a meeting in a foreign town, work in the field, e.g. face-to-face interviews for scientific research, work when travelling, e.g. writing reports while sitting in a train, work in the emergency services, e.g. firemen and emergency physicians, and working at a customer's premises, e.g. ICT developers visiting potential customers.

- *"Pendulums"* alternately work at two different fixed locations, such as the employer's premises and a home office or a client's premises. This type includes home-based telework.
- *"Nomads"* work in multiple places and are constantly moving from one location to another. Several kinds can be distinguished, according to the time the workers spend at a certain location. For example, an insurance agent may visit many customers a day, while others may change their working place after some days, weeks, or months. Examples are traditional cattle nomads and circus performers, as well as managers moving to a different subsidiary every other year or diplomats moving to a different country after some years.
- *"Carriers"* work on the move, transporting goods or people. Examples are train conductors and ticket collectors, airplane stewardesses, sailors, and deliverymen, as well as taxi and bus drivers.

Space and time criteria can be used to distinguish the types of physically mobile workers. *Space criteria* are (Lilischkis 2003): the number of locations, recurrence of locations, whether there are headquarters to return to, whether work takes place while moving or at a destination, whether work can be done at fixed locations without changing it, whether there is a limitation of the work area, and what the distance between locations is. *Time criteria* are: frequency of changing location, the time spent moving between work locations, and the time spent at a certain work location if not moving. Each type of mobile work has its constitutive criterion: "On-site movers" work in a limited work area, "Yo-yos" return back to a head office, "Pendulums" have two recurrent work locations, "Nomads" work in more than two places, and "Carriers" cannot do their work at a fixed location while moving.

Lilischkis also relates physically mobile work to ICT tools and traditional telework. Fig. 2.4 shows the place of physically and virtually mobile work in this context. Both mobile work and traditional telework at home can either be supported by ICT tools or not. Some mobile work is done without using any ICT tools, and some telework is done at only one fixed location. The most interesting type is "Mobile ICT Work", which was earlier defined as physically and virtually mobile work.

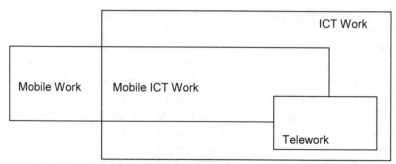

Fig. 2.4. Mobile ICT work (Lilischkis 2003, p. 9)

The increase of eWork in its various forms is an indication of emerging new organisations, whose effects on job demands and content, group processes, and on individual well-being and performance are only vaguely known. It is assumed that new technologies, especially mobile technologies and services, will be implemented more in the future, creating pressures to develop and possibilities to work flexibly in different places and over time. Whether this development is a nuisance or a blessing for employees is a dilemma and a question of choices and decisions between alternatives. Information technology should, of course, be an instrument or medium through which new forms of organisation are made possible, but not determined. In contrast, it is the forms and requirements of the task and of the social interaction of the employees collaborating that should shape the actual work process and determine the performance and quality of the business they are designed for. Consequently, ICT technologies should meet work-oriented social requirements in order to support work rather than be a hindrance to it.

2.6 Mobile work systems in distributed organisations

The purpose of this section is to provide a framework for the analysis and description of mobile virtual work systems, for example, teams and projects and their activities. It is claimed that physical, as well as virtual mobility, is just one feature of a distributed work system that, however, strongly influences its functions. In the following section, distributed and mobile work groups are used as the units of work system analysis. They are seen as activity systems in their environment striving towards their task-related goals. Groups in organisations are their fractals[3] that include all the critical elements of any activity system: they have purposes and goals, assignments and tasks to do, collaborative interactions for the regulation of internal and external action, and they are embedded in their environment. It is also good to remember that not all distributed groups are mobile, but all mobile collaborative groups are distributed by definition.

The analysis of a work system starts from its purpose and ends with its outcomes, i.e. its functionality and performance, and the well-being of employees (Fig. 2.5). Three intertwined and partly embedded factors influence the outcomes. First, the complexity of individual and collective assignments and tasks, i.e. is mainly routine or creative task execution required in work? Second, the complexity of context or space, i.e. in what kind of physical, virtual, and mental/social spaces is work done? Third, these two factors influence the internal regulative processes of individual or collective subjects, i.e. what internal mechanisms and tools are needed to regulate relations and boundaries between subjects, objects, tasks, and the environment? Mobile virtual work units always have some purpose for their activity, which expresses itself as the motives for and objectives of actions. These factors not only result in positive and negative performance outcomes, but also provide descriptions of user needs and specifications for work system design and development.

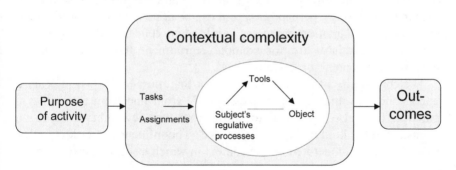

Fig. 2.5. The factors influencing the outcomes of work systems

Next, the three determining factors are discussed in more detail. The purpose is to provide starting points for their analysis and description.

---

[3] 'Fractal' is a term used in chaos theory referring to a self-similar structure at all scales, i.e. parts resemble the whole.

2.6.1 Complexity of tasks

In working life, common objectives drive joint efforts and a commitment to their achievement. The goals are autonomously self-defined or set from outside. The content of assignments may vary from routine to problem-solving and creative tasks (Andriessen 2003). At one end, the task is creative and demanding. At the other end, the task is in its simplest form, i.e. work is routine-like.

Bell and Kozlowski (2002) claim that task complexity has critical implications for the structure and processes of virtual teams. Simple tasks require less co-ordination and their competence requirements are lower than in the case of complex tasks. The main criterion when selecting support technologies is often the complexity of communication and collaboration tasks. This is underlined in the media richness model (for example Picot et al. 2001), which relates the richness of information content to the complexity of tasks. According to the model, the most effective communication is to be found by combining different media to meet the demands of the tasks and by paying attention to the disturbances that result from excessive information and the barriers created by inadequate information. The media richness model has been criticised on the grounds that the fit between task and medium is not a one-to-one relation but falls within quite a wide band of good fit. If the situation falls within this band, performance of the task with the media is not perhaps easy, but can be done with more or less mental effort and adaptation processes (Andriessen 2003). Various adaptation mechanisms available are, for example, recruitment, training, or changing the tasks, the context, or the tools.

The complexity of the task is the factor that must be known in order to understand why intra-group processes vary from one team to another in practice. It is also beneficial to know from the viewpoint of managing teams, i.e. what kind of support is needed? The influence of task complexity is, however, moderated by the context in which tasks are performed.

2.6.2 Complexity of context

Tasks are always carried out in some space. Space can be characterised as a context or an environment or a scene where actions take place. Roughly speaking, contexts can be seen as being both physical and psychological or 'objective' and 'subjective'. Each individual exists in a psychological field of forces that determines and limits his or her behaviour. Lewin (1972) called this psychological field the 'life space'. It is a highly subjective 'space' that deals with the world as the individual sees it. 'Life space' is embedded in the objective elements of physical and social fields. The physical and social conditions limit the variety of possible life spaces and create the boundary conditions of the psychological field. 'Subjective' and 'objective' elements are not strictly divided, but the context is blended and layered, as analysed in the concept of *ba* (Nonaka et al. 2000). Today's working life and the contexts of individuals and groups are combinations of physical, virtual, psychological, social, and cultural working environments.

'Public' and 'private' spaces are interestingly intertwined in the work and life of mobile employees, while work is more and more done at home, in moving places, and in third workplaces, e.g. hotels, cafés, and meeting rooms. According to Cooper et al. (2002, p. 295): "the decentralisation of work activities and the practice of 'assembling the mobile office' on the part of 'nomadic workers' entail the simultaneous management of private activities, as when mobile teleworkers coordinate their work life from/at home. 'Public' work activities may be drawn into 'private' spaces, with a variety of effects on an individual's home and family life (both positive and negative)".

Dimensions of contextual complexity

From the viewpoint of mobile employees working in distributed teams, the complexity of their context or space is described by the following six dimensions (Fig. 2.6):

1. *Location*: employees work face-to-face in the same location or they are geographically dispersed in different places. For example, some of the team members or teams in a project work in one place and others in other places.
2. *Mobility*: employees may be physically mobile and change their workplaces or they may stay in a fixed place, working mainly in one location.
3. *Time*: employees work either synchronously or asynchronously in different time zones or sequentially in the same time zone. In addition, they work only for one team or project or divide their time between several teams and projects, doing a part-time job in them.
4. *Temporariness*: the collaboration of employees and their social structure may be permanent or temporary. Most teams are project teams which have a start and an end to their life cycle.
5. *Diversity*: the background of employees, i.e. their age, education, sex, nationality, religion, language, etc, is more or less similar or different.

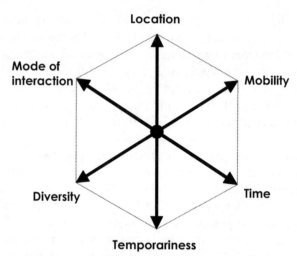

Fig. 2.6. The physical, virtual and mental context features of team work systems

6. *Mode of interaction*: communication and collaboration take place directly face-to-face or are mediated via different media and technological systems in a virtual workplace.

The six features can be used to characterise the degree of complexity that mobile team work reflects. They are related to the *ba* as spaces to work in the following manner: the variables of location (distance, mobility) and time (asynchronity, temporariness) characterise the physical space; the variable of interaction (mediatedness) indicates the virtual space; the variable of diversity (differences in backgrounds) shows the potential relations between people as the basis of mental space.

Dynamics of contextual complexity dimensions

The six dimensions are closely related to and dependent on each other: a change in one of them results in changes in others or in all of them. At one end of the continua (= spot in the centre in Fig. 2.6), there are traditional co-located work groups, such as assembly workers around a production line, and at the other end, there are global, highly mobile virtual teams and projects, such as marketing and sales teams and new product design teams, whose members are constantly moving and may never meet each other face-to-face. In practice, teams and projects are only seldom fully distributed and 'virtual' in the meaning of being at the extreme ends of the six dimensions. Next, the dimensions of contextual complexity are discussed from the viewpoints of physical place and mobility.

Location and mobility

Work is always done somewhere, either in a physical, virtual or mental space. Physically dispersed workplaces in a distributed organisation imply that its members may work in the same building but in different rooms and on different floors, or they may work while distributed in different buildings or districts or even in other countries. Usually some employees are located in distant places while others work in the main office. As can be concluded, most organisations are physically distributed workplaces.

The degree of a team's or a project's *physical dispersedness or distance* as a dimension of contextual complexity can be evaluated and described by answering three questions (Fig. 2.7). First, in how many locations are members of a team or a project, or entire teams in a case of an organisation, working? Second, what types and combinations of places are used for working? Work can be carried out in five different types of physical surroundings: at home, in the main workplace, in moving places, e.g. in a train or plane, in other workplaces, e.g. on a customer's or partners' premises, and in third working places, e.g. in hotels and cafés. Thirdly, what are the distances of workplaces from each other? Moving on-site in the same building or in nearby buildings and areas is sometimes called *micro-mobility* and *campus mobility*. Moving regularly between many places is called multi-mobility, and moving all the time between different sites is called *full or total mobility*. The more workplaces there are to visit, and the more distant they are from each other, the higher the contextual complexity related to the location is.

Physical mobility as a contextual complexity factor can be evaluated in the following manner. First, how many places do team or project members visit because of their job? Secondly, how often do they change locations? Thirdly, what is the nature of their physical mobility? This can be described by using the five categories (Lilischkis 2003): 'On-site movers', Yo-yos', 'Pendulums', 'Nomads', and 'Carriers'.

The number of places, their distance from each other, and the frequency with which they are changed because of the variety involved in an assignment, have an influence on the manner and quality of communication between people (Handrick and Hacker 2002). A classical study (Allen 1977) measuring the frequency of communication of 512 individuals in seven organisations over six months showed that working at a distance of 30 metres does not differ from working 3000 kilometres apart in terms of communication frequency! Even a small distance matters!

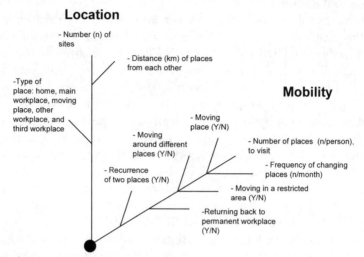

Fig. 2.7. Location and mobility in mobile, virtual work (n = number, km = kilometre, Y/N = yes – no, n/person = number of places an employee visits because of his job, n/month = how often an employee visits workplaces during a month)

Time and temporariness

Time as a contextual complexity factor manifests itself in many issues (Fig. 2.8) and especially as the degree of synchronous and asynchronous working time. The following indicators and questions are used to clarify time as a contextual factor. First, how much time is used in different places, e.g. how much time is worked at home, in the main workplace, while moving, at a customer's premises, and in hotel rooms? Second, the time dominance of a workplace, i.e. what is the ratio of move-time to time used in different workplaces? Third, team members' or teams' concurrent working time on the same object, e.g. are the team members simultaneously working on the same document? Fourth, what is the number of team members working in different time zones? Fifth, how many employees are available at the same time? For example, in global teams some team members are still sleeping while others are working.

Temporariness is also an aspect of time and also a complexity factor. It is manifested first as the length of a team's or a project's life cycle, i.e. what is the time span of the project? Only a few teams are permanent organisational structures varying from a couple of weeks to some years. Second, the time each team member or a team devotes to a specific project, i.e. in how many projects is each team member or team involved? The more projects each member has, the less (s)he can invest in one of them. Third, each member's working time in a team or a project, i.e. is a team member working in the team on a permanent basis or is a team involved in a project only in some of its phases? Fourth, the stage of a team's or project's life cycle, i.e. has a team's work or a project just started or is it about to end?

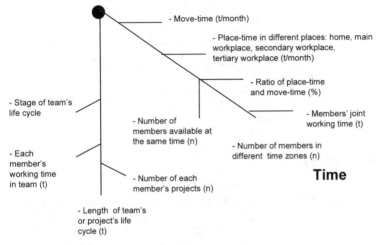

- Move-time (t/month)
- Place-time in different places: home, main workplace, secondary workplace, tertiary workplace (t/month)
- Ratio of place-time and move-time (%)
- Stage of team's life cycle
- Number of members available at the same time (n)
- Members' joint working time (t)
- Number of members in different time zones (n)
- Each member's working time in team (t)
- Number of each member's projects (n)

Time

- Length of team's or project's life cycle (t)

Temporariness

Fig. 2.8. Challenges of mobile distributed workplaces to collaboration (t/month = how much time is used during a month, % = percent, t = hours, n = number)

Temporariness is also an aspect of time and also a complexity factor. It is manifested first as the length of a team's or a project's life cycle, i.e. what is the time span of the project? Only a few teams are permanent organisational structures varying from a couple of weeks to some years. Second, the time each team member or a team devotes to a specific project, i.e. in how many projects is each team member or team involved? The more projects each member has, the less (s)he can invest in one of them. Third, each member's working time in a team or a project, i.e. is a team member working in the team on a permanent basis or is a team involved in a project only in some of its phases? Fourth, the stage of a team's or project's life cycle, i.e. has a team's work or a project just started or is it about to end?

Diversity
The greater the physical mobility of an employee is, the more likely (s)he is to meet people from diverse backgrounds (Fig. 2.9). To find out the complexity of a team's or project's composition, the following questions can be asked: what is the team or project members' native language, nationality, educational background, sex, religion, and age? Employees are

also diverse as regards their personality characteristics. This is, however, difficult to analyse without special specific psychological expertise.

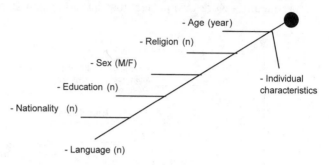

Diversity

Fig. 2.9. The diversity indicators in mobile virtual work. (n = number, M/F = man – female)

The more distributed an organisation is, the higher the probability is that one will meet different people in mobile work. The members of distributed organisations come from different organisations. In addition, customers, suppliers, and other interest groups are involved in the working network. Each collaborating person brings his own cultural background and habits into the interaction and communication. In a global team, there are different languages, life experiences, values, norms, and beliefs. There are big differences in age, sex, education, and work experience even in a distributed team in one country. As well team members' perceptions of time or time visions differ and influence on the teams dynamics and performance (Saunders et al. 2004). Cultural diversity affects team behaviour in many ways. Multicultural teams have potentially higher levels of creativity and develop more and better alternatives to a problem than teams with less cultural diversity. Such teams, however, can also have difficulty in developing a task strategy and troubles solving conflicts, creating cohesion, and building trust. Different languages and cultures make communication among team members complex.

Mode of interaction
In order to overcome temporal, spatial, and organisational disablers, ICT is used both as a means of communication and collaboration and as a collective memory to collect, store, access, and utilise knowledge (Fig. 2.10).

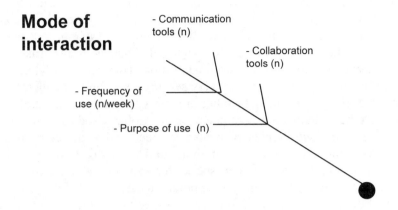

Fig. 2.10. Communication and collaboration tools in mobile virtual work (n = number)

The number of communication and collaboration tools, the purposes for which they are used, and their frequency of use indicate roughly the complexity of communication between team members. Physical mobility can be decreased by virtual mobility, i.e. by using and working from afar with communication and collaboration technologies and developing integrated virtual workspaces. The concept of 'virtuality' in the context of distributed organisations refers to the sole use of ICT as communication and collaboration tools without face-to-face interaction. 'Virtuality' in this sense is, however, just one of six features determining the preconditions for working in a mobile virtual team or a project.

The central dilemma is: to what extent can electronic media and communication and collaboration tools replace face-to-face communication, with all its richness, or is it a question of learning new competences and skills and changing culture so as to overcome the deficiencies of the existing technologies? From the viewpoint of an employee, the challenges of mobile distributed collaborations are, especially, related to two issues: what is the ability and resources of technology to create the *feelings of presence and awareness* to its users? A shared physical space, such as an open office, provides a rich social environment for employees, which makes it possible to be aware of others' tasks, activities, locations, intentions, and feelings. This awareness helps a team to work efficiently.

Interdependence of dimensions
The six dimensions that are described above form an inter-related totality. Even the simplest combination of dimensions generates several types of contexts, which describe the variety of demands that different working en-

vironments impose on employees. As shown in Fig. 2.11, distance between workplaces increases the need for physical mobility, unless it is replaced by ICT. Complexity also increases when there are a number of places to visit and when the places are often changed. Challenges also arise for the design and development of the organisation. How to co-ordinate work? The relationships of features are very sensitive and fluid, and their balance unstable. If a group and its members are physically mobile, the realisations of the other features are contingent on it. Mobility indicates more locations, an increased number of people to meet, and a greater need to co-ordinate joint actions for collaboration, etc. Depending on the dimensions and their combination, we can speak, for example, about co-located or multi-site teams, permanent or temporary teams, etc. A fully distributed virtual organisation can be described as a specific, "extreme" constellation of the six dimensions.

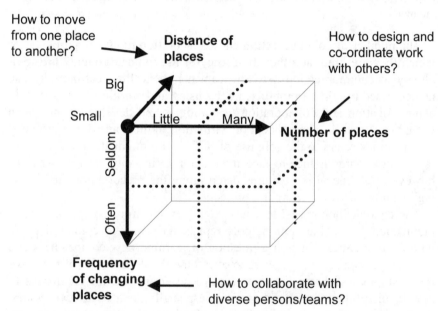

Fig. 2.11. Challenges of mobile distributed workplaces to collaboration

2.6.3 Internal processes of individual and collective subjects

The six dimensions of contextual complexity form, in addition to task complexity, a set of activity requirements for mobile employees and teams. The characteristics, features, processes, and actions of individual and collective subjects modify the influence of task and context complexities on the performance and outcomes of activity systems. By internal processes a subject can regulate and overcome the external influences. Individual actors may be seen as open systems existing and capable of existing only through processes of exchange with the environment.

Rice (1969) described individuals as multi-task systems capable of multiple activities (Fig. 2.12). The activities become bounded and controlled task systems when they are directed to the performance of a specific task and the fulfilling of some specific purpose. Different goals and tasks (T) on different sites (S) require the individual to take different attitudes (A) and roles (R). The roles and attitudes needed on sites S_2 and S_3 overlap to the extent that they use some, but not all, of the same capabilities of the individual. In contrast, the tasks on site one (S_1) require quite different capabilities. As can be concluded, the increasing degree of contextual complexity creates pressures for individuals' mental and physical self-regulation, as well as for collective regulation. In principle, the more distributed and virtual a group or a project is, the more flexibility in its activities it needs.

In mobile dispersed teams, getting to know each other's individual characteristics and 'life space' is more difficult than in co-located groups. The clarity of common goals and tasks, others' roles and accountability, etc may be vague. Additionally, knowledge about the practices of communication and information sharing and the availability of technologies for communication and collaboration may differ. All this may influence intragroup processes such as co-operation and collaboration, trust, and cohesion. It is inevitable that knowledge sharing and mutual learning become more complicated when the task and context complexities increase.

In spite of all these challenges, groups and projects should fulfil three functions to be effective (McGrath 1991): the production function, member-support function, and well-being function. The *production function* implies that team performance meets or exceeds the performance standard set by clients. The *member-support function* requires working in a team to result in the satisfaction, learning, etc. of individual group members. The *well-being function* is related to the degree to which the attractiveness and vitality of a team is strengthened.

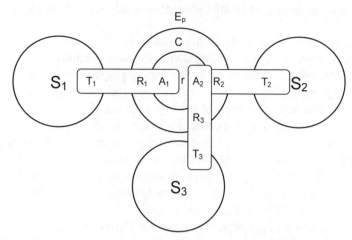

Fig. 2.12. Individuals as acting subjects in dispersed work *Ep* external environment of a person, S_1-S_3 dispersed sites, *C* cognitive functions, *r* internal world of a person, T_1-T_3 different tasks, R_1-R_3 roles, A_1-A_2 attitudes (Modified from Rice 1969)

2.7 Outcomes and challenges

This chapter concludes with the presentation of some examples of societal, economic, social, and psychological outcomes and challenges that are related to implementing physically mobile work and using mobile technologies in distributed organisations. The observations and conclusions are based on reasoning and partly on a few existing empirical studies concerning mobile work and mobile virtual organisations.

Traffic, travelling and the environment
In principle, the use of virtual connections could decrease the need for commuting, because work can be done anywhere and any time by using ICT and moving only mentally and virtually. Applying mobile technologies to vehicles could decrease traffic jams and emissions. This could have a positive influence on the environment by decreasing pollution. However, physical mobility has increased. For example, passenger kilometres in the EU have in fact increased, from 2142 billion in 1970 to 4839 billion in 2000. Goods traffic tripled during the same period (European Commission 2002).

Economic benefits
Hayes and Kuchinskas (2003) argue for the economic benefits of mobile working, though critically: "despite the plethora of mobile applications

that are available, and the substantial number of companies that have implemented at least basic mobile or wireless extensions to information, there
is very little firm data on how much of a return on the investment such deployment will offer or on when it will do so". Real estate savings are one
of the most commonly expected benefits from using mobile working practices. There are examples that confirm this positive view. For example,
"using better technology, online processes and 'hot-desking', British Air-
ways was able to increase the occupational density of space at its Water-
side headquarters by up to 80%. The building uses the 'club' concept of
office configuration – allowing 180 people to be allocated to a floor plate
that, with a conventional one-desk-person policy, would have accommo-
dated only 100 staff. Extrapolation using conventional measures of density
shows that this reduces space requirements by some 5000 square metres."
(Lilischkis 2003). Low average use percentage of office space by employees indicates the potential for savings related to premises in the future.
Work is done anywhere, and sometimes also in the office.

Employment and labour relations
In three years, 1999-2002, the number of eWorkers grew annually by
around 30 per cent (Collaboration@Work 2003). The number of mobile
and self-employed eWorkers doubled annually, and supplementary home-
based eWork grew by 40 per cent. Only the number of traditional, home-
based teleworkers remained on the same level. In principle, because mobile ICT allows mobile work to be coordinated more effectively, some
jobs, for example, transportation and delivery, can become superfluous. In
a survey (Lilischkis and Meyer 2003), mobile workers were not, however,
more concerned than non-mobile workers about their job security. It is
evident that in virtual mobile groups employees and managers are likely to
work in different places. This makes direct control of employees in a traditional manner difficult. It is likely that a new work policy will be needed in
the future. Though collective labour agreements may not change, there is a
need for psychological contracts that state norms and values for new practices and modes of action in distributed teams. (See also Helle in this volume).

Mobile divide
The danger of deepening social gaps has been connected to the use of mobile ICT (Lilischkis 2003). According to him, the impacts, however, vary.
There are differences between European countries in utilising mobile work
and technologies. Inside countries, mobile ICT work offers opportunities
to disadvantaged regions, because people may not need to move to affluent
regions but can work from home and commute to their offices. Some industrial sectors are likely to benefit from mobile work, for example, the

real estate sector, as a result of savings because of office space being used more effectively. Large companies have more investment resources than small- and medium-sized ones and can invest more in mobile ICT work. On the individual level, mobile ICT at work may favour those with a better education. Mobile devices are not easily usable for people with manual disabilities, because screens are small and not easily readable.

Work-family balance

Work intervenes more and more in family life, and in part also vice versa. Mobile work appears to place greater strain on families and partnerships than non-mobile work (Lilischkis and Meyer 2003): while 27 per cent of the mobile workers agreed with the statement that the job often "prevents you from giving the time you want to your partner or family" and 39 per cent said "sometimes", the shares among non-mobile workers were only 21 per cent who answered "often" and 35 per cent "sometimes". The statement "partner/family gets fed up with job pressure" was answered with "often" by 14 per cent and with "sometimes" by 39% of the mobile workers, contrasting with only 11 per cent and 30 per cent among non-mobile workers. This finding is true for all professional groups. In another study (Hill et al. 1996), some mobile respondents perceived their possibilities of achieving a balance between work and home as being better than before. On the other hand, others considered keeping the balance to be difficult or very difficult. Availability is one of the potential impacts of using mobile technologies. As Cooper et al. (2002) note, the time spent getting to and from work can now be reconfigured as potentially productive time. To be available all the time may be stressful, but people seem to develop different strategies to maintain boundaries, for example between work and leisure. In all, the influence of mobile virtual work on family life is evident, and it seems to have positive or negative consequences that depend on the situation and the interpreter.

Job content

The content of mobile work content may be richer than that of stationary work. Mobile devices and services allow the same tasks to be performed elsewhere as had earlier been performed in the main workplace. Mobile employees meet more people, which increases the social requirements of the work. Communicating and collaborating via ICT is more abstract, which makes it cognitively more complex and demanding. Autonomy in work is greater: mobile employees can start and end their work more freely than non-mobile workers.

Competences

It is evident that mobile employees need new competences. Moving around increases the number of new people met, which requires new social skills and flexibility. Using mobile ICT for communication and collaboration requires new skills as well.

Well-being and stress

Increasing contextual complexity and mobility as one of its features change the requirements of work, and they are also potentially stress factors for employees. For example, feelings of loneliness and isolation could be expected. Only little is, however, known about the well-being outcomes of mobile virtual work. Lilischkis and Meyer (2003) found out that overall work satisfaction is slightly higher among mobile workers than among non-mobile workers. They note that mobility may be just one feature of an interesting job that leads to higher satisfaction. The fact is that mobile workers are more often self-employed or employed professionals and managers than manual workers. In a questionnaire study (Borg and Kristensen 1999), the main stressors of travelling salespeople were long working hours, many customers, non-day work and high perceived psychological demands in general. Borg and Kristensen did not find any association between poor mental health and factors such as the number of working hours away from the firm, nights away from home, and a low degree of perceived support from colleagues and superiors. (See also Richter, Meyer, and Sommer in this volume).

Social relationships

The capability of communication technologies and applications to support mobile employees' intra-group communication has been questioned. Mediated communication has been said to be socially impoverished in comparison with face-to-face communication when e-mails, teleconferences and videoconferences are used for meetings, and mobile devices and the internet for communicating with family and friends.

At least two approaches are provided to explain possible impoverishment (Watt et al. 2002). The first is the engineering concept of communication bandwidth, which refers to the relative information-carrying capacity and efficiency of communication channels. The low capacity to transfer great volumes of rich information quickly results in reduced social cues, and further also misunderstandings of messages and disturbances in intra-group relationships. The media richness model (Daft and Lengel 1984) relates the richness of information content to the complexity of tasks: the more complex the task, the 'richer' the media that are needed, and the more structured the task is, the more effective the 'poor (or simple)' media are. According to the model, effective communication is to be found by combining different media to meet the demands of the tasks and by paying attention to the disturbances caused by excessive information and the barriers raised by inadequate information.

It is not clear what the right balance is between face-to-face and virtual interaction in the arrangement of communication in mobile work. If necessary, people seem to be able to work and create trustful relationships in hazy situations. On the other hand, face-to-face meetings seem to remain the basic glue for social cohesion.

In all

The number of physically and virtually mobile workers and organisations that utilise mobility is increasing greatly. The main drivers are economic benefits and emerging new connections, devices, applications, and services. On the level of people, new opportunities are seen and found, though the workday has become more blurred and its practices are still underdeveloped. Factors that slow down progress are costs, inconsistencies and deficiencies of technologies, and the attitudes and competences of management. In the following chapters of this book, both the opportunities and the possible threats are discussed in more detail.

Acknowledgements

I want to thank Ministry of Labour in Finland for funding 'Challenges of Mobile Work' project and National Technology Agency of Finland for funding the 'Distributed Workplace' project. For detailed information I refer to: http://vmwork.tkk.fi.

References

Allen TJ (1977) Managing the flow of technology. MIT Press, Cambridge

Andriessen JHE (2003) Working with groupware. Understanding and evaluating collaboration technology. Springer-Verlag, London

Baecker RM (1993) Readings in groupware and computer-supported cooperative work assisting human-human collaboration. Morgan Kaufmann Publishers, San Francisco

Bell BS, Kozlowski SWJ (2002) A topology of virtual teams. Implications for effective leadership. Group & Organization Management 27(1):14–49

Byrne JA (1993) The virtual corporation. Business Week 8(2):98–103

Collaboration@Work (2003) The 2003 report on new working environments and practices. http://europa.eu.int/information_society/topics/ework/information/

Cooper G, Green N, Murtagh GM, Harper R (2002) Mobile society? Technology, distance, and presence. In: Woolgar, S (ed) Virtual society? Technology, cyberbole, reality. Oxford University Press, Oxford, pp 286–301

Daft RL, Lengel RH (1984) Information richness: a new approach to managerial behaviour and organization design. Research in Organizational Behavior 6:191–233

Davidow W, Malone M (1992) The virtual corporation. HarperBusiness, New York

DeSanctis G, Staudenmayer N, Wong SS (1999) Interdependence in virtual organizations. In: Cooper CL, Rousseau DM (eds) The virtual organization. Trends in Organizational Behavior 6:81–104

ECATT (2000) Benchmarking progress on new Ways of working and new forms of business across Europe. (ECATT final report. IST programme, KAII: New methods of work and electronic commerce. See: http://www.ecatt.com, Brussels

Engeström Y (1987) Learning by expanding. Orienta-Konsultit, Helsinki

European Commission, Directorate-General of The for Energy and Transport (ed) (2002) European Union energy and transport in figures 2002

Franke U (2000) The knowledge-based view (KBW) of the virtual web, the virtual corporation, and the net-broker. In: Malhotra Y (ed) Knowledge management and virtual organizations, Idea Group Publishing, London, pp 20–42

Handrick S, Hacker W (2002) Mobilität und psychische anforderungen. arbeitsgruppe "Wissen-Denken-Handeln", heft 12. Institut für Psychologie, TU Dresden

Hanhike T (2004) EWork in Finland. The Ministry of Labour, Helsinki

Harrison A, Wheeler P, Whitehead C (eds) (2004) The distributed workplace. Spon Press, London and New York, pp 56–57

Hayes K, Kuchinskas S (2003) Going mobile. Building the real-time enterprise with mobile applications that work. CMPBooks, San Francisco

Hill EJ, Hawkins AJ, Miller BC (1996) Work and family in the virtual office. Perceived influences of mobile telework. Family Relations 45:293–301

Jackson P, Wielen J van der (1996) (eds) New international perspectives on telework. In: Proceedings of workshop 'From telecommuting to the virtual organisation'. vol I and II. WORC, Tilburg University

Leont'ev AN (1978) Activity, consciousness, and personality. Prentice-Hall, Englewood Cliffs

Lewin K (1972) Need, force and valence in psychological fields. In: Hollander EP, Hunt RG (eds) Classic contributions to social psychology. Oxford Univesity Press, London

Lilischkis S (2003) More yo-yos, pendulums and nomads: trends of mobile and multi-location work in the information society. (STAR (Socio-economic trends assessment for the digital revolution) Issue report no 36, www.databank.it/star)

Lilischkis S, Meyer I (2003) Mobile and multi-local work in the European Union – empirical evidence from selected surveys. (STAR (Socio-economic trends assessment for the digital revolution) Issue report no 37)

Lipnack J, Stamps J (2000) Virtual teams. People working across boundaries with technology. Wiley & Sons, New York

McGrath JE (1991) Time, interaction, and performance (TIP). A theory of groups. Small Group Research 22(2):147–174

Nonaka I, Toyama R, Konno N (2000) SECI, *ba* and leadership: a unified model of dynamic knowledge creation. Long Range Planning 22:5–34

Oravec JO (1996) Virtual individuals, virtual groups. Human dimensions of groupware and computer networking. Cambridge University Press. Cambridge

Pekkola J (2002) Telework in Finland: physical, virtual, social and mental speces as working environments for telework. Ekonomi och Samhälle 104. The Swedish School of Economics and Business Administration, Helsinki

Peters T (1992) Liberation management: Necessary disorganization for the nanosecond nineties. Alfred A Knopf, New York

Picot A, Reichwald R, Wigand RT (2001) Die grenzenlose Unternehmung. Gabler, Wiesbaden

Pratt JH (2003) Teleworking comes of age with broadband. Telework America Survey 2002. (A Telework America Research Report of the International Telework Association & Council)

Rice AK (1969) Individual, group and intergroup processes. Human Relations 6:565–584

Saunders C, Van Slyke C, Vogel DR (2004) My time or yours? Managing time visions in global virtual teams. Academy of Management Executive 18:19–31

SIBIS, Statistical Indicators Benchmarking the information Society (2002) Topic Report no 5. (Topic: Work, employment and skills. http://www.sibis-eu.org obtained October 2002)

Snow CC, Lipnack J, Stamps J (1999). The virtual organization: promises and payoffs, large and small. In Cooper CL, Rousseau DM (eds) The virtual organization. Trends in Organizational Behavior 6:15–30

Toffler A (1980) The third wave. William Collins Sons & Co, London

Vygotsky LS (1962) Thought and language. The MIT Press, Cambridge

Watt SE, Lea M, Spears R (2002) How social is Internet communications? A reappraisal of bandwidth and anonymity effects. In: Woolgar S (ed) Virtual society? Technology, cyberbole, reality, Oxford University Press, Oxford, pp 61–77

3 Mapping the Mobile eWorkforce in Europe

Karsten Gareis, Stefan Lilischkis and Alexander Mentrup

Empirica: Gesellschaft für Kommunikations- und Technologieforschung, Germany

3.1 eWork and physical mobility

Because they enable time-space compression (Harvey 1989), information and communication technologies (ICTs) tend to make human labour less bound to place. They do not, however, automatically lead to a decentralisation of work locations across territory. Neither do they necessarily lead to a friction-less, fully mobile society where workers roam about as free agents and produce the allocation of labour, which at any given time and space produces the highest possible added value. While there are examples of persons who have exploited the potential for working at a distance from their central office, and of companies who turn their staff into a mobile workforce in order to get in closer contact to customers, research suggests that the overall relationship between ICTs, location and physical mobility is a highly complex one. Only very seldom do ICT-based structures substitute full-scale for traditional ways of carrying out work. More often, they supplement to and transform existing structures in a way, which best accommodates the capitalist imperative as well as the inertia which is a built-in feature of all social systems.

Recent empirical evidence, for example, tells us that telework has in practice developed in ways which have not been expected by the proponents of this type of separation between work location and employer's premises. Telework has not lead to decentralisation of work, but is more likely than not to take place inside of urban agglomerations (Ellen and Hempstead 2002). Teleworkers also show higher rates of work-related geographical mobility than persons in traditional work settings, enabled by mobile office technology, which has liberated work from being bound to a particular space and time (Gareis 2003).

Instead of the home becoming a near-permanent second workplace, we face a situation where much work has become more locationally flexible, and workers settle down temporarily wherever it suits their job, tasks and personal preferences best, all the time staying connected to the networks they need for their work. For many, the home has been turned into a touch-down office, together with a (potentially infinite) number of other locations where work can – and increasingly does – take place. We are calling the people who practice this way of working *mobile eWorkers*. While life-style magazines are bristling with futuristic depictions of "anywhere, any-time" work, surprisingly little statistical data exists about the actual size and structure of this section of the EU workforce. Moreover, there is only limited understanding of which workers are most involved in mobile activities. Certainly, ICT-enabled mobility does not affect all workers to the same extent (Valenduc et al. 2000), as is sometimes indicated in futurist depictions. A differentiated view is necessary in order to identify future challenges for social cohesion and the health of the labour market.

To shed some more light on the discussion around ICT-enabled mobility of work, the authors use a database from a recent, representative EU-wide survey (SIBIS[1]) to explore in more depth the key characteristics of mobile workers and mobile eWorkers. The findings will allow us to gain a better understanding of the reality of mobile eWork in Europe today.

Before doing so, this chapter will discuss the background against which mobile forms of working are developing. Section two looks at some of the main drivers behind worker mobility in general and mobile eWork in particular. This will allow us to relate the phenomenon to more general developments in work organisation and labour markets in the EU and beyond. Section three will then present a conceptual framework for making sense of the interrelations between ICTs, work/task characteristics, and work mobility. This will include discussion of the mobility term itself. Increasingly, there is talk of so-called "virtual mobility", that means relations in which not the workers themselves, but only the "work", that means work inputs, work products, are moving across space, for example, inside of value chains. While in this chapter, mobility is always meant as physical mobility unless stated otherwise, we need to always bear in mind that, in times of virtual reality and ambient intelligence, the purposes which have traditionally required physical mobility might increasingly be achieved through electronic means.

---

[1] The SIBIS database stems from population surveys, which were undertaken in 2002/2003 in all current EU25 Member States plus the USA, Switzerland, Romania and Bulgaria. For more information on SIBIS (Statistical Indicators Benchmarking the Information Society), see www.sibis-eu.org. The project was funded by the European Commission through its Information Society Programme.

3.2 Drivers

3.2.1 Drivers of worker mobility

The following is a brief discussion of the factors and developments, which have been important driving forces for increasing the physical mobility of workers in recent decades.

We can distinguish between economic, technological and socio-cultural drivers without neglecting that the three domains are closely interrelated and should not be explored in isolation from each other.

Economic drivers for worker mobility have their origin in the restructuring of western capitalism since the economic crisis of the late 1960s and early 1970s. Via growing interconnectedness of market participants, this trend has lead to an increasing division of work at a global scale (Massey and Megan 1979) and growing market power of multi-national corporations (Dicken 2003). Intra-company transactions which stretch across locations, regions, countries and continents have multiplied. The organisation of the production process has also changed towards greater parts being executed as market transactions instead of intra-organisational movements of goods and information. Collaboration and network-building between independent enterprises have increased. A higher number of employees spend more time collaborating with external parties. All of this has directly resulted in more travel activity, longer distances and more time spent on travelling.

Another outcome of the economic restructuring in the last third of the 20th century has been a sharp increase in competitive pressure. Enterprises have reacted in a number of ways, often by adopting more flexible production systems, whereby flexible transport services have become an integral and essential part of the production process (Gareis 2003). This is, for example, the case with just-in-time production systems, where input deliveries are made in close co-ordination with production schedules, leading to more frequent deliveries of smaller quantities of materials. And just as just-in-time production transfers the warehouse onto the roads to respond more quickly and adequately to changes in demand, mobile eWork transfers work onto the streets so to better respond to the demands of the customer, what the authors have termed "just-in-time-working" before. In a push for enhanced customer orientation, value chains have also been redesigned to take better account of what customers ask for, thereby gaining competitive advantage (Davidow and Malone 1992). In many cases, companies strive to spend more time and effort on learning what customers want. This implies getting in touch with customers, which (still) means more often than not face-to-face interaction. Physical proximity to great numbers of customers spread over the territory requires mobility.

Recent years have seen much emphasis being put on cost cutting. Because office space is expensive, and rates of utilisation are often shockingly low, because workers are in meetings, visiting customers, teleworking, or on holiday, companies have started to exploit possibilities of distributing office space more effectively, what is called desk-sharing, hoteling or hot desking. There is a growing feeling that reserving personal workspace for the exclusive use of individual workers is a thing of the past that just does not match the flexibility needs of modern businesses any more. But once employees lose their "own" desk, they are more likely to spend more time at mobile locations. In this case, mobile eWork is not only a driver behind new concepts of office space management, but can also result from these: both developments are mutually reinforcing.

Technological drivers include the developments in ICT, which have boosted time-space compression. In combination with progress in transport technology, these have dramatically reduced the time it takes to move humans, physical goods and information across distance. Harvey (1989) illustrated the concept with maps of the world that shrink over time proportionately to the increasing speed of transportation. The world of the 1960s then is about one-fiftieth the size of the world of the sixteenth century because jet aircraft can travel at about fifty times the speed of a sailing ship. Time-space compression decreases the costs for physical mobility, thereby inducing demand. Transportation costs have fallen continuously in recent years, most drastically for air transport.

Closely related to the above, *socio-cultural drivers* have caused increases in the demand for transport. A powerful process in this regard is what is called urban spread, which is a long-standing process that was set in motion by private car traffic and the telephone. In its course, population and businesses have been relocating away from city centres towards the urban fringes and towards major transport arteries (CSP 1999). Notwithstanding recent evidence that city centres are becoming more attractive again, urban spread is continuing with the same speed as ever, leading to more complex and diffuse patterns of commuting and business transport, and overall higher levels of individual transport. Other developments in society of relevance here include the growing numbers of dual income households with partners who work at distant locations and as a consequence have high mobility requirements. Moreover, increasing household incomes imply a higher level of personal mobility, for example, holiday abroad several times per year, because demand for leisure travel has very high income elasticity (OECD 2000).

3.2.2 Physical and virtual mobility

Having listed a number of the most important drivers of worker mobility, it is important to recall that in the world of work, physical mobility is not an end in itself. It serves economic interests and underlies considerations of (pecuniary) costs and benefits. In general, worker mobility is being utilised to achieve an optimal allocation of human capital in the production system. The costs involved in working in a mobile rather than fixed setting can be significant, as the chapter by Mark Perry and Jackie Brodie in this book lies out when discussing "mobilisation work". In general, human capital is today by far the least mobile of all production factors. Companies are, therefore, constantly seeking out alternatives to physical mobility in order to control costs while still enjoying the benefits from close interconnectedness with value chain partners and customers. One way of doing so, much discussed in the futurist literature, is to supplement ICT for physical mobility. An example would be to conduct a video-conference instead of calling persons for a face-to-face meeting, which implies physical travel. Other examples for virtual mobility include all kinds of computer supported collaborative work (CSCW). Complex documents such as construction drafts that used to be presented and discussed in meetings can be circulated and discussed through the Internet. Such forms of work are already quite wide-spread, as EU data from SIBIS indicates (see Sect 3.4.3 below).

While physical and virtual mobility serve similar purposes – namely to make work (products, inputs) available where it produces the highest added value at any given time – there is much evidence which suggests that both do in practice not so much *substitute* for each other as they are *complementary*: the more people interact with others through ICTs, the more likely they are to seek face-to-face interaction as well (Niles 1994, OECD 2000). One reason for this is that ICTs not only provide potential substitutes for physical travel, but they are at the same time also making mobile working much more efficient and effective than ever before. This is briefly outlined in the following section.

3.2.3 ICTs as drivers of mobile work

ICTs play a powerful role as drivers of physically mobile work. For a discussion, it is useful to start looking at problems surrounding mobile work *without* ICTs.

Mobile work can cause a number of problems related to an interrupted communication flow between the mobile worker and colleagues, superiors and customers. Mobile workers who are co-operating with a fixed-location basis are separated from on-going business processes, resources, infrastructures and face-to-face communication opportunities. In a situation where a division of labour exists, the problem of assembling the results of work from different workers arises. Typical challenges that may arise from mobile work without ICTs are *non-accessibility* that means mobile workers not or not fully reachable, *unknown location* that means current location of the mobile worker is unknown; particularly important for emergency medical services and forwarding agencies, *limited ability to carry resources* that means limited ability to transport and process information, *limited resource access* that means lack of full access to databases, secretary services and other resources, and *media breaks* that means detachment from on-going business processes causing media breaks between the fixed and the mobile part of the value chain (Schulte 1997).

ICTs may reduce these problems of mobile work significantly. In fact, many activities could not be accomplished on the move at all until ICTs enabled mobility. Writing documents and analysing data requiring a machine was not possible on journeys until portable computers were created to do such work while sitting in a train or in the premises of a distant customer enterprise. Other examples of the ways ICTs can facilitate, enable and support mobile work include:

- *Swifter data processing*: ICTs allow a more efficient way of data processing and, in an ideal case, data flows without media breaks in spite of different, partly mobile locations involved. Mobile devices for salespersons, for example, enables them to take new orders at the customers' site and enter them immediately into the central computer system. At the headquarters, the order is then transferred to the company's computer-based order and logistic system in real time.
- *Time saving*: Instant data processing can also lead to considerable savings in throughput times, as business processes can be fully integrated regardless of the distance involved between parts of the value chain. This decreases the costs of mobility compared to static work environments.
- *Location independence*: Mobile end devices allow instant communication when the need for it arises, independent of the location. Without a mobile phone, for example, persons working in the field would have to search for a public phone or ask clients to allow them to use their phone. Mobile computing devices also depend much less on fixed access to data networks than desktop equipment.
- *Instant information retrieval*: While on a journey, mobile telephony and online access allows users to retrieve information from company or public sources – including timetables, restaurant guides and hotel finders.

- *Weight reduction*: In many cases, ICTs reduce the weight of work material. For example, digitised files have made work locationally flexible, which was bound to a single location before because of the need for instant access to archived data.
- *Cost reduction*: ICTs have played a vital role in pushing down travel costs per mile traveled – a long-term trend which has gained speed in recent decades. Computer networks are a central component of all modern travel systems, no matter whether on rail, road, water or in the air.

The advance of 3G and later generations of mobile networks will further strengthen these advantages by offering broadband connections, and all applications made possible by them, for mobile use.

3.3 Conceptualising mobile eWork

The term "eWork" has been promoted mainly by the European Commission (CEC 2003) to indicate a step onwards from previous notions of telework. From the research and practitioner literature, it appears that the ways in which eWork differs from the earlier concept of telework are: (a) while telework in the traditional sense is mostly focussing on individualised changes of work location, most prominently at home, eWork also includes remote work in shared office premises, such as call-centres and other remote back offices (Huws and O'Regan 2001); and (b) in addition to traditional telework, eWork is understood to also cover *tele-collaboration,* i.e. telemediated work forms carried out by workers located in traditional office environments, as in the case of virtual teams, which stretch across the boundaries of single organisations (Eichmann et al. 2002). In order to distinguish between such tele-collaboration and traditional types of telework, it is useful to describe the latter as *principal/agent relationships* (see Eisenhardt 1989) to highlight the fact that they consist of a principal, i.e. somebody, such as a superior, who does not act directly but instead by giving incentives – such as money, career prospects – to other persons, and agents who carry out the work on their behalf. In collaboration, there is not necessarily any hierarchical relationship between co-workers, but rather a situation where two or more people work together to create or achieve the same thing (Hanhike and Gareis 2004).[2]

---

[2] A more precise definition of tele-collaboration needs to address what kind of information is transmitted, and for what purpose. This can be operationalised by defining collaboration as being based on an explicit, e.g. written, but not necessary legally binding, agreement about common aims.

We define *telemediation* as the transfer of work inputs and/or outputs via data telecommunication links. *Remoteness* refers here to the physical distance between persons involved, either principal and agent or various collaborators. Any definition as in "remote work" either leaves much room for interpretation, or must appear rather arbitrary. Nevertheless, most often remote work is being (implicitly) defined as meaning different sites, locations and addresses. For example, telemediated work exchange between two establishments, even if they belong to the same organisation, should be considered eWork if they do not share the same address. On the other hand, co-located workers who nevertheless make extensive use of computer supported collaborative work should not count as eWorkers, because distance does not play any significant role in their case.

Work in this context is any type of gainful employment. We define collaboration in virtual teams as a group of individuals who or some of whom, are located remotely from each other and who work together to create or achieve the same thing, and in which interaction takes place exclusively or almost exclusively via telemediation (compare Lipnack and Stamps 1997). They can, but do not have to stretch across organisational boundaries.

A definition of eWork, therefore, should comprise *any type of telemediated remote work* and include the following types:

- individualised or shared-office based referring only to the physical workplace of the worker, not to the fact that they share an office with the principal or collaborators;
- collaborative work that means tele-cooperation or virtual teams, or work which is performed in the context of principal-agent type relationships;
- work interaction, which is inter-organisational, i.e. coordinated over the market such as in client/contractor relationships and freelance work, or work interaction, which is intra-organisational that means coordinated internally in organisations.[3]

Accordingly, Table 3.1 presents a typology of eWork, based on previous work by Huws and O'Regan (2001). The grey cells contain the main types of eWork, while the last line lists some types which do not fall in the eWork category.

---

[3] It should be noted here that this distinction has become less clear-cut in recent years, since many transactions inside of companies are nowadays managed very similarly than market transactions, e.g. in the case of individual profit centres, which together make up a larger, often multi-national corporation.

Table 3.1. Typology of eWork

	Coordination mechanism			
	Principal/agent		Collaboration	
	intra-organisational	inter-organisational	intra-organisational	inter-organisational
Individualised eWork (away from office premises)	Telework in employment relationships	Freelance telework[4]	Work in virtual teams composed of teleworking employees from a single company	Work in virtual teams made up of teleworkers from different companies (or self-employed)
eWork on shared office premises	eWork at other site of same company (e.g. back offices)	eOutsourcing	Work in virtual teams composed of employees from a single company	Work in virtual teams composed of employees from different companies
Non-eWork (examples)	*Employed agents co-located with principals*	*Self-employed co-located with clients*	*Work in co-located teams composed of employees from a single company*	*Work in co-located teams composed of employees from different companies*

(Left margin label: **Work environment**)

Source: based on Huws and O'Regan (2001); Hanhike and Gareis (2004).

Some of these types of eWork can also have a strong component of physical mobility, in which case they can be considered as mobile eWork. This refers to individualised eWork only, since eWork on shared office premises is by definition stationary. For identifying mobile applications of eWork, we need to define mobile work more clearly.

According to Perry et al. (2001), mobile work activities involve "working at multiple (but stationary) locations, walking around a central location, travelling between locations, working in hotel rooms, on moving vehicles and in remote meeting rooms". However, for the purpose of this chapter, we exclude mobile work of the type "walking around a central location" since it does not comply with our criterion of remoteness (see above). In order to distinguish mobile workers from non-mobile workers, one may also need to add the temporal dimension, i.e. set a lower threshold of time spent in mobile work activities for a worker to be considered as mobile.

---

[4] For persons who conduct the major part of their work through networked work environments, we can use Laubacher and Malone's term "*eLancer*" (Laubacher and Malone 2001).

Other important dimensions include the mode of working, i.e. to what extent the mobile activity is supported by technology and how much the mobile worker is integrated in company information networks, and the purpose of worker mobility (Heinonen 2004). While the former concerns the distinction between mobile work and mobile eWork, the latter is linked to the question whether mobility requirements are work-related or not[5].

3.4 Mobile work and mobile eWork today

This section presents some quantitative evidence about the spread of different types of mobile eWork in Europe. Section 3.4.1 contains data on the spread of mobile work in general, while section 3.4.2 discusses the diffusion of mobile eWork and presents an analysis of the development of all individualised types of eWork in recent years. Albeit the amount of statistics available is very limited, there is evidence which suggests that mobile eWork is growing in significance in comparison to other types such as alternating, home-based telework. Section 3.4.3 then presents early findings on the diffusion of types of tele-collaboration, that means "virtually mobile" eWork.

3.4.1 Mobile work

SIBIS defined *mobile workers* as those who "spend some *paid* working time away from their home and away from their main place of work, e.g. on business trips, in the field, travelling or on customer's premises" at least once per month. *High-intensity mobile workers* are those who do so for 10 hours or more per week. In both cases work commutes are not included.

According to the data from SIBIS, 28% of EU15 workers spent some paid working time doing mobile work in 2002. The number of high-intensity mobile workers was roughly half of this (15%).

The share of mobile workers differs considerably between countries (see Table 3.3). In the EU15, the range is from 46% in the Netherlands and 45% in Finland to only 8% in Portugal. There appears to be a North-South divide with above-average levels of mobile work in Finland and Sweden and below-average levels in Greece, Italy, Portugal and Spain. In the 10 New Member States and Acceding Countries covered by the SIBIS data, average shares of mobile workers are lower, although some of the smaller

---

[5] In this respect, Bell (2002) distinguishes between production- and consumption-related mobility.

countries do have figures which are similar to the EU15 average; this applies to Slovenia, the Baltic countries, and Slovakia.

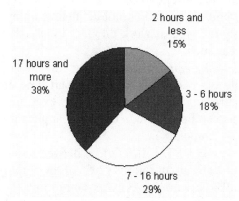

Fig. 3.1. Time spent on the move by mobile workers in %[6]

Regarding the intensity of working at mobile locations, mobile workers were grouped into quartiles of 2 and less hours, 3 to 6 hours, 7 to16 hours and more than 16 hours. According to the results, many mobile workers spend a large share of their working time away from home or their main place of work. In the EU15, 15% of mobile workers work two and less paid working hours per week away from home and the main place of work, 18% between 3 and 6 hours, 29% between 7 and 16 hours, and 38% work 17 hours and more at mobile locations (see Fig. 3.1).

Closer analysis of the data using logistic regression analysis (see Annex) sheds some light on the factors, which determine the likelihood of a worker practising mobile work:

- *Education*: There is a clear correlation between the likelihood to do mobile work and educational attainment, measured by the age at which initial full-time education was finished. A post secondary degree increases the likelihood of doing mobile work by 236% as compared to workers with only basic education; a higher secondary does so by 132%.

- *Occupation*: When broadly distinguishing between blue collar, white collar and managerial or professional workers, we find that the latter two are significantly more likely to do mobile work (106% and 227%, respectively).

- *Employment status*: 26% of paid employees do mobile work, while 42% of self-employed belong to this group. However, when controlling for

---

[6] Unweighted average for EU15, CH and USA. Source: SIBIS General Population Survey 2002, Empirica. Base: All mobile workers (n = 1277)

other factors such as occupation, educational attainment, gender and country, we find that workers with a contract of employment are 68% more likely than the self-employed to do mobile work. The fact that the self-employed tend to be more mobile than employees does reflect, therefore, mainly the type of work they are involved in rather than employment status as such.

- *Full-time or part-time employment*: 31% of full-time employees do mobile work, while the respective value for part-time employees is only 18%. When controlling for third factors, however, no significant effect of working hours can be detected. The same applies for *type of contract* (unlimited versus temporary).
- *Public or private sector*: The differences between mobile work practice in public or non-profit organisations (26% of the employees) and private organisations (30%) are not large. After controlling for third factors, we find that workers in the private sector are 25% more likely to do mobile work compared to public sector workers.
- *Company size class*: Although the share of mobile workers is highest in large establishments with more than 250 employees (30%), all in all differences by size class are negligible.
- *Gender*: Of all male employees, 38% reported to do mobile work, while the figure is only 18% for female workers. This is partly caused by the fact that women are less represented in management positions and among the self-employed than men. Still, after controlling for these and other factors, women remain 67% less likely to do mobile work then men.
- *Age*: The effect of age on the likelihood to be engaged in mobile work practice is insignificant.
- *Country*: As stated above (see also Table 3.3), there are huge differences in the number of mobile workers across EU countries. It can be assumed, however, that these are partly explained by third factors such as sectoral structure, educational attainment, the share of white-collar workers etc. Multivariate analysis allows us to single out those Member States, in which country-specific factors seem to account for a high or low share of mobile workers. Taking as a reference country France, which has a share of mobile workers, which is close to the EU25 average, Finland, the Netherlands, Sweden and Slovenia have a significantly higher incidence of mobile work, while workers in Romania, Portugal, Poland, Bulgaria, Hungary, Spain, Luxembourg and the Czech Republic are significantly less likely to work in a mobile setting.

As this analysis shows, there are a number of factors which have a considerable influence on the odds of doing mobile work. Most obviously, occupational category and educational attainment play a dominant role. Gender, employment status, and in many cases the country also significantly affect the likelihood of doing mobile work. This has a number of implications for policy as well as research, which are discussed in section 3.5.

3.4.2 Mobile eWork

Mobile eWork is defined as high-intensity mobile work in the course of which an online connection to the Internet and/or to company computer systems is being used. 4% of the EU15 work force are mobile eWorkers. Switzerland is the leader here among the countries in the survey, followed by Finland, the USA, Germany and Italy. The penetration in Eastern and Central Europe is again much lower with an average of about 1%, although Estonia and Slovenia have impressively high figures.[7]

The main purposes of mobile eWorkers to use online connections is sending and reading e-mail (92%), but three quarters each also browse the Internet and connect to their company's internal computer system. O'Hara et al. (2002) found in an empirical study of a group of mobile eWorkers that e-mail was used less for outgoing than for incoming communication, and it was much less used for managing urgent situations than the mobile phone. Furthermore, e-mail was only used by those survey participants who stayed overnight away from home. The typical scenario was to check e-mails at a hotel.

Table 3.2. Mobile eWork (in %, EU15)

Mobile eWorkers (use computer connections when travelling)	4.0
thereof (multiple response): Purpose	
for accessing the Internet	*73.4*
for sending or reading e-mails	*92.4*
for connecting to their company's internal computer system	*72.4*
thereof (multiple response): Location	
hotel, conference site or similar location	*68.7*
another company's premises	*52.0*
Internet café or commercial teleservice centre	*5.4*
on the move using mobile device for data transfer	*37.0*

---

[7] Data from Lithuania is missing for this indicator.

Table 3.2. (Cont.)

Other high-intensity mobile workers	11.4
Low-intensity or non-mobile workers	81.8
DK	2.8
Total	100.0

Base: All persons employed (N=5,100); weighted by EU15 population.
Data source: SIBIS 2002, GPS.

Table 3.2 also presents the means by which workers connect to electronic communication channels. One potential access point are teleservice
centres, which offer travellers a temporary workplace equipped with PC,
Internet access, printer, fax etc. Such service providers are emerging at the
nodes of international traffic networks, i.e. at central locations in large cities as well as airports. They may contribute to making mobile work attractive for more and more travellers. However, currently only 5% of all mobile eWorkers make use of telework centres, whereas most choose the
hotel room or conference site, another company's premises a similar location for going online. More than a third use truly mobile technology, i.e.
data transfer via mobile devices, for the purpose.

Table 3.3. Spread of mobile work and mobile eWork (in % of employment)

	All mobile workers	High intensity mobile workers	Mobile eWorkers	Tele-cooperation
Austria	22.4	13.6	3.7	35.9
Belgium	25.7	12.5	2.4	37.5
Denmark	26.8	14.0	2.7	55.8
Finland	44.5	19.7	6.2	55.5
France	25.7	15.5	2.1	25.9
Germany	31.8	16.3	5.7	45.8
Greece	21.5	15.2	3.5	12.6
Ireland	30.3	19.7	4.2	37.3
Italy	24.8	14.1	5.5	35.2
Luxembourg	20.7	6.8	1.5	42.4
Netherlands	45.5	19.6	4.1	46.7
Portugal	8.4	4.3	0.3	9.3
Spain	17.4	9.1	0.8	21.2
Sweden	39.8	19.4	4.9	52.3
U.K.	32.8	18.9	4.7	48.9
EU 15	*28.4*	*15.4*	*4.0*	*37.8*

Table 3.3. (cont.)

USA	32.1	19.0	5.9	53.2
Bulgaria	17.5	11.8	1.0	15.6
Czech rep.	20.9	14.6	2.1	20.7
Estonia	26.5	13.7	3.9	31.3
Hungary	19.3	16.8	0.9	12.7
Latvia	24.1	14.9	2.4	20.3
Lithuania	24.8	16.9	n.a.	21.1
Poland	12.3	8.5	1.0	16.8
Romania	6.1	5.3	0.6	8.5
Slovakia	24.9	16.3	1.8	14.4
Slovenia	34.8	20.9	3.0	31.9
NAS 10	*15.8*	*11.2*	*1.2*	*16.0*

Base: All persons employed (N=5,901), weighted; averages weighted by EU15/ NAS10 population. Source: SIBIS 2002/2003, GPS.

The share of mobile eWorkers among overall EU15 employment has grown from 1.5% to 4% in the course of only three years (1999-2002)[8], as is shown in table 3.3. This is likely to benefit employers, in particular, as the efficiency of business process increases because of more continuous communication flows (Julstrud 1998; Gareis 2003). This increase can be explained by a number of factors, as outlined in section 3.2. There is much evidence that mobile computing technology and online access are being increasingly used for work. According to the Working Life Barometer 2002 in Finland, a forerunner country with respect to mobile phone usage, almost 40% of wage and salary earners have been carrying out work tasks in their leisure time by means of a connection to their employer via mobile phone or ICT network (Ylöstalo 2003). The boundaries between work at a central office, on the road or in the field, at customer's premises, at teleservice centres and at home are likely to further disappear step by step. The same applies it seems, to the boundaries between working time and leisure time (Voß 1998).

---

[8] 1999 data stems from surveys conducted in the context of another EU research project (ECATT), which made use of very similar methodology including survey questionnaires, see CEC 2000.

Table 3.4. Development of individualised telework in % of all persons employed (weighted averages) in EU15

Type	EU15	
	1999	2002
Home-based telework (at least 1 day/week)	2.0	2.1
Supplementary home-based telework	2.0	5.3
Mobile eWork (SIBIS definition)	1.5	4.0
Freelance telework in SOHOs	0.9	3.4
All individualised telework (excl. overlaps)	6.0	13.0

Base: All persons employed; weighted by EU15 population. Data source: Empirica 1999, 2002.

While the number of mobile eWorkers appears to be growing rapidly, the same is not true for traditional, home-based telework as long as this takes up at least one full working day per week, which implies that some form of agreement between employee and supervisor/employer exists about the issue. The share of such home-based teleworkers has remained stagnant over the period 1999-2002 in the EU15.

Permanent telework by persons with a contract of employment is so rare in Europe that it could not be measured in a statistically significant way using the SIBIS sample of ~ 12,000 interviews in the EU15. Among the self-employed, permanently working from home is more wide-spread, for obvious reasons. It has become more and more obvious in recent years that permanently teleworking at home is in most cases not sustainable with regard to psychosocial (Huuhtanen 1997) and economic factors (Gareis 1999). The FAMILIES project (Cullen et al. 2003) has reported evidence from a major Danish company according to which telework's mid-term effect on productivity was slightly negative in case of permanent or near-permanent telework, while it was very positive for alternating teleworkers. The reasons given for the poor performance of permanent teleworkers refer to the lack of social and informal interaction with colleagues, which resulted in a loss of motivation and insufficient access to intra-company information flows.

But while permanent teleworking at home remains an exotic phenomenon, and alternating home-based telework is hardly increasing at all, supplementary home-based telework that means working for less than one full day per week at home is on the rise (see Table 3.4). In 2002, there were more than two and a half times more supplementary teleworkers in the EU15 than three years before.[9]

These findings have been confirmed by research carried out at the national level (USA: ILO, quoted in Di Martino 2001; UK: Di Martino 2001; Finland: Statistics Finland 2003). They suggest that there is a shift among home-based teleworkers towards less time spent at home. Obviously, the progress in the availability of cheap and powerful remote access technology has not led to workers spending more and more time working at home, but rather to more and more workers spending only a fraction of their weekly working time at home. This points towards a greater flexibility in the use of individual working locations, but at the possible expense of some of the traditional advantages ascribed to telecommuting such as savings on miles travelled.

Freelance teleworkers in SOHOs are self-employed persons who work from home, on the same grounds as their home or with their home as their base, and use online ICTs for interaction with their clients. The survey showed that 3% of EU employment belongs to this group, which translates into 21% off all self-employed. The share of teleworkers is, therefore, considerably higher among the self-employed than among workers with a contract of employment. Telework seems to be on the way to becoming the standard working mode for the majority of freelancers. Between 1999 and 2002, the number of SOHO-based teleworkers has grown from 1% to more than 3% as a result of annual growth rates averaging more than 50%. The candidate countries (average 2%) are somewhat behind the EU, but to a lesser extent than it is the case for the other types of telework.

It has been suggested that to categorise teleworkers as either "home-based" or "mobile" distracts from the fact that many teleworkers spend their working time at a number of different locations, among which the home might be only one option. This trend has obviously been enabled by mobile office technology, which has liberated work from being bound to a particular space and time. For this phenomenon, the term "multi-locational telework" has been invented (CEC 2003; Gareis et al. 2004b). It implies that persons work wherever it suits their work tasks, business schedule, and/or lifestyle.

---

[9] It is important to note here that this definition of supplementary home-based eWork and all related figures presented in this chapter requires that paid working time is spent at remote locations. Definitions, which also include unpaid work-related activities quickly arrive at figures of between a quarter and half of all workers doing work at home (Di Martino 2001; Ylöstalo 2003).

Table 3.5. Multi-locational telework – working locations

Base →	(a) at home or the same grounds	(b) on another site of employer	(c) at customers/ clients	(d) at a hotel/ meeting venue	(e) on the move
at home or the same grounds	100.0	40.4	42.2	39.1	42.5
on another site of employer	11.5	100.0	52.5	57.4	55.6
at customers/ clients	17.4	76.0	100.0	64.6	71.9
at a hotel/ meeting venue	9.2	47.4	36.9	100.0	50.1
on the move	14.2	65.2	58.3	71.0	100.0

Base: all multi-locational workers. Data source: BISER RPS 2003, weighted.

Data from the BISER survey can be used to assess in detail how much time eWorkers have spent at each of five "atypical" working locations (Gareis et al. 2004b). Table 3.5 shows the share of those teleworking from one of these locations (columns) who also do telework at each of the other locations (rows). For example, of persons teleworking from the home (a) 11.5% also work at a second location of their employer and use online connections to stay in contact when doing so. Another example: 42.5% of those who telework from mobile locations (e) also spend time teleworking from home.

The figures in the table provide evidence that multi-locational work has indeed become a normal way of working for a considerable share of total employment. Only persons teleworking from home are unlikely to spend time teleworking from other locations. The reason for this might be that the equipment in home offices is often fixed in space, i.e. cannot be used for teleworking from other locations, such as desktop, home-bound Internet access. On the other hand, once workers have access to mobile computing equipment, they seem to choose any of a number of different working locations, including a second location of their employer, the premises of customers or clients, hotels and meeting venues, and temporary locations while travelling.

3.4.3 Tele-collaboration: "virtually mobile eWork"

SIBIS collected data on the extent to which the EU labour force is involved in tele-cooperation already. For this, a very basic definition was used which included everybody who regularly uses e-mail or the Internet to communicate with work contacts located at other business sites, either in other organisations or at other sites of the same organisation. Table 3.3 shows that more than every third worker in the EU15 is involved in regular tele-cooperation, if defined in that way – about three times as many as there are teleworkers.

3.5 Conclusions and outlook

This chapter has discussed a conceptual framework for eWork, which attempts to include established forms such as home-based telework as well as types of ICT-enabled work which have entered the debate only recently, such as locationally flexible work taking place in traditional office environments, and work relationships which are collaborative rather than following a principal-agent pattern. We think that progress in the conceptual underpinning of research on ICT-enabled work forms is strongly needed because:

- much research suggests that traditional (home-based) teleworking is unlikely to ever achieve the significance for the labour market which was predicted only a few years ago;
- it is increasingly acknowledged that networked work environments – which make extensive use of ICTs for interconnecting workplaces across space and time, but do not necessarily involve a relocation of physical workplaces from central offices – play a key role for economic competitiveness.

The chapter has also tried to contribute to a better understanding of the relationship between physical mobility and applications of ICTs for work, namely in the form of ICT-supported environments for mobile work, i.e. *mobile eWork*. While general opinion still tends to equate the application of ICTs in work settings with a substitution for physical mobility, ICTs also give powerful support to mobile working, thereby allowing for closer contact with customers and value chain partners, more efficient use of spare time during travel, and abolishment of traditional disadvantages of work mobility such as disconnection from communication networks. Since there are a number of powerful drivers, which increase the demand for work which is physically mobile, mobile eWork can be expected to keep growing rapidly over the coming years.

This is not meant to suggest that what may be called "virtually mobile work", i.e. collaboration through online data networks such as the Internet, would be insignificant. Quite the contrary, tele-collaboration is starting to affect an increasing share of the EU workforce, as witnessed by the 2002/2003 data from SIBIS (see Table 3.3). According to the definition of SIBIS, already every third worker in the EU15 is involved in tele-collaboration and 16% in the New Member States of Central and Eastern Europe. These figures are based on a simplified definition of collaboration. More research is clearly needed in order to develop and apply more advanced indicators which are able to distinguish between different degrees and intensities of collaboration, and differences in the significance of online tools for collaborative work.

Such research will enable us to better understand the size and shape of the change, which is currently ongoing in the world of work. For policy-making, it will be essential to establish quantitative evidence about the effect of eWork on key variables of competitiveness such as productivity, innovativeness, and time-to-market. While recent research has provided insight into impacts of traditional telework on, for example sustainable development (e.g. Schäfer 2004), only little is known about the effects of "virtual mobile work". This is, of course, mainly due to the elusive nature of these applications of ICT. This must not, however, deter us from trying to establish more evidence.

In addition, policy-makers need more information about the barriers and facilitators of eWork applications, and these need to distinguish carefully between developments, which can be assumed to be compatible with current policy goals, and developments, which are in danger of undermining the effectiveness of policy-making. Gareis et al. (2004a) have found indicative evidence, which suggests that take-up of eWork as well as tele-collaboration is negatively correlated with the degree of employment protection legislation, and also with an index of risk aversion at national level. Such evidence alone, however, does not give us any indication whether eWork is being applied in ways, which optimally exploit potential benefits for society, or not. Against this background, research on the economic, ecological and social sustainability of eWork applications appears to be of highest relevance.

Statistical annex

Analysis of SIBIS data

As we deal mainly with non-metric variables, it is not useful to apply a linear regression model since no linear association can be expected. For our purpose, logistic regression is most appropriate. The logistic regression model is simply a non-linear transformation of the linear regression. For a case with two variables, the logit model is described as:

$$\ln(\frac{p_i}{1-p_i}) = a_1 + bx_i \tag{3.1}$$

whereby:

ln is the is the natural logarithm, $\log_{exp}$, where exp=2.71828…,

p is the probability that the event Y occurs, p(Y=1),

$\dfrac{p_i}{1-p_i}$ is the "odds ratio", i.e. the probability of the event divided by the probability of the non-event,

$\ln(\dfrac{p_i}{1-p_i})$ is the log odds ratio, or "logit",

a is the coefficient on the constant term,

b is the coefficient(s) on the independent variable(s), and

x is the independent variable(s).

The logistic distribution is an S-shaped distribution function which is similar to the standard-normal distribution, which results in a probit regression model, but easier to work with in most applications, i.e. the probabilities are easier to calculate. The logit distribution constrains the estimated probabilities to range from 0 to 1. The dependent variable can be dichotomous and nominal, i.e. discrete not continuous.

To analyse the impact of different demographic, socio-economic and work related variables on the uptake of mobile work, we use the *binary logistic regression* procedure in SPSS. The variables included in the calculation are mostly non-metric variables. In fact, the dependent mobile work variable selected for the analysis is nominally scaled and dichotomous, which is one constraint for the chosen statistic model. The independent variables are of interval level or categorical, one is metric scaled.

For interpretation we use the effect coefficient exp(b), which is the effect of the independent variable on the odds ratio. The last column of **Error! Reference source not found.** displays the increase/decrease of the odds ratio as percentages.

Table 3.6. Determinants of incidence of mobile work (logistic regression, Exp(b))

	Mobile work	
	Exp(b)	in %
Gender (reference: male)		
female	0.334**	-67
Age class (ref.: 14-24)		
25-34	1.126	13
35-49	1.078	8
50+	1.024	2
Educational attainment (ref.: none and basic)		
low secondary	1.506*	51
high secondary	2.317**	132
post secondary	3.364**	236
Occupation (ref.: blue collar)		
white collar	2.065**	106
managerial or professional	3.267**	227
Employment contract (ref.: self-employed)		
with employment contract	1.683**	68
Working hours (reference: part-time)		
full-time	1.166	17
Type of contract (reference: fixed term)		
permanent	1.172*	0
Company size class (ref.: 50-249)		
0-49	1.121	12
250+	1.113	11
Sector (ref.: public and non-profit sector)		
private sector	1.255**	25
Long standing illness (ref.: long standing illness)		
not impaired, no long standing illness	0.898	-10
Size of residential locality (ref.: small city/village)		
city	1.032	0
big city	1.096	10
	Exp(b)	in %
Country (ref.: France)		
Austria	0.802	-20
Belgium	0.737	0
Germany	1.242	24
Denmark	0.870	-13
Finland	1.943**	94
Greece	0.495**	0
Ireland	1.003	0
Italy	0.784	-22
Luxembourg	0.614*	-39
Netherlands	1.653**	65
Portugal	0.227**	-77
Spain	0.570**	-43
Sweden	1.515*	52
Switzerland	1.011	1
UK	1.264	26

Table 3.6. (cont.)

USA	0.875	-12
Bulgaria	0.473**	-53
Czech Republic	0.707*	-29
Estonia	0.879	-12
Hungary	0.534**	-47
Latvia	0.820	-18
Lithuania	0.729	-27
Poland	0.366**	-63
Romania	0.138**	-86
Slovakia	0.928	-7
Slovenia	1.453*	45
Constant (b)	0.008**	-99

References

Bell M (2002) Measuring circulation in developed countries. Paper presented at the 1st International Conference on Population Geographies, International Conference on Population Geographies, July 19-23, St Andrews

Commission of the European Communities (eds) (2000) Benchmarking telework and e-commerce in Europe. (ECATT Final Report) Commission of the European Communities, Brussels

Commission of the European Communities (eds) (2003) eWork, Competitiveness, productivity and sustainable development. In: Proceedings of the 9th European assembly on telework, Paris,

Committee on Spatial Development (CSP) (1999) European spatial development perspective – towards balanced and sustainable development of the territory of the EU. Office for official publications of the European Communities, Luxembourg

Cullen K, Kordey N, Schmidt L Gaboardi E (2003) Work and family in the e-work era. IOS Press, Amsterdam et al

Davidow WH and Malone MS (1992) The virtual corporation – structuring and revitalizing the corporation for the 21st century. HarperCollins, New York

Dicken P (2003) Global shift, 3rd edition. Sage, London

Di Martino V (2001) The high road to teleworking. International Labour Organization, Geneva

eBusiness Watch (2003) The European e-business report 2003, 2nd Synthesis report. Commission of the European Communities, Brussels

Eichmann H, Saupe B, Schwarz-Wölzl M (2002) Critical issues pertaining to the code of practice for global e-work (Project document, Centre for social innovation, Vienna)

Eisenhardt KM (1989) Agency theory: An assessment and review. Academy of management review 14(1):57–74

Ellen IG and Hempstead K (2002) Telecommuting and the demand for urban living: a preliminary look at white-collar workers. Urban studies 39(4):749–766

Empirica (2002) Work, employment and skills. (SIBIS topic Report no 5. Commission of the European Communities, Brussels)

European foundation for the improvement of living and working conditions (2002) Third working conditions survey. Office for official publication of the European Communities, Luxembourg

Gareis K (1999) Benchmarking progress on telework and other new ways of working in Europe. (Paper presented at the fourth international workshop on telework, August 31 - September 3, Tokio)

Gareis K (2003) Home-based vs. mobile telework, the interrelationship between different types of telework. In: Rapp B, Jackson P (eds) Organisation and work beyond 2000. Physica, Heidelberg, New York, pp 171–185

Gareis K, Hüsing T, Mentrup A (2004a) What drives e-work? An exploration into determinants of e-work uptake in Europe. (Paper presented at the 9th International Telework Workshop, Heraklion, Greece, September 6–9)

Gareis K, Kordey N, Müller S (2004b) BISER Domain report no.7: Work in the information society. Retrieved 25 April 2005 (www.biser-eu.com/results.htm)

Hanhike T, Gareis K (2004) Modelling e-work – towards a better understanding of information technology's impact on workplaces and work locations. (Paper presented at the 22nd Annual International Labour Process Conference, Amsterdam, 5–7 April)

Harvey D (1989) The condition of postmodernity. Blackwell, Oxford

Heinonen S (2004) Mobile telework at the crossroads of social, environmental and cultural challenges. (Paper presented at the 9th International Telework Workshop, Heraklion, Greece, September 6–9)

Huws U, O'Regan S (2001) eWork in Europe: the EMERGENCE 18-country employer survey. IES Report No. 380. Institute for Employment Studies, Brighton

Julstrud TE (1998) Combinations and tracks: an investigation of the relationship between homework and mobile work. In: Suomi R et al. (eds) Telework environments, Proceedings of the third International Workshop on Telework. TUCS General Publication, no. 5, pp 148–163

Lilischkis S (2003) More yo-yos, pendulums and nomads: trends of mobile and multi-location work in the information society. STAR issue report no. 36, Databank, Milano

Lilischkis S, Meyer I (2003) mobile and multi-location work in the European Union – empirical evidence from selected surveys. STAR Issue Report no. 37, Databank, Milano

Massey D, Meegan R (1979) The anatomy of job loss: the how, why and where of employment decline. Methuen, London

Niles, JS (1994) Beyond telecommuting: a new paradigm for the effect of telecommunications on travel. United States Department of Energy, Washington

Nurmela J, Ylitalo M (2003) Tietoyhteiskunnan kehkeytyminen, suomalaisten tietoyhteiskuntavalmiuksien ja – asenteiden muutos 1996–2002. Tilastokeskus Katsauksia 3/2003, Statistics Finland, Helsinki

OECD, Austrian Federal Ministry for Agriculture, Forestry, Environment and Water Management (2000) Environmentally sustainable transport – futures, strategies and best practice. OECD, Paris

O'Hara K, Perry M, Sellen A, Brown B (2002) Exploring the relationship between mobile phone and document activity during business travel. In: Brown B, Green N, Harper R (eds) Wireless world. Social and interactional aspects of the mobile age, Springer, London, pp 180–194

Perry M et al. (2001) Dealing with mobility: understanding access anytime, anywhere. ACM Transactions on computer-human interaction 8(4): 323–347

Schäfer RA (2004) Ökologische beurteilung von telearbeit – konzeption und realisierung eines bewertungsmodells of basis einer verhaltensbilanz. Shaker, Aachen

Schulte BA (1997) Organisation mobiler arbeit: der einfluss von IuK-technologien. Gabler, Wiesbaden

Valenduc G et al. (2000) Flexible work practices and communication technology. (Final report of the FLEXCOT project, Commission of the European Communities, Brussels)

Voß G (1998) Entgrenzte arbeit und entgrenzte arbeitskraft. eine subjektorientierte interpretation des wandels der arbeit. mitteilungen aus der arbeitsmarkt- und berufsforschung 31(3): 473–487

Ylöstalo P (2003) Working life barometer october 2002. Työpoliittinen tutkimus no 250, Ministry of Labour, Helsinki

4 New Forms of Work in Labour Law

Minna Helle

AKAVA: the Confederation of Unions for Academic Professionals in
Finland, Finland

4.1 New forms of work as legal challenges

Working life has seen a tremendous change in the way work is organised
in the recent years. An increasing amount of work is being performed
away from the employer's premises: at home, when travelling, at the customer's premises and even at airports and hotels. In distributed work, access to work is more decisive than its physical location. At the same time,
there are more opportunities to take employees' private matters like family
and hobbies into consideration.

New forms of work organisations have also meant that employees have
more autonomy in relation to the content and location of work as well as in
relation to working time. This, combined with the increase in professional
knowledge-related work, has led to a situation in which management and
supervision by the employer do not exist any more in their traditional
senses. This challenges the way in which, for example working time legislation functions, as it is traditionally based on detailed working timetables
where work has previously planned times for starting and finishing.

The emergence of new forms of work is usually more rapid than the development of law and contracts. This tends to raise questions about the applicability of labour legislation to them. What does the situation mean to
the employment conditions and the legal position of the worker?

Work organisational concepts such as mobile or virtual work *do not
have automatic implications in labour law*. This means that in principle the
employment conditions remain unchanged. Accordingly this means that
new forms of work cannot be used as a method of diluting the employment
conditions of employees.

This is not entirely true, however. In the case of mobile work, for example, situations have arisen in which protection of employees has not been
adequately guaranteed or the situation has given rise to unclarity as to what

employment conditions are applicable. This has pushed more responsibility onto the contracting parties – the employer and the employee – at the workplace level to agree on the details of employment conditions because legislation and collective agreements have not given all the answers.

If legislative gaps appear, legislation should adapt or be changed. This seldom happens very quickly. New frameworks can be established also by collective agreements at the European level, nationally, sectorally, or at the workplace level. Ultimately an individual employment contract can fill the gap if none of the above does.

In the case of *telework*, which as a legal concept covers also a large part of mobile and virtual work, a European legal framework is being built up at a contractual level. The European Framework Agreement on Telework, which was adopted in July 2002, sets European minimum standards also for certain type of mobile and virtual work. Telework has, therefore, gained a foothold also as a legal concept.

The objective of this chapter is to evaluate mobile and virtual work as new forms of work from the perspective of labour law. What are the legal implications to labour legislation and what is the legal status of mobile and virtual workers under the European legal framework, mainly under the framework agreement on telework?

In the first part of this chapter, the concepts of mobile and virtual work are discussed in relation to the concept of telework, and its meaning in the European framework agreement on telework. After that the boundary to entrepreneurial relationships is discussed while it will certainly become more difficult to define than before. This chapter will also describe in general the employment conditions of mobile and virtual workers, especially under the framework agreement. Finally, the need for specific contracts between employer and employee is dealt with in different situations as well as the future challenges these new forms of work pose to labour legislation.

New forms of work have also other legal perspectives than the one of labour legislation. In particular, the use of information technology and close co-operation between people from different organisations bring up questions related to privacy and immaterial legal questions such as copyright. These perspectives are not dealt with here.

It should also be remembered that the detailed legal status of a mobile or virtual worker can differ from country to country and even from one sector to another in the same country, depending on the content of applicable national legislation and collective agreements.

4.2 Mobile and virtual work in labour legislation

The purpose of labour legislation is to ensure the protection of employees in a labour relationship. At the same time it has to allow for adequately flexible working arrangements in order to organise work efficiently. The objective of European legislation in the area of social protection is to find a balance between flexibility and security. This objective has been a starting point of the EU Employment Strategy, the Lisbon strategy, which aims at making undertakings more productive and competitive.

The changes in forms, nature, location, organisation and management of work force us to develop and change labour law. On the other hand, labour law cannot be changed every time a new method of organising work emerges. Legislation has to provide for stable yet flexible answers. It cannot offer casuistry but has to provide for a more general framework. This means that *organisational concepts*, such as mobile and virtual work, telework, e-work, flexiwork etc. do not automatically have implications for the concepts of labour law and contracts.

Mobile and virtual work do not have official legal definitions at the EU level. In fact, they *are not* legal concepts at all. They are organisational concepts, which describe the method of organising work and the environment of working rather than the legal status of the worker. From the labour law viewpoint, the question is about a *way of organising normal work* done in an employment relationship. The same applies to teamwork, for example. Being a team worker or not being one does not make a difference towards labour legislation. The general starting point is that labour legislation and collective agreements are applied normally to mobile and virtual workers. Therefore, there is actually no need to have legal definitions of them.

The principle is established also in article 3 of the framework agreement on telework[1] according to which

> *"The passage to telework as such, because it only modifies the way in which work is performed, does not affect the teleworker's employment status."*

Another question is that distributed working locations pose surely new challenges to personnel policy inside a company with more than only one location. The increased distance of employees from each other and from the employer sets bigger demands to the *transparency and integrity of per-*

---

[1] The framework agreement on telework can be found on the internet, for example, from: http://europa.eu.int/comm/dgs/employment_social/key_en.htm.

sonnel policy. Also the questions of equality between workers at different locations will come forward (see section 4.5.1).

Even though the legal status does not change, mobile and virtual work have certain characteristics or dimensions which may have implications from the legal point of view. These include, for example, an untraditional working location. In mobile or virtual work organizations, work is often done at home, "on the move" or otherwise outside the employer's premises. Because of these characteristics, mobile and virtual work is different from work done under "traditional" working circumstances, i.e. at the employer's premises. For example, there tends to be more autonomy in relation to working time and work organisation, which has implications for working time.

Another characteristic is the use of information technology, which is usually an integral part of mobile and virtual work. It is also increasingly used as a method of transferring data and even as a method of locating and monitoring people. This dimension has implications especially for privacy and cost issues. The same questions, for example privacy, also relate to other work done at the employer's premises, but they are even more evident in mobile and virtual work. For example, the employer might want to monitor the mobile workers by technical means because traditional monitoring, such as visual supervision, is not possible because the worker is not present at the employer's premises.

In the area of health and safety, it must be ensured that the new forms of work organisation are covered by health and safety legislation and that specific rules are established, if needed, to cover the characteristics of this kind of work. All these characteristics need attention both at the legislative and at the contractual level.

But *as such* the method of organising work according to the location, the devices used etc. do not and in fact cannot have implications for the status of the worker in labour legislation. Mobile and virtual workers should, therefore, have the same protection as workers at the employer's premises. Rather, mobile and virtual work has certain typical characteristics that bring forward new types of questions but this does not change the underlying picture. This means that the same questions of privacy or working time may arise at the employer's premises as well, but they are more likely when working outside employer's premises.

A more decisive factor will in practice be, for example, the division into permanent and fixed-term relationships or the division between labour and entrepreneurial relationships. The latter can be very problematic in mobile and virtual work. When work is being performed from distributed locations outside the employer's premises it is even more difficult than before to draw the line between an employment relationship and entrepreneurship. While distributed work and subcontracting increases, there is also an increase in the number of self-employed persons, economically dependant workers, i.e. self employed workers who have only one or primarily one client, and freelancers who formally work as entrepreneurs but in fact work under similar conditions to employees.

4.3 The European framework agreement on telework

4.3.1 Purpose and background

Telework has been "officially" defined in the European framework agreement on telework, which was signed in 2002. This agreement is the first agreement of broad scope in which the principles and employment conditions of teleworking are established. In addition to this general EU framework, there are also some sectoral European level agreements and guidelines.

The agreement was negotiated between the EU-level organisations of workers and employers, European Trade Union Confederation ETUC, The Union of Industrial and Employers' Confederations of Europe UNICE, The European Association of Small Craft and Small and Medium-Sized Enterprises UEAPME and The European Centre of Enterprises with Public Participation and of General Economic Interest CEEP.

The agreement was negotiated under the procedure of article 139 of the EC Treaty, and it will be implemented by the members of the abovementioned organisations in accordance with the procedures and practices specific to management and labour in the Member States.

The agreement provides for a general framework, which will be useful at the national, sectoral and workplace levels also when introducing mobile and virtual work into practice. The agreement is currently being implemented by the social partners in each EU member state. The deadline for implementation is July 2005. The practical effect of the agreement depends on the method of implementation chosen in each EU country. The methods used vary from binding legislation and collective agreements to recommendations depending on the labour market practices of the country.

The framework agreement was adopted because there was a need to establish a general legal framework to guarantee the balance between security of employees and the flexibility of the work organisation when using telework. This was because teleworking had already become a very common way of organising work and the problems related to the employment conditions of teleworkers were very similar in all European countries.

The European social partners saw telework as a way for companies and other organisations to modernise their work organisation, and as a way for workers to reconcile work and social life and give them greater autonomy in the performance of their tasks. The social partners also saw that, if Europe wants to make the most out of the information society, it must encourage this new form of work organisation and that the framework agreement was necessary in order to do this. As long as the contents of the employment conditions of teleworkers remain unclear, there might be reluctance among employees and employers to adopt the new working arrangements.

4.3.2 The definition of a teleworker

Telework includes by definition a wide range of technology-assisted work done outside the employer's premises. The definition covers also most mobile and many virtual workers. Workers falling under the telework definition are entitled to those rights established in the agreement and correspondingly have obligations towards their employer. *Those mobile and virtual workers who do not meet the criteria of a teleworker are still covered by EU and national labour legislation, providing they work under an employment relationship.*

The difference between the employment conditions between those who are or are not covered depends on the national legislation. The difference is not necessarily very great. The telework agreement establishes some important principles, such as a non-discrimination clause in employment conditions, the principle of the voluntary character of telework, and a clause on covering the costs of telework. Many of these are currently lacking in national legislations and the agreement will improve the status of teleworkers when in force.

The definition of telework according to article 2 of the agreement is as follows:

> *"Telework is a form of organising and/or performing work, using information technology, in the context of an employment relationship, where work, which could also be performed at the employer's premises, is carried away from those premises on a regular basis."*

Anyone who performs work as mentioned above is a teleworker and thus falls under the scope of the agreement. Telework covers a wide and fast evolving spectrum of circumstances and practices. For this reason, the social partners have chosen a definition that makes it possible to cover various forms of telework. The social partners, taking into account the rapid development of mobile technology, did not want to make an exhaustive list on the forms of telework, which the agreement covers and which at the time of the negotiation were usually being discussed. During the negotiations of the framework agreement, at least telework from home, mobile telework, work in telecenters and work done in virtual organisations were being discussed as forms of telework that are covered by the agreement, on the condition that the other criteria in the definition are met.

The complex definition of telework has many elements, all of which have to be fulfilled in order for a worker to be covered by the agreement. They are as follows:

1. *Telework is a form of organising and/or performing work, not a separate form of employment relationship.* This means that telework is normal work in which work is only organised in a different way. This does not change the basic starting point, which is the employment relationship and the applicability of both EU and national labour legislation. The agreement does not cover work done outside an employment relationship, i.e. self-employed work, freelancing, etc.
2. *Information technology is used.* The use of information technology is an integral part of the definition of telework. It must be noted however that the agreement does not say that information technology has to be used in *performing* the work. According to the agreement, using information technology in the *organisation* of the work is sufficient. This means, for example, that if communication between the employee and his or hers superior is by e-mail, the criteria are met, even if information technology is not used when performing the work itself. Information technology has a wide meaning here including the use of the internet, e-mail and mobile phones.
3. *Work is carried out outside the employer's premises but it could also be performed at the employer's premises.* The agreement does not define the location where work is done as long as it is done outside the employer's premises. The agreement, therefore, covers work done at home, at a holiday home, at telecenters, mobile work done at hotels, airports, in vehicles, and at the customer's premises, as well as virtual work done outside employer's premises.

   However, not all work done outside the employer's premises is telework. There is a precondition according to which the work *could also* be performed at the employer's premises. This precondition is hypothetical and it does not mean that the employee would have to have a concrete space at the employer's premises reserved for him or her. Therefore, the agreement covers also situations in which the employer only has a virtual office and situations where the employer has premises but the employee in question does not have his or her own working space there. This condition describes rather the nature of work, which is meant by the agreement. For example, copying machine repair work done at the customer's premises is excluded because of this condition, i.e. it can be done *only* at the customer's premises.

4. *Telework is done on a regular basis.* The agreement covers only work which is done outside the employer's premises on a regular basis. Occasional telework, therefore, falls outside the scope of the agreement. Telework is occasional, for example, in a situation in which an employee agrees on a single day of teleworking as a non-recurring event. "On a regular basis" does not mean that there would be a beforehand confirmed schedule, as long as telework is done regularly, for example approximately one day a week.

It must be noted that the framework agreement does not include any limits on how many hours a day, week or month telework must be performed in order for the agreement to apply. Work done partly at the employer's premises and partly elsewhere, as well as part-time telework, are covered by the agreement if other conditions are met.

Only telework that meets the criteria explained above is covered by the framework agreement. In the case of mobile and virtual workers, they are covered as long as the criteria in the definition are met. It is not relevant whether the worker is called a teleworker in practice or not. Mobile and virtual workers who fulfil the criteria are always teleworkers within the meaning of the agreement and the agreement applies to them.

4.4 Employment relationship and entrepreneurship

Sometimes when using organisational concepts, such as telework or mobile work, not only work done under employment relationships but also work done in other relationships, such as freelance work, is referred to. In these cases, the question concerns a phenomenon which relates to the working environment, not the legal nature of the working relationship.

The legal status of mobile and virtual workers depends first and foremost upon the status of the working relationship. When work is being performed under an employment relationship, both national and EU labour legislation apply, in addition to the applicable collective agreements. Mobile and virtual work may also be performed under an entrepreneurial relationship, i.e. as a self-employed person, freelancer or equivalent. These fall outside the scope of labour legislation and contracts, meaning that the relationship is usually governed by entrepreneurial laws only (Fig. 4.1). The criteria, which define the boundary between these two, vary to some extent from one European country to another.

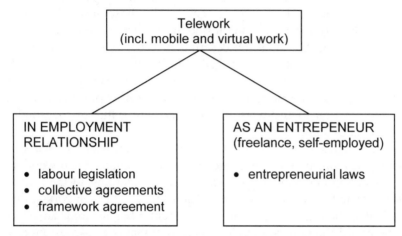

Fig. 4.1. The legal status of a teleworker

There are some exceptions to this general starting point, however, also at the European level: for example, certain EU labour law directives on equality and discrimination have wider scope and they also cover self-employed work.

In recent years, there has been an expansion of the "grey area" between employees and entrepreneurs. This goes with the emergence of new forms of work organisation. When work is distributed outside the employer's premises, the grey area widens because it becomes even more difficult to separate the real self-employed and freelancers from "bogus" self-employed who should actually be working under an employee status. This is because the main characteristics of an employment relationship – the supervision and management by employer – are attenuated if work is done outside the employer's premises.

The boundary between these two is extremely difficult to find in some cases. The working environment of a mobile or virtual *employee* or that of a mobile or virtual *entrepreneur*, for example a freelancer, will in many cases be very similar. One reason for this is that the location of the work is not as decisive as it was before in determining whether the case is of an employee or a self-employed person. Both might work from a home-based office or work on the move. Nowadays there are also increasing numbers of freelancers working at the customer's (employer's) premises. These might even have only one, or primarily one, customer, in which case they are often called economically dependant workers.

The scope of the labour law is mandatory, which means that an employment relationship may exist even if the parties have agreed on something else. In most cases, it is clear if the question is of an employment relationship or not. Unclear situations are usually those in which a person is recruited directly for a location outside the employer's premises, i.e. telework is a part of the initial job description. When telework - be it home-based, mobile or virtual – is engaged in later during the employment relationship, i.e. the employee enters telework from the employer's premises, unclear situations are more rare. This is because, in the latter situation, only the location of the work changes, not the status of the employee, which remains unaffected.

It is not unusual that the parties do not know themselves what kind of working relationship they have intended to agree upon. When work is carried outside the employer's premises already according to the initial job description in the beginning of the relationship, it is very important to clarify whether the question is of an employment relationship or an entrepreneurial one. This must be done in such a way that both parties understand what the status of the worker is and what duties relate thereto.

It must also be remembered that work, which is actually done under an employment relationship cannot be agreed to be self-employed or equivalent entrepreneurial work. Even if this kind of an agreement were made between the parties, it would not be valid.

4.5 Employment conditions in mobile and virtual work

4.5.1 The outline of employment conditions

The employment conditions of mobile or virtual workers are mainly established by EU labour legislation, national labour legislation, applicable collective agreements (if any) and the individual working contract. If the work falls under the definition of telework in the framework agreement, this is also applicable (Fig. 4.2). It must be remembered, though that the effects of the framework agreement might differ to some extent from one country to another depending on the method of implementation chosen by the social partners at each country.

```
Mobile and virtual work – existing legal framework

  • EU and national labour legislation
  • Framework Agreement on Telework (if applicable)
  • Collective agreements (if applicable)
  • Individual employment contract
```

Fig. 4.2. Mobile and virtual telework – existing legal framework

Because of the other than traditional working location, i.e. outside the employer's premises, there are certain particularities that relate to this kind of work. Many of these are covered by the framework agreement on telework, which indicates concrete rules on how to solve possible gaps (for example costs). If the framework agreement is not applicable and if the national legislation and/or applicable collective agreement does not provide for an answer, the matter has to be dealt with in the individual agreement. In certain cases even the framework agreement leaves the detailed solution to be agreed upon locally.

4.5.2 The principle of equal treatment

As regards employment conditions, mobile and virtual workers have the right to the same employment conditions by applicable legislation and collective agreements as comparable workers at the employer's premises. This principle of equal treatment is established in article 4 of the framework agreement of telework, although it is in force already through national legislation in many European countries. Mobile and virtual workers cannot be treated less favourably than other comparable workers.

The term "comparable workers" refers primarily to those employees who perform the same work as a mobile or virtual worker. If there are no employees who have the same job, then a comparable worker is a person carrying out equivalent tasks. It is important to note that, according to the agreement, employment conditions of mobile and virtual workers are compared to comparable workers at the employer's premises, not to other mobile and virtual workers.

Teleworkers, mobile and virtual workers etc. *do not form a specific group* in relation to employment conditions; instead, they belong to the group of employees according to their tasks and position in the enterprise.

If comparable workers do not exist, employment conditions must be compared to a hypothetical comparable worker.[2]

When employment conditions of mobile or virtual worker and a person working at the employer's premises are compared to each other, it must be evaluated when different location or other characteristics of mobile and virtual work constitute a *real and acceptable reason* for different treatment. Less favourable treatment of mobile and virtual workers would, therefore, be possible only in relatively rare situations. Certain situations could constitute valid grounds for less favourable treatment, for example, a home worker does not need a parking space at the employer's premises even if all the other employees have one.

4.5.3 Working time

When work is done outside the employer's premises it is by no means unusual that responsibility for organising the individual employee's working time has in practice been transferred to the employees him- or herself, while the employer has only formal responsibility. This is especially true in relation to professional and managerial staff, that carry out their tasks independently and are also a major group of teleworkers, mobile workers and virtual workers.

In addition to this, in virtual work other members of a virtual team may be working from other countries and continents, which means that traditional working hours are not always suitable.

Poor organisation of mobile and virtual work can lead to an increase in working hours as well as confusion between working time and leisure time. If work is done outside employer's premises, the workload is estimated to increase, because the traditional official control of working time and social control are lacking.

Mobile and virtual work is covered by the EU working time directive.[3] The directive establishes, for example, maximum working hours and minimum rest periods. If work is done outside employer's premises and the work includes a great deal of worker autonomy in the organisation of working time, it can in practice be difficult to control maximum working hours and rest periods. They apply nevertheless.

If the work falls under the scope of the framework agreement on telework, there are some additional rules provided in this agreement. Accord-

---

[2] See EC Court ruling Macarthys Ltd. v. Wendy Smith, case 129/79.
[3] Directive 2003/88/EC of the European Parliament and of the Council of 4 November 2003 concerning certain aspects of the organisation of working time.

ing to article 9 the workload of the teleworker is equivalent to those of comparable workers at the employer's premises. If the job description of the mobile or virtual worker is very autonomous, i.e. the worker manages the organisation of working time him/herself under certain conditions, it is in practice advisable to adjust the workload carefully so that it can be done within normal working hours. This will make it easier to separate overtime hours from normal working hours.

The worker also has the right under the framework agreement to receive appropriate training in the characteristics of this kind of work organisation. The worker's supervisor and his or her colleagues may also need training for this kind of work and its management. Working time management is an example of a training that could be useful.

4.5.4 Equipment – costs and liability issues

Costs are an important consideration in mobile and virtual work. If working on the move or at home, the worker will need appropriate equipment and usually information and communication hardware and connections. Often a worker will need two sets of equipment, one at the employer's premises and another when working elsewhere.

The framework agreement on telework includes a fairly clear provision on costs. This provision is one of the most important in the agreement because many European countries were lacking clear provisions on costs and there has been unclarity as to who pays and for what. If the framework agreement does not apply, cost issues are solved by the national framework and individual agreement.

According to article 7 of the agreement, all questions concerning work equipment, liability and costs must be clearly defined before starting telework. As a general rule, the employer is responsible for providing, installing and maintaining the necessary equipment for regular telework. The precondition of "regular" means, for example, that the employer is not liable to provide the equipment for an occasional teleworking day at home. The teleworker can also use his or her own equipment if agreed upon. In this case, the parties have to agree on how this is compensated.

The framework agreement establishes also that the employer must compensate or cover costs that are caused directly by the work, in particular those relating to communication. These may in practice include phone bills, ADSL connections, materials etc. The employer also has to provide the worker with appropriate technical support facilities and appropriate training for the technical equipment at the worker's disposal.

Liability issues turned out in the framework agreement negotiations to be a difficult point because European legislation varied from country to country and a general provision proved to be too difficult to create. This is why liability issues are determined solely on the basis of applicable national legislation. They might be relevant, for example, if the employer's property is stolen from employee's home. Adequate insurance policy is essential.

According to the agreement, the employer has liability regarding costs for loss and damage to the equipment and data used by the employee. The particularities of the liability are determined according to national legislation and collective agreements. The employee has the obligation to take good care of the equipment. The liability of the employee in cases of misconduct is determined according to applicable national legislation and practices.

4.5.5 Health and safety

The occupational risks to health and safety differ from work to work. Mobile and virtual work entail certain specific risk factors, which may include, for example, risks to mental health, ergonomic risks, and safety risks related to traffic.

According to article 8 of the framework agreement on telework, the employer is responsible for the protection of the employee's health and safety in accordance with Directive 89/931/EC[4] and relevant daughter directives, national legislation and collective agreements. EU health and safety legislation applies also to those mobile and virtual workers who are not covered by the framework agreement.

In addition to the general responsibilities emanating from the legislation, the employer must, according to the framework agreement, inform the employee of the company's policy on occupational health and safety, in particular requirements on visual display units arising from Directive 90/270/EC[5]. The directive includes provisions on the requirements that are set for equipment and working place.

---

[4] Council Directive 89/391/EEC of 12 June 1989 on the introduction of measures to encourage improvements in the safety and health of workers at work.
[5] Council Directive 90/270/EEC of 29 May 1990 on the minimum safety and health requirements for work with display screen equipment.

4.5.6 Data protection

Data protection is a very important consideration for all employers but especially for those employers that have employees using communication technology outside the employer's premises. From the perspective of labour law, the framework agreement on telework includes provisions that establish the main responsibilities of the employer and the workers. The responsibility for adequate data protection measures lies with the employer but employees also have an important role because their actions in practice play a vital role in the protection of data.

According to article 5 of the agreement, the employer is responsible for taking appropriate measures to ensure the protection of data used and processed by the employee for professional purposes. The employer, therefore, also runs a risk if appropriate safety measures are not in place.

It is the employee's responsibility to comply with the rules the employer gives to protect data. In order for this to happen, the employer must inform the employee of all relevant legislation and company rules concerning data protection. According to the framework agreement, the employer has to inform in particular of any restrictions on the use of IT equipment or tools. Sanctions in case of non-compliance must also be declared.

4.5.7 Privacy issues

Labour legislation concerning the protection of employees' privacy is only under development in Europe. In certain European countries, there is already specific legislation concerning privacy issues in working life.[6] This kind of legislation is becoming increasingly necessary because information technology permits increasing opportunities to monitor people by technical means.

A directive on the protection of employees' privacy in working life is currently under preparation in the EU. Until it is ready, the issues remain to be determined under national legislation. Privacy is safeguarded as a fundamental right also by many international conventions, such as the Council of Europe Convention on Human Rights, and by national constitutions.

The framework agreement on telework establishes only in article 5 that the employer must respect the privacy of the worker. What this means in practice remains somewhat unclear. The employer also has to inform and

---

[6] This is the case for example, in Finland (Laki yksityisyyden suojasta työelämässä 8.6.2001/477).

consult the workers and/or their representatives in advance if any kinds of monitoring systems are put in place.

4.6 Contractual issues

4.6.1 Individual contracts in mobile and virtual work

The employment conditions of mobile and virtual workers are, as explained above, partly outlined in the individual contracts between the employer and the employee. Every employee has an employment contract – written or oral - which contains provisions on salary, working time, duration, place of work, etc.

In mobile and virtual work there exists in some cases a need to have "specific" provisions on certain issues. These can include issues such as costs, monitoring, reporting arrangements, working time, etc.

Mobile and virtual work, as well as telework, covers a very wide spectrum of work. Not every situation requires specific provisions, as legislation and collective agreements apply just as much as at the employer's premises.

4.6.2 Particularities of mobile and virtual work

As mentioned above, mobile and virtual workers are normally covered by labour legislation and applicable collective agreements, and benefit from the same rights as other comparable workers at the employer's premises.

The need for specific contract on mobile or virtual arrangement, other than a "normal" employment contract, between the employer and the employee depends largely on the situation (see 6.2). If a worker moves from the employer's premises to a home-based office, the need for a specific written contract about the telework arrangement is evident. If a part of the worker's job description is to be on the move, for example, to go to meetings outside the employer's office, there is usually no need to have any specific contractual arrangements in addition to the normal employment contract. If teleworking is part of the original employment contract, the particularities of telework are taken in the employment contract.

The national legal framework also has a great impact on the need for specific contracts or provisions and the contents of the issues that need to be addressed in a contract for mobile or virtual arrangements. This may, for example, be due to the fact that the national legislation includes restrictions on its applicability to some provisions in relation to work done on the move. The situation varies from one country to another.

For example, in Finland there are two major exceptions to the basic starting point of labour law applicability to mobile workers: Firstly, the Finnish Working Time Act does not apply to work which an employee carries out at his or her home or otherwise under such conditions that it is not feasible for the employer to supervise the organisation of the employee's working time.[7] Mobile workers have in legal praxis been a group that can fall outside working time protection, depending on the degree of autonomy.

Secondly, according to the Finnish Occupational Safety and Health Act, it is the employer's responsibility to take care of an employee's health and safety also when he or she works outside the premises. The responsibility is, however, somewhat restricted when the employee works at home or some other location that the employee him/herself has chosen.[8] This kind of restrictions, if applicable, can sometimes create a need for special contracting.

These two exceptions are purely national and do not indicate the situation in other European countries, but they illustrate that there may be issues that need to be covered by an individual contract because legislation does not provide adequate solutions.

The framework agreement on telework provides some answers to questions like working time and health and safety. It does not, however, eliminate the need to have specific provisions/contracts, because in terms of details many issues remain open. This applies, for example, to reversibility of telework: according to the framework agreement, telework is reversible if it is not a part of the initial job description, but the modalities of reversibility remain to be established between the teleworker and the employer or in the collective agreement. In the case of reversibility the framework agreement merely establishes a general rule but leaves the details to be decided at the individual or collective agreement level.

4.6.3 The need for specific contracts in different situations

The introduction of mobile and virtual work at the workplace can cover either individual employees or more generally an entire working place or a part of it. Mobile work done while travelling, at the customer's premises, etc., usually relates to the nature and requirements of work. It is, therefore,

---

[7] Työaikalaki 9.8.1996/605, 2.1§.
[8] Työturvallisuuslaki 23.8.2002/738, 1:7.1 §.

usually a part of the original job description and the particularities have to be taken into consideration already when making the employment contract.

In virtual work, the need for specific provisions or contracts depends mostly on the location of the work: if virtual work is done at the employer's premises, the situation does not differ from the situations that the other employees have at the employer's premises. If the virtual worker changes over to telework, i.e. starts working from home or telecenter, there is certainly a need to agree in writing on the particularities of the new situation in accordance with the principles of the framework agreement on telework.

In all of these cases, whether a specific contract is needed or not, there is usually a need to prepare some kind of common *workplace policy*. In mobile work, this may include, for example, issues concerning availability, working time records and the methods and safety protocol of transferring data as well as safeguarding the privacy of employees if technical surveillance is in use.

If the mobile or virtual work in question is covered by the framework agreement on telework, it must be noted that according to article 2 of the agreement telework is voluntary for the worker and the employer concerned. This means that if telework is not a part of the initial job description, and the employer makes an offer of telework, the worker may accept or refuse this offer. And vice versa, if a worker expresses the wish to opt for telework, the employer may accept or refuse this request. A worker's refusal to opt for telework is not, as such, a reason for terminating an employment relationship or changing the terms and conditions of employment of the worker.

The need for a specific contract when changing to mobile or virtual work from employer's premises depends on the situation. Not all situations require special agreements (Fig. 4.3). The entering into telework requires usually a written agreement on teleworking arrangements between the worker and the employer if the entire working time or part of it will be done outside employer's premises. This is advisable, for example, if an employee starts working from home instead of the employer's premises.

A written agreement is not as necessary if teleworking arrangements are occasional, for example, when the worker is at home with a sick child, irregular or used in overtime work or while travelling (mobile work). In these cases, it is usually enough that telework is carried out in accordance with an oral agreement between the worker and the superior or telework is performed according to the workplace practice or policy.

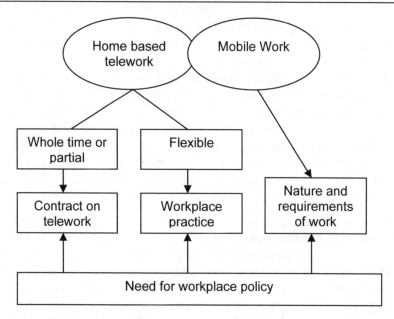

Fig. 4.3. The changeover to telework in the workplace and the need for specific contracting in different situations

From the *contractual point of view* and considering especially the need for specific contract about the arrangement between the worker and the employer, telework may be:

- *Full-time home-based telework*, where the employee works entirely outside the employer's premises at home or an equivalent place. In these cases, a written contract on the arrangements is advisable also when changing over from the employer's premises to another location. In this case, an employee and an employer agree only on those issues that are in some way affected by the change of location/the new way of organising work, for example, reversibility, costs, reporting systems, monitoring working time, etc. This is because the employee already has an employment contract in force.
- *Partial telework*, where part of the working time is performed at the employer's premises and part elsewhere (at home, etc.). In this kind of telework, the agreement includes recurring teleworking days, for example, one day a week.
- *Flexible telework*, the amount of which changes depending on the situation. This kind of telework is done depending on the needs at hand and it is usually done without special written contracts. Usually a worker agrees on telework on a case-by-case basis with his or her superior, the

situation covering single teleworking days or teleworking during a certain task. Oral case-by-case agreements or the accepted practice is usually enough from the contractual point of view.

- *Mobile telework,* which means that work is carried out when travelling, at the customers' premises, in hotels, airports, etc. Mobile work is usually done because of the nature of the work and the requirements the work sets on the worker, and it does not have its basis on any separate contracts. Mobile work is usually an integral part of a growing number of job descriptions. This means that mobile work is already a part of the initial job description or it becomes an integral part of the tasks of the worker through time.

Even though entering into mobile work organisation does not require specific employment contracts, it is necessary to agree on certain issues: these include especially the monitoring of working time and overtime, including the question of how travelling time is compensated as well as availability, privacy and data protection issues. The framework agreement on telework also contains provision on these issues (see section 3). National legislation and collective agreements may also contain applicable provisions.

4.6.4 The content of a specific contract

As explained above, not all situations of mobile and virtual work require specific contracting between the employer and the employee, i.e. other than what is normally included in the employment contract. If the work in question meets the criteria of telework, there usually is a need to agree on special arrangements compared to "normal" cases, i.e. working at the employer's premises.

Even though labour legislation covers mobile and virtual workers, it has not prepared to all the particularities of this kind of work. Because of this, labour legislation and collective agreements may include unclarity and even gaps that have to be covered using an individual agreement between the employer and the employee.

The framework agreement on telework answers some of these, but in many cases the issues covered in the framework agreement are also left partly open to be agreed on either in collective agreements or individual employment contracts.

Legislation does not include exhaustive lists as to what the issues are that need to be included in a contract for telework (or mobile or virtual work). EU Directive 91/533/EC[9] contains a list of the employment conditions that the employer has to inform the employee about. This list includes issues such as duration, place of work, work description, salary, working time, periods of notice, etc. These are examples of conditions that have to be included in any employment contract.

Apart from these basic conditions, a telework contract might need special provisions on issues such as reversibility, reporting arrangements, liabilities and costs, privacy and equipment. According to article 2 of the framework agreement on telework, the employer has to provide for additional written information on matters such as the department of the undertaking to which the teleworker is attached, his or her immediate superior, and reporting arrangements. Further information on the content of these issues can be found in the framework agreement.

4.7 Conclusions

New forms of work and work organisations are generally covered by the same rules established in legislation and agreements as old ones. New concepts, which are used to describe present and future phenomena in the field of organisational research and practice, do not and should not, have automatic effects on labour law. Workers should be granted the same rights, whether they work at the employer's premises, at home or elsewhere.

This being said, it must be admitted that at the same time these new forms put pressure to develop legislation to correspond better to modern work organisation. The general labour legislation should be developed to cover the new phenomena better. It is not desirable that labour legislation is split into parts, which cover different forms of work organisation in a different way - or, even worse, offer less protection if work is not carried out in a traditional way. The difficulty is to find a balance between general and overly vague legislation on the one hand and explicit and unduly narrow legislation on the other.

Major challenges are faced, for example, in legislation on working time. How can traditional working time with its detailed provisions be applied to autonomous work in which an employee in practice decides by him/herself when to start working and when to do what and when to stop working? While facing this dilemma, we see at the same time that exhaustion, stress, problems of coping at work, and other mental problems become increas-

---

[99] Council Directive 91/533/EEC of 14 October 1991 on an employer's obligation to inform employees of the conditions applicable to the contract or employment relationship.

ingly frequent (see also Richter, Meyer and Sommer in this volume). This leads us back to the need for properly functioning working time legislation also for those people who work autonomously and to the need to have skilled people to lead, manage and supervise the organisation of work with enough time and resources to do this.

In health and safety, there is an increasing need to tackle problems of stress, to identify the risk factors of new forms of work in time, and to prevent and manage new risks. The problem is that it is extremely difficult to recognise situations in time because mental exhaustion and stress develop gradually. It becomes even more difficult if the worker performs his or her job somewhere outside the employer's premises. The employer has a duty to take care of the employee's health and safety at work. But how to take care that the virtual worker does not work too hard at his or her home office and suffer mental exhaustion? These questions need also practical workplace solutions to make legislation work in practice.

Distributed working locations also pose major challenges to personnel policy. It has to be even more transparent than before, and questions of equality between the personnel in different locations will certainly arise. Measuring work performance will have to change: it can only be done by results if the employer and the employee are working at a distance from each other. There has to be a move away from the traditional "supervision of presence".

More challenges are posed by the increase of cross-border working situations and the dispersion of the boundary between employment relationships and self-employed work. The position of many self-employed workers is precarious and unclear. Also the protection of the privacy of workers needs a European framework before monitoring practices become disproportionate for the purpose.

Legislation adapts – usually with a time lag – to new phenomena in order to create a framework for controlled and managed change. Existing legislation can create barriers to new forms of work organisation, in which case it must be evaluated if these are justifiable or not. The need to protect the employee establishes in many cases a need to maintain or even add restrictions, as in the case of precarious working relationships like fixed-term, part-time and temporary agency work. Sometimes, on the other hand, new frameworks are needed in order to promote something new we want to promote.

References

ETUC (2003) Interpretation guide on voluntary agreement on telework. European Trade Union Confederation, Brussels

Helle Minna (2004) Telework. Edita Publishing Oy, Helsinki

Part 2

Mobility in Work

5 Virtually Connected, Practically Mobile

Mark Perry[1] and Jackie Brodie[2]

[1]Department of Information Systems and Computing, Brunel University, UK
[2]Centre for Entrepreneurship, School of Management, Napier University, UK

5.1 Chapter outline

This chapter addresses a central issue in studies of mobile work and mobile technology – what is the work of mobile workers, and how do they use the resources that they have to undertake this work (i.e. the work they have to do in order to do their work)? In contrast to many of the other papers in this collection, the objective of this chapter is to examine individual mobile work, and not teamwork and co-operation other than where it impacts on the work of individuals. We present data from a study of mobile workers, examining a range of mobile workers to produce a rich picture of their work. Our analysis reveals insights into how mobile workers mix their mobility with their work, home and social lives, their use of mobile technology, the problems – technological and otherwise – inherent in being mobile, and the strategies that they use to manage their work, time, other resources and availability. Our findings demonstrate important issues in understanding mobile work, including the maintenance of communities of practice, the role and management of interpersonal awareness and co-ordination, how environmental resources affect activity, the impact of mobility on family/social relationships and the crossover between the mobile workers' private and working lives, how preplanning is employed prior to travel, and how mobile workers perform activity multitasking, for example through making use of 'dead time'. Finally, we turn to the implications of this data for the design and deployment of mobile virtual work (MVW) technologies for individuals and a broader organisational context.

5.2 Designing mobile technology to 'fit' the work

One of the most important things that we can say about mobile technology is that it has the potential to support and even change the way we work – the very topic of this collection of papers on mobile virtual work being based on this notion. However, whilst it is a commonplace observation to say that mobile technology can improve and transform work, there is very little evidence to support how this might happen, or the real benefits that mobile technology will bring to its users. Moreover, we know very little about the way that mobility itself is used to support the performance of work. There is an interesting parallel to be made here with studies of collaborative work arrangements – academic theorists often talk about the work needed to make collaboration happen: the additional work on top of the task needed to manage collaboration, known as 'articulation work'. As yet there is no parallel term in the area of mobility, but clearly, when people are mobile, they need to do additional 'mobile' work to be able to accomplish their work when they are mobile. Perhaps there is no simple differentiation between the two forms of work, as people are often mobile because the work itself requires this, but there are clearly areas where some form of alignment is required to marshal and co-ordinate the resources and work around the constraints posed by the mobile settings with the mobile individual's ongoing work activities.

   This then, is the area that we have chosen to explore in this chapter – making the point that whilst users of the so-called 'Martini' solution technologies (enabling "anytime anywhere" connectivity) may be connected to a communications network, they have very practical constraints that arise from the nature of the technology, the sorts of work that they are doing, the environment that they are working in, and the broader context of the work (including temporal, social and political contexts). This then, is the 'practical' aspect of mobility, and as such may greatly affect the 'virtual' world of work that is promised by the marketing rhetoric of mobile solution providers. This practical set of considerations is crucially important in improving existing technology and in motivating new mobile technology designs – only by understanding users' needs and wants, and the problems and importance of mobility to users, can we set about doing this in a principled way. There are really only two ways to examine the role and potential value that mobile technology could play in supporting its users, and these are i) to examine user activities (part of which may involve mobile activity or may be constrained by users *not* being able to be mobile) and ii) to give users technology with new capabilities that allows them to explore new ways of going about their activities. We address both in the chapter, reporting and reflecting on our own research.

Certainly, it would be hard to imagine a world without the mobile telephone, and increasingly, laptops and handheld computing applications, and a multitude of hybrid information technology and communications devices are visibly proliferating within certain market segments. Go to any international airport and see a hinterworld of hunted and exhausted executives tapping into their mobile devices, trying to maintain a connection with their offices in the outside world and keeping up with their ever-increasing workload. Yet we must ask ourselves how much of this activity is bound into mobility and where the mobile devices fit into this work – and whether they actually support it (and if so, how?).

The goal, therefore, of this chapter is to work through the conceptions of mobile virtual work, and then to present a 'vision of the future', developing this to generate design guidelines for effective and sustainable MVW systems (which we see as synonymous with mobile information and communications technology and mobile information systems). The next section examines the nature of mobility and the various literatures contributing to our understanding of mobile virtual work.

5.3 On being mobile

5.3.1 Addressing Mobile Virtual Work

The title of this paper "Virtually connected, practically mobile" comes from the central problem of the mobile worker, that is, whilst technology now gives them the potential to make some kind of a connection, this opportunity is constrained by the very practical concerns and constraints that they face when they are being mobile. There is a play on the term 'virtually' here, in its double meanings of supporting a remote presence, but also meaning 'almost succeeding, but not quite'. Its dual connotation is that whilst allowing a remote and connected presence, that this presence may be inadequate or failing in some way. This is very much the reported evidence from the mobile workers that we have studied and in the academic literature.

There is currently no truly effective 'anytime, anywhere' solution that allows its users to work as effectively as they could when they were not mobile. There is, of course, a corollary here, in that workers obviously find a value in mobile work and could not work as effectively when they are static[1]. This is an important point to make – we should not think of mobile work as a constrained form of static work, but as a type of work that has different values for people, opportunities for action, and methods of performing that work. This clearly has implications for technology design, although what these implications actually are is not so obvious – all that we are immediately able to say is that designers should *not* attempt to simply reproduce the work resources from an office into mobile technology, as the practical and occasioned requirements of the mobile workers are likely to be different to those of office-based workers. The much-lauded 'mobile office' should not just duplicate the desktop office (see also Laurier 2000). However, a cursory examination of many current, commercially available mobile technologies does not appear to demonstrate that this has been fully taken on board, so, for example, we have mobile devices that duplicate many of the functionalities of the desktop computer (e.g. running Microsoft Office's Word and Excel) that are simple ports (admittedly with some concessions to the device's form factor) of their desktop counterparts. Perhaps the mobile office is an inappropriate metaphor.

Of course, users may be demanding this advanced functionality from their mobile devices (known as 'creeping featuritis' in the trade), but this point only serves to illustrate that the conceptual models of the mobile technology that many designers are presenting users with are themselves inadequate – is it a computer? a personal assistant? a telephone book? or even a camera/address book/telephone/mini-computer/videoconferencing suite/media station? Fieldwork has shown that users generally have suites of technology that they select from to take with them which is dependant on their plans and expectations of the demands that they will have made on them. Each of these technologies has particular strengths for particular activities, and compression of the whole set of office resources (some of which may not be even currently computer-based) into a miniaturised computer workstation is to misunderstand and misrepresent their users' needs and capabilities.[2]

---

[1] The term 'static' may not be ideal, but we are using it as the antithesis of 'mobile'. In reality, both terms are descriptively limited, in that they do not allow us to convey the full richness of the work and the inherent crossovers between them. However, for pragmatic reasons, whilst recognising this limitation, the two terms suit the purposes of this discussion.

[2] A growing literature in *appliance design* (Norman 1998; Sharpe and Stenton 2002; Bergman 2000) examines this, offering solutions to the problems of usability posed by the general-purpose PC. However, this is not solely concerned with the nature and problems of mobility.

5.3.2 'Mobility' in the research literature

Whilst it is a frequently used term in the research literature, the term 'mobility' has been used in a number of different and occasionally conflicting ways. Typically, mobility denotes some form of movement in space and time. However, within the corpus of research material addressing mobility in work, this description has ranged from Luff and Health's (1998) discussion of 'micro-mobility' (shifting the orientation of resources, such as paper, between people) to notions of mobility that embrace spatial, social, temporal and contextual elements (Kakihara and Sorensen 2002). More typically, the focus of research into mobility is centred on the notion of travelling (local or remote), and can involve working *'at multiple (but stationary) locations, walking around a central location, travelling between locations, working in hotel rooms, on moving vehicles and in remote meeting rooms'* (Perry et al. 2001). However, each of these environments have their own challenges in terms of resources for/and constraints on communication unique to their own circumstances. Within this chapter, we again take this broad view of mobility.

Generally, mobile technology and research into mobile technology has developed at an increasing pace as mobile technology components have improved, getting smaller, faster, more energy efficient, networked and making effective use of protocols for technology 'convergence'. Yet hindering the design and take-up of these technologies has been a largely insufficient understanding of the social and or organisational backdrop against which these technologies are deployed, and how it has the potential to change them. Much of the recent research that has attempted to address this has largely arisen from the fields of CSCW (computer supported cooperative work) and information systems. This research has, unsurprisingly, tended to focus on that most pervasive and visible mobile technology, the mobile telephone. Social interaction around the telephone, using voice and text (SMS) messaging has formed a body of evidence demonstrating the role that mobile technology has taken on in the lives of a variety of user groups and in a range of settings: novices users (Palen et al. 2000), teenagers (Grinter and Eldridge 2001), mobile knowledge workers (Perry et al. 2001), and in restaurants (Ling 1999), waiting at bus stops (Tamminen et al. 2004), on public transport (Weilenmann and Larsson 2002) and in cars (Laurier 2000), amongst others.

This research focus on the particularities of specific user groups and settings, whilst important in understating mobility and mobile technology, has often resulted in the design of prototype mobile technologies that support particular workers, work types or settings, for example, supporting the efficient handling of electronic documents in large-scale mobile knowledge work (Flynn et al. 2000), or the work of mobile service engineers (Kristof-fersen and Ljungberg 1999). Moreover, the commercial focus on what is seen as the 'early adopters' and high value customer segments have also skewed the development of technology towards white-collar knowledge workers in favour of what we have called a document-centric perspective (O'Hara et al. 2001). Unfortunately, these digital tools can be ineffective or inappropriate for other types of mobile work. What we require for the design of more generic mobile technologies is to understand the impact of these technologies on a broader section of society in a more widely scoped study of users, with more abstract generalisations on use practices and user needs that can be applied back into the design process.

Of the more generalised findings that have come out of the literature, the core issues on mobility that face users and which form the backdrop of why they employ mobile technologies include awareness (e.g. Laurier 2000), general work maintenance when mobile (e.g. Perry et al. 2001), and a need to make use of lightweight (e.g. Churchill and Bly 1999) and inter-actionally appropriate technologies (e.g. Luff and Heath 1998). We revisit these issues and examine other issues arising from the incorporation of technology in the performance of mobile work.

5.3.3 Articulating mobile work: 'mobilisation work'

Mobile work, as with other forms of work, requires resources (most visi-bly, information, technologies and social networks) to be brought to bear on the tasks being undertaken. Work that involves the co-ordination and meshing of task activities (above and beyond the core work itself) is known as 'articulation work' (Strauss 1995). Articulation work allows people to manage contingencies that arise out of the performance of work, and is contrasted against predefined work processes. Articulation work goes beyond the everyday conception of what one of our reviewers has called 'co-ordination work' by explicitly delimiting the boundaries of co-ordination activity, as well as placing it within a theoretical and analytic context. As an analytic tool, articulation work is commonly used in the analysis of the divisions of labour in work that involves multiple individu-als. Schmidt and Bannon describe that when workers are *interdependent* on one another in their collective work, this cooperation:

> ...*involves a number of secondary activities of mediating and con-trolling these cooperative relationships. Tasks have to be allocated to different members of the cooperative work arrangement: which worker is to do what, where, when? [...] Furthermore, the cooperat-ing workers have to articulate (divide, allocate, coordinate, sched-*

ule, mesh, interrelate, etc.) their distributed individual activities [....] Thus, by entering into cooperative work relations, the participants must engage in activities that are, in a sense, extraneous to the activities that contribute directly to fashioning the product or service and meeting requirements. That is, compared with individual work, cooperative work implies an overhead cost in terms of labour, resources, time, etc. (1992, p. 14)

As noted above, the majority of the research on articulation work within the area of computing has been in the analysis of multi-person activity, and not so much in the arrangement of individual tasks. Yet, the nature of articulation work is not limited to collective activity performed by ensembles of people. Strauss is clear about this: the division of labour (which involves articulation work) may be carried out over a unit of any size.

How can this research on articulation work be of relevance to mobile work? Well, there is a considerable co-ordination overhead to being mobile: mobile workers are often impoverished in terms of their social, informational and technological resources. They need to perform additional work be able to achieve their goals when they are mobile. This is a form of articulation work, but is sufficiently unique to warrant a unique term for itself, one that we will call 'mobilisation work', from the work required to mobilise resources that are not in themselves necessarily suitable for use outside of a resource-rich, static and unique work location.[3] Mobilisation work underlies many of the challenges and opportunities for mobile technology design, in supporting the secondary co-ordination efforts that users have to perform in order to complete their primary work objectives and goals. This focus on mobilising work cannot be the only factor in the design and choice of mobile technologies (for example, aesthetics and entertainment value may figure as important issues), but it is a crucially important one that will help determine the work-related utility of the mobile technology for users.

---

[3] Mobilisation work has a counterpart in the work that is being mobilised. In articulation work, this counterpart has been called 'co-ordinated work' (see for example Simone et al. 1999). Rather than calling our parallel term 'co-ordinated mobile work', we have opted to differentiate it simply as the primary mobile work objective/s. This lack of formal nomenclature is mainly for reasons of confusion, 'mobile work' being the term used in common parlance for the totality of all mobile activities, but also as the mobilisation work can itself shift levels to become a primary objective, and may itself require further mobilisation work to resolve contingencies arising from local circumstances (c.f. Gerson and Star 1986).

There is an interesting point to note here in the choices that people make about going mobile: being mobile may be a less efficient way of fulfilling the work tasks than working at a fixed workplace. The required degree of mobilisation work may make their work so inefficient that the costs of being mobile exceed its benefits. This is not a choice that some of mobile workers are able to make (due to the nature of their jobs), but it explains why many workers have a work*place*. Rather than thinking of the static workplace as the norm for a working environment, perhaps we need to think about it as being a necessary workaround for the failures of the mobile work environment.

In this chapter, we do not simply attempt to understand mobility for some abstract reason; we examine mobility – specifically mobilisation work – to better support it through the design of appropriate technologies. The bulk of the rest of this chapter therefore undertakes to examine the mechanisms of interaction that are used by mobile workers in order to perform this mobilisation work, concentrating on the practices and strategies used by mobile workers. However, first, we document the methods used in collecting data for the study.

5.4 Examining mobility

5.4.1 Data collection methods

We employed two main techniques to collect data on mobility, supported by additional research methods allowing us to triangulate our analysis. These methods were entirely qualitative, as we were interested in the rich picture, or the 'thick' descriptions of our informants' mobile activities to look at the detail and lived experiences of those people. The first of these methods was based on an interview-based examination of the day-to-day activities of mobile workers. The second used a 'technology probe' approach. Hutchinson et al. (2003) describe technology probes as simple and adaptable technologies that are assessed by users with three primary goals:

> 'the social science goal of understanding the needs and desires of users in a real world setting, the engineering goal of field-testing the technology, and the design goal of inspiring users and researchers to think about new technologies.' (p.18)

A technological probe is assumed to influence the behaviour of the user and allow designers to gather use-data related to this. A probe is not a prototype in the traditional sense: its purpose goes beyond design and allows further data to be gathered about users, their needs, social contexts, and the 'fit' of the technology (and its transformative qualities) with their work practices. In support of these two techniques, a range of other methods was also used, including observational fieldwork, scenario-based design, paper prototyping, and breakdown analysis. However, for the purposes of this chapter, we concentrate on the interview and probe data, as these lie at the core of the arguments that we make.

5.4.2 Primary data collection

Our initial research focused on the underlying patterns of mobile communication activities. Fifteen users of digital mobile technology were interviewed for between 1 to 2 hours, where possible, in their usual working environments, surrounded by their everyday work tools. We sought to get a broad mix of participants: all came from different organisations, with different jobs; there were 11 men and 4 women; they varied by employment type, both employed and self employed; by the distance travelled, international, national, regional and local; by mode of transport (various); frequency of travel; destination (same, different); and the extent of collaboration in their work. These individuals fall across the categories noted in this volume (on-site movers, yo-yos, pendulums, nomads and carriers), although many of them could be described as working across more than one of these categorisations, simultaneously, or changing over time. We recognise that there are different types of mobile worker by sector, work type, position in the value chain, communication style, etc., and that mobile workers themselves may (or may not) be 'structurally' different to non-mobile workers. However, the set of participants used in this study was intended to reflect a broad range of mobile work types and to examine work practices in detail, not as a large set for statistical sampling.

We focused the interviews on the communicative activities of mobile workers when they were mobile (including local, distributed and global mobility). We also examined the way workers used space and supporting artefacts when they were mobile, and any collaboration in their work. Beyond the mobile event itself, we examined the activities undertaken before and after travel. In order to encourage users to present us with real, and not idealised accounts of their activities, we used a diary technique in which participants recorded a typical working day in detail, including the resources used and information collected over their whole day, and not just the work they did, thus emphasising sequential activities and interrelated activities.

In addition to examining the communicative requirements that users have and the contexts that they work in, we also wanted to see how users make use of the communicative tools that they currently use to see how any new device would fit within an existing web of technology. As might be expected, most of the workers studied only had access to mobile phones and not other mobile technologies (e.g. laptop computers and PDAs), and consequently the findings reflect this. This is not to say that the only mobile technology that we were interested in is the mobile telephone, and we have tried to emphasise the nature of the need for mobile information and communication by those interviewed rather than simply focusing on their use and application of the mobile telephone in their work.

5.4.3 Technology probes and user evaluation

The probes were trialled with six users in the autumn of 2003. Two of the participants had been interviewed in the original study and had offered some interesting insights into mobile work in their particular professions so it was felt useful to return to them to gauge their opinion on the effectiveness or otherwise of the probe technologies (the hairdresser and electric meter installer). The others included a telecommunications engineer, an electrician, a plastic sales specialist and a chiropodist. All were highly mobile (in a variety of different ways), and their work covered a range of different forms of activities.

Each of the interviews lasted between one and a half to two hours. Each of the participants was interviewed, wherever possible, in their typical working surroundings, and the interviews were taped and later transcribed. Following initial background information being collected on the users, the probes were shown to users. Taking each probe in turn, the participants were presented with three 'future use' scenarios. Following on from each scenario, they were shown the technology probes running on a mobile device. For the purposes of collecting data, the probes were 'chauffeur' driven by the second author during this initial interview stage. After a detailed run-through of each of the probes, questions were asked regarding the probe and its potential role in the participants' working lives.

5.5 Analysis

The analysis of our initial interview study is loosely grouped into two main categories, although, as keen readers will note, many of these issues are interdependent. Moreover, we recognise that the boundaries between cognitive and social behaviour are not absolute, and different schools of philosophical thought have differing views on this. However, these analytic segmentations of the data serve to detail something simpler than a fundamental point about human thought; they separate the solutions that individuals have created to manage their own work (cognitive activity and planning behaviour) from the methods that the participants used to manage and co-ordinate their social interactions (social interaction and home/work relationships). In using the term 'social' here, we are using it in the broad sense of living within a community of some form, and not as a synonym for leisure. Within these two categories, we have broken down some of the behaviours that constitute them, and examine the mechanisms of interaction used in resolving problems arising from mobility and the social practices that enable mobile work to be conducted.

5.5.1 Cognitive activity and planning behaviour

Environmental resources and mobile activity

This issue covers the interplay between the primary work objectives, the resources (or lack of them) in the mobile work environment, and the mobilising work required to repair this. With respect to mobile technology use and design, it demonstrates the changes that may result in the nature of mobile work as users employ more, or different, mobile communication technologies.

Communications technology often necessitated environmental rearrangements. Individuals working on the move needed to take account of the resource deprivation they experienced because the majority of the informational resources available in static environments are missing. Mobile workers frequently sought out flat surfaces to work on in the venues observed, e.g. tables in restaurants and bars in airports. The requirement for a flat surface to colonise with their array of tools (including notepads, notebooks, laptops, PDAs or mobile phones) stemmed from the problem that mobile work often requires users to employ several different information artefacts simultaneously, and they need therefore need these immediately available at hand. Ironically, the configuration of this communication space actually hindered movement through physical space, tying mobile users to the table-top.

An inappropriate 'form factor' for existing mobile technologies often led to 'breakdowns', with users unable to work effectively just anywhere. Fellow passengers were observed on trains having to balance their paper work on their knees to accommodate the considerable table space demanded by the simultaneous use of several mobile communication devices (e.g. PDAs and laptops by themselves and others). Another reason that a flat surface was sought out was the form factor of some mobile communications artefacts. These mobile devices often tried to replicate the PC by having, for example, keyboard input, which meant that to use them effectively, during the inputting of data, two-handed input was needed, which required the device to be placed on a flat surface during these interactions.

Beyond the devices themselves, companies often did not take into consideration that their employees may need to be mobile in different locations. For the communications manager, this meant that when he spent a few days a week in Bristol he was unable to access the network in that location because the firewall prevented him from logging on from more than one location (in his case London), but this meant problems printing in Bristol, which he had devised a workaround for:

"Because it is a network printer and because I am not on that server I can't connect and I am only on a phone line. So I plug-in and what I do is I end up emailing people in the same room as me with a document which they then open and print. And that has been going on for a year because there isn't a technical way around it; as our infrastructure has not caught up with the fact that loads and loads of people work semi-location independent."

In another example, the plumber had tried to take his phone into some extreme conditions, and he had lost his mobile several times in attics and lofts. He now preferred just to leave it in a 'safe place' rather than carry it about in extreme conditions. He also opted to switch it off when working on a roof or somewhere else where answering it may be dangerous. For the traditional knowledge workers interviewed, their locations also sometimes limited their communication choices, such as when they were driving. Socialisation effects also played a part in this: the communications manager noted that he did not like to make work-related phone calls in public places, such as on trains, because he felt it was disruptive to others around him.

What we see here are the frequent effects of environmental constraints and resources impinging on mobile work and their activities having to be developed to accommodate to these conditions in either temporary work-arounds or in reorganising their practices so that these problematic conditions did not occur. Environmental conditions have a strong impact on the potential use of MVW technologies, so that whilst there is a theoretical possibility of always on connectivity, this is highly limited in practice.

Preplanning for mobility

Although in situ flexibility is important for mobile workers, planning prior to travel was also an important work strategy (c.f. Perry et al. 2001). Part of the planning those mobile workers engaged in involved determining which artefacts and information they *might* need. For example, when going from London to Bristol for a few days, the communications manager would take his car to accommodate all his work artefacts. However, if he were only staying overnight, he would travel by train and just take his laptop and briefcase. For the blue-collar workers interviewed, daily planning was crucial. Often work would be issued by control rooms in the order that the jobs were requested by customers. This meant, for example, the telecommunications engineer and the electric meter installer having to sit down and re-organise the order of their jobs around their location (ensuring that jobs near each other were dealt with after each other), the job difficulty, and whether other people would be involved. Both thus needed an A to Z map to hand and notebooks to write their new working day structure in.

A very important issue emerged in our observations, that whilst mobile workers are mobile, and particularly when they are travelling, they are not easily able to carry on with their day-to-day work, keeping their 'heads above water', and there was a constant danger of their being swamped with work on their return to their offices or when reporting to a client or supervisor. Many of them tried to make best use of 'dead' time (Perry et al. 2001) or 'wasted' time when on trains and planes to keep up with their workloads (e.g. carrying on with email communications on laptops and PDAs), and even planned for this ahead of time. Unfortunately, given the poor access to resources that they had when mobile, and the unpredictability of their circumstances, this was not always possible to do as effectively as when at their static workplace. Clearly the mobile telephone was an important tool in making use of this dead time (largely because of its minimal interaction requirements during travel), and several mobile workers reported delaying and lining up several telephone calls for precisely these times.

The data emphasises that mobile work is at least partially predicable, allowing mobile workers to determine which resources that they may require to take with them. Even when work is not predictable, mobile workers can at least plan for that unpredictability, taking task-relevant paperwork 'just in case' it is required. Paradoxically, mobilisation work may therefore take place whilst at a static workplace location. This extends mobilisation work beyond the mobile event itself – something that is not typically considered in the research on mobile work.

5.5.2 Social interaction and home/work relationships

Communities of practice

From the interview transcripts, it is evident that much mobile work re-volves around the idea of social 'contacts', which formed communities of practice (of varying intensity) that they could call on. These communities of practice were also important in the performance of ongoing mobile work, perhaps even more so in blue collar work (although not exclusively). Often the blue-collar workers would help out other tradesmen working in their vicinity if they requested help, even if they were personally unknown to them. As examples of this, the builder gave a surplus barrel of sand to other builders who had run out, the mobile hairdresser did a hairstyle for a fellow hairdressing colleague and the painter helped a plasterer move fur-niture. As the gas boiler installer noted, the relationships with others on a building site may become mutually beneficial:

> "...the builder might say ... I need some hot water here or cold water and I can't be bothered to walk back upstairs where the bathroom is any chance in running me an outside tap, and so you say to them 'Yeah, right when I finish the boiler instead of me getting on the ladder, if you are a builder with all the equipment,' he might even have the scaffolding up, 'instead of me getting on the ladder to get up with my sand and cement will you do it for me?'"

Overall then, in the data, there is as general sense of mobile workers possessing a sense of shared identify and community with others in their own profession, or other mobile workers they often come into close con-tact with, even if these people are not know to them personally. This sense of community did not just surface among the blue-collar workers, but was also evident in the interviews of the art director, arts workshop co-ordinator, and the academic. We see here how mobile workers make use of others when mobilising their work. Although this is often *ad hoc* and un-planned, communities of practice form an important resource in mobilising work, usually (though not always) through reciprocal arrangements.

Colleague awareness when mobile

Mobile workers rarely did their jobs in isolation from others, even if they were often alone whilst mobile. As we have seen, mobile workers often had to organise and coordinate their work activities around each other as part of a community of practice. This led to a need for others to know what the particular mobile worker's schedule was and for the mobile workers in turn to know other peoples' schedules so that collaborative activities were carried out effectively. This was often resolved by *ad hoc* agreements being made over the telephone and using paper diaries. However, the extra effort of using a long-term diary – even a paper one – is clearly evident in an extract from a self-employed informant:

"I am really crap at diaries and like, for instance, you having to phone me today and remind me. You see my diary is basically empty. I just don't bother! ... Basically, everything goes in the day-book or scraps of bits of papers." (Art director)

Similarly, the communications manager noted that although current groupware calendaring technology like Lotus Notes fitted into desk-bound work well and had a high value for co-ordination with co-workers, it required too much maintenance and effort for dynamic work on the move.

For the most part, the people interviewed were heavy mobile phone users (when this was not the case, it was because their firms refused to pay their mobile phone bills). The majority of the calls made on the move were for logistical coordination with other co-workers, or to give others an awareness of their activities and updates on their current work situation. The data suggest that current digital technology often fails to support the need for constant communication between co-workers who may just be in the next building or room but who need steady progress updates from each other to manage their own workloads.

Often, the mobile workers described how they would often waste time phoning colleagues about something urgent, but their colleagues' mobile phones would be engaged or switched off. The painter also pointed out another problem, relating to other people's awareness of a mobile worker's activities. He noted that since his working schedule had to be highly dynamic (he would paint one coat then go onto the next job, often returning the following day to finish the job off), the companies he went to visit had limited awareness of his planned activities, so his working schedule had to be very flexible. This meant that he often found when he arrived at a company, their staff was not prepared for his visit and he was requested to return the following day to do the job because the staff had to arrange to sit somewhere else for their lunch or meetings when he was painting.

Mobile workers would often record the planned activities of others that they worked with ahead of time, even if they were not directly involved in those future activities themselves. This would remind them of the availability or lack of availability of close colleagues and help them coordinate their activities at a later time/date. Even on a day-to-day basis, mobile workers often described keeping their "eyes and ears open" to background information when talking to colleagues to find out what was happening to them:

*"You ask each other where you are working and what you are do-
ing...that is mostly the topic of the conversation in the morning
where have you been working and who have you been working with.
How do you get there 'cause usually they are quite far away... in
case... during the day the boss could phone and say 'nip up to
wherever' and if you have been speaking to someone you have a
rough idea how to get there because they have been there."* (Painter)

Such a need to know what others were doing in case they had to help
out was common. Similarly, mobile workers frequently had to make their
own job activities known to their managers and others over the mobile
phone in case they needed help themselves. Awareness information from
colleagues therefore has a high value in reducing the effort required to
mobilise the resources available to mobile workers, and a large part of the
mobilisation work observed fell into monitoring this awareness information, both actively and passively, and before and during travel.

5.5.3 Mechanisms of interaction in mobilising work

What the data show are a number of strategies through which mobile
workers make use of the resources available to them and how they are able
to work around their actual or expected constraints that arise through mobility. In performing these activities, they are *mobilising* their resources in
order to be able to conduct their primary work objectives: by developing
workarounds to environmental conditions and preplanning for their expected constraints, and by enabling awareness information and communities of practice, mobile workers are able to build an infrastructure around
which they are able to conduct their primary work activities. An interesting
point to note here is the granular basis of this mobilisation work, ranging
from the broad appropriation of social contacts into the co-ordination of
work, to the opposite end of the scale, in the highly localised reorganisa-
tions of artefacts in space to better manage available resources.

5.6 Technology probes: design and functionality

5.6.1 Design of the probes

Following a review of the data, a list of initial core functions was drawn-
up for three probes. For each function of the probes, the function was
named (e.g. opportunistic communication) and a description of the support
that this will provide for the users' work was given (e.g. facilitate the ar-

rangement of opportunistic meetings between co-workers). We do not go into the design processes for each of the probe technologies as this is not of concern here (see Brodie 2004); our concern is demonstrating the functionality of the technology and the opportunities that they offer their mobile users in supporting mobilisation work. In the rest of this section we describe the prototypes.

5.6.2 VMail

The effective management of incoming communications and the use of information received while on the move presents a challenging design problem if we accept that mobile workers will not always be available to communicate synchronously. One of the main sources of this incoming communication is the mobile phone. However, even when mobile workers made an effort to respond to voice messages on a regularly basis, they often found that they could not work '*anytime, anywhere*', and mobile voice calls were left unmanaged for several hours. When eventually picking up their voicemails, mobile workers may have to deal with a lot of information sequentially, unaware of the importance or trivial nature of each message in advance.

In the first probe technology, V-mail, we established that it would be valuable to support two important functions: *awareness* (being aware of incoming information while using the system, for e.g. how many messages a user has received while unavailable in a meeting), and *managing incoming information* (ordering and archival of incoming information based on user preferences, to allow effective use of that information). V-mail supported the management of incoming verbal communications through a voicemail application. The ability to search previous voicemail messages was also seen as important if a mobile worker wanted to access all calls from a particular caller in sequence or to re-find a particular call but were unsure of the time the call was made.

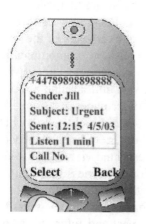

Fig. 5.1. A V-mail entry

As figure 5.1 shows, a V-mail entry shows the phone number of caller, the caller's name (if in the mobile phone's address book), the subject header, the time/date and length of the call and the option to listen to it. After a caller has received a V-mail notification, they can select to 'read' the message and this will take them to a list of all unread V-mail notifications. By scrolling down they can highlight and then select the call they would prefer to listen to first. In its simple mode (see Fig. 5.2) calls are presented by recency, but in a more advanced mode, users can opt, for example, to have calls ordered in terms of other personalised prioritising criteria, such as who the voice call is from, regardless of the time of arrival of the notification, or they can chose to have notifications with topic headers such as 'urgent' listed first.

Fig. 5.2. V-mail listing (simple mode)

5.6.3 Dynamic-List

We have seen that mobile workers organise and coordinate their activities in conjunction with one another as part of their wider communities of practice. However, the need for an ongoing and up-to-date awareness of other people's activities and location was not always possible when mobile workers were mobile and so the possibility of re-organising their own work more effectively in real-time would often be lost.

For Dynamic-List, we identified several issues that were important in supporting *ad hoc* mobile co-ordination: *awareness* (information available to users of the system about other users, from being aware that someone is in the same area as the user, or that they free to collaborate); *lightweight interaction* (without the interactional and logistical overheads of the computer); and *opportunistic communication* (a 'constant' communication channel should allow users to communicate with one another quickly and receive responses). The Dynamic-List prototype was built around a shared dynamic time and activity to-do-list schedule. It provides its users and their colleagues with real-time information on schedule changes to help them re-organise their own work around each other. Individual privacy needs are supported, with mechanisms such as restricted viewing of to-do-list entries marked 'private'. It allows information awareness through visual 'notification' of incoming verification requests or automatic updates of lists, and allowed limited read/write capacity for a user's colleagues. Finally, it provides an easily accessible archive of past and future to-do-list schedules.

Fig. 5.3a. Dynamic-List (awareness screen)   **b** Adding a to-do-list entry

The 'desktop' view of Dynamic-List (Figure 5.3a) shows activities that the user has listed to do that day. The application has its own small 'peripheral awareness' screens on the PDA home screen. These show a miniature version of the user's to-do-list and also two of their chosen colleagues' to-do-lists. These miniature screens can be extended, by dragging the top right corner with the stylus to present a larger 'awareness' screen for quick viewing of a user's or their colleagues' schedules. Using a combination of drop-down lists and stylus writing, users can also enter requests to meet up with other users (Fig. 5.3b).

In a Dynamic-List page (Fig. 5.4a) a user's activities are listed in time order. Users can choose which day or start time they wish to view by selecting the arrows on the date and time toolbar. Users can access each other's to-do-lists for viewing, and edited if permission has been granted. The application allows users to choose who they want to view their lists as well as choosing 'special' others who have read/write access (see Fig. 5.4b).

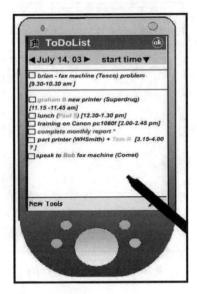 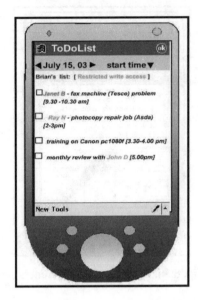

Fig. 5.4a. To-do-list page   **b** Viewing another user's to-do-list page

Dynamic-List therefore supports opportunistic face-to-face meetings by providing notification about local potential colleagues to interact with. The user can either choose whom to be alerted about in advance, when in a particular location, or allow the system to 'react' to any of their colleagues when they are close to the user's current location. Alerting users to colleagues nearby is achieved through an audio alert (or vibration) accompanied by a flashing of the display and an accompanying text notification indicating who the other user is.

5.6.4 Connect-Talk

Mobile workers frequently collaborate with other mobile people. However, current mobile technologies often fail to support the need for communication and awareness among mobile co-workers. Connect-Talk was primarily intended to investigate the interactional potential of a mobile device to support work and relationships within mobile communities of practice. Criteria guiding the development of the talk-mode operations of Connect-Talk included the facilitation of *ad hoc* coordination between mobile workers and their co-workers by providing a constant audio communication channel. This would provide a community of practice with passive awareness of each other's activities and communications while mobile. It was intended to support opportunistic face-to-face meetings by showing colleagues in the user's environment that they could interact with through the location positioning technologies.

Connect-Talk's core functions were *awareness, lightweight interaction and communication, coordination* and *presence.* The final function, presence, refers to information about the user being made available to other users. The system provides mechanisms to share a user's status (e.g. 'online', 'offline', etc.) with others, and allows a user's on-line presence to switch between different 'buddy' groups (similar to instant messaging technology).

Connect-Talk was designed as an 'always-on' awareness device, utilising a radio/walkie-talkie metaphor of use. As noted in the analysis, mobile

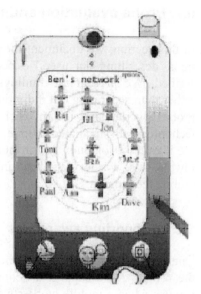

Fig. 5.5. Connect-Talk concept device

workers often found themselves asking their colleagues on their mobile phones their exact whereabouts to aid smooth coordination. We therefore sought to make use of location-based services for Connect-Talk so that users could easily locate each other when in the same local area should they wish to arrange an opportunistic meeting to carry out face to face conversations.

When a user is present in a given location, and the device is in 'talk' mode, the interface shows iconic representations of co-workers using Connect-Talk in the area (see Fig. 5.5). Users of the Connect-Talk device are alerted to the status of co-workers by colour coding (availability), audio/vibration (new buddies' devices detected nearby), and concentric circles showing the approximate location of colleagues (in relation to the user), so that buddy proximity can be established at a glance. Switching between different 'buddy' networks (e.g. different communities of practice) that a user may wish to view or to allow adjustment of a user's status (e.g. when they are no longer available or engaged in hazardous activities) is possible. A change of icon colour, from blue to green, informs users who is talking on the system.

5.7. Probe evaluation and implications for design

In this section, we document the use of the probes from the user evaluations, describing our users' expectations and the problems that they described. We present the findings for the probe interviews collectively, rather than separating out individual probes, as the findings for each of the probes overlap and inform each other, allowing a richer picture about technologically mediated mobile work to be offered than would be possible if each set of findings for the technologies were presented alone. Following this, we develop these into implications for the design of future mobile technologies.

5.7.1 Supporting awareness

One of the main themes that emerged from the user evaluations was that the probes could support a heightened sense of awareness of other colleagues when a mobile worker was out on a job. For example, the electrician noted that one of the key benefits of the Dynamic-List system was being able to know exactly where his colleagues were. Similarly, the plastic sales specialist noted that it was advantageous to know when a colleague or client was close by:

"If you could spare 15 minutes you could quickly go and see the person. I appreciate that. That is good. Whereas with a mobile phone you wouldn't know that unless you call the number."

However, there was a negative aspect to this greater awareness: while the technology allowed them to know the precise whereabouts of their remote colleagues it also allowed colleagues and family to know their own exact location. Indeed, the hairdresser noted that by supporting greater awareness of a user's activities and location, the technology could actually lead to restrictions on her activities because, for example, if asked for help through the Dynamic-List system:

"There was no way you could lie and kid on that you were at the other end of the city!"

While the three probe technologies were deemed successful at supporting effective awareness for mobile workers and their communities, this 'heightened' awareness did not always 'mesh' well with the users' current work practices. Mobile technology adoption would be improved if mobile technologies that include support for greater awareness of a user's activities also offer users mechanisms to restrict colleagues' awareness of their activities when deemed necessary.

5.7.2 Supporting effective communication

Over-hearing of conversations through the Connect-Talk device was considered to be mutually beneficial:

> *"It has advantages too if other people hear your conversation. If it is work related. If the two of us don't know, someone else may be able to give some knowledge on that."* (Telecommunications engineer)

The electric meter installer echoed this, noting that Connect-Talk could overcome the need for fruitless rounds of phone calls. One of the potential benefits that the participants could envision with V-mail was that it would help them maintain awareness of their contacts, even when they were unavailable to receive phone calls. Instead of having a barrage of voice messages to listen to, the header part of V-mail would allow users to respond quickly to important messages.

The plastic sales specialist was also appreciative of the way V-mail could allow busy salespeople to cope with the demands of communicating whilst driving. However, despite the participants expressing optimism about the benefits of V-mail, the telecommunications engineer noted that he would be reluctant to activate it – in some organisations there is an *expectation* of 'anytime, anywhere' accountability for mobile workers:

> *"Sometimes the manager wants to get hold of you because you have done something wrong or something. Or maybe he wants some explanation because someone is screaming his head off or something. So these things, they can't wait. If you don't answer they come looking for you and I would be in more trouble because maybe I am not in the place I am meant to be."*

Another problem identified with Dynamic-List was the need to focus attention on the device to the detriment of the other ongoing activities. As we already know, mobile work can be cognitively demanding. Tools that make heavy demands are likely to be left in vans and cars (like the laptop) in favour of other technologies that facilitate more fluid and flexible communications when mobile.

In summary, while the mobile workers saw some of the technologies as potentially supportive of more effective communication, those that were more cognitively demanding may not be as effective at supporting communications in very dynamic mobile work environments because of the need to actively monitor the device and manually update it.

5.7.3 Transforming work relationships

Evaluators noted that the probes could potentially affect their relationships with colleagues. In current work practice, those interviewed admitted that they would contact the colleagues that they get on best with if they needed physical help, rather than the colleagues who may be physically nearer. However, by explicitly showing who was physically nearest, Connect-Talk allowed users to choose to ask for help from their nearest co-worker. Other criteria for asking for help, in addition to proximity, could also be potentially established through Connect-Talk:

> "*I would maybe state, and sort of ask, who is the closer to me and who hasn't got as many calls left for the day. Maybe to help me out for the rest of the afternoon or whatever...Tom may be further away, but he might only have one call left and, such and such, may have two or three more left.*" (Electric meter installer)

The electric meter installer also described how Connect-Talk could bring his colleagues 'closer' together and support more face-to-face exchanges:

> "*Maybe see them more, through the job, either helping each other or helping each other out more because you know exactly who has got what and who is closer in your area.*" (Electric meter installer)

The Dynamic-List application differed in this respect: for the hairdresser, even if the application allowed more communication between colleagues, it was not allowing the *right kind* of communication. She went on further to explain that she could envision wasting time meeting a colleague to borrow some supplies when they did not have the exact stock she was looking for because of the absence of verbal communication through the system. The plastics sales specialist also noted that relationships between him and his colleagues would become impoverished if verbal communications were taken out of the equation for negotiating meetings. A critical problem with Dynamic-List then, is not that it does not allow rich enough communication between co-workers to facilitate coordination and collaboration, but that it threatens to supplant verbal communication and the specific qualities that verbal communication brings to exchanges between co-workers.

Another problem identified for 'always-on' awareness technology was that it might adversely affect the way the users would respond to their obligations as members of their respective communities:

> *"It's got benefits ... but if you were maybe tired and just wanted to go home you couldn't kid on you were no-where near them, and you would feel obliged to go help them..."* (Hairdresser)

It would appear then that the introduction of such technologies *could* adversely affect community bonds if they are designed and adopted without sensitivity to the needs of group dynamics.

5.7.4 Building and maintaining social and domestic bonds

The mobile workers interviewed noted how Connect-Talk could support their social activities. For example, although the plastic sales specialist felt his colleagues and clients had good access to him while he was working (because of his company mobile and landline phones), he usually switched his personal mobile phone off on working days or put it onto a silent ringing profile. In light of this, he felt that V-mail would be useful for managing his personal phone calls:

> *"...for emergencies that would be ideal. Just stating 'urgent' – I would be looking that immediately. It could be family or loved ones just phone you up."*

Overall, the work life and home life of our mobile workers were often intertwined: work colleagues could become personal friends, and personal friends could become clients or co-workers. As users, they tended to assess the probes from both perspectives.

5.7.5 Privacy and 'user control'

During the interviews the mobile workers often brought up 'privacy' and 'control' concerns. For example, while discussing the scenarios for the Dynamic-List, the mobile workers identified instances of potential use that they considered an 'invasion' of privacy, something they were keen to avoid:

> *"...it's always the case that you don't want management to know what you are doing but they are always the opposite. They are your enemy aren't they? ... whereas colleagues - it doesn't really matter."* (Plastic sales specialist)

Although the electric meter installer did not mind his colleagues knowing his work activities, the risk of colleagues finding out personal activities was also a very real concern. Conversely, the hairdresser was worried about hairdressing colleagues in her neighbourhood finding out about her work activities, not because of embarrassment over personal matters, but instead for the very real threat that other hairdressers would try to steal business away from her if her activities were too open.

Another issue raised by the mobile workers was that of user control over the management of their own work activities. Some of the mobile workers grudgingly admitted it would be acceptable for their managers to do it, but except for the chiropodist (who was not in control of her own daily work plan), the participants were not positive about their work colleagues changing entries in their dynamic to-do-lists without asking their permission:

> *"Oh, no, I wouldn't like anyone changing it... No! Let me know and I would 'okay' it beforehand."* (Electrician)

To summarise, 'privacy' and 'user control' issues are important elements to consider, although they have not been widely addressed in mobile systems, other than with respect to encryption and data access. Yet, as we have seen from our research these concerns are often more socially contested, and such concerns are very important to individual users in terms of their willingness to accept new technology.

5.7.6 Technological implications

While the implications of the study are limited to the participants selected and the forms of probe technology examined, they offer important insights into mobilisation work and the communication and informational requirements of mobile workers. What we have seen from the data is that a central focus for the design of future mobile technologies is on connectivity with other people, and whilst remote document and file access may be occasionally desirable, this does not appear to figure highly as a necessary function, whether or not those interviewed were involved in knowledge-intensive professional work, or other forms of work.

1. *Supporting lightweight mobile interactions*: Low-effort/quick-to-operate interactions were highly valued. Without this, participants may employ workarounds or reject the technology. When supporting lightweight interactions mobile technology should not distract unnecessarily from the main activity at hand or it is likely to be rejected. Similarly, attention-distracting technologies can cause safety issues for mobile users.

2. *Support for verbal communication when mobile*: The data emphasises the primacy of voice over other forms of interpersonal connectivity. Media spaces, like that supported by Connect-Talk, can be successful at supporting mobile work activities through providing effective awareness of the activities of others. In contrast, Dynamic-List failed, in part, to support many forms of mobile work because it ignored how mobile workers often rely on voice communications to support negotiations when organising meetings.

3. *Balancing social awareness with individual privacy*: While the mobile workers often needed to know where others were and what activities they were engaged in, it was noted that the technology should avoid 'invading' their privacy. For example, it is often enough to effectively support awareness if it is merely indicated that someone is unavailable to talk on the system, without displaying why they are unavailable to talk. Mobile work is different from that carried out in open plan environments, where supervisors and colleagues are usually well aware of co-workers activities; it often involves a mobile worker working at their own discretion, and making quick decisions in response to dynamic circumstances. Extra sensitivity needs to be exercised when supporting more awareness of this kind of workers' activities to avoid resentment or misunderstanding developing between managers and employees. Mobile technologies then, should provide enough awareness to accommodate effective action but not so much that privacy is threatened. The thin line can easily be crossed, and technology should accommodate different users' sensibilities by providing those users with control mechanisms over their presentation of awareness information to others.

4. *Flexibility to support individual and community needs*: Different mobile communities need different types of support to aid effective work practices. In mobile communities, issues of trust, privacy and accountability are important constituents of the work situation, and these issues need to be flexibly supported by mobile technology to accommodate a whole range of users and their individual needs. Mobile technologies should also seek to support not just the work activities of mobile workers but also their lifestyles, as much of this is bound in with the mobile component of their work.

5. *Supporting obligations and accessibility in communities of practice*: In mobile communities, social and organisational obligations and accountability are part of the job. During the probe evaluations, several mobile workers expressed worries about being obligated to help out other colleagues, or worried about their accountability to management who could be constantly aware of their current whereabouts through the use of location-aware technologies. This suggests that the mobile communication

technologies of the future need to be sensitively designed to support the nature of the communities that people work in. One way to approach this is to allow different levels of technological accessibility to other mobile workers, for example, by allowing private conversations as well as more open conversations. While this approach is already apparent in technologies like Internet chat-rooms, more research needs to be done to see how to implement such mechanisms to effectively support the interactions needed for mobile work.

5.8 Discussion and conclusion

One of the critical questions that we set out to examine was to understand the work that people had to do in order to be able to conduct their jobs when they were mobile. The data documented in the studies gives an important insight into this: how mobile workers make use of the environmental resources around them, plan ahead, make use of travelling time, build and exploit communities of practice, maintain an awareness of colleagues and organisational changes, and manage and connect their private and working lives. This all contributes to developing a clearer picture of what mobile work is beyond the individual work scenarios themselves.

Yet disconnecting mobilising work from its primary work objectives is to miss an important part of the larger picture: work and the co-ordination of that work are intimately bound together, the one meaningless without the other for those that it concerns in their daily, lived experiences. At the risk of over-labouring this, we could say that understanding the work of doing the work is analytically inconsequential without considering the achievement of the primary work objectives. This rather academic point has an important role to play in the design of mobile technology. The simple provision of technological mechanisms for mobile interaction that allow work to take place will not, by themselves, enable mobile work, or more effective mobile work. Such mechanisms can only be effective when they mesh with the individual particularities of the work contexts and the working practices of the people concerned. Providing an opportunity to support mobilisation work will not necessarily be useful where the work practices are in conflict with the design. By providing flexible opportunities for action, and resources that can be adopted when they are found to be useful, we can give users of mobile technology access to different and a richer set of mechanisms for interaction that can be used to mobilise their own work. In this sense, a formal mobile information system that requires a particular form of engagement to perform mobile virtual work will probably fail because it does not support existing practices and contexts.

What we are getting at here is that when we consider the terms 'mobile virtual work' and the 'mobile virtual organisation' and try to understand the nature of these activities, these terms are only really useful as placeholders for the diverse range of applied practices and technologies that constitute the material experiences of mobile workers. The work is itself not virtual (ah, wouldn't that be a welcome treat!); rather, by placing resources and technologies so that they are accessible through a 'virtual' technology, work can be conducted 'as if normally'. The attentive reader will notice a good deal of gloss here: 'normally' is being used in its broadest sense to accommodate performance, and not practice.

The 'virtual' part of work then, needs to accommodate aspects of mobilisation work, and more so than through the provision of a 'virtual desktop', even if that desktop is designed to accommodate the ergonomic restrictions of the mobile users. Access to information on the activities and accessibility of other people (whilst accounting for the reservations exposed by the probe study participants) is clearly one such criterion. Whilst this requirement for 'awareness' information can be also seen in the literature in remote CSCW and groupware applications, being mobile, and accessing (or making available) this information has its own particular design problems. Similarly, and building on awareness, creating and maintaining links with a community of practice (or even a *mobile* community of practice) also presents designers with a complex problem: how can mobile users contribute to and gain value from communities that they spend much of their time physically remote from. Work-time, as well as family and social relationships are important too, in ways that we have seen that demonstrate how the demands of mobility cut across traditional work/leisure time and occupational/social boundaries, and these offer very different resource sets to mobile workers than the canonical office worker.

Extending the findings beyond the individual worker, we can envisage how mobile technology can have impacts on a wider organisational picture. An important finding from the research, and which can be seen indirectly in the work of much of the mobile academic literature on mobility, is that a very large part of the connectivity that is required (and used) by mobile workers is directed towards remote *people*, and not remote *things* (e.g. documents and remote devices). This aspect of connectivity is not supported by most mobile technologies, apart from the mobile telephone, interestingly, the most common MVW device in use. There is an argument here that the participants' requirement for this access to other people may be to use them as a proxy to access currently inaccessible remote things (see Perry et al., 2001), but close inspection of the data does not appear to bear this out for a large number of the instances reported. What we see is a great deal of social interaction and community building, activities that cannot be reduced to simple goal driven action. The organisation then, as both a closed commercial entity and open community of practice, is clearly a valuable informational resource for enabling the mobilisation of work.

In terms of the implications of the research for organisational theory, it is harder to speculate on outcomes, as these are related to phenomena that extend beyond the technologies available, encompassing governmental policy (e.g. the move away from or towards self employment), and social change (e.g. fragmentation of the family unit or an increasing geographic dispersal of social relationships), as well as other factors, such as demographic shifts, which may for example affect norms of social interaction. Nevertheless, mobile technologies do offer resources to mobile workers that free them from the boundaries of their employer organisation. We see networks of organisation emerging that appear atypical of office work, as friendships and occupational alliances are appropriated in the performance of an individual's work. At its simplest level, we see this as people keep their (personal, and occasional work) mobile telephone numbers as they move between jobs. At the other level of the scale, mobile workers can work for multiple organisations simultaneously, keeping abreast of awareness information and other ongoing organisational activities.

References

Bergman E (2000) Information appliances and beyond: interaction design for consumer products. Morgan Kaufmann, London

Brodie JEA (2004) Supporting communication on the move: investigating user activities and implications for mobile technology design. PhD Thesis, Brunel University, UK

Churchill EF, Bly S (1999) It's all in the words: supporting work activities with lightweight tools. In ACM Proceedings of the International Conference on Supporting Group Work, ACM Press, Phoenix, pp 40–49

Flynn M, Pendlebury D, Jones C, Eldridge M, Lamming M (2000) The satchel system architecture: mobile access to documents and services. In: Mobile Networks and Applications, 5(4):243–258

Gerson E, Star S (1986) Analyzing due process in the workplace. In: ACM Transactions on office information systems, 4(3):257–270

Grinter R, Eldridge M (2001) Y do tngrs luv 2 txt msg? In: Proceedings of the 7th European conference on Computer Supported Cooperative Work, pp 219–238

Hutchinson H, Mackay W, Westerlund B, Bederson B, Druin A, Plaisant C, Beaudouin-Lafon M, Conversy S, Evans H, Hansen H, Roussel N, Eiderbäck B, Lindquist S, Sunblad Y (2003) Technology probes: inspiring design for and with families. In: Proceedings of the International Conference on Computer-Human Interaction (CHI 2003), ACM Press, Fort Lauderdale, pp 17–24

Kakihara M, Sorensen C (2002) Expanding the 'mobility' concept. In: Proceedings of the 35th Annual Hawaii International Conference on System Sciences, Volume 5:131–140

Kristoffersen S, Ljungberg F (1999) "Making place" to make IT work: empirical explorations of HCI for mobile CSCW In: Proceedings of the International Conference on Supporting Group Work, ACM Press, Phoenix, pp 276–285

Laurier E (2000) Nomadic Talk: assembling a mobile office. In: Proceedings of Wireless World: Social, cultural and interactional issues in mobile communications and computing, DWRC, University of Surrey

Ling R (1999) Restaurants, mobile telephones and bad manners: New technology and the shifting of social boundaries. . In: Proceedings of the 17th International Symposium in Human Factors in Telecommunication, Copenhagen, pp 209–221

Luff P, Heath C (1998) Mobility in collaboration. In: Proceedings of the Conference on Computer Supported Cooperative Work, ACM Press, Seattle, pp 305–314

Norman DA (1998) The invisible computer: why good products can fail, the personal computer is so complex, and information appliances are the solution. MIT Press, Cambridge

O'Hara K, Perry M, Sellen AJ, Brown B (2002) Exploring the relationship between mobile phone and document use during business travel. In Brown, Green and Harper (Eds). Wireless world: social and interactional implications of wireless technology, Springer-Verlag, London, pp 180–194

Palen L, Salzman M, Youngs E (2000) Going wireless: behaviour and practice of new mobile phone users. In: Proceedings of the. ACM Conference on Computer Supported Cooperative Work, pp 201–210

Perry M, O'Hara K, Sellen A, Harper R, Brown BAT (2001) Dealing with mobility: understanding access anytime, anywhere. ACM Transactions on Human-Computer Interaction, 8(4): 323–347

Schmidt K, Bannon L (1992) Taking CSCW seriously: Supporting articulation work. Computer Supported Cooperative Work, 1(1):7–40

Sharpe WP, Stenton S (2002) Information Appliances. In: Jacko and Sears (eds) The human-computer interaction handbook: Fundamentals, evolving technologies and emerging applications, Lawrence Erlbaum Associates Inc

Simone C, Mark G, Giubbilei D (1999) Interoperability as a means of articulation work. In: Proceedings of the ACM Conference on Work Activities Coordination and Collaboration, pp 39–48

Strauss A (1985) Work and the division of labour. The Sociological Quarterly, 26(1):1–19

Tamminen S, Oulasvirta A, Toiskallio K, Kankainen A (2004) Understanding mobile contexts, personal and ubiquitous computing, 8(2):135–143

Weilenmann A, Larsson C (2002) Sharing the mobile: mobile phones in local interactions. In: Brown, Green, Harper (eds) Wireless world: Social and interactional aspects of wireless technology, Springer-Verlag, London, pp 92–106

6 Collaboration in Mobile Virtual Work: a Human Factors View

John R Wilson

Institute for Occupational Ergonomics, University of Nottingham, UK

6.1 Starting position

There are two strong and related implications of possible increased incidence of mobile technologies and virtual work, to do with collaboration and the human factors of such collaboration. The first implication is that to be of real benefit such work, and the related technical and organisational systems that are necessary, must provide improved support for collaboration in distributed teams and organisations. In a corollary, collaboration in all senses will be required to ensure that organisations and communities get any benefit at all from the technical and organisational investment required by mobile systems and virtual organisations. By extension the people involved, the human factors, must be genuinely, participatively and innovatively accounted for in mobile and virtual work system design and implementation. The second implication is that to properly understand the nature and needs of mobile and virtual work and to develop the related technical and organisational systems to make it work will require substantial contribution from the human factors research and application community, in theory and practice. This means that human factors (and particularly cognitive ergonomics) must increasingly move its focus from "one operator-one interface-one task" to joint cognitive systems and distributed cognition, and related studies must more often be embedded in actual practice rather than carried out in the laboratory.

This chapter will first set the notion of collaboration at work in the context of mobile work and virtual work. Then there is emphasis given to the requirement for understanding the nature of collaboration and how to support it before beginning to implement future information and communications technologies (ICT). The relationship between collaboration and key facets of participation and teamworking are then explored. General criteria for ICT in collaboration are described, and then the particular requirement that interaction and interactivity be supported by sensor-based technologies is examined further. In order that we better understand people at work, and especially in distributed socio-technical systems, great care is needed in research study methodology, and a short note is provided on this. Then examples of studies of various types of collaboration at work are given, chosen so as to reflect various aspects and levels of mobile virtual work and collaboration, and to illustrate the ways in which we can study and understand the jobs and roles of people working in this way, before some final conclusions are drawn.

This contribution takes an explicitly sceptical position. Sceptical about the capabilities of ICT and the successors to the artificial intelligence community to be able to deliver anything approaching some of the visions of the promoters of ambient intelligence and virtual working. Sceptical of the extent to which those promoting an agenda of "collaborative work" actually understand anything about collaboration as a psychological and social process – or even think such understanding is important; for instance the recent report Collaboration@Work is remarkable for the absence of any real insight into the nature of collaboration – it is taken as real and much more attention is paid to the minutiae of teleworking or of mobile technology and networks (European Commission 2004). And sceptical of the degree to which many of us will actually need or – just as important – want many of the technologies suggested as supporting virtual work, mobility and collaborative work of the future. As Olson and Olson (2000) put it, paraphrasing Mark Twain, "reports of the death of distance are greatly exaggerated" (p. 397). Never has the need been more marked for a good balance between user and task pull and technology push.

Nonetheless, there are work activities, communities and organisations where the need to work in a distributed fashion, on the move, or at least not at a common central location, and collaboratively, is increasingly acute, and some of these will be examined in this chapter for the lessons they hold about requirements for work systems design and for the well-being of the individuals concerned.

6.2 Future work, mobility and virtuality

In the last few years we have seen a great broadening in conceptualisations of what is meant by the workspace and work environment. These have moved beyond the traditional view, that they embrace the physical space, i.e. desk, seat, console, access and egress, where someone works, the physical environment around them, i.e. lighting, noise, climate, space, and notions of reach, clearance, fit and sight lines. Now, to take a particular example, if work is carried out by teams who meet physically at some times and virtually at others, using a variety of technical systems, then the workspace includes the virtual media in which they meet and the social structures they form there, as well as the equivalents of these in physical and co-located space. In the Future_Workspaces Roadmap project[1] new ideas for work and living spaces were said to now be stimulated by moves to service and knowledge-based economies, global networking and customer responsiveness, underpinned by rapidly developing ICT. New ways of working were predicted, unsurprisingly, to include teams of all types, collaborative networks, remote agents, virtual environments, advanced visualisation and ambient interface tools, knowledge communities, and self-directed home-, tele- and hotel working. Even if we are cautious about how many of these developments will really happen in any widespread fashion, and how much is really desirable, it is evident that our conceptions of what are workspace and work environments, i.e. physical, social, psychological and emotional, must change, and therefore so must our research methods, design criteria and design guidelines.

The examination of collaboration and collaborative work in this chapter is in a context of virtual work structures and groupings and in circumstances where people and/or their work are mobile. Therefore a brief word or two is in order about these concepts of mobility and virtuality at work, although of course more substantial contributions to the debates and discussions will appear throughout this book.

Descriptions of work as mobile and virtual can refer to many different types of organisational structure. Virtual is used in many ways to describe work, and the roles and structure of individuals, groups, systems and organisations – as in virtual enterprises, virtual manufacturing, virtual teamwork, virtual reality (VR), virtual environments (VE) etc. In other words, the meaning of "virtual" is rooted in the noun it is used to modify. The implications of "virtual" include: being not physical or not real, as in a digital simulation; being not anchored to a specific (central) location, as in a virtual worker; being computer-or simulation-based, as in VR/VE or virtual manufacturing; implying flexibility and a temporary nature, as in a virtual project team; involving a distributed network, as in virtual communities; and implying cooperation and collaboration, as in virtual teamwork. The most common use of virtual as a description is where there is an absence or reduction of hardware or solid artefacts: that is, there are no bricks and mortar to make offices which house project teams and allow co-location

---

[1] www.avprc.ac.uk/fwf/

and face to face meetings; or no metal and other materials making up process lines and machines for a manufacturing system.

Mobile also can be used in several different – and valid – ways to describe how people work. The individual can be mobile, either continually or from point to point. The equipment and computer systems can be portable or moveable, wearable or personal, or at least relatively easy to pack up and move. Or the experience itself can be mobile, basically allowing collaborative networks to cooperate.

In some senses virtual mobile work has always been with us – the travelling salesperson or delivery driver for instance. But technical opportunities and business needs are changing work systems even for these groups and moving many more functions into the ambit of mobile virtual work. To these jobs we now add those who are able to be peripatetic and mobile by virtue of technical – computer – systems support, whether this is fairly standard conferencing and networking equipment or more advanced VR/VE and personal and ambient technologies. Such systems of work usually make up complex distributed sociotechnical systems which include remote agents – train drivers, meter readers, inventory checkers, and repairers – as well as centralised staff – control room or head office – and distributed computers (Wilson 2000).

A typification of mobile virtual and collaborative work in terms that are predicated on the technology being available, and therefore necessary, is dangerous. As well as virtual working not being new in itself, it also may not be required or wanted in many cases. Before any decision is made on what technical systems to implement in support of mobile and virtual work, we need to question: Why would mobile virtual work be of value? Who would gain from it and in what way? What functions carried out where and when should be performed in this way? Only after addressing those questions should we then consider the "how" – what technical support should be specified, assessed, trialled and implemented. In this, implementation of mobile and virtual work is no different to other systems change in which human factors are key: thorough business- and end-user, domain, function, task and social system analyses must be carried out. Businesses need a clear understanding of the advantages and disadvantages from mobile virtual work. The former include: greater flexibility, mobility and collaboration amongst a work group, reduced costs, of central facilities including buildings, improved performance in terms of quality, quantity or time measures, improved capacity for knowledge management, greater work satisfaction, and better work/life balance. Set against these will be any potential losses and downsides, including costs, ineffective – even white elephant – technology, loss of inter-personal relations, changing work practices that eliminate some former unacknowledged yet highly valuable flexible or innovative activities or skills, and removal of chances for personal broadening of horizons through travel.

6.3 Collaboration

Collaboration is critical for mobile virtual work, in both a direct and indirect sense. Organisations will often install technical and organisational systems to allow a mobile worker to be part of a virtual team, and hence to collaborate. Also, a critical success factor for any virtual network or grouping is the extent to which it can coordinate itself to communicate and achieve common goals – in other words, to collaborate. In its simplest sense, collaboration means any number of people engaged in interaction with each other, within a single or series of episodes (meetings) to reach common goals; in this it is close to defining what true teams are about.

As yet our research understanding needed to underpin design of complex distributed socio-technical systems is not substantial, although there are interesting and potentially valuable contributions from the computer supported cooperative work community (CSCW) (eg McNeese et al. 2001) and from approaches such as distributed cognition (eg Hutchins 1995). Even where theories, approaches and methods exist to help with explanation of collaborative working, it is only with great difficulty, at best, that these can be translated into usable design support for systems and other engineers.

There is a surprising lack of real understanding of what it is to collaborate (or not) and how to best support this. Such lack of understanding is found for "traditional" work settings as well as for newer digital communities. Ironically, although it is near certain that the key human factors contributions of the future will be based around understanding of complex systems, distributed groups and collaborative activity, the discipline of human factors (ergonomics) to date shows only little evidence of a shift in focus away from the purely (and individually) cognitive to the social (Boff 2000; Wilson 2000). McNeese (2001) differentiates a focus on what is inside a person's head from a focus on what a person's head is inside. There is a glut of theories and models for the former, much less for the latter. There appears to be little to build on for development of understanding in such settings as virtual teams, collaborative virtual environments and video and electronic conferencing. Our own work in trying to understand social organisation, social work artefacts and complex distributed socio-technical systems led us in 2003–4 to join a network with Universities of Oxford and Manchester amongst others. This network – CABDYN – was set up to integrate the study and understanding of complexity, and in particular complex networks. Because the state of knowledge about collaboration and complexity in socio-technical systems was insubstantial, we wished to try to learn and adapt lessons from others in the network, in terms of their work on complexity in domains such as zoology, biology, mathematics and financial systems.

The difficulties in understanding collaboration and collaborative work, and by extension in contributing to better design and implementation of mobile and virtual work, to an extent reside in the ill-defined, rapidly changing and unstructured nature of such work. Cooperative activity, embracing teamwork and collaboration, is dynamic, situated and influenced by its context. Social activity is fluid and relies heavily on nuance; exceptions are normal and goals are multiple and frequently conflict (Ackerman 2000). In addition, collaboration embraces conversation – an intellectual and a social process – and social cues (Erickson and Kellogg 2000). Extending from a study of design teams, Arias (2000) adds to these requirements for collaboration and the relevant ICT, the support of exploration of alternatives, providing a meaningful structure, allowing 'what if' simulations, supporting reflection and giving a common language, both cultural and technical as well as linguistic.

Of course studies of collaboration and collaborative work activities have taken place over a long time, for instance carried out by sociologists and anthropologists (eg Goffman 1967; Argyle 1969; Kendon et al. 1975). Those promoting the ideas of distributed cognition have used this framework to try to understand, in a unified sense, all the entities and activities involved in collaborative work (e.g. ship navigation – Hutchins 1995; network engineers and hospital radiologists – Rogers and Ellis 1994). In a forerunner to studies that will take place of ICT for future collaborative networks, there have been a number of researches into audio conferencing, video conferencing, CSCW etc (e.g. Gaver et al. 1993; Finn et al. 1997; Hindmarch et al. 1998), despite, or perhaps because of, the many usability and utility problems found with such media. More recently the wider human factors community has started to get to grips with understanding such collaborative work systems accepting that cognition is not just purely thinking but embraces embodied action (e.g. Clark 1997), through studies within the naturalistic decision making field and in domains such as emergency control rooms (Artman and Waern 1999), air traffic control (Mackay 1999; Cox et al. 2004) and rail network control (Farrington-Darby and Wilson 2005).

So, to sum up: although there are studies of collaboration in the literature, focussed on both collocated physical workplaces and distributed networks, this is still not a dominant theme in cognitive ergonomics research.

The bias towards laboratory studies in academic fields such as psychology still tends to support research into individuals with individual tasks and interfaces. Where field studies exist, some of these tend to describe cultures and behaviours rather than provide structured ideas for design, especially the ones by researchers from an ethnographic persuasion. And anyway, field studies are extremely difficult and time consuming to carry out, interpretation is often open to question, and translation into design or implementation guidance is not straight forward.

6.4. Examining mobility

If so little is known, or at least widely accepted, about what collaboration at work really is, it may seem strange that we can propose requirements for the implementation and support of mobile and virtual collaborative work. However, we can make some suggestions for this based upon best practice in fields such as participation and participatory management, teamworking, virtual teams and human computer interaction. In this section we first of all address social and organisational support and then more on to requirements for technical systems support.

6.4.1 Social and organisational support

There are strong parallels between the notions of collaboration and participation – as philosophies, approaches, processes and structures. Moreover, and following the socio-technical system principle of compatibility, if we want a successfully collaborative, or participative, work system then this should be implemented through collaboration and participation. We can then learn much from the widely accepted requirements and success factors for participation (see Haines et al. 2002 and Morris et al. 2004).

At the outset, as we are preparing to implement participatory processes and systems, then – as with all change implementation – there is a need to cultivate interest, involvement and agreement amongst all those involved: "you can take a horse to water but cannot make it drink". Moreover, both the organisation and the individuals within it must perceive gains for themselves from setting up and working within a participatory or a collaborative culture. The need for commitment must be widened; senior management interest and support, being more than lip service, is vital, and trade unions must also be embraced in the early pre-planning stages.

Critically, again as with any change implementation, a champion is desperately needed. The role and attributes of such champions are interesting.

Often they will become the facilitator also, a role fraught with difficulty which is paralleled by the role of the co-ordinator when collaborative work becomes operational. Although in principle collaboration between colleagues should occur naturally in circumstances where there are no great internal relationship problems, in fact like participation it usually needs someone to drive it (gently), someone who can give direction but without being dictatorially directive, who can be empathetic yet decisive, who is comfortable with both people and technical systems, respected by all involved. In other words, the collaborative work facilitator or co-ordinator is a rare beast indeed.

Collaboration, like participation, will thrive best in a culture and climate where there is already a very good experience of change initiatives, where industrial relations are not damaged, and especially in organisations with appropriate knowledge at all levels of an open, communicative structure. Ideally, participation and collaboration will snowball; we can see this as a virtuous circle. As people collaborate more they gain confidence, pick up technical, organisational and inter-personal skills and improve the process and outcomes of work, and therefore generate the motivation to use these skills in further and deeper collaboration, and so on.

Three concepts related to team working have particular relevance to collaboration at distance and especially to virtual teams (Edwards and Wilson 2004). The first concept is trust. In the context of collaborating teams this has several manifestations. There is the trust that each team member has in each other, to be able to do their own job and to perform in such a way that the overall performance of the team is not impaired. There is also the trust that team members need to have about the inputs that they receive from other team members, in particular how reliable communications are and the quality of hardware and software that are passed amongst the team members. A particular case of this is uncovered in the author's current research into knowledge management (KM), where those providing their knowledge to be incorporated into KM systems must have trust that their services will not be dispensed with as a result, and those using the systems must trust in the advice or instructions that are delivered. The third manifestation of trust is less to do with the actual work for which the team is employed and more to do with trust in the sense that we have confidence in colleagues not to let us down and not to side with a higher authority against us. All these aspects of trust are difficult enough to develop and support in co-located teams, and difficult to measure; for virtual teams there is the added point that it is generally going to be harder to build trust since day to day and face to face contact are lacking. Trust is a vital ingredient in a successful organisation, but is very fragile and is compromised at a company's peril.

The second concept of interest from co-located and virtual teams is the shared or team mental model (Bristol 2004; Langan-Fox et al. 2004). A mental model refers to the way in which we perceive and conceive of a situation, a product, a system or a task. It is made up of our own expectations as we approach a task or a product and of what confronts us at that time. One way of thinking about mental models is that they are simulations that we run inside our own heads to help us with tasks or use of products or dealing with other people. A team mental model, then, is an explanation of the types of beliefs, perceptions and knowledge that might be held across a whole team; they may well be variable in number and quality, and may be concerned with the form, functions, state or purpose of things or people. A shared mental model is the extent to which individuals in a team will have parts of a mental model in common, so that they can work with common understanding of problems and can hand over tasks or functions to each other without there being a breakdown in their performance. In some situations a distributed mental model may be preferred, where individuals differ in their model but the bringing together of the different views and perspectives can be very powerful. Such notions of team and shared mental model are of great interest when we look at collaboration in, for instance, air traffic control or emergency coordination centres. Considerable research is required to know how we can support a team mental model and the sharing of mental models when people are distributed in space and time within mobile and virtual collaborative work.

The third concept is that of the team boundary and its management. Team boundary usually means the limit of functional responsibility and authority. For instance, with a co-located manufacturing team the extent to which they are responsible for process quality and how they liaise with the quality engineers are amongst the indicators of where we set the boundary to the team and then how we manage transfer of information and decision making across it. In general we have to decide what lies within the boundary, which is to do with the selection of team members and determining the size of teams and their composition. Then we have to specify the boundary, deciding on the clarity with which we set roles for the team and how we allow the team to identify with itself and its place within the wider organisation. Boundary permeability is the extent to which the team is open to external inputs and to which the wider organisation is open to contributions from the team. Boundary spanning is to do with the actual interactions that take place with other groups or personnel and how these are done. Finally, boundary crossing is to do with how we enable members of the team to exit or leave the team, and how we allow new members to enter or join the team. In developing, setting up, implementing and managing mobile, virtual collaborative work systems, all aspects of the boundary must be carefully considered, as should structures and processes to promote trust and to inculcate an appropriate team mental model.

6.4.2 Technical systems support

When we consider the ICT to support mobile virtual collaborative work we have a choice of philosophies. If we wish to try to replicate face to face collaborative activity we will want to develop and implement ICT which provides a structure for common "language", supports reflection, subtlety, nuance and exploration, allows a fluidity in relationships and ideas, gives social cues, and enables co-operative diagnosis, prediction, problem solving and decision making. These requirements are, of course, easier to define than to achieve, and the alternative philosophy is to accept that mobile, virtual ICT will be very limited in some respects and so not try to replicate those subtle or sophisticated elements of face to face communication, instead applying the processing resources to functions the ICT can do very well. As just one example, if provision of facial expressions on avatars in collaborative virtual environments, or high definition pictures of faces in video conferencing, still do not give participants the feelings they get face to face then there is an argument not to bother, and to apply the processing resources to another part of the system or else use something else entirely, for example audio conferencing.

Only after understanding user needs, including whether collaborative computer systems are needed at all and the settings and circumstances for use, should we consider the technical systems to support collaboration. Decisions about technical support for virtual and mobile collaborative work should be made against a number of criteria. By reviewing the resulting profiles in the light of needs for their own organisation, companies can start to make rational technical choices (Edwards and Wilson 2004).

Functionality is the capability of the ICT system and its interfaces; in other words, what can it deliver? Functionality can be a two edged sword, with the danger of providing either too little or too much, the latter being especially relevant with mobile and virtual technologies. Virtual teams and their facilitators must first address the question of what it is they really need to do, now and in the future, and how they wish to collaborate. Then they should think about: who will be doing this, when and where; how they will be working in practical terms – i.e. on the move, at home etc; and why they will be working in this way. Only then should they consider which ICT best meets their needs. Two particular elements of functionality are archiving and security. Archiving is the capability of the technology to create a historical record of team information exchange, interactions and decision-making. The very nature of virtual work – with people working out of the office, often in relatively insecure homes or on the move in public, and information being transmitted over external networks – means that security takes on extra importance, with all that overly aggressive fire walls bring.

At the heart of human factors of ICT is the notion of usability. Organisations should consider ease of learning, interface consistency, on-line and off-line help, support for navigation, comprehensible coding systems, health and safety and the motivation of the worker to actually employ the ICT rather than to work around it. Good usability will mean that users can get the most out of the system's functionality, giving it high utility. Lessons learned from collaborative technologies in the past are that the sheer effort of using the interface sometimes takes time, concentration and energy away from the actual collaborative tasks. The quality of human-human, human-computer, and human-computer/telecommunications – human interactions will be crucial for usability of the ICT and for good collaboration. Sensor-based interaction will, arguably, be the most important technical support for the mobile and virtual worker, collaborating using personal devices or devices embedded in the environment. Rogers and Muller (2003) define opportunities for the sensor-based system designer to support perception, awareness, reflection and dealing with uncertainty and unexpectedness, and such capabilities will be of great value for distributed collaborative socio-technical networks.

The functionality and usability of a system combine to create the values of social presence, information richness and salience. Social presence is the extent to which a technology makes people feel a personal connection with others. Interactions with high social presence tend to be synchronous and have an open and friendly environment. Face to face meetings should have high social presence (but in practice many may not!), and video-conferencing attempts to provide this (although technical deficiencies often detract from this). High social presence is not always a good thing; some communication may be easier when not faced with the reactions, emotions and gestures of others or of their avatars, and in such cases it may be better to use systems with lower social interaction. Reduced social presence is inherent in systems such as email, which are relatively asynchronous, but this does not detract from the fact they are very useful for many purposes. Information richness reflects the variety in the content and format of information that will be transferred between team members. An information rich resource – for instance providing graphical images and audio as well as text - can reduce confusion and misunderstanding, but additional complexity may come at a price of less reliability. Figure 6.1 illustrates several forms of technology to support collaboration, classified on the time dimension of asynchronous/synchronous and the dimension of information richness. Salience is the meaning of the message or interaction implied by the technology and especially the user perceptions of this.

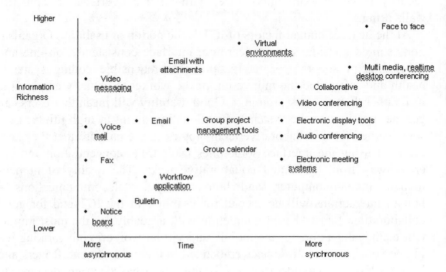

Fig. 6.1. Classification of information and communication technologies to support collaboration in virtual teams. Source: Edwards and Wilson 2003

People may be more responsive if there is the increased (virtual or real) human interaction. Surface mail in these days of email overload may assume a greater subjective importance, because of the sender's care that it implies.

As well as attributes of the ICT system itself, technical choice should also be based upon organisational parameters. There needs to be clear understanding of the organisational readiness for implementation of different ICT to support virtual teams, a mobile workforce and for collaboration itself. Particular attention should be paid to the in-house ICT support capability that a company has. An organisation will usually want to choose ICT which matches the existing infrastructure if possible and which can be implemented and supported and serviced by their existing staff. Some local area networks may only have a relatively small bandwidth, and a rich communications media will suffer consequent quality problems – which will impair communications and give low motivation for use. Cost is an obvious criterion, whereby the benefits from being mobile and collaborating virtually must outweigh the costs of implementation (tangible and intangible). Highly related to this is the project life or period of time over which the ICT will actually be employed.

6.5 Methodological considerations in studying collaborative work

The development of mobile virtual work should be based upon research to investigate and analyse current collaborative work networks, both co-located and distributed, and including formative and summative evaluation of the full socio-technical system that emerges, not just of the technical systems. Such research is not straightforward however. The traditional laboratory setting will be of only limited value, with the main need being for careful field research. Good quality simulations – of social as well as technical systems interactions – may have a role for future systems at the concept stage, but these would be very difficult to design, especially to capture all the social interactions – planned, contingent and serendipitous – that characterise collaborative work in complex distributed systems. For future and current systems we can use scenario walkthroughs and scenario analysis in which groups of, scientific or subject matter, experts assess the structure, processes and outcomes for collaboration in any proposed or actual system of work.

Where people are currently working in collaborative settings, field methodology may borrow from ethnography (e.g. Engstrom and Middleton 1996; Heath and Luff 2000), naturalistic decision making (e.g. Klein 1998), distributed cognition (Hutchins 1995; Rogers and Ellis 1994) and work domain analysis (Vicente 1999). We may use questionnaires and interviews to establish opinions and collect evidence of successes and failures. Various techniques of direct observation of behaviours and events, interviews, archive analysis, verbal protocol analysis, textual and content analysis will help us to examine what is happening within a collaborating group, why and how All of these methods have strengths and weaknesses, and in most studies we would certainly use more than one. A period of familiarisation and examination of archives and incident reports for domain analysis may be followed by extensive periods of observation and interviewing, followed by debriefing, further group or individual interviews, and validation exercises. The data collected must be collapsed otherwise they cannot be reported in any coherent form, but the process of reduction must be transparent and supportable at every stage and can take a long time (e.g. Farrington-Darby et al. 2005 in press). In our studies of planners and schedulers, which is presented below, each investigator spent weeks at a time shadowing one focus job holder, returning several times to gain greater insight into what had been observed and to validate the interpretations that had been made; such studies can take months and years.

This sort of study is difficult enough when we are trying to understand and focus on individuals in a single workplace. It will be even more difficult when trying to understand, or even predict when the systems are not yet in place, collaboration in virtual enterprises and for mobile networks, teams distributed in space and perhaps in time and where several members will be moving. At a simple level, it has been suggested that we might make a first examination of how people within distributed computer-mediated networks collaborate, and who with, by adapting techniques from social network analysis to allow electronic traces of activity. We could track and interpret email traffic and construct and analyse resultant social networks, but that could only tell us so much surface detail about frequency and perhaps direction of interactions. This might be of use in a very cursory and initial understanding of the type of work that goes on when people are collaborating within mobile and virtual teams, but it is certain that something else will be needed to generate deeper understanding. An equivalent in virtual environments presented via networked VR systems is to use a "play/replay" facility to track what happened in the VE.

A richer study would possibly require a distributed research team in a kind of mapping onto the focus collaborating team being studied, whereby each member of the work team is shadowed by a member of the research team so the same events, communications and decisions can be observed from the different points of view involved. Such methodology will not be easy but is currently under discussion in our own work studying the interaction of pilots and air traffic controllers in the light of new technical systems, and in studies of distributed team working amongst railway signallers, train drivers, controllers and planners.

6.6 Cases of collaborative working

In order to illustrate some of the points made in this paper, and to raise some new ones, details are given of four very different examples of collaboration, or of settings and domains that require an understanding of collaboration, taken from the work of the author and his colleagues.

6.6.1 Collaborative virtual environments

Collaborative virtual environments are a hybrid, combining the real time visual and auditory interaction and presence allowed through virtual reality with the online communities possible through computer networks. In work carried out from the mid-1990s through into about 2002 we studied the performance of groups of participants in collaborative virtual environments (CVEs), deriving methods and measures to assess the manner and extent of their collaboration (Tromp et al. 2003). However, even familiarity with the literature in computer supported cooperative work at the time provided us with little clue as to how we should conceptualise collaboration and its quality and therefore how to measure and evaluate it.

There are few structured accounts of usability evaluation in virtual environments, and even fewer for CVEs outside technical guidance for developers. There is little agreement on what functions are most important, especially to support collaboration. Our role in a much larger project was to develop processes and methods for formative evaluation of CVE prototypes.

Much of our evaluation work was carried out on a CVE designed to support virtual meetings. Participants (actually situated hundreds of Km apart) represented by their avatars made contact with each other, exchanged information in papers and files, and arrived at simple decisions. Literature on human-human collaboration was used to develop a set of identified interactions that take place during collaboration, and which were used to underpin much of our evaluation methodology. These are: verbal communication, phatic communication, spatial regulation, proxemic skills, turn taking, peripheral awareness, trust building, reciprocity, indexicality and gaze patterns.

The methods we developed were a usability inspection cycle technique comprising both a cognitive walkthrough and a heuristics evaluation checklist, an adaptation of a task analysis method, assessment against usability guidelines, a consumer report and evaluation procedure, and observation based on ethnographic studies of sequence interactions, turning into a sequence process analysis technique. The series of questions used in the inspection cycle were:

- "Can the user locate the other user(s)?"
- "Can the user recognise and distinguish the other users?"
- "Are the communication channels effective?"
- "Are the actions of the other user(s) visible and recognisable?"
- "Can a user act on a shared object while keeping the other user(s) in view?"
- "Can the user easily switch views between objects, locations, and other users?"
- "Can the user get an overview of the total shared space and all other users in it?"
- "Can the user tell when there are interruptions in the attention of other users?"

In general, the CVE as it was implemented at the time of the tests – i.e. as a prototype – did not perform well on the tests or against the benchmark criteria, although as software it was the most advanced CVE of its time. A significant issue was that the very need to operate and deal with the technology can detract from the sense and maintenance of collaboration; our observations showed only about 30% of activity was to do with the collaborative tasks that were set, and the rest to do with keeping the technical systems, and thus the means to collaborate, going (see also the chapter by Perry et al. in this volume). However, it is the types of testing and the issues that were addressed, especially as regards collaboration, which are of interest in this chapter. For further information the reader is referred to Tromp, Steed and Wilson (2003).

6.6.2 Studies of planners and schedulers

We have made many studies of the work of people in planning, scheduling and control. These studies have been in industries that include steel, railways, aircraft manufacturing, electronics, textiles and bakeries. The catalyst for the research has been the relatively poor performance of IT scheduling tools and the lack of understanding of how expert schedulers actually work. Questions we have asked include (MacCarthy and Wilson 2001; MacCarthy et al. 2001):

- How do schedulers handle information and make decisions?
- How do they fit in with – and indeed catalyse – social networks in the work place?
- What makes a good scheduler and schedule?

Although one aim has been to study and analyse the cognitive work involved, and the knowledge and skills required for people to carry this out successfully, it became apparent that a distinguishing feature of such work is social network understanding and use of social work artefacts (Jackson, MacCarthy and Wilson 2004; Wilson et al. 2003). In most of the cases the people we have studied have been part of formal and informal collaborative networks of people who are both co-located and distributed, often moving into different locations, and these teams and groups therefore fit very well within the mobile virtual collaborative work paradigm. In all the domains we have studied we have found a dearth of understanding of the role of social collaboration. We developed models and methods starting from a number of different backgrounds including naturalistic decision making, distributed cognition and ethnographic work analysis (see Crawford et al. 1999). For example a method to record and analyse decisions –

the decision probe – was developed to capture all the factors that were involved in the scheduler's decision-making process – scheduler decisions tend to be mediated through a web of social interactions and are rarely made at one location at one point in time. In order to validate the data captured, the method had to allow for subsequent retrospective assessment by the schedulers and researchers. The overall aim of the method was to be rich enough to capture all relevant decision information yet structured enough to allow us to assess the scheduler's decision making within the context of their work, so that we could make valid and useful suggestions for the design of future supportive IT systems and of the cognitive work supported.

6.6.3 Railway maintenance

Current work on human factors on the railways (e.g. Wilson et al. 2005) has thrown up a superb example of a distributed network of mobile workers, who need to collaborate in order that their jobs are carried out safely, efficiently and reliably to a high quality. This is the work to undertake maintenance of the railways, whether this is inspection, repair, enhancements or major renewals. Differing numbers of specialists from different functions have to come together into teams with varying degrees of integration, and must coordinate and cooperate together whilst distributed over time and space. The roles include planners and managers, engineering supervisors, PICOPs (Persons In Charge Of Possession), COSSs (Controllers Of Site Safety), overhead line engineers, trackside workers, engineering vehicle managers and drivers, and inspectors. The wider collaborating network will also include signallers, controllers and passenger and freight train drivers.

Amongst the studies we have undertaken has been a recent one of the work of the engineering supervisor (Slamen et al. 2004). The nature of their role means that their activity is, or ought to be, highly collaborative. The engineering supervisors are responsible for a number of work sites along a length of track that can be anything from a few metres to several kilometres. Their collaborative activity stretches over time, translating outline and detailed plans made hours, days or weeks before into activity on the shift, and handing back a safe track to the railway operations, and space, with their work gangs spread out along the track, the signallers and controllers many kilometres away. The teamworking is virtual in the sense that they are not all co-located and work for several different companies. And they and their gangs are mobile. Early observations and interviews revealed the critical aspects of the role to include communications, shared planning and conducting briefings, all central to collaborative work.

In such settings a conceptual framework of the issues must be built up in parallel to the collection of empirical evidence, and this underpins understanding and eventual recommendations. Tasks and interactions between all the actors concerned were observed with different degrees of detachment and obtrusiveness according to circumstance and the requirements of rich data collection. A variety of interview techniques were employed, dependent on whether the focus was individual performance or group/collaborative behaviour. The critical part of such studies, apart from gaining access in the first place, is making sense of all the rich data from various sources, combining, sorting, reducing and representing these in a manner so as to be useful but at the same time so that there is a traceable evidence trail. A previous study of track workers and maintenance supplied support in how to represent the data in tables and diagrams to help see visually where problems and issues lie (Farrington-Darby et al. 2005).

Those who are interested in the availability and subsequent integration of personal and ambient technologies to allow mobile and virtual work to take place, find a number of interesting requirements from this example of rail maintenance work. The information, needed in pre-planning and in re-planning actually while carrying out the maintenance, includes knowledge of safe access routes, potential dangers at the site, maps and drawings, job history at that site, and lists of resources needed and available including skill sets for the teams. Also of great value will be the potential for updating position information, for the engineering supervisor and their team, perhaps via GPS. There is also a requirement for record keeping using video, photographs, graphics and text in order to support better knowledge management, sending such new information to a central store and drawing down from that store when required. All this is as well as the straightforward needs for robust, high quality, and flexible communications media as would be found with any collaborating group.

6.6.4 Multiple decoupled interaction in virtual environments

The fourth example differs a little from the first three in that it does not posit collaboration needs or problems but rather describes a solution we have developed to allow greater collaboration between participants in a virtual environment (VE). The VIEW of the Future (IST 2000-26089: Virtual and Interactive Environments for Workplaces of the Future) project developed best practice for industrial use of virtual environments, with applications in product development and testing, and in training (Wilson and

D'Cruz 2005). Amongst the project objectives were to produce a mobile VE concept and mobile systems and to enhance people's participation in virtual environments. Thus all the central issues of this book were covered; work with the systems was to be virtual (in both senses of being a simulation and being distributed), the participants and the equipment were to be mobile, and the active participation or collaboration of all users was to be supported. Here we briefly mention one technical development to enhance collaboration (for other innovative technical developments in VR/VE from the project see Hoffman et al. 2005 and Ronkko et al. 2005).

Multiple Decoupled Interaction (MDI) (see Bayon et al. 2005) was developed on the basis of a highly successful project on distributed computing systems for collaborative story-telling by children (e.g. Bayon et al. 2003). MDI employs user company models of VIEW applications such as for vehicle design, converted to run within the commercial package Virtools. It allows a number of users to actively collaborate using a virtual environment, either at the site or remotely, by using PDAs, mobile phones, gyro mouse, speech or laptop. Different participants can simultaneously control the viewpoint, aesthetics, interaction, or can grab video clips or screen dumps, interacting collaboratively with the VE (generally displayed on a large screen). The MDI differs from collaborative virtual environments (CVEs) – such as in the work described earlier – in that participants collaborate in performing the tasks enabled by the VE rather than with each other through their representation within the VE. The MDI will allow active collaboration by a group of users, say in a design team, whereby one might manipulate the viewpoint using a gyromouse, another interact with the model by opening a door using speech, a third use a PDA to modify the model aesthetics and another team member, perhaps remote from the others, grab screen dumps or video clips for later client review, using a laptop. To date the system has been evaluated in laboratory trials and has undergone initial approval trials with aerospace and motor company design engineers. As with the other cases, one key area of relevance of the MDI to the discussions of this chapter are the requirements it makes on the human factors community to be able to understand more about virtual social networks and distributed collaborating teams.

6.7. Concluding discussion

Fine words about the excitement of virtual and mobile work and adventurous visions of ambient technologies in the future are all very well, but there is a worrying feeling that the push of technology development, or even worse, the need to make sales of existing and proposed new technical systems, rather than the real pull of real user needs might be at work. Users in this view embrace individual employees including managers, organisations, local and regional communities and governments. To what extent are the visions of how we will work in the future those of businesses such as PR, marketing, publishing, investment houses rather than those of locally-embedded productive industries? As a simple example, does the notion of hotelling or bed-and-breakfasting, i.e. employees booking space and facilities at HQ for a defined period only, have any relevance to a family construction company in a southern French village, or a machine tool manufacturer in the north east of Spain? We must beware of being swept along on the tide of developer euphoria or, even more dangerous, the dreams of self appointed "visionaries" who are often marooned mid-Atlantic with some vision that the whole of Europe - from the design houses of Milan and the PR agencies of London to the woodworking factories of Genova and the metal foundries of Birmingham – will be wired into a Grid, part of a knowledge economy with open knowledge availability and exchange, and employing ambient intelligence (whatever this might be).

Collaboration in its true sense has several critical components, and these must be supported by any new organisational and technical systems of mobile virtual work. Systems must allow people to orientate themselves and participate in collaborative activities, supporting direction and leadership even if this is not vested in one permanent leader. The teams who are collaborating must be able to handle rich, high quality, open, flexible and yet disciplined communication and coordination. Collaborators should be able to monitor and be aware of each other's activities, give and receive feedback from colleagues, fill in and back up team members who are unable to complete a particular task, be sensitive to each other's workload and performance and adapt and reform as a team according to changes in the environment. There seems little point in providing mobile virtual work if it does not improve the quality of knowledge creation and knowledge management, imagination and creativity, learning, exploring and discovery, engagement and reflection. Moreover, in order that mobile virtual workers have trust and confidence in new systems, they must feel a sense of ownership and of privacy. It never ceases to amaze me how naively some technologists talk of systems for knowledge management that will somehow monitor instances of use of knowledge by employees and capture them, for future use by others in the organisation. We do not have to be of a particularly suspicious nature to feel that we are not very happy about giving our knowledge in this way. It is such issues of competence, trust and ethical concerns generally which must be satisfied for mobile virtual work and also for collaborative activity of all kinds.

This chapter has discussed collaboration within mobile virtual work with the implication that this will be through new advances in ICT. However such collaboration will not always be carried out and supported remotely via ever more sophisticated ICT. Many mobile workers will continue to perform successfully using fairly traditional methods of communication, and others will carry out their activities through face to face contacts supported by technical tools when appropriate. It is the depth and quality of collaboration that is critical and it is this that we need to better understand.

Acknowledgements

Whilst the views in this chapter are the author's own its writing has been aided immeasurably through collaboration with his colleagues at the University of Nottingham and with colleagues in a number of European Commission projects, notably Irene Lopez de Vallejo, Maria Cristina Brugnoli and Paul Wheeler.

References

Ackerman MS (2002) The intellectual challenge of CSCW: The gap between social requirements and technical feasibility. In: Carroll JM (ed) Human-computer interaction in the new millennium. Addison-Wesley, New York, pp 303–319

Argyle M (1969) *Social interaction*. Methuen & Co.Ltd, London

Arias EG, Eden H, Fischer G, Gorman A, Scharff E (2000) Transcending the individual human mind: Creating shared understanding through collaborative design. In: Carroll JM. (ed) Human-computer interaction in the new millennium. Addison-Wesley, New York, pp 347–362

Artman H, Waern Y (1999) Distributed cognition in an emergency co-ordination center. Cognition, Technology & Work 1:237–246

Bayon V, Wilson JR, Stanton D, Boltman A (2003). Mixed reality storytelling environments. Virtual Reality 7(1):54–63

Bayon V, Griffiths G, Wilson JR (2005) Multiple decoupled interaction: An interaction design approach for groupware interaction in collocated virtual environments. (Paper to appear in special issue of International Journal of Human Computer Science)

Boff KR (2001) Foreword. In: McNeese M, Salas E, Endsley M (eds) New trends in cooperative activities. Human Factors and Ergonomics Society, Santa Monica, pp v–vi

Bristol ND (2004) Shared mental models: Conceptualisation and measurement. (PhD thesis, School of Mechanical, Materials and Manufacturing Engineering, University of Nottingham)

Clark A, (1997) Being there: putting brain, body, and world together again. MIT Press, London

Cox G, Nichols SC, Stedmon AW, Wilson JR (2004) The flight deck of the future: Field studies in Datalink and Freeflight. In: McCabe PT (ed) Contemporary Ergonomics 2004. Proceedings from the Ergonomics Society Conference. Taylor & Francis, Swansea. London & New York.

Crawford S, MacCarthy BL, Vernon C, Wilson JR (1999). Investigating the work of industrial schedulers through field study. Cognition, Technology and Work 1:63–77

Edwards A, Wilson JR (2004) Implementing virtual teams: A guide to organizational and human factors. Gower Press, London

Engstrom Y, Middleton D (1996) Cognition and communication at work. Cambridge University Press, Cambridge

Erickson T, Kellogg WA (2002) In: Carroll JM (ed) Human-computer interaction in the new millennium. Addison-Wesley, New York, pp 325–342

European Commission (2004) Collaboration@Work: The 2004 report on new working environments and practices. Office for Official publications of the European Communities, Luxembourg

Farrington-Darby T, Pickup L, Wilson JR (2005) Safety culture in rail maintenance. Safety Science 43(1):39–60

Farrington-Darby T, Wilson JR, Norris BJ, Clarke T (2005) Expertise in rail network control. (Submitted to Ergonomics)

Finn K, Sellen A, Wilbur S (eds) (1997). Video-mediated communication. Lawrence Erlbaum, New Jersey

Gaver WW, Sellen A, Heath C, Luff P (1993) One is not enough: Multiple views in a media space. In: Proceedings of INTERCHI'93, pp 335–341

Goffman E (1967) International ritual: Essays on face-to-face behaviour. Pantheon Books, New York

Heath C, Luff P (2000) Technology in action. Cambridge University Press, Cambridge

Hindmarch J, Fraser M, Heath C, Benford S, Greenhalgh C (1998) Fragmented interaction: Establishing mutual orientation in virtual environments. In: Proceedings of CSCW'98, pp 217–226

Hoffman H, Stefani O, Patel H (2005) Extending the desktop workplace by a portable virtual reality system. (Submitted to International Journal of Human Computer Studies)

Hutchins E (1995.) Cognition in the Wild. MIT Press, Cambridge, Massachusetts

Jackson S, Wilson JR, MacCarthy BL (2004) A new model of scheduling in manufacturing: Tasks, roles and monitoring. Human Factors 46:533–550

Kendon A, Harris RM, Ritchie Key M (eds) (1975) Organization of behavior in face-to-face interaction. Mouton Publishers, The Hague

Klein G (1998) Sources of power: How people make decisions. MIT Press, Cambridge

Langan-Fox J, Anglim J, Wilson JR (2004) Mental models, team mental models and performance: Process, development and future directions. Human Factors and Ergonomics in Manufacturing 14:331–352

MacCarthy BL, Wilson JR (eds) (2001) Human factors in scheduling and planning. Taylor and Francis, London

MacCarthy BL, Wilson JR, Crawford S (2001). Human Performance in Industrial Scheduling: A framework for understanding. Human Factors and Ergonomics in Manufacturing 11:299–320

Mackay W (2000) Is paper safer? The role of flight strips in air traffic control. ACM Transactions on Computer Human Interaction 6:311–340

McNeese M, Salas E, Endsley M (eds) (2001) New Trends in cooperative activities: Understanding system dynamics in complex environments. Human Factors and Ergonomics Society, Santa Monica

Morris W, Wilson JR, Koukoulaki T (2004) Developing a participatory approach to the decision of work equipment: Assimilating lessons from workers' experiences. TUTB, Brussels

Olson GM, Olson JS (2002) Distance matters. In: Carroll JM. (ed) Human-computer interaction in the new millennium. Addison-Wesley, New York, pp 397–413

Rogers Y, Ellis J (1994) Distributed cognition: an alternative framework for analysing and explaining collaborative working. Journal of Information Technology 9(2):119–128

Rogers Y, Muller H (2003). Stop making sense: Designing sensor-based interaction to facilitate exploration and reflection. Technical Report Equator-03-002, Equator. (Submitted to International Journal of Human Computer Studies)

Rönkkö J, Markkanen J, Launonen R, Ferrino M, Gaia E, Basso V, Patel H D'Cruz M, Laukkanen S (2005). Multi-nodal astronaut virtual training prototype. (Submitted to International Journal of Human Computer Studies)

Scott J (2000) Social network analysis. 2nd edition. SAGE Publications, London

Slamen A, Schock A, Ryan B, Wilson JR (2004) Human factors analysis of the work of the engineering supervisor. (Restricted report of Network Rail, London)

Tromp JG, Steed A, Wilson JR (2003) Systematic usability evaluation and design issues for collaborative virtual environments. Presence: Teleoperators and Virtual Environments 12(3):241–267

Vicente KJ (1999) Cognitive work analyses: towards safe, productive and healthy computer based work. L. Erlbaum, New Jersey

Wilson JR (2000) Fundamentals of ergonomics. Applied Ergonomics 31:557–567

Wilson JR, D'Cruz MD (2005) Virtual and interactive environments for work of the future. (Paper to appear in special issue of International Journal of Human Computer Science)

Wilson JR, Jackson S, Nichols S (2003) Cognitive work investigation and design in practice: the influence of social context and social work artefacts. In: Hollnagel E (ed) Cognitive Task Design, pp 83–98

Wilson JR, Norris BJ, Clarke T, Mills A (2005) Rail human factors. Ashgate, London

7 Model-based Design of Mobile Work Systems

Ludger Schmidt and Holger Luczak

Institute of Industrial Engineering and Ergonomics, RWTH Aachen University, Germany

7.1 Introduction

The fast development in the area of information and communication technology and especially in broadband internet access and mobile computing has changed the established ways of communication, learning, entertainment and work in professional and private lives. Undoubtedly, mobile devices, network applications and services offer a wide range of new possibilities. But besides technological feasibility it is not always clear what features are really essential, useful or handy for a particular person in a particular work context. Therefore, to create mobile work systems that enable efficient and effective work in a new way or improve current work processes, it is necessary not only to focus on technology, but to look at the users, their qualifications and tasks, as well as to include aspects of work organisation in an integrative approach. Especially in the area of mobile work applications, the time to market and the half-life period of products gets shorter and constantly new versions of products are launched. Accordingly, the time frame for design phases decreases, calling for an efficient and reliable design process.

Hence, to meet these challenges a structured and model-based framework has been developed that includes a human-centred and task-oriented design approach. It is supposed to help mobile work systems' designers to think about what is required for particular work context in terms of technology, organisation and personnel. Against the background of trends in mobile work, this framework is presented in this chapter and illustrated by a case study to exemplify the proposed design process.

7.2 Trends of mobile work in Europe

In 2002 the EU-Commission published the Action Plan "eEurope 2005 – An information society for all" (Commission of the European Communities 2002) which identified key targets like the connection to broadband networks and the review of legislation affecting e-business. Similarly the German report "Information Society Germany 2006" (Federal Ministry of Economics and Labour & Federal Ministry of Education and Research 2004) set a focus on a digital economy aimed at growth and competitiveness and pointed out that in 2005 75% of the German population should use the internet and in 2010 50% of all homes should be connected to a broadband line.

In 2003, more than one out of three EU citizens was an internet user, whereas Sweden had the highest share of internet users with 57 per 100 inhabitants. In the EU, there were 80 mobile phone subscriptions per 100 inhabitants in 2003. Luxembourg (120), Sweden (98), and Italy (95) had the highest number of subscriptions per 100 inhabitants, Lithuania (62), Latvia (52), and Poland (46) the least (Eurostat 2004).

The future of work is supposed to demand a high degree of mobility, multifunctional applications and flexibility concerning the aspects of time and space. Relevant prognoses and statistics that concentrate on the mobile market support these requirements. Working persons need to adapt to working circumstances, which call for flexibility and mobility, for instance (tele)commuters or moving people.

The technological development is progressing and computer technologies are becoming smaller as well as more advanced and create various possibilities of mobile data transfer. Besides offering these options of innovative applications and services the current progress presents new perspectives and research demands in the field of industrial engineering and ergonomics.

Actual trends in the development of mobile work can be summarized according to six aspects characterizing the use of mobile technologies (Scheer et al. 2001, Pousttchi et al. 2003):

- *Mobility*
  The most obvious advantage of mobile technology is a gain in the freedom of movement. The user is not attached to a certain location or to a fixed frame of time. The freedom of movement will only be ceased if provision of mobile networks is terminated.

- *Ubiquitous access and processing*
  The term ubiquity refers to the omnipresence of information systems, thus, ubiquitous access means ad-hoc access to the virtual world from every spot in the real world. The user is permanently online, no boot procedure is necessary; the services are applicable at any time and at any place. Mobile end devices can be taken along everywhere. Furthermore, ubiquitous access provides permanent reception and sending of data as well as direct data processing.

- *Context sensitivity*
  Context sensitivity means shaping information to the actual needs of the user. This is also known as tailoring (Rumelhart 1980). Tailoring is to design information in a way it fits the target group, for example presenting different information to a tourist than to a business man when visiting a particular town. The user's environment can be recorded and evaluated with mobile technologies. Therefore, user services can be offered for each specific context. For example, for a tourist visiting a city information about different events can be tailored to location of the person (local context), to the persons actual activity (action-related context), to the time of the day or year (time context) or to personal preferences like non-smoker, sportsman (personal context). Therefore, local, action related, temporal and personal contents are to be considered for designing a mobile work environment.

- *Reach ability*
  Mobile users are connected to information structures at any time. They cannot only access information, they can also be contacted anywhere. Pro-active services can be provided by permanent availability, e.g. intelligent agents are supposed to give particular advice. For example these advices could refer to buying or selling stocks if the stock quotation falls beneath a threshold. The permanent availability of users enables a synchronous communication among users. The availability is realized technologically by the infrastructure of mobile networks.

- *Remote control*
  The internet already provides the possibility to operate or configure stationary machines from far distances. Mobile end devices are supposed to control other devices in close distance via for example an infrared or Bluetooth radio interface. Medium and far distances can be by-passed by WLAN (Wireless Local Area Network), GPRS (General Packet Radio Service) and UMTS (Universal Mobile Telecommunication System). The device that is being controlled can also be mobile, for exam-

ple a car or a train. If a malfunction occurs then a mechanic can analyse the data from the car (or train) computer online. Ideally the mechanic can eliminate the error source by reconfiguring the system from his office. If that error is a structural problem of the production process, all vehicles could be reconfigured, even before the disturbance occurs.

- *Unequivocal allocation and security:*
  Security in mobile communication and unequivocal allocation are crucial for future applications. It is of major importance that the user can be identified quickly and explicitly via a call number, pin, card number, or even unmistakable biometrical data. Thus, the security in data communication and use can be extremely increased.

These trends and the referring new options in the use of mobile technologies and the fast progress in the development of mobile devices and services as well as its increasing spread within private and professional areas require innovative ways of work design. As a result these technological developments affect the working person and the operational organization of the company (Bradley 2001). However, these effects still have not been investigated completely (Carayon 2001, Luczak et al. 2003). Dimensions of mobile work are presented in this article against the background of the classical fields of industrial engineering and ergonomics. Combining a design space for mobile work with a human-centred design process, a model will be introduced, which aims at shaping and designing mobile working systems in a human-centred and task-oriented way. Its application will be demonstrated by exemplary research questions, which have been developed in a real world case study.

7.3 Mobile work in the context of industrial engineering

Over the past few years, mobile work has been forwarded especially by technological developments and innovations and new kinds of information and communication systems enable to work at different places and times. This trend – as mentioned above – is supposed to increase even stronger. The spread of computer technologies in private households is the basis for mobile work and home office work. In addition mobile work offers a very promising potential for the gain in efficiency, cost reduction and proximity to customers as well as new flexible working concepts with the creation of an interesting value for the employees in the meaning of work and life balance.

Against this background many questions concerning the effects and the relevance of mobile work and mobile technologies on the working environment and the design of new infrastructures arise. Similar to Vartiainen's concept (cf. chapter 2 in this volume), the Stabsgruppe arbeit 21 (2002) proposed the following dimensions for new mobility of work, that should be considered in the design process.

- *Mobility of the individual*
  The first dimension is the mobility of the individual (in this context only work areas are concerned in which the individual needs technical support devices). Mobility of the individual is characterized by the individual being able to work at different places. An example would be a design engineer being not only able to work at his company's office, at the client, but also at home or at some other place he might feel comfortable or inspired. That is, people are able to do their job regardless of their physical location. This dimension would facilitate the combination of leisure, family and job-related activities.

- *Mobility of work contents*
  Due to stationary machines, there is a strong attachment to a certain location in traditional work settings, whereby the work force is rotating dynamically. Today many work contents can be mobilized independently from the individual. This for example applies to cases in which different agents work on one issue in sequential steps (like 24h of product development per day with three teams around the world in a time zone oriented process chain). Thereby different actors or individuals have to access one pool of work-related information either consecutively or simultaneously. The infrastructure of new communication technologies should facilitate the de-centralized provision and availability of work contents, for example the design engineer supported by a version and history management system being able to finish some parts that his colleague from a team in another time zone has started working with. At the same time there are cases in which both, the working individual and the work content have to be mobile.

- *Mobility of working tools*
  The mobility of tools is supposed to be understood in terms of mobile end devices, distributed software and interactive software agents. The working tools should incorporate a variety of mobile functions to activate, control and end work processes. They should be platform independent in order to achieve ubiquity of the working environment for a particular agent. Imagine for example the construction engineer being busy with the installation of a plant at the customer. Now problems

arise, because a particular part seems not to have the right identification number. His company uses software for the plant's particle lists which is not present at the customer, but the engineer carries a mobile version of the software with him on a personal digital assistant (PDA), thus, he will be able to check the particle list. The trend towards the mobile office via the ubiquity of tools is facilitated by the progress of the development of small, flexible and lightweight technical tools, which are independent from power supply systems.

- *Mobility of work relations*
  The mobility of work relations is growing in complexity. In the past it was a topic to talk about dynamics between operational attachment to a certain location and the mobile (but permanently allocated) work force. With the increasing amount of dynamical actors on the supplier side as well as on the side of the customer, the amount of dynamical work relations will grow, too. As dynamic teams have to communicate with mobile clients, the quantity of dynamical interactions is growing. One can assume an increase of the number of dynamic work relations between local/mobile companies and local/mobile employees as well as mobile task forces and mobile and dynamic problem solution teams. Examples would be the outsourcing of software engineers to newly industrialising countries or virtual companies as temporal joint ventures of different core competences (supplier-program in the automotive industry).

- *Virtual mobility*
  An increasing amount of partially virtual work environments requires new intellectual demands from the employees for being mobile in different virtual work settings without physical mobility. Work forms with combined or separated virtual rooms confront employees not only with real-to-virtual, but also with virtual-to-virtual interactions. The change from real to virtual environment comprises more than a mere shift in support by technical devices, because virtual mobility is not only a one-to-one mapping of physical mobility, but an addition of new interaction possibilities, e.g. by the use of avatars in a virtual environment. Partially enhanced, modified or limited interaction possibilities need suitable qualification and practical experience.

7.4 Design space model for mobile work systems

These dimensions form one axis of the model that is developed. In essence, these dimensions are possible design fields of mobile work settings. These work settings vary in their characteristics and not all fields need to be considered for all cases. Thus, these dimensions are supposed to be taken into account when developing alternatives and concretizing a design solution of a mobile work environment. After a first analysis of the planned work setting regarding these dimensions of mobile work, it is the designer's task to decide which and how these dimensions have to be met.

For instance, a mobile application for parcel delivery would have a need for mobility of the individual (when the deliverer is on the road), mobility of the work content (needs to have addresses, information about payment conditions, etc.) and mobility of tools (PDA for signing or registering deliveries). Mobility of work relations has to be taken into account, if communication between changing colleagues in a dynamic team is necessary to handle short-term orders. This aspect is irrelevant, if there is a headquarter using localization technologies such as GPS (Global Positioning System) to determine all drivers' positions and sending the courier closest to the client or the driver with the fewest orders. It is questionable whether virtual reality is possible for this example context; the designer has to decide whether different forms of mobility account for particular problems. Maybe work designers can imagine future mobile systems in this regard where virtual reality plays a role for delivery of packages.

A well-known perspective on designing work systems is to distinguish between technology, organization and personnel in a TOP approach (Luczak 1998). By incorporating these three ergonomic aspects into the model, an ecological approach is constituted, that is, system elements and relations, task and environmental variables can be considered. The variables of the TOP approach form the second axis of the proposed model. Thus, the dimensions of mobile work and the TOP approach are used to derive a matrix for design-related issues (Fig. 7.1). An explanation of how this matrix can be used for designing mobile work settings and what needs to be filled into the cells will be explained below. It is noteworthy that this model is predominantly aimed at helping to organize the design of mobile work systems and thereby creating a tool for effectively thinking about the design process. It should help to give an account of problems related to that topic.

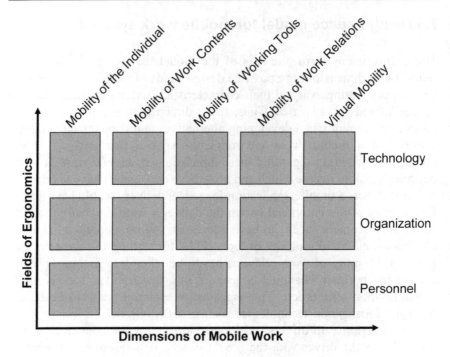

Fig. 7.1. Design space for mobile work systems

In the following section the application of the model is exemplified by explaining how the matrix can be used in a human-centred and task-oriented design process. In order to illustrate this in more detail, a case study will be introduced in the ensuing section.

A two-way table with the dimensions of mobile work in the columns and TOP in the rows emerges from the model. The corresponding cells of the matrix at the intersections are supposed to be used for the design process. For this purpose, not all combinations have to play a role in every case of an application, but it may be useful to think about all possible combinations and to decide which one to focus on.

For example the intersection of the column "mobility of work contents" with "technology" provides a cell (Fig. 7.2). In this cell it has to be pointed out, how mobility of the work content can be realized in a technological manner, that is, what technological functions need to be implemented in order to derive the mobility of work contents. This realization should be worked out by means of a human-centred and task-oriented process for that particular design problem. The procedure described in the ISO 13407 standard "Human-Centred Design Process for Interactive Systems" (ISO 13407 1999) can be selected and adapted for this purpose. The standard describes four principles of human-centred design, which are an active involvement of the users, an appropriate allocation of functions, an iteration of developed design solutions, and a multi-disciplinary design. Additionally, four key human-centred design activities are covered in this standard, which can be assigned to four main design phases. Passing iteratively through these phases of (1) analysis, (2) conception, (3) integration, and (4) evaluation gives a possibility of ergonomic design and redesign (Fig. 7.2).

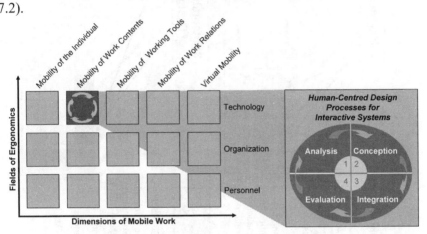

Fig. 7.2. Human-centred design process for mobile work systems

Potentially, these phases have to be run through several times, as long as reasonable results can be obtained from the process. It is noteworthy in this regard that not all cells in all levels need to be filled in. Sometimes it is even advisable to leave some cells in order to reduce redundancy. A more detailed description of these phases and some examples for methods, which can be used to pass through these phases are given in figure 7.3.

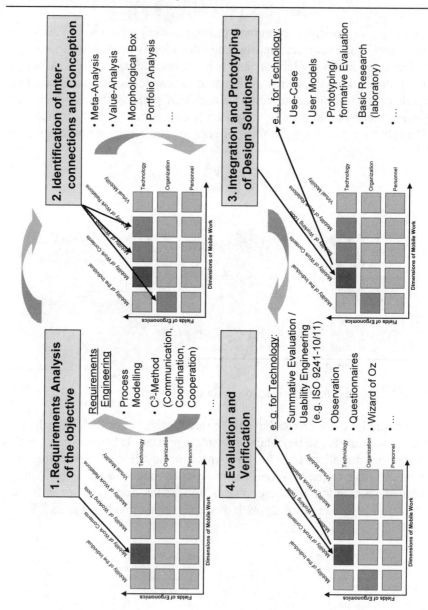

Fig. 7.3. Design phases and examples for methods

In the first step the state of affairs is analyzed and the main research question is localized in the matrix. Methods of requirements engineering like process modelling could be applied. Then the matrix is scanned for interconnections with other matrix elements within the design space regarding further research aspects. The relevance of the research question for the other fields of the matrix is specified by the results of analysis-methods. A first conception of possible design solutions is generated at the end of this phase. In the third step both the core research field and the identified secondary fields are integrated by modelling specific use-cases, building user models etc. in the example field of technology. Prototyping of first design solutions gives the possibility of further analysis according to ergonomic principles. In phase 4, an evaluation and verification of the design solutions takes place on the basis of criteria defined before. As an example for technology, criteria represented in part 10/11 of ISO 9241 (ISO 9241 1996 and 1998) could be used. The results of phase 4 can be integrated in a further run of the cycle in phase 1 in order to reach a result optimization in an iterative process.

In the following section a case study will be illustrated in terms of the proposed model in order to exemplify the design process. This study is based on the recently finished project ARVIKA (2005, Friedrich et al. 2001, Friedrich 2004, Luczak et al. 2004), which deals with Augmented Reality for the support of partially mobile work systems in industrial applications.

7.5 Case study on augmented reality work

Augmented Reality (AR) is a form of human-machine interaction where information is presented in the field of view of an individual e. g. through a head mounted display, thus augmenting his or her perception of reality. This occurs in a context-sensitive manner that is in accordance with and derived from the observed object, such as a part, tool or machine, or his or her location. In this way, the real-world field of view of a skilled worker, technician or design engineer is augmented with superimposed notes to present information that is relevant to this individual in order to enhance his or her situation awareness. Situation awareness (SA, Endsley 1995a and 1995b) is a major determinant of performance, although not in all cases. Different factors seem to have effect on SA and individuals differ in their capability to develop SA. One influencing factor is the amount of experience. As the amount of experience increases, SA increases also after practice. Basically SA contents three levels: The first level is the perception of elements in the environment, secondly, comprehension of the current situation and thirdly, the projection of future status. AR-Systems may help to create a facilitating environment for a good SA and thereby increasing productivity.

The current state of the art and the available appliances of AR are mostly at a prototype stage and do not yet permit a product-oriented application of the technology. However, AR enables a new, innovative form of human-machine interaction that not only places the individual in the centre of the industrial workflow but also offers a high potential for process and quality improvements in production and process workflows. While Virtual Reality, especially in the development phases of a product, supports the design and improvement of products without any real environment, AR focuses on the real product and the real environment and augments this reality in a situation-sensitive manner with information right on the object that can enable or facilitate the design, manufacture or maintenance of an industrial product.

Within the ARVIKA project several applications in the fields of product development, production, and service in the automotive and aerospace industries, for power and processing plants and for machine tools and production machinery were created. For example, a generic AR assembly process was developed and tested for production tasks in an airplane (Fig. 7.4).

Fig. 7.4. Assembly task and superimposed information in the mechanical engineer's field of view (Schmidt et al. 2004)

In this scenario, the mechanical engineer retrieves the work schedule including virtual parts information from the shop floor job management system and virtually views the assembly space in order to locate the assembly position. Then he visits and identifies the real work environment, assisted by the virtual advance information, uses reference points to assess the real world and synchronize it with the virtual world, and activates the tracking feature. For assistance in the assembly process, the real-world view of the mechanical engineer is superimposed with virtual textual, graphic, and multimedia information. In an assembly environment like this, AR replaces the traditional assembly manual and provides additional updated information that are relevant to the process, such as pressure, temperature, rpm, etc.

In addition to this situation-sensitive interaction, the use of computers that can be worn on the body enables AR applications that require a high degree of mobility as well as process, measuring or simulation data to support the workflow. In contrast to stationary computer systems AR systems also require new interaction concepts. These concepts have to provide a possibility to present information in an HMD modus as well as the possibility to use hybrid interaction devices in order to ensure an optimal support for the worker (push and turn input device and navigation by speech). However, in what extent these new approaches can be put into practice and mean an additional work load to the worker's regular work, respectively, has not been investigated thoroughly, yet.

7.6 Application of the model based design process

Using the design space for mobile work systems and the proposed design phases for an AR application in the field of service is illustrated in this section.

Globalization and reduced lifecycle costs as motors for investments are two prevailing trends not only in the machine tool industry: Many enterprises produce their goods in production sites located at a considerable distance away from the consumer. The machine tool industry, for example, is characterized by small and medium-sized enterprises that cannot establish service branches all over the world. At the same time, there is an increase in task complexity placing more and more demands on the service personnel. Lifecycle costs require optimizing reliability and maintainability as well as fast service when needed. Traditional technologies in service are poorly adapted to support complex diagnosis and repair processes. But many of these processes are already planned on the basis of data. These data can be used to superimpose real objects in a technician's head-mounted display (HMD) for the support of disassembling and assembling tasks. Furthermore AR allows cooperative work for a locally distributed problem-solving process. A remote expert can be consulted from everywhere in the world by AR-telecooperation, which could be very important for the machine tool industry.

The model described in the section above was used in order to advance the user-centred and task-oriented development of Augmented Reality technologies for this work setting. This ensures that the developed AR systems meet the requirements of users and work processes, that the user interfaces are ergonomically designed and that AR functionality enables improvements of the work organization.

7.6.1 Requirements analysis of the objective

To begin with, the customer or user requirements, respectively, in terms of the assistance of work processes by AR systems were assessed in the requirements analysis phase. By using a scenario-based method, it was possible to assess typical activities in the fields of applications along the value chain and prioritized with regard to potential user- and task-oriented improvements. In this case study ten German enterprises participated in 11 focus groups (n=60) with their potential future users of AR-systems. These focus groups were structured in the following way: after an introduction in the new AR-technologies and the possibility to test a first and simple AR-prototype the participants were asked to describe their problems in work tasks. These problems were structured and classified by their importance for the work process, their sector of activity and their frequency. In the next step the participants were asked to describe their personal work processes for the most important tasks for which a support with new human-machine interaction could be advantageous. Work processes were modelled with the so-called "metaplan technique", which allows a participatory design of the work tasks together with the describing persons. Also the descriptions of alternative and weakly structured subtypes of tasks were included in the modelled work processes. As modelling technique the "K^3-method" was used, which was developed especially for weakly structured processes (Killich et al. 1999, Foltz et al. 2001). For the description of the tasks as a dynamic model, the K^3-task model was applied. At the end of the modelling process a participant was asked to present the process model to the other participants of the group. Additional tasks which occurred during the presentation were noted by the group and integrated afterwards by the supervisor of the focus group.

After the verification and the validation of work processes the participants were asked to write down their problems in the process description and to attach the tasks related to the problem. The identified problems were discussed and later on ideas for a future support by new human machine interaction were explored. The participants were asked to form metaphors for these new interactions and not to focus on the AR-prototypes demonstrated at the beginning of the focus group.

Subsequent to the focus groups the results were documented by the supervisors and reports were presented to the tested group. The comments given by the group were integrated afterwards.

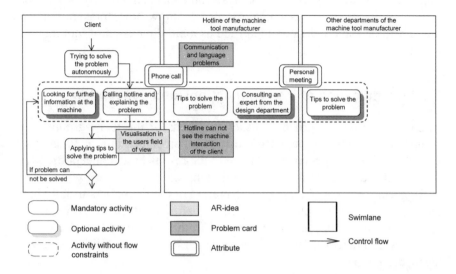

Fig. 7.5. Example for process modelling and task related problems (Luczak et al. 2000)

Figure 7.5 gives an example result for the analysis of a work process represented in terms of a K³-Task Network. It shows the model of a communication scenario between a client's service technician, a manufacturer's service hotline and a specialist of another manufacturer's department. In the beginning the client's service technician tries to diagnose the cause of the machine problems, but he does not manage to solve the problem. The client's reaction is to call the hotline. The client tries to explain the problem and the steps that have already been performed for analyzing the machine's fault. Sometimes there can be problems in the understanding between the client's service man and the manufacturer's hotline. These problems are often caused by language barriers or simply by information transfer limited on the auditory channel. If the hotline personnel do not know how to help the client, they try to find an expert in the design department. This expert tries to find a solution for the client's problem and he transfers the information to the hotline or to the client. In a further step the client executes manufacturer's advice. If he cannot solve the problem, he will phone the hotline again. This is just a little segment of the whole process, but it already shows the problems of service in a concrete way.

From a technology-driven point of view, the main focus in this ARVIKA project phase was on requirements for a better support of the crucial service processes by the new way of AR human-computer interaction. Based on the requirements analysis, an enhanced mobility of the work contents (diagnosis of machine problems, know-how transfer between manufacturer and client) was identified as main dimension of mobile work ("1" in Fig. 7.6).

7.6.2 Identification of interconnections and conception

In the second design process phase the results of the focus groups were compared with other groups from different companies in a meta-analysis. Together with AR-specialists and due to the results basic conceptions were developed and are described in the following.

Bigger enterprises like car manufacturers or their suppliers usually have their own service branches with highly qualified personnel. Nevertheless for the last years they have been reducing their personnel or abandoning their service branches. Operators have taken the responsibilities for maintenance and repair.

According to different levels of an enhanced support for the service personnel, three conceptions can be described, that can be used for identification of cells representing interconnected research fields concerning the technology design for a mobility of work contents ("2a", "2b" and "2c" in Fig. 7.6):

a. The client could be supported with an up-to-date electronic manual to execute his or her work. A similar type of support but more sophisticated regarding to navigation in the electronic documents and search tasks could help the service technician, who repairs a machine at the client's place. Using that electronic manual also refers to a mobility of working tools, if it can be installed on a notebook or PDA. In contrast to paper based instruction this also can enhance the mobility of the service technician, especially if a small end device like a PDA can be used.

b. When clients need an expert's advice, they can use the manufacturer's telephone hotline. In doing so they very often have the problem, that the experts cannot see the worker's field of view and thus lack a common visual basis of reference. To facilitate the hotline's considerations, there should be some means of pointing at certain objects in the user's field of view. Comparable to giving advice at the client's location by pointing, this concept is related to virtual mobility of the manufacturer's expert.

c. AR can play an important support role in service applications but will be also very exacting in terms of mobility, robustness in an industrial environment, etc. The most advanced concept could be a mobile AR-system, which can assist service personnel and end users in trouble-shooting, commissioning, maintenance and repair in the field or through direct interaction with the service centre. In the case of a malfunction of a machine tool, the AR system provides the service technician with component-related assistance from an information system provided in an augmented field of vision. The defect can be located based on the error description. To correct the problem, a workflow guides the service technician step by step through the maintenance instructions for this component. If required, the service technician can be supported by a remote expert in the service centre by means of video and audio communications (including concept b)). Concerning the design space the same technology-oriented fields as in a) and b) can be identified as interconnected cells in the matrix, but in contrast to this conceptions, a comprehensive change in work organization especially regarding the work contents can be ascertained. This comes along with a modified qualification profile for the technician required for his or her service work.

a.

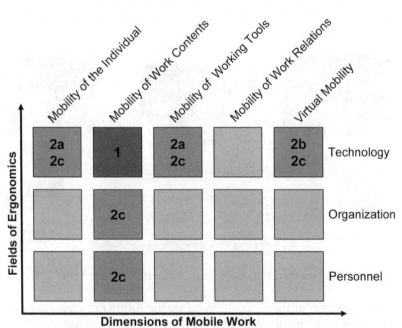

Fig. 7.6. Main research objective and interconnected cells in the case study

7.6.3 Integration and prototyping of design solutions

Mock-ups and prototypes are an essential part in design and implementation of new solutions. In the presented design process of AR-systems rapid prototyping and early user interaction testing are very important for an ergonomic and user-friendly system. This phase of the design process refers to first mock-ups, which are used for formative evaluations.

First ideas of systems integrating new technologies can easily be presented in computerized images. For first mock-ups, these ideas of new concepts were realized with software integrating simple browser and image display functionalities. These mock-ups were used in discussions with potential future users of AR-systems and technology developers. They were also evaluated in parallel with a second session of the described focus groups.

The next and more difficult step was to integrate AR-functionalities or other interaction modes in the mock-ups. First use-cases for new AR-processes had to be defined. Therefore, the processes elaborated in the second focus group session and in the very first mock-ups without AR-functionalities were used to create storyboards. Here, the new AR-process for the mock-up was described.

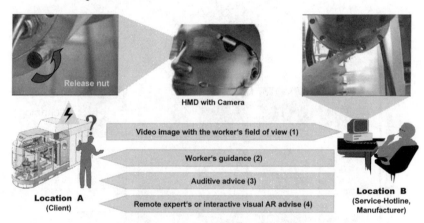

Fig. 7.7. AR-mock-up for the machine tool industry (Schmidt et al. 2004)

The mock-up in figure 7.7 is based on the following scenario (according to concept 2c): The machine tool manufacturer's client has a problem with his machine. He does not manage to repair his machine himself. The machine tool manufacturer's hotline tries to support the client with a conferencing tool, which allows the manufacturers' specialist to have the same field of view as the client's worker. The remote specialist can guide the client by auditive advice as well as pointers and graphical information in the field of vision.

When the problem is detected and the repair procedure is well known, the hotline can start an interactive AR-application, which explains the repair procedure step by step.

The mock-up was realized with one Silicon Graphics SGI workstation for image capturing, processing and tracking. In addition, two PCs were connected for the remote expert's IP-based videoconferencing.

In this design phase, four design teams were formed that worked in parallel to create corresponding design suggestions. This resulted in a first version of the "Style Guide for AR Systems" as the central document for the application designer, combining findings from the empirical research of the displays and the work system ergonomics, from usability tests and from the relevant literature. It documents initial design rules and requirements for AR systems that can guide application developers in the implementation of application-specific prototypes. After two loops in the human-centred design process an evaluated version of the "Style Guide for AR Systems" was available for further applications.

7.6.4 Evaluation and verification

In this stage of the design process prototypes including much functionality of serial products are concerned, which are sometimes already integrated in their future environment. To ensure a user-centred and task-oriented system design from the perspective of hardware and software ergonomics, in addition to basic research dealing with issues such as the minimum required display size of information in head mounted displays, usability tests and prototype evaluation are required with regard to the application specific use-cases (Schmidt et al. 2002). Commercially available AR products and AR technologies such as visualization components, tracking systems or interaction tools are examined in the respective field of application from an information technology point of view. It has to be tested where and in which way AR can be used most efficiently in the product lifecycle. Before such a system can be realized some crucial steps in data preparation, tracking and other fields have to be done. Mobile applications also require an adequate frame rate per second that often exceeds capabilities of the currently available mobile computers. The information display is generally limited to circles, arrows, and short texts. However, the information to be delivered must meet high requirements. In the case of a service call e. g. on a production machine, the entire documentation of a machine plus current process data must be available. These data should be centrally stored in an

AR-ready format so that they can be retrieved by a mobile device over a network.

The first step was to conduct basic ergonomic studies with head mounted displays. In particular, human reaction times and errors as a function of relevant types of tasks and display sizes as well as the question of a minimum display size were observed. As a result of these studies, design recommendations could be made based on display type and type of task (Oehme et al. 2003, Oehme 2004).

After the realization of mock-ups the described AR-functions are realized in terms of a mobile prototype and this prototype was tested with the potential users. Thus different interaction modes and support functions are evaluated. The empirical research enabled the verification of the design recommendations for the AR assistance of work processes in a context that is close to reality.

Concerning the service application the remote expert system was investigated (Wiedenmaier et al. 2003). This system with augmented and tracked pointing capabilities enables a hotline agent to provide the assembly worker with superimposed position and additional information in the field. In addition to the remote expert system two alternative variants for assistance via a hotline were evaluated (hands free phone and videoconferencing system). The AR system in its current form competes with traditional videoconferencing systems and cannot yet be considered to be fit for everyday use. However, while the videoconferencing system performs better in an assembly task, the AR system supports the necessary "hands free" operations. The investigation indicated advantages of AR especially for the cognitive process of finding the place of a part or during the process of reading, hearing, and comprehending the support media (Wiedenmaier 2004).

The criteria of the evaluation focus on ergonomics and acceleration of processes and their influence on the working person. In addition to time and quality, the perceived strain as well as utility- and application-driven criteria are evaluated (according the design principles of the ISO 9241: suitability for the task, suitability for learning, suitability for individualization, conformity with user expectations, self descriptiveness, controllability, and error tolerance).

The test persons were selected from the user population that represented the target audience for subsequent use in order to ensure that the experience-based knowledge of the testers was the same as with the later users. During the usability tests (Krauss and Quaet-Faslem 2004), the test persons were required to use the prototypes to execute real-world work tasks in order to allow the use of observation and questionnaire methods (video recording, thinking aloud, structured interviews, etc.) to evaluate the systems. In order to be able to include new, not yet implemented integration concepts in the tests, methods like "Wizard of Oz" were used.

In further iterative loops AR-mock-ups and prototypes were improved, displays were tested and design guidelines were established for the design of mobile AR systems for service applications. As this section has pointed out, making an AR system user-friendly requires several stages of examination and redesign. This is an iterative process which can be organized in the framework of the model.

7.7 Conclusion

In conclusion, a model-based design of mobile work systems was presented. Therefore a two-dimensional design space was introduced. In the first dimension five aspects of mobile work are differentiated, which are (1) mobility of the individual, (2) mobility of work contents, (3) mobility of working tools, (4) mobility of work relations, and (5) virtual mobility. The second axis comprises aspects of technology, organization and personnel (TOP). This framework can be used as a guideline to order and integrate several aspects of mobile work. Combining this design space with a design process according to ISO 13407, a model was introduced, which aims at shaping and designing mobile work systems in a human-centred and task-oriented way. Its application was demonstrated by exemplary research questions, which have been developed in a real world case study.

The case study, presented in terms of the model dimensions, dealt with new possibilities of service support in the machine tool industry by augmented reality. Four iterative design phases were passed through to analyze, design and evaluate AR-mock-ups and prototypes together with the potential users. Thus different interaction modes and support functions were evaluated. The criteria of the evaluation focused on ergonomics and acceleration of processes and their influence on the working person and work organization.

The surplus of mobile work systems needs to be identified and analyzed in terms of its target group specific and dimension specific requirements. The example as presented above can only give a rough overview of the complex set of difficulties and numerous questions with regard to the mobilization of work within the context of industrial engineering. Regarding the idea of mobile work, even traditional fields of human oriented organization of work such as working hours, division of labour etc. can be considered from a new perspective. This perspective represents a great challenge in order to enrich industrial engineering science and to explore possible chances and risks of mobile working holistically. In addition requirements and abilities of humans and organizations involved need to be considered concisely. In the future, the application of the proposed model for the design of mobile work systems should be realized in other domains to validate its suitability.

References

ARVIKA (2005) http://www.arvika.de/www/e/home/home.htm, 01/21/2005
Bradley G (2001) Information and communication technology (ICT) and humans: How we live, learn and work. In: Bradley G (ed) Humans on the net. Information & Communication Technology (ICT), Work Organisation and Human Beings. Prevent, Stockholm, pp 22–44
Carayon P, Haims MC (2001) Information & communication technology and work organization: Achieving a balanced system. In: Bradley G (ed) Humans on the net. Information & Communication Technology (ICT), Work Organisation and Human Beings. Prevent, Stockholm, pp 119-138
Commission of the European Communities (2005) eEurope 2005: An information society for all. (Action plan to be presented in view of the Sevilla European Council 21/22 June 2002. http://europa.eu.int/ information_society/eeurope-/2005/all_about/action_plan/index_en.htm, 01/21/2005)
Endsley MR (1995a) Toward a theory of situation awareness in dynamic systems. Human Factors 37: 32–64
Endsley MR (1995b) Measurement of situation awareness in dynamic systems. Human Factors 37:65–84
Eurostat (2004) Portrait of the European Union – science & technology. http://epp.eurostat.cec.eu.int/cache/ITY_PUBLIC/KS-60-04-523/EN/KS-60-04-523-EN.PDF. Luxembourg, p 25, 01/21/2005
Federal Ministry of Economics and Labour Division, Federal Ministry of Education and Research (2004) Information society Germany 2006 – action programme by the Federal Government. BMWA & BMBF, Berlin
Foltz C, Killich S, Wolf M, Schmidt L, Luczak H (2001) Task and Information modelling for cooperative work. In: Smith MJ, Salvendy G (eds) Proceedings of HCI International 2001. Volume 2: Systems, social and internationalization design aspects of human-computer interaction (New Orleans 2001). Erlbaum, Mahwah, pp 172-176
Friedrich W (ed) (2004) ARVIKA – Augmented reality für entwicklung, produktion und service. Publicis Corporate Publishing, Erlangen
Friedrich W, Jahn D, Schmidt L (2001) ARVIKA – Augmented reality for dDevelopment, production andsService. In: DLR Projektträger des BMBF für onformationstechnik (ed) International Status Conference – Lead projects "Human-Computer Interaction" (Saarbrücken 2001). DLR, Berlin, pp 79–89
ISO 13407 (1999) Human-centered design process for interactive systems

ISO 9241 (1996) Ergonomic requirements for office work with visual display terminals, Part 10: Dialogue principles

ISO 9241 (1998) Ergonomic requirements for office work with visual display terminals, Part 11: Guidance on Usability

Killich S, Luczak H, Schlick C, Weissenbach M, Wiedenmaier S, Ziegler J (1999) Task modelling for cooperative work. Behaviour & Information Technology 18:325–338

Krauss M, Quaet-Faslem P (2004) Evaluation von AR-realisierungen im service. In: Luczak H, Schmidt L, Koller F (eds) Benutzerzentrierte gestaltung von augmented-reality-systemen. Fortschrittberichte VDI, Reihe 22, Mensch-Maschine-Systeme Bd. 17. VDI, Düsseldorf, pp 83–93

Luczak H (1998) Arbeitswissenschaft. 2nd edn. Springer, Berlin

Luczak H, Wiedenmaier S, Oehme O, Schlick C (2000) Augmented reality in design, production and service-requirements and approach. In: Marek T, Karwowski W (eds) Proceedings of the 7th conference Human Aspects of Advanced Manufacturing: Agility & hybrid automation (Krakow 2000). III. Institute of Management, Jagiellonian University, Krakow, pp 15–20

Luczak H, Bruns I, Oehme O (2003) Mobile workplaces. In: Luczak H, Zink KJ (eds) Human factors in organizational design and management – VII. Proceedings of the Seventh International Symposium on Human Factors in Organizational Design and Management (Aachen 2003). IEA Press, Santa Monica, pp 1–10

Luczak H, Schmidt L, Koller F (eds) (2004) Benutzerzentrierte gestaltung von augmented-reality-systemen. Fortschrittberichte VDI, Reihe 22, Mensch-Maschine-Systeme Bd. 17. VDI, Düsseldorf

Oehme O, Schmidt L, Luczak H (2003) Comparison between the strain indicator HRV of a head-based virtual retinal display and LC-head mounted displays for augmented reality. International Journal of Occupational Safety and Ergonomics 9: 419–430

Oehme O (2004) Ergonomische untersuchung von kopfbasierten displays für anwendungen der erweiterten realität in produktion und service. Dissertation RWTH Aachen. Shaker, Aachen

Pousttchi K, Turowski K, Weizmann M (2003) Added value-based Approach to analyze electronic commerce and mobile commerce business models. In: Andrade RAE, Gómez JM, Rautenstrauch C, Rios RG (eds) International Conference of Management and Technology in the New Enterprise (La Habana 2003), pp 414–423

Rumelhart DE (1980) Schemata: The building blocks of cognition. In: Spiro RJ, Bruce BC, Brewer WF (eds) Theoretical issues in reading comprehension. Erlbaum, Hilsdale, pp 33–58

Scheer AW, Feld T, Göbl M, Hoffmann M (2001) Das mobile unternehmen. Information Management & Consulting 16: 7–15

Schmidt L, Oehme O, Wiedenmaier S, Beu A, Quaet-Faslem P (2002) Usability engineering für benutzer-interaktionskonzepte von augmented reality-systemen. it + ti – Informationstechnik und Technische Informatik 44:31–39

Schmidt L, Depolt J, Luczak H (2004) Analysis of telecooperation in the German automotive industry. In: Khalid HM, Helander MG, Yeo AW (eds) Proceedings of the 6th International Conference on Work with Computing Systems (Kuala Lumpur 2004). Damai Sciences, Kuala Lumpur, pp 184–188

Schmidt L, Wiedenmaier S, Oehme O, Luczak, H (2004) Augmented reality als neue form der mensch-technik-interaktion. In: Luczak H, Schmidt L, Koller F (eds) Benutzerzentrierte gestaltung von augmented-reality-systemen. Fortschrittberichte VDI, Reihe 22, Mensch-Maschine-Systeme Bd. 17. VDI, Düsseldorf, pp 1–14

Stabsgruppe arbeit 21 (2001) MAP verändert arbeit 21: Basispapier 2 – Annahmen über folgewirkungen und soziale ausgestaltungen. Obtained on 21 January 2005 from www.map21.de/projekt/arbeit21/a21_basispapier-02.pdf.

Wiedenmaier S, Oehme O, Schmidt L, Luczak H (2003) Augmented Reality (AR) for assembly processes – Design and experimental evaluation. International Journal of Human-Computer Interaction 16:497–514

Wiedenmaier S (2004) Unterstützung manueller montage durch augmented reality-technologien. Dissertation RWTH Aachen. Shaker, Aachen

8 Usability in IT Systems for Mobile Work

Niklas Johansson[1], Torbjörn Lind[2] and Bengt Sandblad[1]

[1]Uppsala University, Department of Information Technology, Human-Computer Interaction, Sweden
[2]UsersAward, Swedish Labour Organisation, Sweden

8.1 Usability in mobile IT systems

Today mobile IT systems are increasingly deployed as technical support tools in various mobile work situations. In order to contribute to, or at least not prevent, usability and a healthy and efficient work environment these mobile support tools must fulfil a number of requirements.

In our research concerning usability of mobile technology, we are mainly interested in usability of mobile IT systems used in a professional work context. Such work support systems are found in various work settings, e.g. in health care, in technical maintenance and in sales and consultant organisations. IT systems support mobile work activities and are sometimes necessary for making work mobile. However, in some occupations work is, and has always been mobile, such as in home care or in technical maintenance field work. For this reason technical support system must of necessity be mobile, otherwise they cannot be used at all. In many such situations lack of appropriate, supporting, technology has resulted in low impact of modern information technology at such work places. Improvements in usability could result in new application areas and progress in development of work organisation and efficiency.

This means that we are facing two different challenges. The first concerns design of mobile IT support systems which are efficient, have a high usability and can contribute to positive development of mobile work situation. The second concerns how we, through design of efficient, supportive and usable IT support systems, can contribute to making a normally stationary work practice mobile. Usability criteria for mobile IT support systems are probably the same in both cases, but the design processes will face different difficulties. Either the work practice already exists and can be studied and analysed, or it must be made mobile and thereby completely redesigned.

There are two main aspects of how technical systems can support development of mobile work situations. One aspect concerns usability in a more traditional sense, i.e. user interface design, how well the technical system as such can be handled by users, whether it supports a good physical and cognitive work environment etc. Another aspect has to do with how well technology can contribute to improvements in organisation, management, work efficiency, communication, competencies, skills etc.

In this chapter we focus on three different issues concerning usability in mobile IT support systems:

- Definition of a set of usability criteria for mobile technology
- Experiences from evaluating usability in mobile IT systems
- Designing work processes enabled and supported by mobile IT systems

The first issue addresses important usability aspects to be considered in the design of IT support systems for mobile virtual work. It is our experience, that if technical support systems are not appreciated as efficient by professional users, technology will not be used and users will, if possible, find other ways to perform their tasks. This is apparent when introducing mobile technology in a work situation. Moreover, when designing IT-support systems, we must handle relevant requirements concerning work procedures, usability and work environment. Requirements related to 'tacit knowledge' (Polanyi 1967) are especially difficult to specify but important to include in a user centred system design process (Huges et al. 1993). In this way, we will enhance efficiency and be more likely to engender a positive attitude towards new technology. The opposite would result in a deteriorating and unhealthy work environment.

The second issue concerns assessment of usability in mobile systems in the health care sector. The study reports parts of findings from a survey named "Vård-IT-kartan"[1] (Lind et.al. 2004) performed in Sweden in 2004 by the company UsersAward. In the survey, user opinions concerning usefulness in a broad sense are evaluated. The part of that study presented here addresses mobile applications used in the health care sector.

As always, when new technology is introduced in a professional environment, it has to be done carefully and with respect for many complex goals and requirements. Whilst the "On line" mobile technology provides us with an excellent opportunity to develop working life in a positive manner, it also entails many problems to be solved. Some problems can already be foreseen, while others are difficult to predict. The third issue in this chapter is concerned with these issues and the design of future mobile work support systems for home care professionals. The project VIHO is described, where requirements for future mobile support systems to be used by professionals in home care work were studied. The goal of the

---

[1] "The Health care IT map"

project was to develop future work organisation and work processes, as well as mobile technology that could support new work practice. A group of experienced professionals from the home health care area was involved in a participatory process, where scenarios of future work were formulated. Based on these scenarios, general requirements for supportive technology were derived.

8.2 Usability aspects and criteria

It can be argued that a mobile work situation is basically, when usability aspects are considered, similar to any other work situation. Hence, the same definitions, criteria, design requirements etc. that relate to other work situations are also relevant in a mobile context. We share this view, but we have also noticed that in a mobile work situation some usability aspects are especially important and occasionally must be extended. In the following paragraph, we will discuss general aspects on usability as well as some more specific mobile aspects.

8.2.1 General usability in IT-support systems

The definition of usability found in ISO standard 9241-11 (ISO 9241-11 1998), "Ergonomic requirements for office work with visual display terminals", is useful in this regard. Moreover, in the ISO-standard it is stated that usability can be defined as: "The extent to which a product can be used by specified users to achieve specified goals with effectiveness, efficiency and satisfaction in a specified context of use." This definition of usability is based on three parts: effectiveness, efficiency and satisfaction. Effectiveness refers to whether users can reach stated goals, efficiency relates this to resources needed and satisfaction is related to both acceptability of the system and ease of use.

Furthermore, usability can be related to the more general concept usefulness. Nielsen defines usefulness as related to how suitable a system is in terms of achieving a certain goal (Nielsen 1993). Usefulness consists of two concepts: utility and usability. Utility describes if appropriate functionality is at hand, while usability describes if the user is supported as defined by the ISO-standard mentioned above.

Several different sets of more general usability criteria exist, that try to relate operationally useful criteria to design decisions. Some of these are truly general, while others are more or less specific to a work domain.

Examples of more general criteria can be found in e.g. ISO 9241 as principles for design of human-computer dialogue. Dialogue should be:

- adapted to actual work tasks
- self descriptive
- controllable
- predictable
- error tolerant and
- individually adaptable

Nielsen (1993) and others suggest that a user interface should be:

- easy to learn
- easy to remember
- efficient to use
- result in few errors by users
- subjectively attractive

It is obvious that such lists of criteria are too general to guide design of systems and user interfaces. Furthermore more work domain specific sets of criteria exist, such as ISO 11064-1 (ISO 11064-1 2000), "Ergonomic design of control centres" concerning design of operator user interfaces in process control. Even such domain specific standards and style-guides tend to be too general to really support practical design activities.

We have found that use of design heuristics is a method that can give substantial support in design processes. Design heuristics are sets of practical rules for good design of user interfaces, often combined with practical example of good and bad solutions. It is important to understand that it is never possible to specify any criteria or rule that are applicable in all design situations. What is a good design solution in one context can be bad in another context. Any set of criteria must therefore be used with care, and only high competencies of design teams can guarantee high quality of resulting systems and interface designs.

When designing user interfaces for skilled professionals, regardless of work domain, it is always important to focus on criteria related to high efficiency, good work environment and opportunities for future development of personal skills and the organisation. Criteria related to ease of learning, graphical design, cosmetics etc. become less important. Normally a user is a novice for a relatively short period of time, and the potential for development of high skill levels is more important in the long run.

8.2.2 Mobility specific usability criteria

Design of today's mobile devices seems hard to liberate from the established design norms of IT systems in general. Consequently metaphors and interaction solutions like desktop, office applications, icons and windows have been incorporated into new platforms without reflection. However, use of mobile technology differs from "common office use" and it is important to emphasise that systems design for mobile devices is not the same as for a stationary computer. Being mobile implies numerous new prerequisites to consider when designing mobile devices.

Environmental variations

In most cases use of mobile technology occurs in unpredictable and varying contexts. Therefore, when designing IT systems for mobile use, one cannot foresee the precise context where the user, technology and interaction between them will occur.

Variations in context are an innate part of the nature of mobility and are not likely to disappear as technology evolves. Contextual aspects might seem basic and obvious, but are nonetheless important and fundamental. A major failure in one aspect might make a whole system unusable, or result in the system being used in an unexpected manner. Gorlenko and Merrik (2003) illuminate a number of substantial aspects that are to be considered in design of mobile IT systems:

- Environmental variations e.g. temperature, precipitation and lighting conditions might affect performance of mobile hardware. Batteries are quicker consumed, processors are running slower at low temperatures and screens are more difficult to see clearly in bright light.
- Noisy and in other ways distractive environments make mobile system hard to fully interact with.
- Users move, to some extent, from place to place and mobile systems must be able to follow and to be usable on the move.
- Competition for attention in multitask mobile settings where users are engaged in other tasks and at the same time using mobile system.
- Users might need to manipulate other physical objects during interaction with mobile systems.

Hardware limitations

When mobile devices are to be carried, the device itself has to be small and easy to transport. These basic requirements affect its overall performance to a large extent. A number of constraints for hardware in mobile IT systems limit their performance:

- Network connections are still relatively slow and unreliable. This limits data transfer rates when sending larger sets of data, e.g. in more demanding multimedia applications.
- CPUs are slower in the interest of being inexpensive, small and less power consuming.
- Memory size is limited as well as its speed.
- Battery life is short, also in order to reduce price, size and weight. Routines (that are not always desirable) for screensavers, device standby and hibernate modes and network disconnections has been developed in order to prolong battery lifetimes.
- Network connections are today unpredictable and far from geographically complete.
- Screen size is small and information presented is hard to read for people with bad vision. As a consequence of small screens, use of GUI (Graphical User Interface) elements in an application become limited compared to a stationary computer with a significantly bigger screen. This results in bad readability and is one of the most commonly treated issues about usability in mobile systems, the design for mobile graphical user interfaces (Weiss 2002; Nielsen 2000).

Technology is constantly evolving, and as a result limitations in mobile devices will gradually be reduced. Some limits, however, are consequences of the nature of mobility and are not easily dealt with; physical screen size can, for example, not be larger than the device itself.

Interaction with mobile devices

Physical properties of mobile devices, advanced functionality, and mobile context of use require new ways to handle interaction. To meet new prerequisites and requirements in design for new mobile technology, a number of new interaction techniques have evolved. Consequently, mobile devices offer a number of interaction channels for input and output. Where a full-sized traditional keyboard is no longer possible, several methods for data input and output have been tried with varying results. Moreover, in interacting with mobile phones one encounters challenges like entering text while on the move or answering the phone while bicycling. It is not unusual, however, that a mobile device supports several interaction types. Below is a short overview of the most successful interaction channels available at today's devices.

Input

- Write directly on the screen, over the whole screen or in a dedicated area, with a pen, also known as "stylus". Software for hand recognition translates written signs to characters that are possible for computers to recognize.
- Use of buttons 0-9*# for input of text, mostly on mobiles and smart phones. Each button is assigned 3-4 letters which can be selected between by pressing same button repeatedly. The T9 algorithm offers a quicker approach where each button representing 3-4 letters only has to be pressed once for each letter in a word. At the end of a word the algorithm compares the possible combinations with a dictionary and finds the right word, or supplies a list of possible words.
- Dedicated hardware buttons for direct access to e.g. a camera application or to a WAP-browser.
- Devices with a stylus can provide a virtual keyboard, i.e. a keyboard displayed on the screen where the user can tap with the stylus on the letters.
- A small hardware keyboard (that makes you fall back to the hunt and peck system) with which the traditionally QUERTY keyboard layout can be used.
- Researchers are interested in tactile interfaces and on how to use them for output and input. Linjama and Kaaresoja (2004) demonstrate how a tactile interface can be used for input interaction. A ringing phone can e.g. be shut off when it is still lying in the pocket, simply by a gentle tap with the hand on the outside of the pocket.
- Technology for voice control of IT systems has been available in several years now, but is sparsely used in mobile devices. Two categories can be identified; voice commands and voice translation. Neither of them has reached any degree of perfection and both require concessions, like talking exaggeratedly clearly and carefully proof-reading the result.

Fig. 8.1. The traditional QWERTY-keyboard is implemented in various ways in mobile devices. Here on the Siemens SK65 mobile, Sony Ericsson P910 smart phone and the OQO 01 computer

Despite several new techniques for entering text on mobile devices, a stationary computer with a traditional keyboard is still faster and provides richer medium for interaction. Ergonomically, a larger, stationary, computer is also the most efficient device to use for longer periods of work.

Output

Progress in terms of interaction channels for output has not evolved much since the invention of the telephone. Today, about 130 years later, just a few different output methods are used by mobile devices to get users attention or communicate information back to the user.

- Traditional sound and ringing tones are now available in several channels (polyphonic). Context sensitive sounds and other variations in volume and intensity are still seldom used. Today a lot of effort is instead put into making it possible to listen to one's favourite song as a ring tone.
- Attention can also be drawn to artefacts by visual means, e.g. a lamp or a blinking screen. An optical signal requires the device to be in the user's visual field and can be used as an alternative to sound when the device is in some kind of silent mode. During a meeting or when driving a car and listening to music, a blinking mobile phone can be quite effective as a substitute (or complement) to sound. Light can also come into use as feedback when for example pressing a button (the button illuminates) or as an indicator (a small indicating lamp is blinking when a message is waiting or when battery is low).
- The screen is still one of the most important output-channels.
- Tactile interfaces are implemented for output to some extent. Some mobile devices use a vibrator for interaction, mostly as a complement to the ring signal or as a sort of force feedback for games.

- Some mobile devices can be connected to a stationary computer and to some extent synchronized to exchange information. A few devices can interact with users via stationary computers.

8.2.3 Design for mobile systems

Usability criteria for design of user interfaces are normally based on a standard platform consisting of a normal sized screen, a broadband network, keyboard and mouse. When designing devices for mobile use, hardware most often becomes the limiting factor.

Interface interaction

As input of information in mobile devices turns out to be complicated and slow, design should try to minimize the need for data and text input. Fällman (2003) considers text input as a stationary activity, which is partly supported by our findings. However, text input should not be totally ignored. A reduction in text input in more advanced mobile devices can sometimes be achieved using graphical components that are easy and quick to manipulate, e.g. checkboxes, radio buttons, drop lists etc. When it is necessary to enter free text, systems should offer a quick and easy way to do so, without demands for completeness of written text. Entered information should later be accessible from a stationary computer where users can continue to edit text or start to enter more complex text.

When designing software for a certain device, advantage must be taken of the interaction potential of the specific device. Hardware buttons on PDAs and smart phones are, for instance, seldom used except by specific applications from the manufacturer.

Presentation of information

Established HCI knowledge should not be forgotten when designing for mobile devices. It is often said that design should provide for the right information at the right time in the right way. Aspects of the use of mobile devices invite the addition of "in the right place". Due to the previously mentioned aspects of usability in mobile IT systems, presentation of information is even more challenging and emphasises the importance of information being:

- Short and concise (with no need to read unnecessary information)
- Carefully chosen (not to be misunderstood and context adapted)
- Quick and easy to read (not too small letters, good layout etc.)

- Effective (suited to the situation)
- Resource effective (quickly displayed)

Too much information is not good when:

- It takes too much valuable space on a small screen.
- It causes an "information overload" and makes it hard for mobile users to find and remember the right information at the same time as doing other work tasks.
- It should be fast to read, at a glance and on the move.

Hardware and physical design might differ a lot between different kinds of mobile devices. Consequently more attention needs to be paid to hardware and how to handle its limitations and fully take advantage of its benefits.

8.3 Assessment of usability in mobile systems

Participating in a study performed by the company UsersAward, we conducted an extensive survey of Sweden's IT system within the health care sector during spring and summer of 2004. Results are presented in the report "Vård-IT-kartan" (Lind et al. 2004). The survey covers nearly every IT-system in Sweden and approximately 1400 people from almost 300 work places participated. The survey provides information about the user's opinion of their IT systems. This data helps us define and locate IT system success factors as well as reasons for failure of such systems. As a part of the survey, most of the mobile IT systems used within Swedish health care arena participated. Approach, method and results are briefly presented here in order to give a short description of users' opinions of the different mobile IT systems.

8.3.1 Method

We have not been able to construct any specific hypotheses concerning how these systems have been designed and consequences of decisions taken in the process. Evaluation of use of mobile IT systems is difficult and circumstantial. Weiss (2002) gives a short overview of the most popular testing methods from the HCI field. These methods can, to some extent, also be used for testing usability in mobile devices. In the "Vård IT-kartan" survey we have studied broad aspects of how the system is used in its work context. Over all focus of the approach is to describe usefulness of the system and the users' opinion.

To achieve quantitative as well as qualitative results we conducted the survey in three parts. When a part was more extensive, the number of investigated systems where decreased as well as the amount of users involved in the tests. Questionnaires reach many users with a limited number of questions. Group interviews reach a limited number of users but can catch important and informal aspects of usability and how systems are appreciated by users. Finally, observation interviews (Åborg 2003) can give experienced observers a deep insight into how systems really are used in its everyday work context.

Questionnaires

Opinions from users of all investigated systems were collected using an extensive questionnaire. To make the study more effective a web based questionnaire was used. Results from questionnaires were evaluated and a few systems considered more interesting were sorted out for the second phase. Factors affecting this selection were:

- The system had many users
- It was considered to be a successful system
- The system has totally failed and is considered to be a bad system

Focus interviews

Usability in a number of systems was thoroughly investigated using focus interviews with users. Interview sessions proceeded for at most two hours and were based on questions from the questionnaire. Participants were carefully chosen to represent different parts of the organisation using the IT-system, and there were three participants in each group at most. In interviews, users are given opportunity to elaborate their opinion and further describe their experiences. In contrast to drawing conclusions from results of a questionnaire, opinions perceived in a face-to-face situation like an interview are much easier to evaluate. Interview sessions were afterwards summarised in a small report.

Observation interviews

The last and most thorough study of the systems was made through observation interviews, conducted as a short field study. We have here been influenced by the discourse about ethnography in system development (Greenbaum and Kyng 1991).

In this phase practical use of systems was studied in their own environment and in their actual context of use. One user of a system, an informant, was chosen and followed during a part of a working day. Moreover, the researcher conducting the study was well informed about the system in advance. Focus was on how the system is used in practice. Often the user's practical interaction with the system is not seen through the two earlier steps, since described interaction does not necessarily correspond to what they are actually doing. It is our experience that descriptions of interactions with systems are significantly improved by conducting field studies.

8.3.2 Results

Despite an extensive exploration of the market, few functioning mobile systems were found. However, several projects with good ideas and intentions but still in a test or development phase have been identified, but none of them are included in the survey. The mobile survey included eight work places, five IT-systems, and received input from 90 users. Results from the study, together with knowledge gained from earlier research, illustrate key considerations when designing mobile IT systems. The essence of the results is partly presented here and discussed. Selected systems that were examined in the survey are:

- Ambulink – An ambulance patient record system running on a web platform. Manages information about patient's medical condition as well as information about ambulance transports.
- CAK-net – An ambulance patient record system similar to Ambulink but implemented in Lotus Notes.
- Joliv – A system for information management, planning, statistics and quality assurance for home health care services. Running on a PDA and a stationary computer.
- Permitto Care – A web based home health care system running on a Nokia Communicator and a stationary computer. Similar to Joliv.
- Take Care – A mobile version of a medical record system running on laptops. Used by physicians for advanced health care in patient's home.

The chosen systems are all, in various degrees, mobile. Systems used for emergency health care consist of several parts and are mobile to the extent that parts of the system are used inside ambulances. The Take Care system is the same medical record system used at hospitals, but in this case considered mobile when it is run on laptops and used by a group of physicians making house calls. Permitto Care and Joliv are systems developed for home health care services; they run on small mobile devices.

Stationary systems compared to mobile systems

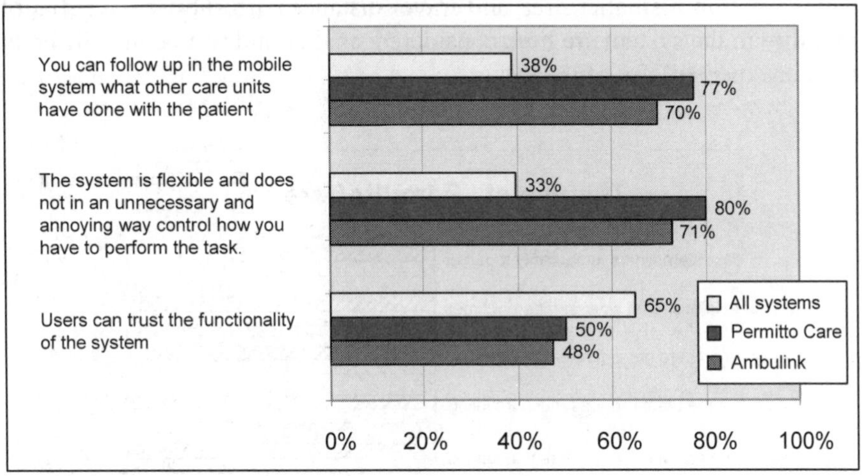

Fig. 8.2. Some mobile systems compared with all other health care systems in the survey. "All systems" refer to all investigated IT-systems in the health care survey

General conclusions from comparison between stationary and mobile IT systems:

- Mobile systems are appreciated when they are considered to add quality, safety and effectiveness to work, and give users a better overview of health care processes.
- Mobile systems better support a flexible work and do not in detail restrict how work can be carried out.
- A system can be considered a useful system, even if it is not considered to be reliable.
- Stationary systems are in general considered to be more available and reliable then mobile systems.

Mobile systems in different environments

Some installations of Permitto Care are in use in the northern part of Sweden, a more sparsely populated area. Large distances between different care takers characterize the organisation, and personnel have to spend lots of time on the road. The system makes it possible for personnel to start their working day at home, without needing to travel to the office. They can log in to the system remotely, read information and thereafter begin their daily route. Sometime during the day, when appropriate, they meet in premises along the route.

The same system is also implemented in Stockholm. Here work is performed within a smaller area and travel distances are shorter. Benefits of mobility in the system are here considered smaller and results in a different (and unexpected) use of the system.

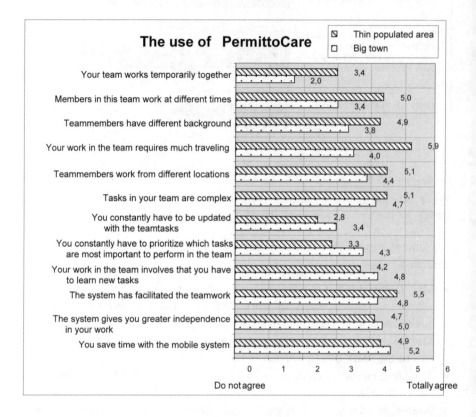

Fig. 8.3. The table shows differences in work settings and use of mobile systems between user groups in a big town and a less populated area in northern Sweden

The table shows that in sparsely populated areas, the system is considered to be more efficient and valuable. That compensates for drawbacks in the system, such as bad connectivity. Usefulness of the system is estimated differently by users depending on the conditions of use. The Permitto Care case is thoroughly discussed in the appendix.

8.3.3 Case study – the ambulance system CAK-net

One of the work places with the largest amount of participants in the survey, the ambulance, was chosen for more extended field studies. Ambulance personnel use several systems, among them the CAK-net system for keeping emergency treatment patient records. A version of the system was tried out, running on a laptop kept in the emergency car and in the ambulance. After a short time the trial was cancelled for a number of reasons; the ambulance is filled with advanced medical equipment and the laptop was considered too large to use in an already overstuffed ambulance. Further, the battery ran out of power and it was hard to manage to reload it between turnouts.

> *"It is squeezed into an already stuffed ambulance and you have to stretch all over the patient to plug in all the cables and stuff"*
> (User of the CAK-net system)

The physical environment in an ambulance is hard and rough. Consequently, hardware (as well as personnel) must endure rough treatment, including bumps and shocks as well as someone throwing up on it. Using a laptop was not suitable in that kind of environment and under these circumstances. As a result personnel went back to using stationary computers at the ambulance station. In interviews it was also mentioned that once at the station it is quiet and therefore easier to concentrate. Another important factor is that information about accident, patient and turnout is automatically imported into CAK-net system from CyberMate, the MobiText system used for communication with SOS alarm central from where the alarm is received. Integration of two systems results in a reduced need for input and provides less risk for mistakes.

Through CyberMate, personnel receive information about the accident they are going to. The system also has capability to position ambulances by sending the coordinates to SOS alarm central. It is a well appreciated system but it generally fails in one aspect:

> *"...The GPS receiver stops searching if it is kept indoors for a while. To make it start searching again you have to restart the entire system"*
> (User of the CAK-net system)

Through the CyberMate system, by use of its GPS-receiver, SOS alarm central knows the position of each ambulance. The system does not provide any information about other units, consequently at a large accident with several ambulances included personnel have to communicate with mobile phones or VHF radios to know the positions of other units. In order to solve all communication and information needs, an emergency car is equipped with no less than nine different systems, in addition to the CAK-net system.

Fig. 8.4. Nine different IT systems are used by ambulance personnel

The different systems are, however, not well integrated. The most obvious example is the PDA necessary to translate the position coordinates received in X-Y format from the CyberMate into longitude / latitude for entry into the GPS map system.

Case conclusions

During the three phases of the survey (questionnaires, interviews and observation interviews) several conclusions have been made. Typical problems and weaknesses of investigated systems imply that:

- Mobile IT systems have to be designed to support all situations and environments where they might be used.
- Information presented in systems has to be carefully chosen, effectively presented and easy to access.

- Well integrated systems are appreciated since they provide good cooperation with other users, effective information handling and thereby help personnel to work well and effectively.

8.4 Design for usability in mobile systems for home care

This study was performed as a part of a large project, VIHO (a Swedish acronym for Efficient Computer Support in Care for the Elderly), performed in Kortedala, a suburb of Gothenburg in Sweden. The purpose was to investigate how new mobile technology could support development of the organisation, efficiency of work procedures and work environment. Researchers with a background in human-computer interaction together with organisational consultants from Komanco AB, a company owned by the Swedish Municipal Workers' Union, were involved in the project.

8.4.1 Background

Today professionals in care for elderly, and especially in home care, normally have few technical support systems. In most cases none at all. Many commercial systems have been developed, but few have had any success at all. It was our hypothesis that this was mainly because systems developed and deployed were not useful enough to be accepted in everyday use. We find that professionals often have a positive attitude and are really trying to use technology, but much too often they experience that technology hinders them rather than supports them in their work. We wanted to try another approach, where we started with development of work procedures according to defined goals, and where we were free to assume any type of technology support. In this way, we could use mobile technology as a driving force in organisational development, without limiting ourselves to existing products. As a second step we identified functional aspects of proposed supportive technologies and started with the design of user interfaces. The process followed a participatory model in all phases (Olsson 2005).

The organisation studied was the care of elderly in Kortedala. The project was originally triggered by economical problems in the organisation and the fact that the population is getting older. Because of this, they started to look for efficiency improvements, at first by implementation of new technology. As no appropriate technology could be found on the market, the project was soon broadened to include how organisation, work procedures etc. could be developed and what kind of technology might actually be able to contribute to this. Objectives of the project were:

- to let elderly people stay longer in their own home, rather than being referred to institutions
- to increase security for elderly people who stay in their homes,
- to increase, or at least maintain, present levels of service, despite budget limitations
- to specify requirements for future mobile technical support systems that could contribute to the other objectives

The main research objective for the VIHO project was to investigate how the organisation of a home-help service can be developed in order to be prepared for increased demands on health care. The project was actually not an IT-project, but intended to show how good use of mobile technology could contribute to an efficient and sustainable work situation in tomorrow's care for elderly people.

Projects like VIHO can be seen as prerequisites for formulation of requirements for more technically oriented IT-development projects. If a new technical support system is introduced in a work environment, it will often change both organisations and work processes. In order to develop efficient and usable technology it is important to first develop organisations and work processes and then, as a second step, new technical support systems. Often this is done in the opposite order, which is probably one of the main reasons for unsuccessful projects.

Another basic standpoint is that it is only in close cooperation with potential users that proper requirements can be gathered and prototypes evaluated. At the same time it is always difficult for users to formulate their visions of future work and requirements for technical support systems. In our project researchers and employees have specified requirements together, according to a participatory development model.

8.4.2 Seminars for requirement gathering

In order to describe both today's work and a potential future work organisation, we conducted a series of seminars together with a group of experienced home care professionals in the local community. Work in the seminar group was organised in several steps. In total we had 12 full day meetings, with time periods between seminars for reflection and for preparation. Main discussion areas were:

- Description of today's work and organisation

- Analysis of today's work: problems, difficulties, need for change etc
- Specification of goals for future work: what do we really want to achieve? Both the group's own goals and goals stated by the organisation were discussed
- Specification of boundary conditions, prerequisites etc that are expected in the future. The group defined a time horizon of 4 years as "future".
- Specification of a set of important aspects that must or should characterize work in year 2008
- Specification of scenarios for the most important work processes, as the group expects them to be in 2008. This was partly made as detailed scenarios of "a day at work in 2008"

Based on this work, and especially on "important aspects of future work" and detailed work scenarios, we have made:

- Descriptions of work activities in future work processes
- Descriptions of information and communication needs in future work activities. I.e. with whom will they communicate, in which context and what is the information content?
- Preliminary prototypes of future technical, mobile and stationary, support systems that can support their new work

8.4.3 Specification of future work

Home care work is complex and consists of different processes and tasks that are administrative, medical and care related. Therefore a technical support system must be well adapted to all different work situations. Today, however, technical support systems are seldom used. We see a significant potential in developing work and organisation in the home care sector and this can be efficiently supported by new technology if systems can be made efficient and usable. We found it important to first specify organisational and care related goals. Main characteristics of future work, as specified through user involvement during seminars, were:

- Autonomous work groups and decentralized economy. The best planning of care activities can be made by work groups themselves, provided that they have relevant competencies, tools and access to all information needed
- Common care plans that are understood by all and shared among personnel involved in the care process, the patient and his/her relatives. If detailed care plans are always to hand, that planning, operational work and evaluation can be made based on correct and up to date information

- Integrated organisation. Today care activities are shared among different organisational teams. Even if they have partly the overlapping competencies they can not communicate efficiently enough, which results in parallel and resource consuming activities
- Evaluation of care delivery process within work groups. Today they work according to old patterns, and mostly do not have competencies, information, tools or time for evaluation. Because of this they do not know exactly what they are supposed to produce or what they have produced. They do not know if they carry out the right things in the most efficient way
- Integrated information support. An efficient care delivery organisation requires efficient information systems. Especially important are integration of different information sources and competencies of the professionals to utilise systems. Connections to other care institutions such as hospitals and primary care units. must be developed and supported by efficient tools

Fig. 8.5. Work within home care is, by definition, done in the homes of care takers. This leads to high demands for a potential mobile computer support system, in order to support usable, efficient and direct access to relevant information sources, communication with other actors etc

We will not further discuss these goals here, since this is not within the scope of this paper. Nevertheless, it is important to understand that it is only when we base our design of information systems and user interfaces on a detailed description of future care organisation and work procedures, that we can specify proper requirements concerning functionality and usability.

Scenarios of future work

Descriptions of future work situations are specified as a set of scenarios. One scenario can describe a larger or smaller part of one professionals work during a day. Specification of scenarios is made so that professionals involved can understand and describe them in their own terms. We have guided the formulation of scenarios in order to assure that they cover the most important parts of future work situations, and so that they are detailed enough for the subsequent steps of the design process.

Scenarios describe what is being done, actions, when, in which context, of what purpose, decisions made, information handling, communication about what and with who etc. When scenarios are analysed, it is possible to identify work activities, i.e. more complete sets of tasks, performed during one limited time period. Identification of activities is important for design of user interfaces.

8.4.4 Design of mobile work support systems

As mentioned in the introduction, VIHO was not a pure IT-project, even though future technical support systems are in focus. The goal is not to implement technology, but to show how work and organisation can be developed with technology as a driving force towards efficiency and a good work environment.

Starting with the specifications mentioned above, we can develop early prototypes of new support systems. When doing this, we consider aspects concerning design of mobile systems as especially important.

Interface metaphor

One problem when designing user interface for mobile systems is visualisation of complex information structures on a small screen. A common solution is to spread information on a number of separate windows, often in a hierarchical structure, and provide access to different windows via a menu system. However, this solution often results in information fragmentation and jumping around in menu systems.

A set of work tasks that together form a work process can be seen as an activity. With an activity we here mean a number of activities that are completed together during a limited time period, in order to reach a specific goal. In user interfaces, complete activities should be, if possible, supported without leaving the activated window and with a limited number of navigation steps. To operate the interface through open, close, move, activate, select etc. draws attention from core work tasks. Therefore, if information processing can be made with a minimum of navigation the cognitive focus can be on work activities.

This design technique is often referred to as the "room metaphor" (Henderson 1986; Lif 1998). When an activity is performed, a "room" is opened in the interface. This room contains a "work space", especially designed to support the works tasks associated with the activity. The "work space" is designed to support the activity in as optimal fashion as possible.

In order to design the complete interface of the technical support system, the following must be specified:

- The activities that constitute the total work processes. Define the different rooms needed in the design. Each room also defines one work space
- Information contents of each room, both information sets and information tools
- Interactions needed for the user when the different tasks are performed in the room

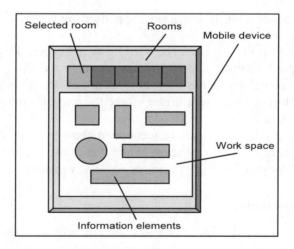

Fig. 8.6. A fictive mobile device with a room selection bar, one selected room and the corresponding work space with its information elements

Design for usability

The following general design rules are a base for design of the user interface. For the detailed design decisions this is not enough, but must be completed with more domain specific rules and design knowledge.

- Design for skilled users. Professional users are novices during a short time period, and the efficiency for the skilled user must have a high priority
- Allow automation of work processes. It must be possible to have a continuous focus on the work process, without spending high mental work load on handling of the supporting technology
- The correct information sets must be available during a complete activity. All information needed and nothing more must be at hand
- Choose an appropriate basic metaphor, e.g. the "rooms metaphor"
- Make the design complete, i.e. the user should not have to make any design activities during use of the system, such as e.g. start processes, open/close windows etc
- Show the whole and the details simultaneously. By doing so it will be possible to always know exactly where you are, which details are available, how to reach these etc
- Allow easy change of work tasks. It will often be necessary to change between work tasks, e.g. when the user is disturbed
- Minimize need for input of data and commands. Especially when somebody is mobile, input is slow and demanding
- Make information coding clear, consistent and consequent. Everything on the screen must be obvious and easy to interpret
- Efficient and minimized use of icons and colours. Use no colours without a meaning
- Use "turning of pages" instead of scrolling when reading texts from the screen
- Make point areas large enough, otherwise the user will be slowed down
- Adapt pointing functions and devices to the work situation, especially when the system is used in a mobile context

8.4.3 Case conclusions

In this case study we have illustrated how it is possible to design future work organisation and work processes according to the organisation's requirements and not according to which technology is available. To achieve this it is necessary to use a participatory model, where representative end-users are given the chance to design the future work processes before the supportive technology.

We have also briefly discussed some basic design guidelines for mobile work support systems. It is our experience that it is possible to specify some general rules that can support good design, but that it is important to base the design on detailed scenarios of the new organisation and work procedures.

8.5 Conclusions

This chapter deals with the question: "How can we understand problems and possibilities related to usability of mobile work support systems?" We have discussed which aspects of usability are especially important to consider when work becomes mobile, compared to more general usability guidelines. There appear to be conflicts between interface aspects that support usability and what is technically possible in a mobile context. As an example, the handling of large amounts of information requires a large screen, something which can be impossible in a mobile system. In many such situations we must find a reasonable compromise between what is useful, from an information retrieval point of view, and what is efficient to use in a mobile context. We have listed a number of important factors where such usability conflicts occur.

In the first case study, we studied a number of mobile systems in professional use in the health care sector. The purpose was to see how usability aspects of mobile systems could be assessed in real work settings using questionnaires, interviews and observations. As far as we could see, there are few truly mobile systems that are extensively used in the health sector. There exist a lot of test systems, ongoing research and development projects etc, but the number of "full scale, in real use systems" is rather limited. Other findings are that technical solutions often are rather primitive and that many systems are intended to be mobile but are used as stationary systems because of usability limitations. By better taking advantage of the technology and knowledge available, better mobile systems could be designed.

In the second case study we studied how the development of usable mobile IT systems could support the development of organisation, work procedures and work environment. We studied the work setting, home health care, that is mobile already but normally lack technical support systems. Our hypothesis was, that through design of usable mobile support systems adapted to the work context, we could achieve positive improvements in the organisation.

The outcome was that in order to manage this some important requirements must be fulfilled. We must base the design process on a detailed description and analysis of the work context, because usability criteria (especially in a mobile environment) are context dependent to a great extent. Moreover it is also necessary to involve the potential end-users in the process since they have detailed knowledge about local needs and requirements. It is necessary to work according to an iterative development model, since the exact requirements are not known in advance. Design decisions can often be based on heuristic rules, but these must be formulated for a mobile situation and for the actual work context.

To conclude. The case study has shown that if well adapted technical systems can be designed, they can significantly contribute to a positive development of an already mobile workplace. The system can give the personnel improved opportunities to plan their work, to document, to communicate and to evaluate their own work. Things can be performed in the right way, the personnel can through their own evaluation improve their work procedures and skills and they can have grater control over all aspects of their workload. In this way personnel can avoid stress, become more efficient and create a better, healthier, work environment.

Acknowledgements

The VIHO project has been financially supported by VINNOVA, The Swedish Agency for Innovation Systems. We also want to thank the home care organisation and personnel in Kortedala, Gothenburg for their participation and support, Users Award for the good co-operation with the survey and Komanco AB for their contributions to the work.

References

Åborg C, Sandblad B, Gulliksen J, Lif M (2003) Integrating work environment considerations into usability evaluation methods – the ADA approach. Interacting with Computers 15:453–471

Fällman D (2003) In romance with the materials of mobile interaction: A phenomenological approach to the design of mobile information technology, Larsson & Co's Tryckeri, Umeå University, Umeå

Gorlenko L, Merrick R (2003) No wires attached: Usability challenges in the connected mobile world, IBM Systems Journal archive, 42(4):639 – 651

Greenbaum J, Kyng M (eds.) (1991) Design at work. Lawrence Erlbaum, New Jersey

Harper R (2003) People versus information: The evolution of mobile technology. In: Chittaro L (ed) Human-computer interaction with mobile devices and services, LNCS 2795, Springer-Verlag, Berlin, pp 1–14

Henderson DA, Card SK (1986) Rooms: The use of multiple virtual workspaces to reduce space contention in a window based graphical user interface, ACM Transactions on Graphics, 5(3):211–243

Hughes J, Randall D, Shapiro D (1993) From ethnographic record to system design: Some experiences from the field. Journal of CSCW 1(3):123–141

ISO 9241-11 (1998) Ergonomic requirements for office work with visual display terminals – Part 11: Guidance of usability, International Organization for Standardization

ISO 11064-1 (2000) Ergonomic design of control centres - Part 1: Principles for the design of control centres, International Organization for Standardization

Landay JA and Kaufmann TR (1993) User interface issues in mobile computing. In: Proceedings of the Fourth Workshop on Workstation Operating Systems, IEEE Computer Society Press, Napa, pp 40–47

Lif M, Olsson E, Gulliksen J, Sandblad B (2001) Workspaces enhance efficiency - theories, concepts and a case study, Information Technology & People 14(3):261-272

Lind T, Sandblad B, Johansson N, Utbult M (2004) Vård IT-Kartan. Sjuhäradsbygdens tryckeri, Borås

Linjama J, Kaaresoja T (2004) Novel, minimalist haptic gesture interaction for mobile devices. In: Proceedings of the Third Nordic Conference on Human Computer Interaction (NordiCHI'04), ACM Press , pp 457–458

Luff P and Heath C (1998) Mobility in collaboration. In: Proceedings of CSCW'98, ACM Press, New York, pp 305–314

Nielsen J (1993) Usability engineering, Academic Press

Nielsen J (2000) WAP usability report. Norman group report, http://www.nngroup.com/reports/wap, obtained 7 March 2005

Olsson E, Johansson N, Gulliksen J, Sandblad B (2005) A participatory process supporting design of future work: Technical report. Department of Information Technology, Uppsala University, Uppsala 2005-018

Polanyi M (1967) The tacit dimension, Anchor Books, New York

Weiss S (2002) Handheld usability. John Wiley & Sons, New York

9 Participative Design for Home Care Nursing

Marion Wiethoff[1], Thierry Meulenbroek[2], Hans Stafleu[3] and Rogier van Boxtel[3]

[1]Faculty of Technology, Policy and Management, Delft University of Technology, The Netherlands
[2]OPTA, The Hague, The Netherlands
[3]TNO Telecom, Delft, The Netherlands

9.1 Home health care as mobile work

Home care is traditionally a branch in which mobile work takes place. Home care nurses, and other workers such as general practitioners (GPs), other (para)medical professionals, e.g. physiotherapists, and voluntary carers provide care for patients at home.

It is recognized in this branch of health care (Hanhart and Janssen 2000) that the professionals, and also the patients, are relatively slow regarding uptake of technological innovations in the field of information and communication technologies (ICT). In this chapter, we will show that this is in spite of the fact that there are important opportunities to improve quality of life and quality of work if the use of ICT is implemented. The reasons for the slow uptake of ICT in this branch of health care are related to the limitations of the patients, and to the organisational limitations faced by health care workers. There is a strong societal need to resolve current problems in this area.

A method will be presented and discussed in this chapter that can be used to design a socio-technical system for stakeholders with very diverse needs, and sometimes restrictive limitations, who have very limited acquaintance with new technologies. The design method is a participative design method, combined with an ethnographic approach. The method is based on the Early Scenario based Evaluation (ESE, van den Anker 2003) and Holtzblatt and Beyer's (1993) Contextual Design approach. The aim is to show convincingly that this method is appropriate for these types of contexts.

Since this chapter is primarily methodologically-oriented, only part of the empirical data concerning the content of the concept will be presented here to serve as examples. A brief description of the aims and the requirements of the phase will be given at the beginning of each phase and the proposed procedure will be outlined. This is then followed by a description of the procedure as it was performed in the study.

9.2 ICT, mobile workers and the chronically ill

In general, the population of Europe is getting older due to lower birth-rates and longer life expectancy, partially that of the aging of the baby boomers (EUROSTAT 2001). Furthermore, the group of chronically ill consists to a considerable degree of elderly people. Evidently, the need for care will increase considerably, but according to the predictions of the RIVM (Salzmann 2004) the capacity of homes for the aged in need for care will be insufficient in the near and far future (up to 2020). However, many chronically ill elderly people would prefer to stay at home independently, for as long as possible. The requests for transmural care will increase for this category; both for professional and voluntary carer. On one hand, it is necessary to increase the number of professionals working in this branch of health care, and in particular in home care, and on the other hand, it is important to support the voluntary carers, especially those who give care on a daily basis[1]. There are, however, more opportunities. The effectiveness and the efficiency of care can be improved by supporting all parties involved in providing and receiving home care, and here is the obvious opportunity for supporting mobile work.

The introduction of new technology in this particular field will meet a number of barriers. One important barrier is the fact that there is a large variety of user groups and roles, and each user group has its own expectations, organisational requirements and personal limitations. Another barrier is the very limited experience with, and high resistance to using, new technologies, and the learning difficulties associated with being elderly and chronically ill.

Still, despite these barriers, there may be solutions which can really improve a patient's quality of life and carers work efficiency. It is necessary to adopt an approach with a high degree of active user involvement to optimize the quality of a design of such a system.

---

[1] There are two categories of voluntary carers: 1. the carers who are usually sent out by an organisation and who give care on a regular basis, e.g. weekly. 2. The carers who are usually closely related to the patient e.g. spouse or child or neighbour and who give care on their own initiative, and sometimes very intensively, i.e. on a daily basis. Whenever members of the last category in particular are referred to, the term *frontline voluntary carer* is used. To address both patients and their frontline voluntary carers, the term 'client' is used here.

9.3 User involvement in design

The development of usable systems (e.g. Kujala 2003, Karat 1997) is achieved by involving the potential users early on in the design process. The ISO 13407 standard concerning the design of interactive systems (1999) stresses the importance of active involvement of users in order to understand the user and the task requirements.

User involvement can take many forms, and ranges from incidental information gathering, to user consulting to participative cooperative design procedures (Damodaran 1996). Kujala (2003) gives an overview of the main different types of user involvement approaches, each originating from its own tradition: user centered design, participatory design, ethnography and contextual design. Over the years, these approaches have grown more closely together. For instance, contextual design involves ethnography, and participatory design also combines with the other approaches.

From a review of studies on user involvement, Kujala (2003) concludes that user involvement usually has a positive effect on the quality of the designed system and that the benefits outweigh the costs of user involvement. However, Kujala also concludes that it is of vital importance that the involvement of users is *carefully managed* in the process. There are various ways in which user involvement can play a role in the design process, and some main design approaches in which user involvement takes place will be presented in the next section. The design cycle approach (Roozenburg and Eekels 1995) form the basis of the other approaches presented below. It involves a process with convergent and divergent stages. The cycle consists of the stages analysis – criteria – synthesis. The design evolves via provisional design, via expected properties to simulation and then to evaluation, on the criteria defined earlier, and finally reaches the stage of decision making on the design. This design cycle approach forms the basis for product design or service design, but it is merely focused on the product or service. It is a well established method and can be considered as a basic unit that is repeated over and over again in more iterative design approaches

9.3.1 Design approaches

Evolutionary design approach

In Boehm's spiral development approach (1988), stages of development, i.e. requirements plan, risk analyses, prototypes, various types of requirements tests and validations, and plans, are successively developed as in a spiral progressing outwards. This approach has been successfully used in many projects for software development (van de Kar 2004), and its method forms the basis for a number of IS development approaches. The spiral design method is more explicit with regard to proposing methods for analysis and evaluation

Participatory design approach

The participatory design approach (e.g. Ehn 1993) has become an important design approach in the past decades. According to this approach, the user's work activities and the integrative context in which applications are used is the starting point for the technological design process. The end users, i.e. those who will be interacting with the final application in order to perform their duties, in their own experience and expertise, form the basis for the criteria of success of the designed product. Therefore, *all* stakeholders affected by the newly organized and performed way of working with the designed application will be involved in the whole design process. Ehn's participatory design method is very important for stressing the cooperation between designer and prospective user in a 'democratic' way: the user participates actively, instead of being consulted from time to time. Therefore the user's participation is more active in comparison to the spiral development method (Boehm 1988).

Contextual Design

The above mentioned approaches require the stakeholders to have a clear view of the new system's characteristics. However, this usually is very difficult to achieve for novel applications. Contextual Design (Holtzblatt and Beyer 1993) is a design approach specifically developed for designing novel products and maximising the innovativeness of totally new products. The design method entails a structured approach for the collection of relevant user information and context information ("Contextual Inquiry") and for structuring and interpreting the information to make it usable for the designers. To this aim, "models" are produced: context models, work models, artefact models, physical models, flow models and sequence models which are used to regulate the communication between designers and users/stakeholders and to prioritize the design decisions. Information is collected using interviews, observations and discussions. This is a very comprehensive approach to the full process of design, from first idea about the technology to final design. This design approach has been applied successfully at the Digital Equipment Corporation (Holzblatt and Beyer 1996), and has served as the basis for the Early Scenario based evaluation approach (ESE, van den Anker 2003). The ESE was taken as the model for the current study, because of its particular strength in very actively involving the end users and all the other stakeholders in the whole design cycle. Furthermore, the ESE is explicit in involving all stakeholders in the later stages in various types of evaluations, after implementation of an application.

The early scenario based evaluation approach

The ESE approach (van den Anker 2003) is oriented towards user-centered design and based upon Holzblatt and Beyer's Contextual Design approach, and applying Ehn's concept of very actively involving users as participants in the design process. In spite of its name, the approach is basically a design method, because the method involves the whole process of designing and evaluating a new technology application. The evaluation takes place in various stages, even at the early stage of the conceptual development; hence the name. Potential problems and opportunities in use and functionalities are identified at an early stage, so they can be accounted for in the design process. Various categories of actors are involved: i.e. the designers, the prospective end users, the service providers, and possibly other organisations involved in providing services attached to the application. The use of scenarios is elaborated.

The evaluation part of the approach is based on Andriessen's (2002) three–stage model for assessment of the usefulness and usability of new technologies. The three stages refer to:

1. *Defining the requirements by scenario-based concept evaluation.* The process methodology implies a contextual analysis of the new technology and of the current situation of the application to be. This is the basis for developing a future work scenario. A future workshop for participatory evaluation of the scenario will then result in the identification of user and context requirements.
2. *Prototype testing* based on a systematic user oriented evaluation of the usability and usefulness of an application in a laboratory setting. This stage results in the identification of renewed user and context requirements.
3. *Operational evaluation*, of socio-technical settings in which new applications are introduced.

In this chapter, we concentrate on the first stage only, i.e. defining the requirements by evaluation of a scenario-based concept.

Early evaluation of implications of novel
ICT applications: ESE

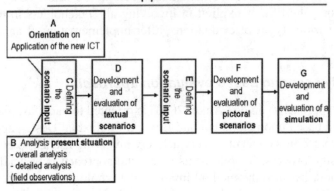

Fig. 9.1. The "Early Scenario based Evaluation" method for evaluation of novel technology applications as it was applied in the current study. Only the stages B - F are specified in this chapter

The context of use is considered extremely important in the phase, defining the scenario input. There are various ways to conceptualize the context of use. One method is to apply Activity Theory (Engeström 1987; Kuutti 1995) to define the content. Activity Theory considers, in particular, organisational issues and the social cultural environment to be very important. In the theory 'activity' is defined as the 'minimal meaningful context for understanding individual actions'. The activity entails: tool, subject, object, rules, community and division of labour. The object is the entity (or goal) that actors manipulate. The actors interact on the object with the help of artefacts (tools), within a context of roles, and under a set of community rules (Fig. 9.2). This definition of an 'activity' is used in the current project to define the elements that need to be incorporated in our scenarios (see further). The activity is the minimum meaningful context for understanding individual actions (Kuuti 1993). For the sake of the present focus on mobile work, the space- time setting is added to define the context of mobile work, i.e. synchronous vs. asynchronous, same vs. different location, mediated by what type of tool, under which rules, and who participates.

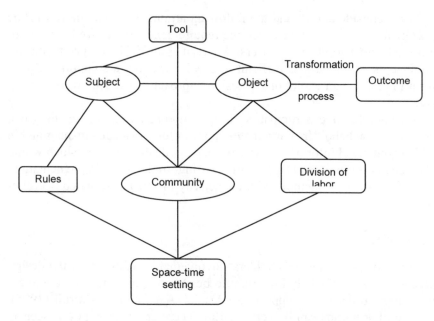

Fig. 9.2. Activity structure for mobile work (adapted from Engeström 1987)

Considerations for choosing the design model

In the context of home care, the design model selected for user participation was chosen on the basis of the following considerations:

- the user group was varied in age, experience with new technology and limitations, i.e. both elderly chronically ill, elderly healthy, young or middle aged carers and professionals
- the user groups had different types of roles, e.g. patients at home and professionals
- some user groups had strong requirements originating from the organisation or professional practice. The applications should carefully fit in the home context and the working context of the user groups
- most of these user groups had little acquaintance with new technology applications, and this means, on the one hand, that they had therefore more difficulty in imagining the effects of new technology applications, and, on the other hand, that it was vital to design applications that follow closely the needs and requirements and limitations of these user groups
- the specific user needs and requirements were relatively unknown to the designers, and also to the prospective users

These considerations, and the following argument of Van de Kar (2004 p 48): "for design cases in which the requirements are not well formed, or not well understood by the users, where it is difficult to specify the requirements or where it is difficult to predict whether a solution will perform in practice an evolutionary design approach is needed" were conclusive.

A comprehensive participative design approach was needed, in which all relevant stakeholders participated in a carefully managed manner and in which contextual information was extensively dealt with, and which would also enable future evaluations of existing tools after implementation. Therefore, the ESE method, with the activity theory incorporated was chosen.

Scenarios

In order to realize the stakeholders' involvement effectively in the design process, it was extremely important to be able to communicate effectively with them to derive the appropriate results. According to Carroll (1995), the use of scenarios can be very fruitful. There are many types of scenarios, e.g. textual, storyboards, moving videos, with and without interactivity, but a very important dimension (e.g. Van den Anker 2003) is *scenario richness*. This entails that scenarios enable interactivity between the audience and the scenarios, e.g. as in an interactive demo, that there are various discussions about the scenario, and that the scenarios have a narrative character. In general, it has been found that narrative scenarios arouse imagery, interpretation, comprehension and recall (e.g. Sadoski 1999), and therefore, rich narrative scenarios are expected to act most powerful in participative design processes. Furthermore, one can expect that a rich scenario will solicit comments at a detailed level.

Several types of scenarios were applied for the design process in the present study. Because of the large variety of user groups, the choice was made to organize focused discussions in working groups in parallel, to aim at early conceptualizations. Furthermore, the decision was made to apply various types of scenarios with increasing degrees of scenario richness, and presented understandably for all stakeholders throughout the whole process.

The textual and pictorial scenarios are presented in this section. Activity overviews (e.g. Fig. 9.3 and Fig. 9.4) were used to define the elements of content in the scenarios. A choice was made to use a limited set of objects for each scenario. A scenario should not contain more than one or two objects, otherwise the discussions on the scenario will be muddled and confused and the results chaotic.

9.4 Application of the ESE design approach

9.4.1 Stage B: Analysis present situation and problems[2]

A literature study, interview study and participative observation is needed to arrive at an overview of problem areas.

The actual analysis is performed

A literature study was performed for the current study of various overviews in books and articles (e.g. Steen 2000, Hoving 2003, Bosma et al. 2001, Van Kammen 2002, Koning et al. 2002) in the field of social medical literature concerning the organisation of care in the Netherlands, as well as of overview articles on medical informatics, and of books and reports on pilot studies for Information and Communication Technology (ICT)projects. Furthermore, a number of interviews were held in two rounds: first, with key persons in the field of care in the Netherlands: scientists, management of national interest organisations, e.g. LOT[3] and NPCF[4] and with organisations involved in implementation of ICT in health care, e.g. KITTZ[5] and NICTIZ[6]. In the second round, workers in the field, were interviewed, i.e. GP's, home care nurses, patients, voluntary carers etc. The main subjects of the interviews were: (1) organisation and problems in home care: in the first round at a more generic, organisational level, and in the second round at a more personal level, and (2) possible options for ICT application development. In total, 14 interviews and a few days and nights of participative observation were carried out.

Results

The following main issues were reported:

- Evidently there will be a capacity problem for home care institutions and frontline voluntary carers in the future. For these carers, the care load can be up to 24 hours a day, for long periods in time, in cases the spouse is the frontline voluntary carer. There are approximately half a million frontline voluntary carers in the Netherlands: 10% below 35,

---

[2] Only stages B, C, D, E and F are presented here.
[3] LOT: National organisation coordinating Home Care institutions and representing them nationally.
[4] National organisation for defending patients' interests
[5] Quality Institute for Innovation in Home Care
[6] National ICT Institute in Health Care

50% between 35 – 60 years of age, 40% over 60, 20% over 75 (figures from the Dutch Coordination institute for Frontline Voluntary Carers). It can be concluded that the high work load for front voluntary carers make them a group with special interests, risks and needs.

- Elderly chronically ill and frontline voluntary carers complain that they have loss of control over their own lives. However, having more control over one's life means a higher task load, and this is a disadvantage for many: but for everyone experiencing a loss of control, *informational control* can be beneficial. Someone with informational control only, feels that it is not possible to influence the occurrence of events, but they know what is going to happen. People *feel* more in control if they have informational control in comparison to no control at all. It is advisable to establish a fit between clients' needs and the type of control provided.
- Clients and family complained about the Personal Care Budget (PGB)[7]. Apparently, managing their PGB carries a high decision load.
- Home care institutions have their own needs. It was reported that they feel a need to be able to acquire information at a distance that is relevant for giving care to a client. This involved specific medical information, but also information concerning the care given and the observations made by GPs and professional carers. This is in line with the utilities reported by Vartiainen (chapter 2 in this volume) that in order to overcome temporal, spatial and organisational disablers, ICT could be used as a collective memory to collect, store, access and utilize knowledge, as well as for communication.
- Clients and frontline voluntary carers tend to become very isolated, and it was reported that there is a great demand for social contacts and social support.

Many of the younger chronically ill patients have discovered the internet as a means for finding medical information, but there are not many older patients for whom this is an option.

---

[7] "Persoons Gebonden Budget"; This is a Dutch regulation according to which chronically ill people can receive a budget to allocate to sources for care, according to their own choice. The "Persoons Volgend Budget" is an improvement in that it reduces administrative burdens.

9.4.2 Stage C: Defining the input for textual scenarios

Procedure

A few main functionalities for support by ICT must be defined from the analysis, performed at the previous stage. Foci for functionalities are defined according to the following criteria: there must be an obvious need for a functionality on a relatively large scale, the functionality must entail to some degree ICT functions, there should be a link to other organisational and ICT developments in the Netherlands, so as to join forces, however the functionalities should not cover pre-existing developments.

Next, rich, narrative scenarios should be defined, and in the first stage the scenarios must be used to attract general comments, while in subsequent stages the comments should become increasingly detailed. The aim of the first set of scenarios is to define the degree of desirability of the functionalities, and the conditions under which these functionalities are desirable, as well as an overall judgement on the realism of the concept. Therefore, the scenario richness of the first set of scenarios is limited, comments about the *appearance* of the applications are not appreciated, and textual scenarios are to be preferred. The scenarios should be validated by stakeholders. Organizing a workshop is a possibility.

The procedure as it was performed and the results

From the analysis of the present situation and problems, the following main issues emerged as relevant types of support needs:

1. Communication opportunities with medical professionals, also visually
2. Social support for clients and frontline voluntary carers
3. Informational support for clients and their family on the PGB, and support for transactions and PGB management

It was decided by the authors that the following types of support were also relevant, but for practical reasons less of a priority for the current study:

4. Support for planning and administration for the home care nurses
5. Support for monitoring bodily functions at home
6. Informational support for the clients and front voluntary carers on medical issues, and concerning giving care

7. Therefore it was decided to continue with three types of scenarios:
  1. Scenarios focusing on coordination between planning of visits by the carer and client in order to provide informational control
  2. Scenarios focusing on communication between clients with the carers
  3. Scenarios focusing on management of the PGB and communication with all other parties, i.e. family, friends, service providers, etc

9.4.3 Stage D: Developing textual scenarios

The central problem in the scenario was centred around low efficiency for the home care institution. The following considerations were leading:

- there is considerable loss of time due to the need for a carer to travel from client to client. Is it really necessary for the carer to come? There may be instances where it is not necessary, e.g. because the patient feels well enough that day to do some tasks by her/himself, or because there is someone else around
- the urgency is not always clear; should someone come immediately, and who should come or is it possible to communicate between client and carer at a distance?

Two textual scenarios were produced for each of the three above mentioned types, one scenario based on use of contemporary technology, and one scenario based on future technology. Each scenario was written as a brief story, a narrative scenario, in which the main user makes use of the application. Central features of the interaction with the application were stressed. The scenarios had a strong narrative character.

The scenarios focussing on *communication* with the carers are presented as an example.

These considerations led to the development of two scenarios: the scenario based on contemporary technology; this was called: 'TV Home care' (Table 1) and the scenario based on future technology; this was called: 'Care always close' (Table 2). The characterizations of 'TV Home care' are shown in the activity overview in Fig. 9.3)

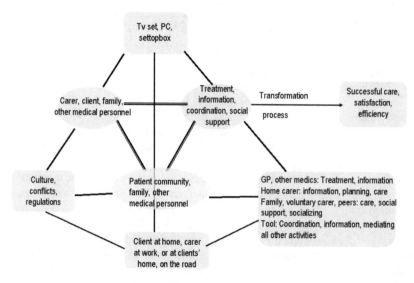

Fig. 9.3. Activity overview: Textual scenario: *'TV Home care'*

In this scenario, the actors were primarily clients, patients and frontline voluntary carers, and home nurses and the GPs. The system and tools were the equipment and the application designed for informing and communicating. The client would use it at home, at a fixed location: the combination of a TV set and a settop box, this combination enables the TV set to be used for the internet, but the client still sees and confidence of a normal TV set. The carers and the GPs will use PCs and internet, also at fixed locations. The object of the activity was communication between the client and carer or GP, in the form of information transmission, social support or treatment support. The client was the actor that initiated communication. The communication would be mainly asynchronous, and meeting dates and moments of the conversations would be recorded. The community behind the actors were the people involved behind the actors, i.e. patient community, family, and other carers. The rules referred to the regulations for providing care, treatment information, rules and considerations on when to visit the patient physically and privacy regulations. In the division of work, communication would take place to a large extent between client and carer, and more incidentally between GP and client, or GP and carer. In this scenario, the clients were mainly at home, the carer could be at work, either in the home care institution or in the clients' home.

Table 9.1. Textual scenario: *'TV Home care'*

Textual scenario: 'TV Home care'	
Personalised home care TV channel *Simple user interface*	Monday morning 09.15 hr. Mrs. Jongemans (79) presses the green button on her CareBox. The television set switches on immediately and turns to the Home Care channel, and she watches her care programme for the day: her regular exercises programme begins at 11.00 hrs. She is also reminded to take her medication during lunch and dinner. Also all previous "conversations" and "dates" are recorded by the carers. She can watch them again.
Personalised information *Client decides when to contact carer*	Mrs. Jongemans presses the orange button she uses to contact Cora, her personal carer. The TV shows a message that Cora is engaged, and it is also audible. Mrs. Jongemans records her video message for Cora, using speech. After one and a half hours, Cora contacts Mrs. Jongemans. Mrs. Jongemans tells her that the black spot on her arm is still hurting considerably. Cora advises her to contact the GP. After the conversation, Mrs. Jongemans switches to the GP and discusses her problem. Then she switches off.
Care history available	At 11.30 hrs. Mrs. Jongemans switches the television set on again, and performs the exercises presented and shown by Cora. She is improving on the exercises. The exercises are recorded, so that Cora can watch how Mrs. Jongemans is doing later on the day.

The characterizations of the textual scenario 'Care always close' are shown in the activity overview in figure 9.5. This is a scenario based on innovative, new (mobile) technology (see Fig. 9.6), involving the same actors, and also the same community as the previous scenario. The tool for the clients at home is the 'care box': a mobile device with a wireless broadband connection, to be used outside or inside the house. The tools for the carers or the GP is a fixed PC, or a similar mobile device. The object of the activity is the communication between the client and carer or GP, in the form of information transmission, social support or treatment support, using audio channels, video channels and data transmission. Communication is mainly synchronous. Both client and carer can initiate communication. The client can also make additional notes. The rules are the same as in the previous scenario, but differently applied because of the possibility for visual contact. The GP and the carer check the state of the client, and can provide more support for the frontline voluntary carer. In this scenario, all actors can also communicate when they are mobile.

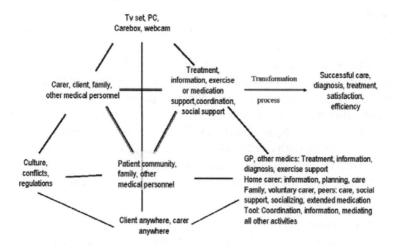

Fig. 9.4. Activity overview: Textual scenario: *'Care always close'*

Table 9.2. Textual scenario: *'Care always close'*

	Textual scenario: 'Care always close'
Communication at home and on the road	Johan van der Kaf (47) is undergoing rehabilitation several months after a traffic accident. He is regaining his mobility and is now able to go out with his metallic rollator. Yesterday, he and his carer Daniel decided that he would perform the afternoon exercises outside.
Personalised Information *Annotated care history*	Johan will have to perform exercises walking on the field and up and down steps. He clicks his mobile CareBox on the rollator and puts a tiny audio transmitter in his ear. Outside, Daniel contacts Johan. Daniel watches Johan moving on the grass and gives directions and they make some dates/assignments for the next day. Later at home, Johan switches on his
Time saving for carer *Call forwarding function*	CareBox, and watches the recordings of his exercises, to see for himself what went well and what not. He adds his own spoken remarks which he can see and hear later again. Just before he wants to switch off his CareBox, the hospital contacts him. His doctor saw how he did the exercises and noticed that he is improving faster than expected. The meeting for next week can be cancelled. Johan closes the connection.

The workshop for evaluating the textual scenarios

Procedure

The purpose of the workshop was to evaluate the potentially usefulness, desirability and feasibility of the scenarios, and to identify the priority scenario, that would be most suitable for further development. The respondents came from key organisations and were scientists, with an overview over the field, each one from their own perspective. The relevant questions for each workgroup concerned functionality: Is it useful, desirable and realistic and what are the necessary conditions for successful use? Is it realistic that the functionality will work as expected, especially given the sociocultural and organisational context, and under which conditions should it work? Then, in a third phase, a voting procedure for each scenario was done to prioritize functionalities.

How it was done

Participants came from the following organisations: scientists from several research institutions, civil servants from the Dutch Ministry of Health, patient interest organisations, branch organisations, Home Care organisations, organisations involved in ICT development in the field of health care, organisation deciding upon the care that patients will receive (RIO). In total there were 38 participants, and 4 discussion leaders.

The respondents attended a workshop at Delft University of Technology. The programme for the afternoon consisted of an introduction by the chairman of the meeting including a brief introduction of the three subjects of the afternoon: (1) coordination of the planning, (2) communication with the carers and (3) management of the PGB. The participants chose two of the three subjects by picking two of three cards from decks on the table. Each card represented admission to one workgroup. There were a limited number of cards available, so all the working groups were equally in size.

The participants attended the first workgroup. The programme was organized as follows: first, an oral presentation of the first scenario, based on contemporary technology, supported by a powerpoint presentation. Then the discussion leader collected the responses from the audience after asking the audience to react to the following questions: "What is your judgment regarding the functionality in terms of desirability and usefulness, what are necessary conditions to be fulfilled in order to be successful? Is it realistic to expect that it could be developed and successful within a few years?" The same procedure was followed for the second scenario, based on future technology.

Subsequently, the participants switched to the other workgroup of their choice for a similar programme as in, but covering a different subject.

Finally, all participants voted on the scenarios they attended (4 out of 6) on the following question: "Which scenario is the most desirable and realistically attainable?"

Results of the workshop

Only some main remarks are given here on the communication concept, to give an impression of the types of comments that were gathered in the working groups. The discussions in each working group were lively, and the remarks were both general and specific, especially on the conditions that had to be fulfilled.

Table 9.3. Examples of remarks on the communication concept

Functionalities: desirability and usefulness	Conditions and realism
The concept absolutely has positive learning elements and opportunities for saving time at both sides	There should always be a possibility to get into contact directly, especially in emergencies.
There is no time for learning to use new communication channels.	Privacy must be guarded.
The concept may be too technical. Can clients learn to work with it?	High requirements on quality and technical reliability, and usability, especially the images.
Positive effects for the client are expected with such a system because the client keeps more responsibility	All parties must be willing to cooperate
The lack of synchronous communication makes the first concept not very useful.	Both client and carer must be able to watch the care history.
If people wish personal contact, they will make sure they get it.	Carer must be able to make notes digitally (on the spot).
Be sure to get a clear functionality. Make the concept accessible for the frontline voluntary carer.	Do not focus on communication only, but also "fun things", e.g. play bingo.
Communication at a distance may increase the risk of mistakes and especially the chance of missing the "last important question". There is a risk of missing important problems.	A doctor wants to see, feel and measure!

Voting

The voting procedure resulted in a preference for both scenarios of the communication concept which received 51% of the votes in total (Fig. 9.5).

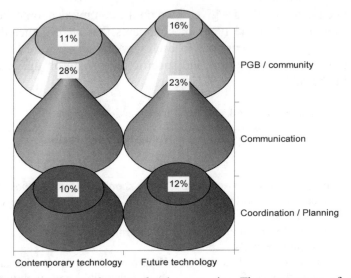

Fig. 9.5. The relative preferences for the scenarios. The percentages of votes attributed to each scenario are presented in the figure

Following the outcomes of the voting procedure and the comments in the workshop, it was concluded that the communication concept was the most important for further development, under the given conditions. Evidently, the importance of providing support for communication to clients, but also to front voluntary carers was stressed.

During the overall discussion afterwards in the workshop, it was concluded that other important functionalities should be:

- peer contact, for patients *and* frontline voluntary carers
- understanding the PGB, reduction of the administrative humbug
- getting transport

Conclusions

All three concepts bore elements that were considered useful, but the communication concept was most viable for further development. Therefore, the communication concept should form the basis for the next phase. However, certain elements from the other concepts, in particular on planning appointments and support for management of the care budget, as well as supporting peer contact were considered important features.

It can be concluded that the textual scenarios were powerful for raising many different types of comments; the participants managed to produce a clear image of the functionalities, the people were very well able to give their votes, and the conclusions gave enough directions for deciding how to continue. A side effect of producing (textual) scenarios is that it helps the researchers to test the logic of their own concepts by producing a coherent scenario, i.e. one is understandable by the participants.

9.4.4 Stage E: Defining the input for pictorial scenarios

The procedure

In the next phase, the scenarios should be increasingly rich to evoke imagery and comprehensiveness and arouse comments at a more detailed level than before to continue the development process into more detail. Narrative, pictorial scenarios was particularly useful for these purposes. The data from the earlier phase on prioritisation should form the input. In this stage, the scenarios should be more visibly accessible, with a narrative character. The main aim of these scenarios is to collect more detailed remarks on type of user interface issues and type of contents. Each scenario should also be limited in content regarding the functionalities shown.

The procedure, how it was done
A list was made with important elements of functionality for the second round of scenarios. This list resulted from internal discussions after analyzing the remarks, the prioritizing of the earlier scenarios and producing a combination of functionalities which formed a unified concept. Seven elements were defined.

Three elements originated from the "Communication" concept. The first was called: 'My Profile', i.e. the availability of some relevant personal medical data both for carer and client, and important phone numbers. The second was 'Digital Care Record, i.e. a system for logging and communication between client and home care nurses and GP's with questions and answers. The third was 'Digital care record for family issues', i.e. communicating and logging by family and friends and the client. One new element arose from the discussions: 'Care .... together', i.e. a system for making and keeping peer contacts. One element Originated from the planning concept: 'Care Diary', i.e. a diary with appointments and other important dates. Two elements originated from the PGB concept: 'Ensure Care', i.e. an overview and assistance by managing the personal care budget, and 'Medical Information', i.e. general information about their clients' disease and treatment.

9.4.5 Stage F: Developing pictorial scenarios

Procedure followed for developing pictorial scenarios

At this stage, it was decided to proceed with a concept for support based on the technology of today and the users of today. Development of a vision on how the concept would be in the future (2015) was postponed. Therefore, the concept entailed no ambient intelligence. Furthermore, it was established that the main users, i.e. elderly clients, voluntary carers, and home care nurses are generally not very accustomed to using computers, and the family of clients, administrators of the home care organisation and other medical personnel (GP's) are accustomed to using computers.

We chose a simple and usable concept, in which the nurses of home care organisations, GP's and family of the clients could make use of the PC at their home or working place. Clients and frontline voluntary carers make use of a television set with settop box and a telephone, and a keyboard for the nurses of the home care organisation when they are on location or a laptop.

The seven scenarios were produced as seven storyboards, containing a series of two or three photographs, with text beside the first photograph and some text displayed on the television set in the photographs.

All the storyboards were glued to cardboard; they were 20 cm x 80 cm or 20 cm x 108 cm.

The workshop for evaluating the pictorial scenarios

The purpose of the workshop was the evaluation of the appearance and the functionality of the scenarios, and to define the priority scenarios, which would be most suitable for further development.

Procedure of the workshop on pictorial scenarios
Because the pictorial scenarios were meant to elicit detailed comments, it was appropriate to choose participants from the end-user population and people who all work very closely with patients, or are patients themselves. Furthermore, more comments can be expected if participants work in small teams instead of large groups. Detailed comments and arguments can be expected if the participants are subsequently required to discuss in detail their opinions with others.At least 4 teams of 2 or 3 participants are needed for the procedure (see below), therefore at least 8 participants are needed. The assignment for each team separately is to evaluate the functionalities depicted on the storyboards, and to say what they feel is missing, what should be different, to rate the desirability of the scenario and finally to give a prioritisation of the functionalities. After the first round of discus-

sions, two teams were combined, and they received the assignment to prioritize the functionalities and in the last round all four teams were combined with the same assignment. The discussions were led and minuted by a discussion leader.

How it was done
Eight participants attended the workshop: 2 patients, 1 frontline voluntary carer (spouse), 2 voluntary carers from an organisation, 2 home care nurses. It was therefore not possible to organize four teams, but we organized three teams and extended the discussion in one team into two phases: phase one similar to all other teams; phase two was a more deeply detailed discussion about the choice of the top 7 of scenarios.

There were seven storyboards: 'My Profile', 'Digital Care Record', 'Digital cahier for the family', 'Planning care', 'Ensure care', 'Medical Information', 'Care together'.

The storyboard for 'Digital Care Record' is presented as an example of a pictorial scenario (Fig. 9.6). The Digital Cahier was based on the concept of the care record, which is usually lying somewhere in the house of the client, and where the nurses for the home care organisation write down their actions and observations. The concept of the digital care record was to extend the original care record to a communication device also accessible from a distance, and also available for family to add notes.

A solution for repeatedly having to tell the story to all home care nurses. All visits, treatments and other care moments are, digitally recorded and accessible on distance. They can be inspected easily. The home care nurse can easily change, annotate and add notes.

Carer arrives at the client's home	Client inspects the pages 'digital care record'	Client and member of the family, or voluntary carer
Carer and client read the care record together	Client adds spoken text through the telephone	inspect the 'digital care record' on the special
Carer types the actions performed and the observations of the visit in laptop/PDA		television pages and listen together to the notes.
Carer transmits the data to the system		

Fig. 9.6. Pictorial scenario for '*Digital care record*': the storyboard. The text printed above is the text which was in reality printed on the left hand side, besides the first picture. The texts below the pictures are reproduced from the texts printed on the photos of the storyboard

Results
The results of the discussions concerning the 'Digital care record' are summarized in this section.

The remarks of the participants primarily concerned privacy and security. It was agreed that the data should only be accessible to authorized persons. Most participants were quite positive about the functionalities, but slightly worried that it would take too much time to use the system. The elderly should be able to inspect and amend the care record. Furthermore, use of the care record must ease administrative burdens. The participants would prefer the cahier to show details about things like what to eat and what not, medicine intake, and provide video support for exercises. The frontline voluntary carer should have prominent use of the care record.

Prioritization discussion

The overall discussions of all the 7 functionalities are summarized in this section. The purpose of the prioritization discussion was threefold. First, it was a way to define which functionalities could be missed out, and which not, second, it was a way to structure the complete concept into functionalities belonging together, and third it was a way to force the participants to discuss in a detailed level the scenarios because the teams had to agree on a prioritization.

Table 9.4. Relative importance rating of the Functionalities by the Teams 1, 2, 3 and 4, and joined Teams A (teams 1 and 2 in the second round) and B (Teams 3 and 4 in the second round). 1: least important; 7: most important

Functionalities	Team 1 and 2	Group A	Team 3	Team 4	Group B
My profile	6	7	5	5	4
Digital care record	7	7	5	7	3
Digital cahier for family	3	3	1	4	3
Diary	4	4	5	6	5
Medical information	6	7	2	2	6
Ensure care	2	2	6	1	1
Care together	1	1	7	3	7

The prioritization lists showed an interesting picture. For team 4, mainly consisting of a patient and a frontline voluntary carer, peer contact appeared to be very important. For teams 1 and 2, mainly consisting of voluntary home care nurses, the digital care record and planning instrument was considered more desirable. Obviously, the patient and family prefer peer contact while the professionals prefer planning instruments. The priorities depend on the perspective of the person. The preference of the patient and frontline voluntary carers was related to the wish: "to live our lives as much as possible and not to be aware of sickness all the time". The home care nurses, however, had the perspective of the need for care, and there own organisation of their work. It was concluded that both perspectives were important, and that both types of functionalities should be part of the final concept, to ensure that it would be useful for all parties.

Furthermore, both teams agreed that a number of functionalities, i.e. the care records and the diary, could be joined together in an extended diary, with past history (care record) and future (diary).

Conclusions

It was concluded in the workshop that all the scenarios together constituted a coherent concept, with basically three main elements. First, the scenarios concerning the care records and the diary were considered inseparable. Second, the scenarios for peer group contacts and non-illness issues were considered most important, and possibly the "killer application". Third, the scenario for medical information and for the personal care budget most risky on realism and quality. The discussions were extremely lively and sometimes difficult to finalise.

Therefore, it can be concluded that the pictorial scenarios were very powerful instruments for soliciting the relevant imagery and discussions. Furthermore, it is extremely important to involve the relevant actors, especially in a complex setting, with clients and service providers, because they clearly have very different priorities based on their conception of duty and needs for providing or receiving care.

9.5 Discussion and conclusions

The results from evaluation of the textual scenarios showed that these scenarios were able to provoke remarks at a rather general level, but one that was specific enough to be able to continue the process up to the next level.

The results from evaluation of the pictorial scenarios showed clearly the importance of involving all relevant actors in the discussion, and the power of more detailed discussions. The differences in expectations and desirability become evident due to organizing the groups in such a way that similar actors are grouped together in one team.

Finally, these scenarios proved to be very fruitful for the next phase, conceptualizing further and building a demo.

Unfortunately, there were a few shortcomings. It was not possible for all attendants to attend all three working groups of the workshop for evaluating the textual scenarios. However, because it was organized in such a way that the working groups were equally sized, we could be confident that we did receive reliable results. This was supported by the fact that the discussions in the future workshops later in the process were consistent when it came to soliciting compatible results.

Another shortcoming was that a number of participants missed the workshop for the evaluation of the pictorial scenarios; if these participants had come, the discussions may have been more complete. The size of the focus group was very limited. Therefore, the reliability of the results should be tested with more stakeholders. One other possible flaw is, that financial and technical conditions were hardly considered; an additional analysis is needed.

The design approach adopted in the process, as far as presented here took in total four months. The whole approach was successful for translating requirements and needed functionalities into very clear ideas about the contents of the design. The ethnographic approach in the early phase helped the designers and researchers to gain an insight into the situation. The early phases evidently showed valid information about the problems recognized in the field of home care, and the user needs and limitations of the user groups. The validity of the information is shown by the fact that through the discussions in the workshops, it became clear that the participants recognized all the functionality concepts, especially the communication concept. The different types of comments on the scenarios is is important, because it shows that the evolutionary character of the approach worked effectively.

An important point is the issue of mobility. The scenarios on future technology allow clients to be mobile and communicating to their carers and the rest of the world. Being able to communicate to carers or family while on the move, or performing exercises is particularly important for people who are dependent on others. The visual and audio contact could also provide valuable information to carers or family on their current state of health, particularly when there is a broadband wireless connection. For carers, especially home care nurses, the availability of all relevant information for the people they care for, both organisational information: ie who is coming next, real time changes in their planning and diary, and possibilities for optimizing planning and transferring information about arrival times are most relevant, and medical information about their patients, was considered to be very important. Two items of general interest were found. One that there was a desire of clients for more contact with others and two that ICTcould be used to support the formation of virtual communities. It will be a challenging issue to study and stimulate the formation of virtual communities for clients and their families.

References

Andriessen JHE (2002) Working with groupware: Understanding and evaluating collaboration technology. Springer Verlag, London

Anker FWG van den (2003) Scenarios@work. Developing and evaluating scenarios related to cooperative work mediated by mobile multimedia communications. Ponsen & Looijen BV, Wageningen

Blomberg J, Suchman L, Trigg RH (1996) Reflections on work-oriented design project. Human Computer Interaction 11:237–265

Boehm B (1988) A spiral model of software. Development and Enhancement. IEEE Computer 21:33–44

Bosma ES, Giezen-Biegstraaten LMGJ, Ruiter P de, Spaltman MCM (2001) Arbeid, zorg en technologie. KwaliteitsInstituut voor Toegepaste Thuiszorgvernieuwing (KITTZ)

Carroll JM (1995) Introduction: the scenario perspective on system development. In: Carroll JM (ed). Scenario-based design. Envisioning work and technology in system development. John Wiley & Sons, New York pp 1–10

Damodaran L (1996) User involvement in the systems design process – a practical guide for users. Behaviour and Information Technology 15(6):363–377

Ehn P (1993) Scandinavian Design: On participation and skill. In: Schuler D and Namioka A (eds) Participatory design: principles and practices. Lawrence Erlbaum, Hillsdale

Eijkel G van den, Maas A, Moelaert El-Hadidy F, Zeeuwen E, Pals N (2002) User requirements and business models. (Full proposal B4U for Freeband Impuls)

Engeström Y (1987) Learning by expanding. Orienta-Konsultit, Helsinki

EUROSTAT (2001) Disability and social participation in Europe. Key Indicators, theme 3: Population and social conditions. European Commission

Gould JD, Lewis C (1985), Designing or usability: Key principles and what designers think. Communications of the ACM 28(3):300–311

Grudin J, J Pruitt (2002) Personas, participatory design and product development: An infrastructure for engagement. In: Proceedings Participatory Design Conference, pp 144–161

Hanhart J, Janssen, MGAJ (2000). Telemedicine, een inventarisatie van initiatieven in Nederland. Electronic-highway Platform Nederland, Den Haag

Hoving D, Koning N de, Pas R van de, Dries J (2003) ICT, health and living: An environmental exploration. (TNO-Report – XHome – Freeband)

Holzblatt K, Beyer H (1993) Making customer centered design work for teams. Communications for the ACM 36(10):93–103

Holtzblatt K, Beyer H (1996) Contextual design: Principles and practice. In: Wixon D, Ramey J Field methods casebook for software design. John Wiley & Sons, New York, pp 301–333

ISO 13407 (1999) Human centered design processes for interactive systems. (ISO TC 159/SC4)

Kammen J van (2002) Zorgtechnologie: Kansen voor innovatie en gebruik. Stichting Toekomstbeeld der Techniek, Beweton, Den Haag

Kar E van de(2004) Designing mobile information dervices. An approach for organisations in a value network. (PhD Thesis, Delft University of Technology)

Karat J (1997) Evolving the scope of user-centered design. Communications of the ACM 40(7):33–38

Koning N de, Limonard S, Pas R van der, Steen M (2002) Multimedia applications in the health care sector. (XHOME /D1/2 deliverable)

Kujala S (2003) User involvement: a review of the benefits and challenges. Behaviour and Information Technology, 22(1):1–16

Kuutti K (1995) Work processes: scenarios as preliminary vocabulary. In: Carroll JM (ed) Scenario-based design: Envisioning work and technology in system development. John Wiley & Sons, New York

Kuutti K (1993) Activity theory as a potential framework for human computer interacton research. In: Nielsen J (1993) Usability engineering. Academic Press, London

Roozenburg NFM, Eekels J (1995) Product design: Fundamentals and methods. John Wiley & Sons, Chichester

Salzmann WH (2004) Zorg met ICT. Een strategische verkenning aan de hand van diabetis mellitus. (Rapport for the minister of VWS, June 2004. College voor Zorgverzekeringen, Diemen, volgnummer 24047636)

Sadoski M (1999) Mental imagery in reading: A sampler of some significant studies. (Reading Online: http://readingonline.org/research/Sadoski.html)

Sandhu J et al. (1995) TIDE-TURTLE: System studies and possibilities. (Deliverable 1, SNRU, UNN)

Steen M (2000) Informatie over de gezondheidszorg. In: Brancheanalyse Gezondheidszorg, KPN Research

Wiethoff M, Meulenbroek T, Krevelen E van, Boxtel R van, Guikema M, Rietkerk O van, Stavleu H (2004) Evita. (Final report B4U WP2a, Concept ontwikkeling evita, Deliverable B4U)

10 Well-being and Stress in Mobile and Virtual Work

Peter Richter, Jelka Meyer and Fanny Sommer

Work & Organisational Psychology, Dresden University of Technology, Germany

10.1 Challenge of well-being in mobile virtual work

The workplace has changed dramatically during recent years. Due to the development of information and communication technologies (ICT) interpersonal communication and the exchange of information has become independent from the limitations of time and space. Personal computers, notebooks and removable storage media enable work that used to be confined by the 9-to-5 work day and four office walls, to be conducted anywhere in the "connected" world. Whether on a business trip or at home, all the information one requires is accessible with the stroke of a key or click of a mouse. Moreover, boundless collaboration with other people is becoming possible through the development of "virtual teams." The configuration of virtual teams shows high variation, which makes it difficult to find a common definition or even to develop general guidelines for identifying them. Vartiainen (see chapter 2 in this volume) proposes a model of dimensions for the description of virtual teams, which rates the teams on the dimensions time, space, mode of interaction (use of ICT) and diversity of team members. This model allows virtual teams to be arranged in groups of similar attributes and compared with other types of virtual work.

Additionally, globalisation and an increasing number of corporate mergers result in growing company networks and wide economic relations. In the course of these changing processes, the flexibility and mobility of employees is becoming ever more important. Mobile work is characterized by working more than 10 hours a week in different places other than the head office (see Andriessen 2003). This may include travelling to see customers, providing on-the-spot support, working overtime at home and many more examples.

People who work in these new business structures hence have to cope with perpetually changing workplaces, colleagues and tasks. Many of them are freelancers or have fixed-term contracts. The American sociologist Sennett (1998) describes this development as the „erosion" of the employee–employer relationship and the break-down of the classical occupational biography. Today's young professionals show patchwork careers characterized by numerous job changes and short-term stays in several cities and countries. They have to be dedicated to their current jobs, adaptable to new work environments and proactive in life-long-learning related to their occupations. Similar demands are found in mobile and virtual work structures. The consequences of this ever-changing work process on well-being and stress have not been clearly identified (Sverke et al. 2002).

This chapter will provide an overview of the terms and theories related to current research on mental work load. Next it will discuss investigations on mental strain and well-being in the context of mobile virtual work. Here, main emphasis is placed on the design of tasks, motivation and collaboration in virtual teams as well as the role of operational uncertainty. Lastly, resources for mobile virtual work will be presented and discussed.

10.2 A framework to mental workload and mental strain

In the past 20 years various studies have collected and confirmed comprehensive knowledge on the relationship between organisational context, job demands and the short-term consequences of ones mental work load, as well as on work-related diseases. The effects of people's work on their health and well-being are studied in an interdisciplinary approach, including ergonomics, occupational medicine, and occupational and organisational psychology. In 1946, health was defined by the WHO as a state of complete physical, mental and social well-being and not merely the absence of disease or infirmity. A later definition of health, proposed by the Ottawa Charta in 1986, focuses on an individual's ability and motivation to actively cope with upcoming demands.

The workload-strain model (see Fig. 10.1), draws a distinction between the effects of external sources impinging upon a human being (mental workload) and the effects of mental workload within individuals, depending on their pre-existing conditions (mental strain) (Richter and Hacker 1998). In mobile virtual work, mental workload can be characterized not only as distinct work tasks, working hours, role conflicts, or personal concerns, but also as an increasing amount of necessary organisational and procedural regulations, and less contact with other colleagues.

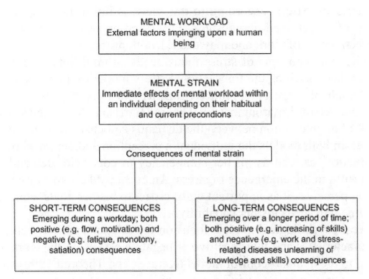

Fig. 10.1. Mental workload, mental strain, and consequences of mental strain (according to ISO EN 10 075)

These factors have an immediate effect on mental strain, which includes an individual's habitual and current preconditions. The consequences of mental strain can be divided into short- and long-term impacts on health and well-being. Depending on the process of mental strain, both positive (e.g. work flow, motivation, further development of the worker's knowledge and skills) and negative consequences (e.g. monotony, mental fatigue, psychosomatic disturbances and illnesses) can occur. In addition, this workload-strain concept in accordance with the international health standard ISO EN 10 075, ("Ergonomic principles related to mental work load" 2002), which defines mental workload and mental strain at work, and identifies its short-term consequences; mental fatigue, monotony, satiation (reluctance to work) and reduced vigilance (see Sect. 10.2.1). Furthermore, this standard includes guidelines for the assessment and design of work conditions. Analytic methods related to mobile and virtual work must be in accordance with this standard, which has been internationally accepted and implemented since its publication in 2002.

According to a new common definition (EUTC, UNICE, UEAPME, CEEP 2004), stress is a state accompanied by physical, psychological or social complaints or dysfunctions, and which results from individuals feeling that their abilities are insufficient for the requirements and expectations placed upon them. This definition is in accordance with stress-concepts that emphasis the interaction between stressors and a person's individual characteristics. Stress, according to this view, is linked to complaints and feelings of anxiety and nervousness. Prolonged exposure to stress reduces the effectiveness of work and may cause health problems.

While some concepts of stress focus on the stimuli impacting an individual, others, such as the transactional stress-model by Lazarus, define it as the result of negative appraisal (Lazarus and Folkman 1984) Alternatively, the Person-Environment-Fit Theory (Harrison 1978) views stress as a result of an interaction between the demands and characteristics of an individual. In both models the individual's perception and appraisal of a special situation, as well as his/her competency to cope with demands, play crucial roles in the emergence of stress. An event is likely to cause stress if a person perceives it as important with respect to his/her goals, while at the same time it exceeds his/her capability.

Several psychological models focus on the relationship between certain job characteristics and their positive or negative effects on the worker. According to the demand-control model (Karasek and Theorell 1990) stress is less likely to occur when a job offers a high degree of autonomy and decision latitude. Likewise, such job characteristics are also correlated to workers' well-being and their development of skills and knowledge (see Hacker 2003). Additionally, a basic feature of work is that it consists of goal-oriented actions. Goals are important for an individual to anticipate special results that should be achieved, to plan courses of action in order to achieve them and to compare realised results with intended ones. As emphasised in the action-regulation theory (Hacker 2003), actions are controlled by such goals, and the setting of specific goals has a motivational function for the completion of work. This theory therefore agrees with what has been said above, i.e. that because goals play an important role for every action, and hence for work as well, stress is likely to occur if a person fears that he/she cannot meet the goals of his/her work, in particular if the achievement of these goals has special importance to the individual, his team, or his employer. (See Sect. 10.2.2).

In contrast to this view, the vitamin model (Warr 1987) postulates curvilinear interrelations between a worker's health and enriched job demands (e.g. task and skill variety, amount of cooperation and communication, decision latitude, autonomy and use of qualification and skills). Enriched job demands are thus believed to contain the risk of overload and therefore, stress. For example, only a certain range of decision latitude can be used optimally in the workplace; if the decision latitude is too high it becomes difficult to keep all available alternatives in mind.

Thus far the impact of virtual and mobile teamwork on employees' well-being has not been investigated thoroughly. Of the studies that do exist, Borg and Kristensen (1999) report that among travelling salespeople poor mental health is associated with greater perceived psychological demands, longer working hours, more customers and the amount of extra work. Furthermore, a few studies on the impact of telework on an employee's health and well-being have been published. Montreuil and Lippel (2003) observe positive perceptions of mental strain in telework, despite problems with the design of home-based work stations, long working hours and social isolation. Unfavourable job tasks (e.g. those with low decision latitude and a low amount of cooperation) are correlated with monotony and feelings of social isolation, yet the level of perceived stress is greater for more favourable work tasks (Treier 2003). Stressors and mental strain seem to be a function of specific social and environmental factors and not dependent on the mode of work, i.e. telework vs. office-based work (Konradt et al. 2003). These findings on telework, however, cannot be applied to work in virtual teams and organisations without taking caution, considering that job conditions are different for these different working structures. Specifically, members of virtual teams and organisations do not necessarily work at home, and furthermore they usually need to work in several teams that exist only for a limited period of time.

To avoid the development of stress and stress-related consequences, and thus to ensure the workers' health and well-being, work and working conditions need to be designed such that both under- and overloading the worker is avoided. Therefore knowledge of conditions that cause fatigue and stress at work is imperative. On the other hand, work does not only contain stressors, but also resources, i.e. work conditions or characteristics of the individual that can be used to attain goals (Sonnentag and Frese 2003). Resources can be separated into three distinct types; organisational (e.g. task variety), social (e.g. social support by others, work-life balance) and personal (e.g. skills, knowledge, optimistic appraisal of situations). Investigations on the resources of mobile virtual work are presented in section 3 of this chapter.

10.2.1 Summary

- Mental workload leads to mental strain which in turn can cause positive (flow, motivation) or negative (fatigue, monotony, and satiation) consequences
- The state of stress is characterized by physical, psychological or social complaints or dysfunctions. Stress results from individuals feeling unable to bridge the gap between their abilities and the expectations placed on them

10.3 Task-related and organisational factors of mental workload

10.3.1 Individual work in virtual settings

Mental workload, mental strain and their effects are strongly associated with working conditions and task characteristics (e.g. ergonomic design of the workplace and decision latitude, respectively). In this section we will provide empirical evidence that this is particularly apparent in virtual settings. These factors can be assessed by means of objective and subjective tools. Objective work analysis tools, such as structured observation, are applied to assess work conditions and task characteristics independently from the workers' perceptions and interpretations (Semmer et al. 2004). The problem of observing the mental and internal requirements of work tasks is addressed through the so-called observational interview, which combines structured observations and interview techniques. This method can be used to assess important stressors and resources at work as well as the workers' personal perceptions and interpretations. This applies to work conditions, job demands as well as processes and consequences of mental strain. The use of both independent observations of task demands and subjective analysis tools provide a more complete and valid estimation, as compared to the exclusive use of subjective data about perceived demands and well-being.

The authors developed a pilot study to measure the differences between tasks in virtual and non-virtual work, with respect to task characteristics and consequences of mental strain. Their findings were based on the observation of 18 virtual teams in Research & Development, IT and Human Resources departments from Great Britain.[1] Members of these teams worked from various locations, co-operated by means of ICT. Some of them took part in temporally limited projects; others had been working together over a long-term period of time.

Furthermore, this study collected data on perceived mental strain from subjects working in 55 comparable jobs in public service and 19 jobs in production. In order to compare their findings from the interviews on job contents with the findings from these traditional work places, the authors used a sub-sample form Debitz (2004).

These teams' task characteristics were evaluated by means of the REBA (Richter et al. 1998). It is based on the Task Diagnosis System (TDS, Hacker 2003) and is used to analyse work tasks from the perspective of the

---

[1] We would like to thank Fred Zijlstra, University of Surrey/Guilford, for his kind support and cooperation in this project.

action-regulation theory. First, information about the job is collected by document analyses and observational interviews, and then the work description is evaluated with respect to 22 task characteristics. Eight of these characteristics play a significant role in predicting the following short-term negative consequences of mental strain: mental fatigue, monotony, mental satiation and stress. The perceived workload was estimated by using an interval-scaled questionnaire for fatigue, monotony, satiation and stress (BMS, Plath and Richter 1984). Additionally, stress, in the form of negative appraisal (see 2.2), and other forms of mental strain were assessed by means of other questionnaires (Job Stress Survey, Spielberger 1994; BMS-questionnaire, Plath and Richter 1984; Rockstuhl 2002).

The findings of the objective and subjective work analyses were compared to data gathered from production and public service jobs. Table 10.1 shows the results.

Table 10.1. Objective job demands, fatigue and stress in virtual teams compared to non-virtual productive and public service activities (Debitz 2004)

TBS/REBA-Scale[a]	Productive jobs 19 activities M	Public service 55 activities M	Virtual teams 18 activities M	Significant differences
Sequential completeness	3.6	3.7	3.7	n.s.
Organisational tasks	3.5	3.6	4.4	$p < 0.001$
Kind of cooperation	4.1	4.7	8.2	$p < 0.001$
Responsibility	3.0	3.7	3.9	$p < 0.01$
Learning requirements	1.9	3.2	3.8	$p < 0.001$
Level of participation	3.5	2.6	6.5	$p < 0.001$
Length of work cycle	4.9	5.4	6.3	$p < 0.001$
Amount of cooperation	3.2	3.7	4.1	$p < 0.05$
BMS fatigue[b]	56..9	53.0	50..5	$p < 0.05$
BMS stress[b]	55.7	56.4	52..2	$p < 0.001$

[a] Higher values stand for enriched job demands
[b] T-scale: T=50+10z, higher values stand for higher levels of fatigue or stress

Compared to the non-virtual activities, the assessed virtual teams have more enriched job characteristics: In virtual teams more organisational tasks and functions are transferred to the members, group work was, to a greater extent, organised by the group itself, members faced significantly more learning demands and responsibilities and were more involved in planning processes. They exhibited a greater amount of cooperation, which took place mainly by means of ICT, and furthermore, their work consisted of longer work cycles. Virtual and mobile work places are more flexible and require intensive interaction with ICT tools. Dynamic work environments, temporally limited projects and network organisations with self-organised teamwork thus cause enriched job demands among virtual teams and organisations. On the other hand, higher levels of stress and lower levels of fatigue were observed in the virtual teams. This corresponds with Montreuil and Lippel's (2003) findings that perceived stress tends to be greater for more favourable, or more enriched job tasks. Measures of mental strain were further correlated to job demands, as shown in table 10.2.

Table 10.2. Correlations between measures of mental strain (JSS, BMS) and job demands in virtual teams

Job demand scale	Job Stress Survey (Spielberger 1994)	BMS monotony (Plath and Richter 1984)	BMS stress (Plath and Richter 1984)
Sequential completeness	.59*		.60*
Organisational tasks	.56*		
Responsibility			.69*
Learning requirements		-.83*	
Level of participation		-.76*	
Length of work cycle		-.90*	
Amount of cooperation			.69[a]

N=19; Significance [a] $p<.05$ (age, gender and working time are partialised out)

High levels of learning requirements, a high degree of participation, and low degree of task repetition (length of work cycle) are correlated with reduced monotony. On the other hand, contrary to existing results of work analyses, rising sequential completeness and organisational demands as well as an increasing level of responsibility and an increasing amount of cooperation were all associated with significantly increased symptoms of job stress in the assessed sample.

Thus, these results support the curvilinear hypotheses of enriched job demands in the vitamin model (Warr 1987): e.g. highly demanding tasks in the virtual environment are associated with stress symptoms and skill utilization, but are also characterised by much higher levels of cognitive and social demands compared to classical co-located work places.

These results can only be referred to as preliminary, and at this point no definitive conclusion of the impact of virtual and mobile work on workers' health and well-being can be drawn. The present studies mainly indicate that certain characteristics of the work, tasks and the team may be associated with ones well-being and health. Thus, further research is necessary to detect what specific conditions of virtual and mobile teamwork may result in risks to the workers' physical and psychological health.

Summary

- Work in virtual teams has more enriched job characteristics (e.g. amount of organisational tasks, learning requirements and the level of participation) than traditional jobs
- Contrary to existing results of work analysis, enriched job characteristics in the context of virtual teams are associated with increased symptoms of job stress
- There could be a curvilinear interrelation between health and enriched job demands (Vitamin model, Warr 1987)

10.3.2 Aspects of collaboration in mobile virtual work

The decision to create mobile and/or virtual work teams is generally based on financial factors, such as economic needs, company mergers or expansionist policies. Virtual and mobile teams enable organisations to connect experts and exchange knowledge by eliminating the barriers of time and space. Most companies expect excellent performance from virtual teams, because such teams are designed to consist of competent people, able to work at locations with optimal conditions on tasks that are often challenging and motivating (for an overview see Andriessen 2003, Furst et al. 2004, Hertel et al. 2005, Vartiainen et al. 2004).

Virtual tools make working life easier and much more difficult at the same time. Technologically-mediated communication allows for cooperation between people located all over the world on one task. Neither the location of a person nor their profession, company or nationality has an impact on membership in a virtual team. These teams may exhibit many advantages compared to traditional organisational structures, like knowledge sharing, building of a common culture between different sides, as well as improved organisational performance. However, difficulties in planning and co-ordination across time zones and cultural differences are barriers to successful performance in virtual teams. Often team members don't know what their colleagues are working on or where synergies could relax the workload. Confusion, frustration and stress could be the resulting consequences for all parties involved.

The following sections deal with factors of teamwork and motivation as well as how these factors affect stress and which coping strategies can be used.

Quality of teamwork

Dispersed locations, asynchronous timetables, and cultural differences call for more precise coordination of teamwork by means of information and communication technology (e.g. telephone, e-mail, internet and groupware). Andriessen (2003) defines coordination as the use of mechanisms to manage interdependence among activities performed to achieve a specific goal. Such mechanisms would involve the allocation, planning and integration of individuals' and groups' various tasks.

Virtual teams often can achieve results comparable to those of face-to-face co-workers, although it generally takes longer and requires more structured interaction. Additionally, misunderstandings may arise faster due to language and culture barriers, and especially due to the loss of social cues in computer mediated communication. Miscommunications can be avoided through common-sense application of information and communication media. For example, giving a colleague a call, rather than writing an angry email is the appropriate way to respond to a setback. Direct conversation, even on the phone, solves problems better than asynchronous communication. The implementation of communicative rules may help to reduce such problems as well. While interaction in virtual teams is often more task-oriented than personal, information about team members' individual abilities, attitudes and preferences help to develop trust within the team. Both forms of conversation are positively associated with high performance and job satisfaction in virtual teams.

In the years that virtual work first started to emerge, it was assumed that workers in virtual settings need very little guidance. Some virtual teams were 'self-regulated', meaning that they only had a team representative, or no team leader at all. In recent years, however, it was realised that virtual teams in fact need strong leadership (Hertel et al. 2005). Therefore, team organisation, encouragement of self-organisation, delegation of tasks and working arrangements, and deadlines are important for the success of virtual teams (Furst et al. 2004).

Motivation

Stress within an organisation does not necessarily influence the performance of its employees (Sonnentag and Frese 2003). A possible moderating factor in this scenario could be the motivation of the virtual team, or more precisely, the setting of goals.

Setting common goals has become a popular method of leading and motivating employees even when they are working in dispersed teams (Hertel et al. 2004). The success of this method is due to the simple but effective way in which goals improve performance. In particular, Locke and Latham (2004) did well-substantiated research on how goals should be set and how they affect the amount of effort people put into their work. According to their research, important attributes of goals are content and intensity. Goal contents can range from vague ("Sell cars") to specific ("Sell ten cars by the end of the month"). Specific and measurable criteria for the achievement of these goals facilitate the evaluation of employees' individual performances. Setting difficult but realistic goals may also lead to higher performance. Ranging from easy ("Sell two cars") to moderate ("Sell five cars") and impossible ("Sell 70 cars"), the perceived difficulty of a specific goal varies among individuals. However, more than 400 studies prove that there is a positive correlation between goal difficulty and task performance. According to Latham and Locke (1991), this outcome is mainly due to the fact that people adjust their level of effort to the difficulty of the task at hand.

Commitment and capability are essential prerequisites for the successful completion of a set goal. Determining and achieving common goals becomes difficult, however, when team members work in different locations and time zones. The result for many workers may be lessened commitment to team goals. Whereas high commitment leads to higher performance, according to Erez and Zidon (1984) less committed people give up their goals earlier, thus exhibiting a lower performance. Affective commitment to the organisation may also represent an important management technique, especially in such dispersed work settings (Allen and Meyer 1990). Up to now little empirical data for mobile virtual work was available. The meta-analysis (Meyer et al. 2002) shows that affective commitment has an important mediating effect between job characteristics and health outcomes. High affective commitment is significantly correlated to broad decision latitudes, well-being, reduced emotional exhaustion, high job satisfaction and innovation. Additionally, affective commitment interacts immediately with psycho-physiological activation processes, thus determining ones basic commitment to his or her assignment (Meyer et al. 2002).

By influencing ones choices, effort, and persistence, setting goals can affect the direction, intensity and duration of ones actions, respectively (Latham and Locke 1991). In specific, goals tend to orient people's actions toward relevant tasks, while reducing the occurrence of irrelevant ones. In the context of mobile and virtual work, goal trajectories may help employees to structure their work, especially when no supervisor is available. Likewise, as mentioned above, people adjust their effort to the difficulty of their goal. The adaptation of ones efforts and energies to meet the demands of ones environment is a basic tenet of human nature. People are capable and willing labourers, when, for example, a project deadline approaches or a customer needs help urgently. Indeed, when there are no temporal or spatial limits to the working day, as often occurs in mobile or virtual scenarios, one runs the risk of working too much. Long hours of intense work may thus result in short and long-term consequences for ones health and well-being.

Investigation on motivation and teamwork in virtual teams

The authors conducted a study to investigate the effects that motivation and quality of teamwork have on performance and job satisfaction in virtual teams. Sixty-four employees of sixteen virtual teams, in the computer services and consulting fields, filled out an internet questionnaire. The survey measured team performance by asking team members to rate quality and quantity of goal achievement as well as adherence to time and financial limits. Job satisfaction was assed using a scale from Baillod and Semmer (1994), which includes satisfaction and resignation. Resignation to the work conditions is closely related to turnover intentions of employees. Turnover intentions and behaviour is known as an important indicator for stressful work situations (Griffeth et al. 2000).

To measure perceived *quality of teamwork* the authors adapted a short version of the TeamPuls instrument (Wiedemann et al. 2000), which was specifically designed for virtual teams. The modified version revealed good psychometric qualities (Cronbachs alpha 0.87 – 0.92; Engel 2004; Meyer et al. 2004) for its five dimensions:

- *Goal- & performance orientation*
  This dimension assesses the way goals are set in the virtual team, the supervision of goal achievement, and its effects on performance.

- *Commitment & responsibility*
  Due to dispersed locations in virtual teams, the responsibility and commitment to common goals is a crucial factor for successful teamwork. This dimension also includes mutual support and self-initiative.
- *Communication within the team*
  This dimension asks for the intensity and openness of team communication as an indicator of inter-personal relations and the handling of conflicts.
- *Team organisation*
  This dimension includes decision making processes, the delegation of tasks, and the organisation of meetings.
- *Team leadership*
  This dimension assesses the way the team leader supports goal-orientation within the team and represents the virtual team to others.

As these results suggest (table 10.3), many aspects of teamwork contribute to performance and job satisfaction (satisfaction and resignation). Regression analyses revealed the importance of team organisation for both team performance and satisfaction (both beta=.77, p<0.001, R^2=.59).

Table 10.3. Motivation, quality of teamwork, perceived team performance and job satisfaction (satisfaction, resignation) in 16 virtual teams (Engel 2004)

		Perceived team performance	Job satisfaction	
			Satisfaction	Resignation
Quality of teamwork (Wiedemann et al. 2000)	Goal- & performance orientation	.48[b]	.73[b]	n.s.
	Commitment & responsibility	.73[b]	.71[b]	-.60[b]
	Communication within the team	.64[b]	.76[b]	-.63[b]
	Team organisation	.77[b]	.77[b]	-.53[b]
	Team leadership	.60[b]	.68[b]	-.57[b]
Motivation (Hertel et al. 2004)	Valence	n.s.	n.s.	n.s.
	Instrumentality	n.s.	n.s.	n.s.
	Self-efficacy	.48[a]	.57[b]	n.s.
	Trust	n.s.	.59[b]	-.54[a]

N=16 teams; Significance [a]p<.05 [b]p<01

The organisation of mobile and virtual teams can be supported in different ways: Face-to-face-meetings (especially in the beginning of a project) should be used to clarify common tasks, responsibilities and decision-making powers. This might enable every team member to react adequately in situations, where decisions are needed and consultation with the team leader or other team members is not possible. Despite of the development of ICT, mobile workers do not have access to all information all the time when they are travelling. Therefore, face-to-face meetings should be organised more frequently in virtual teams than in traditional teams.

Resignation of team members could be predicted by reduced communication within the team (beta=-0.63, p<0.01, R^2=.40). Thus, informal communication, social support and adequate conflict management within the virtual team could have a positive effect on overall job satisfaction. Communication skills should be trained with respect to the context of virtual teams (e.g. use of ICT in conflict situations).

Current studies (Tomaschek 2005 unpublished data) suggest significant correlations between dimensions of TeamPuls and physical as well as mental health in virtual teams. These results point at the impact of quality of team work for health in virtual teams.

The concept of *Motivation* used in this study follows the VIST-model developed by Hertel (2004). This model is derived from general management principles of effective work and was built on the Expectancy x Value concepts (see Vroom 1964), which explain motivational processes in individual work as well as in more complex situations (Karau and Williams 1993). These motivational aspects can be further explained as follows:

- *Valence* refers to the subjective evaluation of team goals (Cronbach alpha: 0.82).Virtual team members often work in multiple teams with conflicting goals. Each team member, therefore, must evaluate these goals of her-/himself. The greater the number of conflicting goals is the lower the valence component, and the lower the team member's motivation.
- *Instrumentality* is defined as ones perceived importance or contribution to the group outcome. (0.78). The more important one perceives his or her contribution to be, the higher his or her motivation to achieve team goals. Limited or absent face-to-face contact within virtual teams, however, may lead to feelings of anonymity or a lack of social acknowledgement, which could cause low perceived instrumentality and hence low motivation (Karau and Williams 1993). Yet, if contributions go unrecognized, who keeps track of decreased effort and motivation? Under such circumstances, performance motivation could decrease considerably even when people value the team goals highly.
- *Self-Efficacy* is ones perceived capability to accomplish the required task. (0.69). Bandura's core concept of self-efficacy, which refers to task-specific self-confidence, has been found to have powerful motiva-

tional effects on task performance (Bandura 1997). When people think that they are not able to accomplish their part of the team task, their motivation is low, and no other motivational factor can compensate for the lack of self-confidence in ones ability.

- *Trust* refers to team members' expectations their efforts will be reciprocated by other team members (interpersonal trust) and that the electronic support system works reliably (technological trust; 0.89). Trust can be seen as a key variable for motivation in virtual and mobile work (Järvenpää and Leitner 1998, Konradt and Schmook 1999, Büssing et al. 2003). It is a determining factor for the effectiveness of activities requiring coordinated action.

The aim of the current study was to test the influence of the four motivational aspects 'valence', 'instrumentality', 'self-efficacy', and 'trust,' on performance and job satisfaction under virtual conditions (see table 10.3). At first, the positive relation of self-efficacy on perceived performance and satisfaction in virtual teams should be emphasized. Self-efficacy in virtual teams can be supported by a detailed preparation of team members for their task as well as constructive feedback and support from the team leader. Further on, self-esteem and self-efficacy are known to have a positive impact on individual's health and well-being (Sonnentag 2002; Tomaschek unpublished data 2005). These results are in line with the investigated negative correlation between self-efficacy and resignation of virtual team members. Additionally, the interpersonal trust could be an important factor to decrease resignation among the team members. Regular face-to-face meetings and frequent opportunities for informal communication via ICT are essential to support this kind of trust.

Summary

- Dispersed locations, asynchronous timetables, and cultural differences call for more precise coordination of teamwork by means of information and communication technology
- Goal-setting can be successful method of leading and motivating employees especially when they are working in dispersed teams.
- The quality of teamwork has an important impact not only on performance, but also on job satisfaction in virtual teams
- Self-efficacy as an aspect of motivation has an influence on team performance as well as reduction of resignation

10.3.3 The role of resources

Resources can be defined as "objects, conditions, personal characteristics, and energies that are either themselves valued for survival, directly or indirectly, or that serve as a means of achieving these ends" (Hobfoll 1998). They refer to conditions within the work situation and to individual characteristics that can be used to attain goals. Individual coping strategies, social support, and work-life-balance may enable people to meet the demands of mobile virtual work.

Coping strategies and social support

Studies on individual coping strategies are mainly based on the investigations of Lazarus und Folkman (1984). At work and in private life, persons are constantly confronted with "changing cognitive and behavioural efforts to manage specific external / or internal demands that are appraised as taxing or exceeding the resources of the person" (p 141). The demands of mobile virtual work spring from attempting to the coordination of labour, the distance to other team members, or perpetually changing tasks.

Moreover, through these studies the crucial role of individual appraisal of the situation in the stress process became more apparent. There are two identifiable steps to the appraisal process. First, an individual must decide whether a stimulus is irrelevant, positive, or negative for ones health and well-being). Stressful appraisals may be harmless, threatening or challenging, but by the second appraisal, individuals must decide how to cope with the perceived stress. Lazarus and Folkman differentiate between problem-focused and emotion-focused coping strategies. Problem-focused coping includes problem-solving behaviour that directly targets the stressor, other aspects of the environment, or ones own behaviour. Possible examples of this type of problem-solving involve the implementation of communication rules after multiple misunderstandings, taking time to educate team members about organisational systems, or conducting face-to-face meetings for team building. Emotion-focused coping refers to attempts to manage cognition and emotion directly. Avoiding situations like missing a team chat, suppressing thoughts on work, or emotional blunting are among some of the many emotion-focused coping strategies. In a sample of 274 white collar public sector employees, Guppy and Weatherston (1997) have found that mental health and well-being is positively related to problem-focused coping, while emotion-focused coping was often found to be associated with poorer well-being.

In addition to individual coping strategies, social support, which is known to be negatively related to stressors at work (Visweswaran et al.

1999), is likely to be a great help in mobile and virtual settings as well. Social support consists of resources provided by others, e.g. superiors, colleagues, friends, and family, and includes emotional, informational, and instrumental support. Especially in the context of mobile virtual work, where team members are at risk of feeling isolated or anonymous, social support plays a crucial role in employees' well-being.

Work-life balance

The balance between work and private life has become an important issue in the context of mobile virtual work. In the 1990s, the development of information and communication technologies was closely connected to the promise of a life where people choose their own workplaces and have increased leisure time. Satisfaction in work and non-work life has always been the main goal. However, in spite of multifunctional support by ICT, work life *imbalance* may have increased during recent years.

The determinants of work-life balance are located both at work and in the home. At work, people deal with the demands of information overload, quick customer response time, the need to be constantly available to customers, and an increased pace of change. Guest (2002) argues that the demands of work are beginning to dominate private life as well and are having a negative impact on people's work-life balance. The resulting imbalance can be seen in the insidious way work assignments seep into family and leisure time. Whereas the demands of private life, such as having children or elderly parents to take care of may take their toll on individuals' attentions, motivation, and performance during working hours. Likewise, personal factors play an important role in perceiving this work-life balance. Guest (2002) suggests that an individual's personal characteristics, including ambition, work involvement, level of energy and capacity for coping with pressures of competing demands, all influence ones orientation toward work versus private life. Also age, gender and stage of career should be considered in work-life balance research.

Some studies (Hill et al. 1998) of telework showed that home-based work increases flexibility, which has a positive influence on both work and personal/family life. Further investigations by Johansson (2002) distinguish between people with reported work-life balance and imbalance in health and well-being among the Swedish work force. More precisely, workers that reported having a work-life imbalance also complained of more gastrointestinal and cardiac problems, more mood and sleep disturbances, and more pain and headaches. It should be considered, however, that work-life balance can have both a subjective and objective meaning and measurement (e.g. cultural aspects of working hours). Judging balance versus imbalance will vary across different circumstances and individuals (Guest 2002).

These investigations show clearly the need for practicable work-life-balance strategies also in the context of mobile and virtual work. Friedman et al. (1998) recommend to companies and policy makers that they set clear occupational goals with respect to individuals' priorities, appreciate employees as individuals with a 'work life' and a 'non-work life', and design jobs due to these changing demands. Conceivable for mobile virtual work are jobs with fixed home office days to relax from travelling ICT tools.

Summary

- Mental health and well-being is positively related to problem-focused coping, while emotion-focused coping was often found to be associated with poorer well-being
- Social support is a source to solve problems in mobile and virtual settings
- Home-based work as an important aspect of work-life-balance needs strategies to separate 'work life' and 'non-work life'

10.4 Conclusions

The consideration of different sources of stress and well-being within the context of mobile and virtual work seems to be a promising approach to stress research. At first, increasing job and learning demands as well as rising amounts of participation and co-operation in comparison to non-virtual and non-mobile work speak for high potential of health and personality promotion (Hacker 2003). Up to now, these findings were only connected to decreasing stress perceptions and healthy cardiovascular behaviour (Rau 2004). Our results, however, point to a curvilinear relation between enriched job demands and mental health. This 'over enrichment' may cause excessive demands by requiring too many qualifications and skills and through informational and social overload. Stress and fatigue are the consequences. With regard to long-term consequences of mental strain, longitudinal studies in mobile virtual work are essential for ongoing research, although the adaptation of existing instruments and the development of new methods will be necessary.

The number of empirical investigations on the influence of motivation and collaboration in virtual teams on mental health are small. Associations between motivation and quality of teamwork with performance of the team can be scientifically proven. Collaboration within the team is an important requirement for achieving success. But, co-ordination of tasks, setting common goals and communication via ICT require a lot of engagement and time. Increased demands and stress are likely to occur in such teams. Therefore, the role of stress as a mediator or moderator and possible resources in realising virtual teamwork should be investigated.

It is the authors' viewpoint, however, that job design should not attempt the goal of decreasing job demands and complexity in mobile virtual work by reducing the operational uncertainty of such systems. Rather employees' competence to cope with its precarious situation should be improved. Christensen (1997) characterised this stressful situation with a nautical image:

"When winds push against the sail, the sailboat tips to one side and looks off-balance. Despite the precarious leaning of the sailboat, however, it is in perfect balance."

References

Allen NJ, Meyer JP (1990) The measurement and antecedents of affective, continuance and normative commitment to the organization. Journal of Occupational Psychology 63:1–18

Andriessen JHE (2003) Working with groupware. Understanding and evaluating collaboration technology. Springer, Berlin Heidelberg New York

Baillod J, Semmer N (1994) Fluktuation und berufsverläufe bei computerfachleuten. Zeitschrift für Arbeits- und Organisationspsychologie 38:152–163

Bandura A (1977) Self-efficacy: Toward a unifying theory of behavioral change. Psychological Review 84:191–215

Borg V, Kristensen TS (1999) Psychosocial work environment and mental health among travelling salespeople. Work and Stress 13:132–143

Büssing A, Drodofsky A, Hegendörfer K (2003) Telearbeit und Qualität des Arbeitslebens. Hogrefe, Goettingen

Christensen K (1997) Countervailing human resource trends in family-sensitive firms. In: Barker K, Christensen K (eds) Contingent work. American employment relations in transition. Cornell University Press, London

Debitz U (2004) Die gestaltung des merkmalen des arbeitssystems und ihre auswirkungen auf beanspruchungsprozesse. Schriften zur Arbeits-, Betriebs- und Organisationspsychologie. Dr. Kovac, Hamburg

Engel A (2004) Anpassung und einsatz von messverfahren zu teamqualität und motivation bei virtuellen teams. Diploma thesis, Dresden University of Technology

Erez M, Zidon I (1984) Effects of goal acceptance on the relationship of goal difficulty to performance. Journal of Applied Psychology 69:69–78

EUTC, UNICE, UEAPME, CEEP (2004) Framework agreement on work-related stress.   http://europa.eu.int/comm/employment_social/news/2004/oct/stress_agreement_en.html visited on 20 May 2005

Friedman SD, Christensen P, Degroot J (2000) Work and life: The end of zero-sum situation. Harvard Business Review on Work and Life Balance, Boston, pp 1–29

Furst SA, Reeves M, Rosen, B, Blackburn RS (2004) Managing the life cycle of virtual teams. Academy of Management Executive 18:6–15

Griffeth, RW, Hom PW, Gaertner S (2000) A meta-analysis of antecedents and correlates of employee turnover: Update, moderator tests, and research implications for the next millennium. Journal of Management 26:463–488

Guest DE (2002) Perspectives on the study of work-life balance. Social Science Information 41:255–279

Guppy A, Weatherston L (1997) Coping strategies, dysfunctional attitudes and psychological well-being in white collar public sector employees. Work & Stress 11:58–67

Hacker W (2003) Action regulation theory: A practical tool for the design of modern work processes? European Journal of Work and Organizational Psychology 12:105–130

Harrison RV (1978) Person-environment fir and job stress. In: Cooper CL, Paye R (eds.) Stress at work. Wiley, New York, pp 175–205

Hertel G, Geister S, Konradt U. (2005) Managing virtual teams: A review of current empirical research. Human Resource Management Review 15:69–95

Hertel G, Konradt U, Orlikowski B (2004) Managing distance by interdependence: Goal setting, task interdependence and team-based rewards in virtual teams. European Journal of Work and Organizational Psychology 13:1–28

Hill EJ, Miller BC, Weiner SP, Colihan J (1998) Influences of virtual office on aspects of work and work/life balance. Personnel Psychology 51:667–683

Hobfoll SE (1998) Stress, culture, and community: The psychology and physiology of stress. Plenum, New York

ISO EN DIN 10 075 (2002). Mental work load. Beuth-Verlag, Berlin

Johannson G (2002) Work-life balance: The case of Sweden in the 1990s. Social Science Information 41:303–317

Järvenpää S, Leitner D (1998) Communication and trust in global virtual teams. Organization Science 10:791–815

Karasek R, Theorell T (1990) Healty work. Stress, produktivity and the reconstuction of working life. Basic Books, New York

Karau SJ, Williams KD (1993) Understanding individual motivation in groups: The collective effort model. In: Turner ME (ed.) Groups at work: Advances in theory and research. Lawrence Erlbaum Associates, Mahwah, pp 113–141

Konradt U, Hertel G, Schmook R (2003) Quality of management by objectives, task-related stressors, and non-task-related stressors as predictors of stress and job satisfaction among teleworkers. European Journal of Work and Organizational Psychology 12:61–79

Konradt U, Schmook R (1999) Telearbeit – Belastungen und beanspruchungen im längsschnitt. Zeitschrift für Arbeits- und Organisationspsychologie 43:142–150

Latham GP, Locke EA (1991) Self-regulation through goal setting. Organizational Behavior and Human Decision Processes 50:212–247

Lazarus RS, Folkman, S (1984) Stress, appraisal, and coping. Springer, Berlin Heidelberg New York

Locke EA, Latham GP (2004) What should we do about motivation theory? Six recommendations for the twenty-first century. Academy of Management Review 29:388–403

Meyer J, Engel A, Richter P (2004). Motivation und teamqualität in virtuellen teams. In: Engelien M Meissner K (eds) Virtuelle organisation und neue medien. Josef Eul Verlag, Cologne

Meyer JP, Stanley DJ, Herscovitch L, Topolnytsky L (2002) Affective, continuance, and normative commitment to the organization: A meta-analysis of antecedents, correlates, and consequences. Journal of Vocational Behavior 61:20–52

Montreuil S, Lippel K (2003) Telework and occupational health: a Quebec empirical study and regulatory implications. Safety Science 41:339–358

Plath HE, Richter P (1984) Ermüdung, monotonie, sättigung, stress. Verfahren zur skalierten erfassung erlebter beanspruchungsfolgen (BMS). Hogrefe, Goettingen

Rau R (2004) Job strain or healthy work: A question of task design. Journal of Occupational Health Psychology 9:322–338

Richter P, Hacker W (1998) Belastung und beanspruchung. Asanger, Heidelberg

Richter P, Hemmann E, Pohland A (1998) Objective task analysis and the prediction of mental workload: Results of the application of an action-oriented software tool (REBA). In: Wiethoff M, Zijlstra FRH (eds) New approaches on modern problems in work psychology. WORC Report 99.10.001. Tilburg University, Tilburg.

Rockstuhl T (2002) BMS-II Modifikationen und beanspruchungsmessung in call centers. Diploma thesis, Dresden University of Technology

Sennett R (1998) The corrosion of character. W. W. Norton, New York

Semmer N, Grebner S, Elfering A (2004) Beyond self-report: using observational, physiological, and situation-based measures in research on occupational stress. In: Perrewe PL, Ganster DC (eds) Emotional and physiological processes and positive intervention strategies Elsivier, Amsterdam, pp 205–263

Sonnentag S (2002) Performance, well-being, and self-regulation. In: Sonnentag S (ed.): The psychological management of individual performance: A handbook in the psychology of management in organizations. Wiley, Chichester, pp 405-423

Sonnentag S, Frese M (2003) Stress in organizations. In: Borman WC, Ilgen DR, Klimoski RJ (eds) Comprehensive handbook of psychology, vol 12: Industrial and Organizational Psychology. Wiley, New York, pp 453–491

Spielberger CD, Reheise EC (1994) Job stress in university, corporate, and military personnel. International Journal of Stress Management 1:19–31

Sverke M, Hellgren J, Näswall K (2002) No security: A meta-analysis and review of job insecurity and its consequences. Journal of Occupational and Health Psychology 7:242–264

Tomaschek A (2005) Commitment in virtuellen Teams. Diploma thesis. Dresden University of Technology

Treier M (2003) Belastungs- und beanspruchungsmomente bei der teleheimarbeit. Zeitschrift für Arbeits- und Organisationspsychologie 47:24–35

Vartiainen M, Hakonen M, Kokko N (2004) Degree of virtuality, the well-being and performance in dispersed teams and projects. (Paper presented at the 8th International Workshop on teamworking, Trier)

Viswesvaran C, Sanchez JI & Fisher J (1999) The role of social support in the process of work stress: A meta-analysis. Journal of Vocational Behavior 54:314–334

Vroom VE (1964) Work and motivation. Wiley, New York

Warr P (1987) Well-being and unemployment. University Press, Oxford

Wiedemann J, von Watzdorf E, Richter P (2000) TeamPuls® - Internetgestützte teamdiagnose.(Final report by Dresden University of Technology)

11 Building Scenarios for a Globally Distributed Corporation

Veli-Pekka Niitamo

Centre for Knowledge and Innovation Research, Nokia, Finland

11.1 Challenge of global working

Nokia R&D operations are located in 59 different sites in 14 countries and in ten different time zones, which cover 24 hours of constant daily R&D activity. Nokia R&D functions employ some 21 000 engineers globally. Besides this, most product creation processes integrate several partner, subcontractor and client sites. On average, each product creation process involves seven sites in three countries and time zones. Current sites are responsible for predefined product process phases and are developed as specific competence centres to carry out these product creation processes.

This chapter identifies some challenges in increasing work productivity in the highly networked product creation communities. Increasing productivity requires an increased mobilization of work, i.e. tasks and processes, as well as the mobilization of engineers. This, in turn, has direct implications for workplace design: the design of work processes and the work environment.

In order to create the necessary new tools, services and facilities for the new way of working, a global team of mobile work developers was established from four global platforms: Human Resources (HR), Security (S), Information Technology (IT) and Real-Estate & Facilities (CRE) (Fig. 11.1).

The objective of this chapter is to show, how a scenario was built in Nokia for optimising the use of available competencies in different sites and time zones in order to shorten the product creation process.

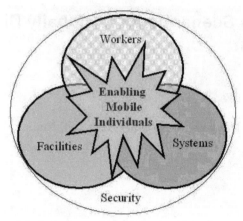

Fig. 11.1. The four global platforms developing enablers for mobility

11.2 Drivers, motivation and context of change

During the time period of 1993 to 2000, Nokia grew by winning more market share in its two primary global business units, Mobile Phones and Telecom Infrastructures, reaching first and second position in the global markets. During this time the company increased its work force in the two business units from 12 000 employees to 50 000 employees primarily by the recruitment of young software engineers. Between 1995 and 2000 it hired more then 50 % of all fresh computer science and electrical engineering graduates from the Finnish universities and technical colleges.

This led to the situation where Nokia was rapidly forced to increase its R&D presence in new countries due to the talent shortage in Finland. Other reasons besides the talent shortage were the market-lead forces to establish R&D units in major market areas and also the need to tap into global talent of distributed software engineers who were not seeking for relocation to Nokia traditional sites.

These initial drivers resulted in the emergence of a truly complex network of crosswise collaborating R&D centres and a more distributed product creation process. It was only later that it became evident that a global network of R&D units distributed in all continents, covering not only interesting talent pool areas but also all time zones, could become a competitive advantage, if the virtual product creation work could be properly managed.

Soon after, it also became evident that the future for global innovation implied collaborating with industries and partner networks. Big global corporations defined their core competencies and made their core context analyses and focused on their comparative advantages. This resulted in the reorganisation of work processes and value chains. Some functions became internally core issues, while others were managed through subcontracting and even through partnering with traditional competitors. A definition of co-opetition, i.e. collaboration and competition, was created, and the extended enterprise or the borderless organisation was defined. The underlying belief was that no single company could dominate the market with appropriate technologies. It became more a competition between constantly changing partnerships and innovation value networks as opposed to the traditional head-against-head competition. Companies that had the competence to orchestrate these value networks became stronger, and companies without this competence were left to be moulded by the market forces.

For Nokia this meant a new era where growth had to be achieved through doing less 'in-house' and more through partnerships. It also implied a strong need for increasing work productivity. All in all, the focus had clearly shifted and the need to create a global strategic program to improve the facilitation of global work processes emerged.

11.3 Globally distributed mobile work environment

Traditional business models for implementation of mobile workplace development projects are very much driven by the urge to save cost. That was initially the easiest and most tangible way to create a buy in from the internal clients. Nokia started the development work with the template shown in Table 11.1. The aim was to maximize the usage of tangible and preferably numeric data.

A study was also conducted on the occupancy rates of personal static desk-places. The utilization capacity was found to be very low (Fig. 11.2), which implied an opportunity to make space savings. As a result of the study an open workspace concept without assigned seats was implemented.

Already during the initial phases of the mobile workplace development it became quite evident that a more general change was underway in the work place. The traditional work paradigm was giving way to the emergence of a new one. The traditional and historical view of working and workplace design assumes that people work in relatively well-defined lo cations ("the office") and during clearly foreseen times ("time in").

Table 11.1. Costs and benefits of the flexispace

Issue	Assumption	Operative costs (kEuro), Benefit/year	System investment costs (occational)	Recurrend costs/ year
Real Estate Cost ■ ▨ ☐	- xx sqm per person/xx in Helsinki - 1700 Noki- ans and 240 externals - Decreases moves by x % and costs of move by x %	- xx kEuro bottomline savings possible ■	- xx kEuro ■	-
Employee Productivity ▨ ☐	-	- Produc- tivity gains ■	-	- Produc- tivity loss ■
Employee Retention ☐	-	-	- x resigna- tions ■	- ■
Showcasing ■ ▨ ☐	- Nokia is able to sell more Busi- ness Applica- tions Products and Base Sta- tions because of showcases that convince customers	-	-	-
TOTAL				

■ = FlexiSpace   ▨ = WLAN   ☐ = Home connection/working from home

Performance is supervised on-site and primarily measured on the basis of individual work. The team members are placed into a common site to allow cooperation and collaboration. In the traditional work paradigm space is designed to reinforce status and hierarchy and the model on the whole is organisation-centric.

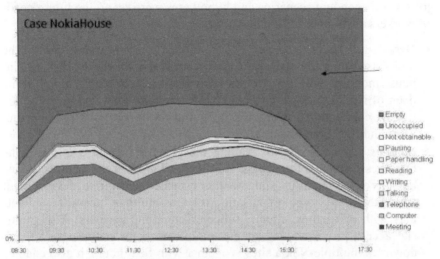

Fig. 11.2. The content of working and the rate of using a worksite in a working day

The emerging new work paradigm was suggesting that work can and should take place wherever and when it needs to. Work was viewed as something fluid and mobile. Productivity was no longer measured solely on the basis of the results of an individual, but also on those of a team. Supervision was giving way to mentoring and coaching, while remotely located team members had to be supported in their need to collaborate in multiple ways. Space was re-engineered to support functions and tasks in a flexible way, which would accommodate the growth and changes in the business environment. Also, an individual-centric model for career, work process and workplace resource allocation began to emerge.

The work paradigm changes taking place in the global enterprise workplace thinking helped us set new targets for shared service models for our employees. To continue the development efforts of the first initiatives such as FlexiWork, FlexiSpace, FlexiHours, FlexiResourcing, a new mobility program was introduced. While the previous initiatives had been carried out in separate platforms, the Global mWork Program combined the efforts of four global platforms: Human Resources (HR), Security (S), Information Technology (IT) and Real-Estate & Facilities (CRE).

The work of the Global mWork Program began with the profiling of approximately 50 globally generic jobs according to two mobility dimensions: a) worker mobility and b) work virtuality (Figs. 11.3 and 11.4). Based on the specific mobility requirements the jobs were then clustered into three broad categories: desk-based, campus mobile and total mobile jobs. Corresponding scenarios and hypotheses were set on the future needs of workers as follows:

- *Desk-based Mobility Scenario.* A hypothesis was set stating that in the desk-based mobility scenario the micro-mobility of the worker, i.e. in-house mobility, will increase primarily due to the implementation of the open office Flexi-space concept. Work virtuality will also increase due to new collaborative teamwork tools and the broad policies on home-work and flexi hours.
- *Campus Mobile Scenario.* Among the campus mobile employees the hypothesis was that the worker mobility will grow in the campus radius, i.e. city level mobility, due to the extended enterprise development where the matrix type organisation requires multiple face-to-face meetings with colleagues, clients, subcontractors and partners. Also multi-site access provision for campus mobile workers enables easy touch downs in multiple Nokia sites. Together with flexi hours, it also enables a better work-life balance and results in savings regarding total transportation times and distances. Another hypothesis was that due to improved work processes and collaborative teamware tools broader, out of town mobility was reducing.
  Work virtuality will also strongly increase due to the high usage of individual wireless tools, i.e. PDAs and Communicators and due to the use of person-to-person and teamware tools, i.e. web cameras, virtual walls, white boards, con-call facilities and Net-meetings, among the campus mobile people.
- *Total Mobile Scenario.* The hypothesis in this group was that cross-border mobility would decrease while in-campus and office micro mobility would increase.

The work virtuality will increase due to the new work processes of the extended enterprise and due to the availability of configured trusted knowledge management shareware tools. Also the heavy use of home access due to the wide distribution of collaboration across many time zones, and the use of multi-site touch down locations increases virtuality.

The analysis of the category profiles provided the mWork team with the necessary information for designing service and tool delivery templates and a service portfolio, which would then be delivered to the incumbents of the jobs in the three categories. After this, the service and delivery templates were tested in different countries, functions and business units. The globally distributed R&D network provided many useful pilot environments. Some testing was also done in subcontractor sites and client premises.

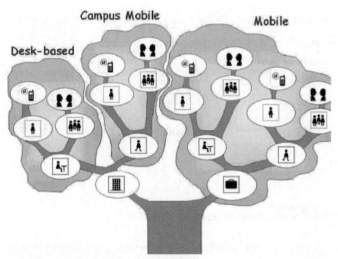

Fig. 11.3. Globally generic jobs forming three broad clusters of mobile, campus mobile and desk-based jobs

Mobile	Campus Mobile	Non-mobile
• Typically works between many locations • Regularly works in a preferred office neighborhood in Nokia sites or in Drop-in centers, no dedicated workspace • Most daily work resources are *or could be* portable or connected remotely; other resources and archives are found in the office neighborhood • May work from home up to 2 days a week	• Typically works in one location but is highly mobile and away from the desk e.g. in meetings or labs a lot • Regularly works in a preferred office neighborhood in one Nokia sites, no dedicated workspace • Solutions for managing storage and personal materials often required • Occasionally uses a drop-in center or works at home/remotely	• Typically uses a dedicated or team workspace in a Nokia location • Most daily work resources (e.g. people, technology, equipment, documents) are and *should be* office-based • Preferred desk is typically used but should be cleared and made available to others when out • Occasionally uses a drop-in center or works at home/remotely

Fig. 11.4. Profiles of different global jobs (CKIR, Helsinki School of Economics)

The current Flexible Working Solutions applied in different Nokia units consist of the three areas of flexibility. These flexibility areas designed by the global human resources unit correspond to space, time and contractual flexibility (Fig. 11.5).

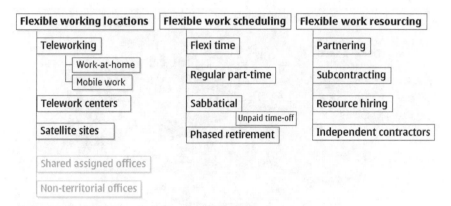

Fig. 11.5. Flexible working solutions

Figure 11.6 shows, how a web-based interface for mobility solutions looks from the user perspective to find required protocols, services, tools and policies. The experiences obtained in the pilot cases using similar web-based interfaces became sources for creating global services, tools, products and policies to be later localized by regional mWork implementation teams. This process is currently under way.

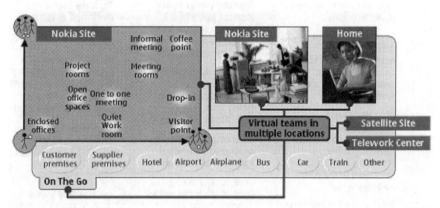

Fig. 11.6. An example of a user centred, web-based interface supporting mobile work.

11.4 Drivers and benefits of flexible working solutions

While the traditional business model based, cost savings driven approaches had made a strong argument, it did, however, prove to be much more strategic to understand the role of other tangible and intangible business benefits of such a productivity raising, globally mobilizing project.

At the current state of the development work, the benefits of the flexible working solution have been identified from various perspectives as follows (Table 11.2).

Table 11.2. Foreseen benefits of a flexible working solution from the perspectives of different stake holder groups

Human resources perspective	Employee perspective	Real estate and information technology perspectives
- Support for resourcing, increased job satisfaction, commitment and tenure as a result of alternative modes of working, i.e. flexibility in terms of how, when and where they work) - Improved efficiency as a result of the innovative, motivating and flexible ways of working - Reinforces the implementation of Nokia values by supporting employees' personal and work-life balance	- Easier and mobile network connections available - Unnecessary commuting and down time between activities reduced, which has a positive effect on work-life balance - Support for ad hoc planning of daily work schedule - Support for choice in work practices regarding how, where and when to work - Allows one to move between teams and work in a more collaborative manner - Improved work-life balance due to flexibility in the way work is organized	- Reduced need for office space due to flexispace solution, i.e. open workspace concept without assigned seats) - IT infra cost reductions due to higher occupancy rate per seat - Increased flexibility and decreased disruption as a result of decreasing need for moving - Supports short-term flexibility, which makes it possible to respond to growth or change needs without continuous investments in real estate and IT infrastructure - Provides showcasing and market-making for Nokia products, while also providing an opportunity to "learn by doing"

There are many external driving forces, which have the potential to become opportunities for such a global mWork program. The new global division of work has brought about a war for talent. Mobile working solutions make it possible to tap into the regional talent pools also in those situations where people do not wish to relocate. The new economies hold bigger pools of talent, but they are also growing market areas. This brings forward the need to establish local R&D facilities as they can significantly improve the local mass-customization of products and services.

The Global mWork Program is finally and foremost Nokia's opportunity to demonstrate, how wireless technology can be used to enable mobility and enhance work performance in enterprises. This is closely linked to its business strategy. As more and more companies define their role in R&D from the core context analysis, the result will inevitably be an increasing need for partnering, subcontracting and collaborating even with competitors, i.e. co-opetition. Innovation and value creation networks are becoming more complex, which also makes the organisational and management arrangements equally complex. The developments raise security, intellectual property rights, confidentiality, trust and other issues. The R&D work done on the Global mWork Program will inevitably also serve as input for the Nokia Enterprise strategy to provide tested solutions to other enterprises in such developments.

11.5 Scenario challenges

When designing a working environment, which supports mobility, some of the key questions that need to be addressed are listed below. The success and arising challenges of the development work depends on the ability of the program to take such matters into account.

- What types of workers are best and least suited for mobile working? User Community Research is needed to investigate this aspect
- What factors or enablers may cause an increase in mobile working for currently static populations?
- How can we sustain and improve teaming across remote or multiple locations? If individual work can take place anywhere, how can we encourage the coming together as a community?
- What kind of activities do mobile individuals choose to do in the office and what do they choose to do elsewhere – and why?
- Which spaces and tools are most commonly used by mobile individuals when they are in the office?
- How do mobile individuals use mobility to enhance their personal work-life balance?
- Change management and enablement: how much and what type of involvement and communication is needed to promote management buy-in and user acceptance regarding the new concepts?

- What support and information is needed to enable the more effective mobile working? This includes technology tools, management training, behavioural protocols, web tools, booking systems, presence indicators, displays at entry space, etc.
- What measures can we develop to ensure a sustainable and socially acceptable productivity improvement?

Individual challenges primarily arise from the complexity of the very matrix type of organisation combined with the network of multiple sites in different countries and time zones integrated into common work processes. The work process can be roughly divided into three phases: first, the planning phase, second, the coding and programming phase, and, third, the integrating phase. Usually most of software engineers are involved on all of these phases. It is quite common for the engineers to also be involved in more than one process at a time, and in some cases even as many as five projects in different phases. Managing the projects requires standardized processes, work practices, collaborative tools, standardized software and system integration inter-phases. Usually the planning phase requires team meetings, which are also physical face-to-face meetings, where relationships based on trust can be created in multinational and diverse groups.

The longest phase, which accounts for 60-80 percent of the total time, is the coding and programming phase, which usually requires individual concentration and an individualized workspace with minimal disturbances. Big challenges arise when this phase is disturbed by other projects in the stage requiring collaboration. A simultaneous cognitive capacity is required to multi-task with highly conceptual problems. The second individual challenge is the work-life balance when one is collaborating with colleagues from other time zones. This is especially challenging for managers and testing and integration engineers.

The team, organisational and work process related challenges are primarily found in the management of the highly talented work force in a networked global organisation. Developmental challenges are needs for multi-skilling and updating the skills of programmers. There is also a period when engineers are motivated on pure programming. In this case, complex multi-tier career plans and paths must be provided for engineers, i.e. a managerial path, a scientist path, and a project path, in order to be able to retain them in an industry where high talent is in high demand.

Significant differences in work practices are also challenging. For instance, should teams be made up of people representing many nationalities and different practices or should diversity be exploited by having internally homogeneous groups collaborate with other homogeneous groups that differ from each other. Work practices differ not only between nationalities but also according to different local or business specific cultures. Because new requirements emerge rapidly with new competence needs, many competencies also become redundant and re-skilling and out-learning needs are also high. A long-term balance of a demographic mix is needed as well as planning for it.

The latest and also future challenges arise from situations where engineers more often work with partners, subcontractors, clients and even competitors. Specific challenges, which are specific for virtually managed satellite sites, are the questions of weak identification to employer, multi-skilling requirements, value for tacit knowledge and less social team related association.

Work process challenges are mainly on the level of collaboration when inter-phasing with other sites. Some work is easily shifted to other trusted partner engineers in other time zones while there remains some tasks where shifting just doesn't yet make sense, because the hand over times are too lengthy. Also quality issues and documentation might be bottlenecks.

Major technical challenges relate to security and especially to challenges on wireless access technologies in Internet protocol. Other big challenges are the lack of the ambient intelligent design in the tool and service user interface. Also the lack of open standards, standard interfaces and intellectual property rights control requirements in using open source software are challenging.

Specific challenges do exist also with collaborative tools such as virtual walls for team inter-phasing, collaborative whiteboard design tools, different collaborating team ware tools and data warehousing techniques, mobile meetings, ad-hoc meetings, different web casting technologies and new multimedia mobile messaging and broadcasting technologies.

11.6 Conclusion

Nokia represents a global ICT company where core competencies exist very much in its innovation capability to design and develop new products to the global wireless datacom and telecom market. One of the competitive edges in this market is to provide solutions and products timely to the market. The global processes enabling it are here called Global Product Creation Processes. The core function enabling the execution is the research and development organisation.

The contextual environment for global product creation is as follows: Nokia R&D operations are located in 59 different sites in 14 countries and in ten different time zones, which cover 24 hours of constant R&D activity. Nokia R&D functions employ some 21 000 R&D engineers globally. Besides this, most product creation processes involve several partner, subcontractor and client sites. On average, each product creation process develops its products between seven sites in three countries and time zones. Current sites are responsible for predefined product process phases and are organized as competence centres to carry out these assignments.

The basic scenario is that managing the global product creation process will rapidly become the major competitive advantage to its holders. Competition and development will take place in the areas of global software talent utilization, the company's attraction and retention, and the orchestration of networked extended partnerships beyond traditional corporate borders. Success will depend on the ability to create management tools as well as collaborative technologies and tools, which foster productivity and innovation. The scenario is based on the following assumptions:

• Global talent and innovation capability will reside in many global locations and work mobility will play higher strategic importance than labour mobility
• Utilization of the whole 24 hour cycle by distributing the product creation process globally will become an a decisive factor in decreasing the time to market
• New innovative ways of global partner collaboration will increase, i.e. battle of changing partnerships
• Technology and development will enable ever more intuitive and collaborative (ambient) new working environments, work enabling tools and services for global R&D.

Nokia related scenarios are hopefully representative for any ICT global company. The rapid development of global collaborative work processes and work environments are key areas for European companies in becoming more competitive. It is challenging to clearly formulate foresights or visions for the future as the progression seems to be very evolutionary and rapid. What can, however, be said is that creating economic and social benefits for Europe will require the management of the emerging value networks, rather than just participating in them.

References

Gartner (2000) The agile workplace: Transforming work and the workplace
Nokia Global mWork Program 2001-2004

12 Case Descriptions of Mobile Virtual Work in Practice

Robert M Verburg[1], Stefania Testa[2], Ursula Hyrkkänen[3] and Niklas Johansson[4]

[1]Faculty of Technology, Policy and Management, Delft University of Technology, The Netherlands
[2]Department of Communication, Computer and System Sciences at the University of Genoa, Italy
[3]Turku Polytechnic, Finland
[4]Department of Information Technology and Human-Computer Interaction, Uppsala University, Sweden

12.1 Setting the scene

The trends toward mobile and virtual work (MVW) appear to be central in a wider process, in which organisations become less integrated, both geographically and in terms of employment. This development may lead to fascinating new forms of organizing and cooperation. It implies a process in which people may become more independent but also isolated both socially and contractually. So, the new possibilities can bring risks; short-term effectiveness may conflict with long-term sustainability. MVW is already a reality in different business areas with mobile customer services, such as sales, logistics, maintenance, professional services or health care. Previous chapters have highlighted a number of experimental settings and examples of small companies. This chapter focuses on the operational processes of mobile work in large enterprises. Four case descriptions of actual practices of mobile virtual work across countries and industries in Europe are presented. Standard techniques for case study research were followed (e.g. Yin 1994). Data were collected through semi-structured interviews, document analysis and observations. Multiple informants were used in all cases. The cases deal with mobile customs employees in The Netherlands, mobile elevator service engineers in Finland, mobile facility management in Italy and mobile home care in Sweden. On basis of the case descriptions a number of current practices for mobile ways of working will be further illustrated and discussed.

12.2 MVW in practice: customs control in the Netherlands

The case study concerns the external control of trade goods by the Dutch customs agency.

The customs organisation is responsible for the control of import and export of goods. A total of 1700 employees are involved with physical control activities. Physical control is done by a single operator or may be performed by teams. Control takes place either on the road or at client sites. Custom control employees are involved with both planned and ad hoc control assignments. The work of custom control employees is mobile in nature.

In 2004 an experiment was performed with a few custom controllers in each of the four geographical sectors of the Dutch Customs: North, South, Rotterdam, West (Schiphol). The controller's task is to perform customs related controls at premises of clients, on roadside trucks, at the Rotterdam harbour or Schiphol Airport.

At present, controllers come each day to the office where they get assignments on paper, which they execute that day. Completed forms are brought back to the office after the controls. In the future, the allocation of assignments is delivered via GPRS to PDA's or laptops; during control digital forms are filled in and central databases, e.g. concerning earlier reports or data of client, may be consulted on-line, filled-in forms are returned electronically.

12.2.1 Mobile setting

The mobile work solution utilizes GPRS connectivity and would be theoretically available wherever the user finds GPRS coverage. In reality the concept is used within the boundaries of the four districts. The case is based on a technology trial including 15 employees and an investment below 50.000€.

The purpose of the experiment was to develop a more automated and streamlined work process and to test the use of certain devices for the support of the controllers. The work process implies that assignments are generated by planners and send to a central control room in each of the four sectors. In the control rooms the assignments are allocated to the controllers, who do the control and then send the results back to the control room. The controllers drive in special cars of the customs organisation. Their tasks are differentiated according to planned and ad hoc assignments, known and unknown clients. Controllers may be specialized in certain areas such as strategic goods, weapons, drugs or textiles.

Presently, assignments are on paper and picked up by controllers at the office. They write the results during the control on a form, which is brought back to the office and then entered manually in the system. In the future large parts of the data exchange will be automated and the communication with the controllers will be done through new devices. In the experiment the following devices were tested: laptops, Smartphones (PDA plus GPRS), and tablet-PCs. Depending on the setting controllers use either a PDA or a tablet PC. Planned assignments are generated by planning systems and ad hoc assignments are allocated through the control room. All assignments are send using GPRS to PDA and tablets of the mobile custom controllers.

The experiment was successful; it has resulted in a Program of Requirements for a full scale implementation in the organisation in 2005-2007. For the technical support a tender is send out for European companies. Both Smartphones and Tablets will be used. Basic principle will be: do not develop company specific solutions but use existing, commercially available, solutions. The objectives of the development are to increase efficiency, i.e. more controls, with less costs, effectiveness, i.e. higher probability of discovering frauds, more flexibility of execution, and better relations with customers, i.e. less disturbance of client logistics, shorter control time.

12.2.2 Implementation

The customs agency is a relatively small case compared to the other cases under review. However, it has been a trial and is decided to be scaled up considerably. Though the organisation made a reasonably small investment, the usage of robust technology allowed to generate quite some positive value impact. The customs agency relied on proven technology for the mobile work solution. Standard internet connectivity and access gateways to the intranet where used in the case. The organisation tested different end-devices as personal equipment for the controllers. At some periods the controllers used Smart phones (wireless connected PDA's), at other times they used Laptops-with-wireless connections. Both have the same purpose, but are used in different physical environments, for example PDA's in hangars, ships and Laptops in offices.

Relying on proven technology resulted in limited technical problems and moderate need for employee up-skilling. However, the experiment identified some technical issues in the area of data transfer speed, battery duration, and certain ergonomic conditions, e.g. use of the tools in rough environments like freeze-cabins.

The technology does not make use of personalization or localization data although this would be possible within the current application. The mobile solution is not yet integrated into other applications within the customs organisation and operates as a stand-alone application. It may be possible to make connections to adjacent administrative systems in the future.

12.2.3 Benefits and drawbacks

The mobile work solution allows for better control of and more efficiency in work processes. The control assignments can be send to the controller much faster, the controllers can send the results of a control almost immediately to the central control room, so controls can be processed faster. As a result, goods can be cleared much faster for the client. This implies fewer disturbances of client logistics.

In the Rotterdam area all custom officials involved were positive for the following reasons:

The tools were perceived as very user-friendly. Employees appreciated the reduction of waiting time between assignments and valued the significant reduction in administrative paper work. Customs information of the assignments could be entered in the laptop or smart-phone during the control, rather than being transferred from a written form into a desktop computer at the office.

The tool enabled customs officials to perform information requests and they could receive relevant information during the trip. The overall benefits of the mobile custom control solutions are the following:

- Improved information availability for controllers
- Higher flexibility of task assignment
- Faster processing of results of controls
- Goods can be cleared much faster for the client
- Less waiting time for assignments at the office
- Positive reactions by controllers
- The tools are very user-friendly
- Data have to be entered only once
- Information can be asked and easily received during the trip
- Improved image and employee motivation

In summary, the new mobile work solution increased employee motivation and is expected to improve the outside image of the agency. Profit and loss implications have not been in the focus of the experiment. We rate the overall value impact fairly high, since the set up of a running solution, and the reduction of the administrative work generated a well-perceived motivation- and image-impulse for the agency. Negative experiences with tool are limited and have to do with the sometimes slow data-communication over the existing network. For security reasons employees need to log on to the intranet several times during the day. Another small concern has to do with limitations such as the duration of batteries.

12.2.4 Conclusion and lessons learned

As described above, the technology deployed to support mobile work in this case is not highly advanced, however it generates a rather positive value impact for the customs agency. The historical lack of advanced technology in this agency makes a relatively moderate technological solution already a success in the eyes of the employees and the organisation. The key challenges for a further improvement of the mobile work environment will be the seamless up scaling of the trial and, possibly, the integration of databases across various governmental entities (e.g. police).

In order to pre-empt isolation among the employees the agency should actively manage the social cohesion. Since it is technically possible to send assignments to the controller at home, who then goes directly to the client, isolation of employees may occur. However, presently controllers come still to one of the offices in the morning and in the evening, to pick up or bring back the tool and the car they use that day. This situation is not likely to change in the future as controllers do not have their 'own' car but make use of a limited number of company cars that are only available at the office.

In summary, the case shows benefits in the area of operational efficiency and in terms of employee satisfaction. Implementation efforts and technological challenges have been minimal, since the project was based on a proven technology.

We recognize that the development in the Dutch custom agency is in line with the general automation trend in the organisation. Organisational processes and actual work practices were not strongly changed, although this was technically possible. Therefore, the introduction of the new devices was quite easily done. Due to earlier experiences, the project was set up with extensive involvement of the organisation and organised by a project team and participative development and evaluation.

12.3 MVW in practice: providing facility services in Italy

Siram is the Italian subsidiary of the leading European provider of facility
management services for public and private companies. Its service portfolio includes the management of heating and air conditioning facilities, the
operation of district heating systems, and industrial energy services. Siram
has locations throughout Italy and the head office is located in Milan. The
number of employees is 700, all of them with permanent contracts, and
450 employees are involved in the maintenance process. There are about
5.500 sites managed by Siram staff. The case focuses on the mobile part of
the maintenance staff. Except for a small group that is permanently located
in big plants the majority of the maintenance employees works mobile.

12.3.1 Mobile setting

The application introduced concerns field force automation and supports
technicians in their daily activities, providing intranet access through WAP
(Wireless Application Protocol) on mobile phones. The project was initiated by the Information Systems department (IS) in order to improve the
maintenance process. IS aimed to automate real time data collection directly from the field, monitoring repairs and having accurate statistical
data, as well as at removing all paper based activities and data transcrip-
tion. Moreover, customers indicated to be not fully satisfied with the information they could receive over the phone and preferred more visual information in order to have a better overview on the overall progress.

Initially, an application with Microsoft Access was developed. This application did not satisfy the needs of the mobile users. It was therefore decided to develop a web-based application with WAP technology for the
remote access. The processes involved are unscheduled and routine interventions management, and energy consumption control.

The current tool provides the following functionalities to its maintenance staff users:

- Unscheduled interventions. The customer reports a system's failure to
  Siram call center, the operator inserts data about the problem in the
  intranet in order to make them available to all local offices. A scheduler
  assigns the call to a technician that receives the data through WAP, or if
  the intervention is pressing, the local office calls the technician by
  phone

- Routine interventions. The scheduling of interventions is available both in the intranet and via WAP; technicians can find data on interventions on a two weeks basis
- Intervention data collection. After every unscheduled or routine intervention, technicians insert data (travelling time, processing time, closure time etc.) that are immediately available on the intranet. Local offices can use such data to inform customers about the status of interventions. Large clients are even allowed to read these data directly from the Siram web page. Before introducing this tool it was not uncommon that customers had to wait a week to get information. Routine interventions are driven by a technical hand-book and a predefined form to fill in, while for unscheduled interventions technical guidelines are not provided
- Energy consumption control. The technician inserts consumption data and an automatic formal error checking controls the data entry online. This makes data entry easier, reduces errors and avoids extra trips to the plant. Moreover, the administrative staff has those data available in real time and can start the invoicing process faster and more easily

The system is composed by a server application and is interfaced by a WAP mobile client that uses GSM/GPRS protocol. In the early stages of adoption some drawbacks related to bandwidth and coverage of WAP connection emerged; some interfacing problems are still unsolved. Mobile phones were preferred to PDA (Personal Digital Assistant). Due to the relative ease of use no training was required for the users. In this case a mobile phone is technically adequate since the amount of data to be transmitted is limited and standardized.

12.3.2 Implementation

The project was designed and managed by IS but eventually top management was directly involved in suggesting applications' improvements. Nevertheless, the implementation process was not easy due to the different stakeholders. The final version of the system is a combination of singular modules developed during the time:

- an access application aimed at supporting maintenance scheduling
- a WAP application, developed by a consulting company
- in-house developed modules aimed at collecting incoming phone calls and at recording energy consumption data

No cost-benefit analysis was conducted: modules have been evaluated one by one, but without going into details. WAP mobile phones were provided by TIM, the largest Italian mobile operator, to replace the old ones. Operating costs are low and predictable and contain primarily telephone costs.

12.3.3 Benefits and drawbacks for the organisation

The system provided some benefits for the organisation. By means of the system it is possible to provide real time data to optimize interventions' effectiveness and improve technicians' productivity. Data are now directly transmitted to a database. No second data entry by someone at the headquarters is necessary anymore. The quality of the energy consumption control process is improved too as formal data entry errors are now automatically checked online. At the moment a formal performance measurement system has not been developed but the positive effects on efficiency and effectiveness have been widely recognized by all the interviewees.

The application is also perceived and sponsored as a tool aimed at improving customer service. During the maintenance intervention, data about technical aspects are collected thus permitting the customer to control them in real time through the web. Previously, information about work in progress and work closure were communicated to customers by means of telephone calls, fax and file transmissions. The real time customer involvement also avoids some of the previous misunderstandings and complaints.

12.3.4 Benefits and drawbacks for employees

At the beginning of the adoption process there was some friction and resistance among the group of technicians. This is often the case when a new information system is introduced. Reasons were essentially related to perceived changes in work habits and difficulties in using the new system. Moreover, maintenance staff perceived the possibility of an increase in control on daily activities as negative. After an introductory phase among maintenance team leaders, the reluctance was overcome. New incentive and reward policies were implemented in line with the changing nature of the work of the maintenance staff. After a period of one year, the maintenance staff was fully used to the system and recurrent practices. As an interviewee underlines:

> 'In my area, Sardinia, there is only one peripheral office of my firm, which serves a large region. I appreciated the tool as it helped me in performing my daily tasks'.

Technicians improved their abilities in scheduling activities and benefit from easy access to updated data about plants. Headquarter and local offices staff benefit from better coordinating technician work. Although the tool provides limited and simple functionalities, because one-way communication was provided and only pre-defined forms could be filled, it fully meets the requirements of the users for conducting their remote maintenance tasks.

12.3.5 Conclusions and lessons learned

Previous research projects (see chapter by Corso et al. in this volume) show that it is necessary to align task characteristics with the characteristics of a mobile support tool in order to contribute to business performance and employees satisfaction. Despite the high number of customers, Siram maintenance tasks do not involve high variety as the firm is focused on a specific type of facilities (heating and air conditioning). Maintenance procedures are repetitive and standardized with known routines for handling them. As well known from Perrow's model of technology and structure (1967), in this case, systems based on procedural guides, operation manuals, task codification and rigid lines of reporting are expected to be effective in terms of degree of control and codification.

The present case study seems to confirm and reinforce the assumption that routine situations with low information needs may benefit mostly from simple systems aimed at supporting users' activities in the mobile environment. The mobile wireless devices adopted by Siram are mobile phones: such devices are cheap, in this case they were even provided for free by the telecommunication operator, and characterized by tiny a screen and a keypad difficult to type on, each key representing more than one character. Nevertheless, they did not provoke frustration among users. The amount of data to be transmitted is limited and standardized (e.g. travelling time, processing time, closure time), and, in the same time, they do not require huge training activities for users. Mobile devices have a limited memory and functionality and wireless connections are slower than those of wired devices but in the described MVW it does not matter because users do not need quick responses or feed-backs, since the communication between mobile workers and headquarter is mainly one way. Furthermore, as already indicated operative costs are low (just the phone calls).

Despite the simplicity of the system, the impact on customer service has been significant (see also Kumar et al. 2003; Zilliox 2002). Now customers may be informed about the status of interventions and this means lower customer service costs, mainly for managing late complains, and higher customer satisfaction. Thus, the presented case may be considered as a success. The solution is technically adequate and fits the way Siram employees work in their settings. Initial friction and "resistance" have been overcome just after one year of use thanks to evident benefits in employees' recurrent practices.

Siram is now planning to completely renew its information system and introduce SAP or Oracle. Both platforms provide a MVW environment. Technicians will adopt PDA technology in order to solve interface WAP problems. Moreover, Siram is now introducing automatic remote control systems to perform consumption reading and failure check in order to reduce technician's manual work, for a foreseen cost saving of about 20 to 30%.

Nevertheless, it is worth noting that, in order to enrich and enlarge the system to other functionalities, management should be aware of the necessity of adequate incentive and rewarding leverages in order to prevent cases of resistance to change.

12.4 MVW in practice: mobile servicemen in Finland

The company under study is a large scale engineering and facility management enterprise employing people globally. Its customers are builders and building owners. The case study observes one group of maintenance personnel (in this section addressed as servicemen) responsible for the maintenance and service of real estate. The persons interviewed (N=7) represent a group of twelve male employees working under one foreman in a maintenance district, which is located in the Turku area. Data were collected during spring 2005. The objective of this case study is to describe the work of one mobile servicemen group and their experiences of testing, implementing and using a new mobile device with support software: palm computer with the Feature programme.

12.4.1 Mobile settings

The real estates that need to be serviced are divided into districts. In the Turku area, there are seven service districts, each with their own responsible foreman. The service districts are further divided into maintenance areas, each with one serviceman responsible for the maintenance. Maintenance work consists of the service tasks defined in the maintenance contract, alarm situations demanding immediate response and possible on-call and specified tasks.

The size of the maintenance area is some 20–30 square kilometres. The number and the type of real estate determine the size. Each type of real estate has assigned points, which influence the bonus for the employee. The division of labour has been implemented in such a way that each serviceman can accumulate the same number of points for his maintenance tasks. Therefore, the number of estates to be serviced varies from 150 to 250 per serviceman. The number of locations to be visited per working day usually varies from 10 to 20 depending on how demanding the maintenance tasks are. Sometimes a whole day can be spent at one location.

The weekly round per serviceman is roughly 50–100 kilometres depending on whether he participates in on-call duties, and other possible special duties in addition to the normal task, for instance, specialised fault services.

Each employee uses a maintenance car, a transit van, for transferring from one service location to another and all necessary spare parts and maintenance equipment are transported in the back of the vehicle. The employees drive directly from home to the service area, where they start work at seven o'clock in the morning. They visit the office only for specific reasons. The servicemen end their working day at four o'clock after which, they drive straight home.

Employees assist each one another in tasks that cannot be completed alone, for instance, for reasons of safety. This adds to their job moving outside one's own maintenance area. The factors impacting the time spent on the move are not only the kilometres driven but also time wasted in traffic jams in the city. Two or three hours can easily be spent in the car daily.

The servicemen visit the main office in Turku perhaps every two weeks, mostly to pick up equipment for the maintenance car. Usually during these visits they may also meet their supervisor. Daily communications with the supervisor are taken care of over the telephone.

Using Lilischkis' (2003) mobile work typology, the servicemen could be characterized as a combination of 'On-site Movers' and 'Nomads': they have a well-defined district to move and work, but they visit the locations in an occasional order. Figure 12.1 shows the requirements of the serviceman job. The spotted circles describe how the servicemen themselves characterized their work and mobility requirements. It is shown that especially visiting many locations, moving physically around and using information and communication technologies increase the complexity of their work, whereas time factors and the diversity of employees are not a special challenge.

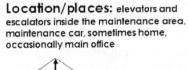

Location/places: elevators and escalators inside the maintenance area, maintenance car, sometimes home, occasionally main office

Mode of Interaction: mediated through palm computer cervices, phone and SMS, both formal and informal; Informal daily face to face meetings between servicemen

Mobility: local mobility all day long

Diversity, similarity of team members; all men with similar education, religion, culture background

Time: mostly synchronous working – "working alone in parallel locations"

Temporariness: permanent, stabile group

Fig. 12.1. Servicemen's job from the viewpoint of contextual complexity dimensions

12.4.2 Mobile reporting with the Palm computer

The Company launched a project during 2003 – 2004 aiming at a paperless reporting routine in the tasks of servicemen. To achieve this, a palm computer with a special programme was implemented. The development of software aimed at creating a transferable service entity applicable to the equipment of various manufacturers. The objective of the development work was also to offer employees a simple, easy to use and portable tool for receiving tasks and reporting on them. The group of servicemen under this study participated in the experiment.

The servicemen receive their work orders via the palm computer and report the jobs they have completed. In the reception of work orders, the servicemen themselves 'commission' monthly service lists into the palm computer, and in acute situations the customer service centre sends a message to the serviceman's palm computer. Reporting on the job takes place immediately after the work has been carried out in the service location directly from the job location. Electronic work reports are the basis of payroll and also act as the basis for the client invoices.

Collaboration between the employees in the service district is mostly built on indirect interaction. Contact between the team members and their supervisor are maintained by telephone and with text messages. The palm computer can also be used for these tasks. The employee need not carry several tools with him. The telephone was relatively recently implemented in the experiment, and only a part of the employees, around 60, are using it.

The service work also has safety risks. Therefore, if the serviceman has not used the software application in one hour, the application sends an inquiry about the situation. If the inquiry is not replied to, the application sends a report to the on-call person in the client service centre. For this reason, the inquisitive palm computer has earned nicknames such as 'Tamaqotchi' or 'Tamara', by the servicemen who use it. The use of Internet features is forbidden because of the lack of virus protection programmes, among other things.

12.4.3 Implementation

From the supervisor's point of view, the challenges in adopting a new operational system have mostly been technological in nature. Uncertainty in the smooth running of the technology has caused problems in the implementation. The user training was taken very seriously from the outset. All users in the experiment have had hands-on training in the use of the system: the main thought has been to openly offer all users the same information and thus underline equality in the development of the implement and the working of the services.

This goal seems to have been reached in the light of interviews. Many of the interviewed persons claimed they were a part of the development work and considered their own participation very important. When the development work shows a person his or her own "thumb prints", a new way of working is easily committed to. The interviewees experienced their participation in the development work as significant, since they understand that by participating, they are developing tools for their own work and for themselves. The interviewees also know to whom they can talk about their experiences of the use of the implements, and of their ideas for development.

12.4.4 Benefits and drawbacks

The need to visit the office has decreased – operations are increasingly focused on the service field. Earlier, the repair task codes were read with a pen, the information of which was downloaded once a week at the main office. At the same time, employees would submit their time sheets, which were then the basis of payroll. The new practice has decreased office visits: now the office is visited once every two weeks to load the van and once every two months for a team meeting. Otherwise, the hours are spent in the service field. Both employer and employees are content with this working mode.

Earlier, assignments and acute work tasks were sent to the device in the van, and in crisis situations the customer service centre had to phone the serviceman on duty in addition to sending the assignment to the device. Now any sudden assignments can be sent to the work location, and the servicemen do not need to return to the van to read the assignment. The new practice has clarified the method of contacting employees.

Not using certain features is ... positive? The palm computer could, according to the interviewees, be used also in the follow-up and control of working hours, since the time of the "first opened job" is recorded into it, and also the out-booking each day is registered in the machine. It would also be possible to monitor the routes taken and locations where employees are. Employees feel that they are trusted, and, therefore, the monitoring of beginning time, out-bookings or routes has not been implemented. Trust is very important to them. On the other hand, servicemen conceive GPS monitoring as a safety factor and an opportunity: if something were to happen, the man on the move could easily be located.

Accelerated customer service is the main value and object. Although the objective for mobile device development was to attain a portable reporting method, the main value has been in customer service. On-the-go reporting from the job location boosts customer service and invoicing. The reports on maintenance acts could be forwarded to clients quicker than before.

Problems are linked with the reliability of the programme operations. The Feature programme operations are unreliable and the programme can, for instance, lose report information. The employee does not receive a confirmation upon reception of the information he has reported. Often, the loss of report information is only discovered when the foreman asks for time sheets. Employees keep a manual double ledger on their work performance in order to remember the details, so that payroll and client invoicing can be taken care of.

The development work on the added features, e.g. text messages and telephone calls, continues. The telephone feature has only been tested for a short period – the telephone development has not been the main issue. Because of the problems in the working mode of the phone some of the tester employees have given up the use of the telephone. Answering incoming calls shuts off the other operations – the caller can hear this as a delay when the call is answered. Some interviewees were bothered by this delay.

The most serious obstacle for work was losing unfinished reports when answering an incoming call. After ending the call, the work had to be resumed from the beginning. Employees would be keen to continue completing the report, which they consider a routine, even during a phone call. And if there are many incoming calls, being able to continue writing the report during them would be a time-saver.

The employees dream about the possibility to answer their incoming calls while carrying out a maintenance task without having to stop working. However, when using for instance the (loud) speaker feature the receiver of the phone call is disturbed by a strong echo that prohibits the message from coming or going through.

Using text message services (SMS) requires reasonably good eyesight. Some interviewees find the service easy to use and say they "even write poems"; some hardly ever use the service because of having trouble seeing the text.

According to both employer and employees the device encompasses countless other possibilities for developing work and its processes. Both groups are well disposed for further development steps. The employees interviewed emphasized the process of continuous joint development.

12.4.5 Conclusions

The design and implementation of a new device and software, and a plan of action succeeded well, although technical problems have also been inherent such as losing information. Technical problems seem to be the main challenge for future developments. Employees are, however, satisfied with their new tool. The main reason for this is the involvement of servicemen in the development work. Training to use the system was also emphasized. The new practice has decreased office visits and time for the core operations in the maintenance area has increased. There are fewer face-to-face meetings of employees and supervisors, and the employees have great autonomy. The relationship between the employer and employees is trustful based on the results of work, and not on monitoring the detailed time usage of employees. An employee starts his work from home and returns there after service visits to customers. Co-workers are contacted to get help and advice via phone. In addition, they meet sporadically on the road in services stations during lunch and coffee breaks and for chatting and exchanging work-related information. In the future, technical deficiencies are improved, and the use of new tools and practices will be disseminated.

12.5 MVW in practice: IT-support for home care in Sweden

A mobile information system for work support in home care organisations, Permitto Care, was originally developed by Telia, a large Swedish telecom company. The initial development was carried out in close cooperation with the home care staff in Nordanstig, a municipality in northern Sweden. Much effort was needed to make the system support the actual needs of the personnel. Nordanstig's community covers an area of 1380 km^2 and has 10.000 inhabitants, i.e. approximately 7.2 inhabitants/km^2. The home care work is characterized by large distances between the clients, resulting in much traveling for the personnel. This gives them limited opportunities to visit the common premises and few possibilities to consult and share knowledge with other colleagues. It also makes it difficult to perform various administrative tasks in the office. Figure 12.2 shows a group of proud Swedish home care nurses with their mobile devices.

The mobile technical support system was very much appreciated by its users and received much external attention; it was e.g. nominated for the "Users price" by UsersAward, Sweden (www.usersaward.se). Other municipalities were also very interested in the system and it was implemented in several other home care services in different communities in Sweden.

Fig. 12.2. A group of home care nurses with their mobile equipment, implemented in a Nokia Communicator 9210i

This case especially focuses on why a system, that is very efficient and appreciated in one setting, is not equally well functioning in another setting. We are here interested in analyzing the effects of introducing the Permitto Care system in a new setting.

12.5.1 Intended use

The mobile IT-system Permitto Care gave its users, the home care nurses, a tool to improve their internal communication. Through the system they could easily get in contact with colleagues, ask questions and share their knowledge. A main objective with the system was to facilitate for the users to start their working day from home, in order to quicker reach the clients and carry out the morning visits. The time needed for administration and planning could be significantly reduced. The mobile system could further make it possible to access and enter information about the care taker before and after each home visit. The events and care activities performed could be instantaneously documented.

12.5.2 The system implemented in another environment

The Permitto Care system is today also used in Hökarängen, a densely populated suburb in the Stockholm area. At the time of this study, the IT-system had been used for one and a half years. Results and conclusions of an interview with representatives from the personnel about their experiences with Permitto Care are here presented.

Group characteristics
In Hökarängen the area to be serviced is relatively small and the home health care personnel can reach their clients on foot. They visit the homes of the care taker often three times per day. The home care district is divided into two areas, where each area is daily served by a team of 10-13 active home care nurses. Each day, the nurses visit about 10-15 clients each. In total, the district serves about 150 clients. The number of personnel is slightly reduced on evenings and weekends.

Aspects of mobility
A normal working day starts with a short briefing in the home care organisation's office, then follows the morning round to the clients, lunch brake, the afternoon round and finally an informal meeting in the office and a rounding up of the day. The personnel mostly perform their rounds alone, but more demanding clients require a coordination allowing help from an assisting colleague or from the separate home health care team.

Communication and collaboration tools
During the home visits, a Nokia Communicator (9210i) running the Permitto Care system is carried along by the personnel. The Permitto Care system provides its users with possibilities for communication and information support needed in the work activities, i.e.:

- Mobile communication with other care givers by text messages and phone
- Access to individual care plans and detailed information about the clients
- Reading and writing care notes about individual clients
- Contact information about the clients and their relatives
- Planning and work schedules for the personnel

The interaction with the Permitto Care system is web-based and has two web interfaces that differ in the layout. The first is for a web browser on a stationary computer and the other one is for the web browser in the Nokia Communicator. To reach data in the system the nurses have to log in with a user name and a password. The interface on the stationary computer contains quite some functionality and is meant for administrative work, while the mobile interface is designed for the operative work and is less detailed. System data are up- and downloaded from a server and never stored locally on the client device for security reasons. Data in the system are sent over an encrypted data connection.

12.5.3 Performance and outcomes

The system is well received by its users at the home health care service in Hökarängen, and is considered relatively easy to learn and to operate. The employees feel appreciated when they are offered a modern IT-system. Appreciated features in the system are the main documentation function, "the care taker record". It makes it easy for the nurses to read and write notes about the care taker they visit. The record keeping is carried out much better with the new system compared to before.

The paper work has also been reduced to a great extent. Now everyone can access information available in the system. By using the system, it is possible for the home care nurses to reach information about the clients. While on the move information about medicines, contact information of their relatives or entry codes to the doors can be easily obtained. Savings in time have also been achieved since the briefing meetings in the morning can now be reduced from half an hour to five minutes.

12.5.4 Unanticipated use of the system

The time it takes the system to create the network connection is quite long. It entails the start of the web browser, to perform the user authorization and to load the Permitto Care web pages is. To start-up and log into the system, in order to write a record note for a certain care taker, takes an average user 2 minutes and 50 seconds.

If one home care nurse visits 15 clients a day, the time waiting for the system would be 2 5/6 min × 15 = 42,5 minutes per day. If this is true for the whole home care team of 10 care givers, working 5 days a week (which is not really true when home health care personnel also works in evenings and during the week ends), that makes 42,5 × 10 × 5 = 2125 / 60 ≈ 35,5 hours per week – almost equal to a full time position!

Just a few days after the personnel at the home health care centre in Hökarängen had started to use the Permitto Care system, it became clear that to log into the system after each visit at a care taker took too much time. The nurses created therefore new routines to use the system. They now carry out just a few logins into the system during a day; in the beginning of the day, at lunch and at the end of the day, i.e. all occasions when the users are meeting in the office. Once in the office it is more quiet and easier to concentrate than when one is on the move. Help and support from colleges is also within easy reach.

The mobile device, the Nokia Communicator, is still carried along on the round to the clients but it is seldom used as a computer. As a mobile phone, however, it is much appreciated and frequently used. Many employees prefer to use a desktop computer at the premises rather than their mobile communicator.

The system's long start up time has the following consequences:

- Users do not write their documentation for each visit at a care taker. Thereby, the intended effects are lost, e.g. the benefits of a frequently updated system, of information written into the system while it is still fresh in the mind, of secure storage of information, and of backup advantages
- Information that is supposed to be documented during the visit to the clients is instead remembered or briefly written on paper notes. The information is entered into the IT-system first when they reach the office. Some users prefer using the stationary computer for entering the information into the system. A stationary computer has much more advantages than a small, mobile one; it is faster, easier to work with (with its mouse and proper keyboard) and has a bigger screen that provides a bet-

ter overview of the system. In this way, the mobile qualities of the Permitto Care system are seldom utilized

- When writing down things to remember, some users prefer to use paper notes or the note-application in the Nokia Communicator, an application that is not a part of the Permitto Care system. Both ways are much faster
- In the same way, entry codes to the client's home are sometimes stored by the nurses in the phones local note application. In this way the codes are much faster available when needed
- While on the move nurses prefer to make phone calls back to the manager at the office in order to report important occurrences and get them entered into the system

12.5.5 Conclusions and lessons learned

The Permitto Care system has, and has been rewarded for, a number of good qualities, e.g. it is easy to learn, it provides the user with the correct information and it is well adapted to the needs of the organisation. However, the system's long connection time results in unintended use, and a more or less total loss of intended efficiency. This becomes even clearer when the system is studied in an environment where long travel distances and solitary work is less apparent.

The slow network connection gives the users a general experience of the system as slow and difficult to handle. As shown in this case, this results in an unexpected way of using the system, caused by their intention to perform well. If the users find better, feasible, ways to achieve their goal without using the system as intended, these ways will be used. In this case the better way to work was e.g. not to use the system frequently as intended.

A professional user tries to perform a task in a quick and effective way, without spending energy in preparing the tool for the task. Our conclusions from this case confirm the notion that professionals will perform their task even if this is hampered by an IT-system that does not fit the nature of their work. In this case, a mobile solution was provided to support the work of home care nurses but the specific nature of the work led to non-mobile use of the system. The case underlines again the great benefits of early user involvement for the design and implementation of IT support tools in organisational context. In order to benefit from mobile solutions a careful analysis of the context of use proofs to be vital.

12.6 Overall conclusion

On basis of our detailed case analysis we have illustrated the use of mobile technology for work in different settings across four different countries. Mobile work is often associated with the nomadic business traveller who can have access to fancy back offices anywhere on the globe through an array of lightweight and preferably integrated gadgets. The cases in this chapter do not focus on this kind of mobile work but highlight the changing nature of the day-to-day activities of service engineers, home care nurses, and customs controllers. The work of these employees was already mobile even before the introduction of tablet PCs, PDAs, and communicators. However, the introduction of mobile solutions has changed the work of mobile employees tremendously. For instance, in case of the service engineers in both Finland and Italy, employees do not start their working day by going to the office but start their work when they enter their car and log on to the central dispatch unit. In case of the custom controllers in The Netherlands the mobile solution has changed their work day as the mobile solution enables the execution of more unscheduled work than before. The introduction of mobile solutions changes the organisation and the involvement of users is therefore of vital importance. The case of the home care nurses in Sweden is an example of what happens when users are not properly involved.

On basis of the cases the following benefits of mobile work come forward:

- Employees experience more efficiency due to less travelling from and to the office
- Employees have much better access to information when outside of the office and do not depend on phone calls to colleagues in the back office
- Employees experience that they have more possibilities to ask for the help and advice of other colleagues on the job

The organisation benefits also in terms of more efficiency of the work processes:

- Data can be stored in the local database directly from the field rather than through additional data entry in the office
- Clients may be updated better, more easily, and more up to date information can be conveyed
- On the move employees can be tracked much easier and unscheduled work can be allocated much better

Overall the cases show a positive picture on the application of mobile solutions in practice. Employees stress the benefits of their mobile work. Possible barriers are of course a lack of user involvement as seen in the case of Sweden, but as long as users are involved mobile virtual work is perceived as a positive change. Potential barriers or possible downsides, such as limitations of decision capabilities, a lack of employee autonomy and stronger propensity for employee control did not feature so much in the cases above. As these factors proof to have negative impacts on employee motivation, those remain a point of concern for the deployment of mobile virtual work in practice.

The four cases described in this chapter show a mere refinement of an already virtual work process through the use of more able tools. So far, there are not many examples of companies that have started new activities on basis of the possibilities that are offered by today's mobile technologies. Further research in the area of MVW would enable such companies to adapt their mobile work practices more carefully. Also, designers of mobile solutions may benefit from the detailed lists of requirements which come forward from the growing research into mobile work in practice. In other words, it is necessary to identify the different enactments of the various mobile practices within different cultures and industries in order to clarify the do's and don'ts of MVW.

Acknowledgement

The authors thank Andrea Giacobbe and Silvia Massa for their work on the Siram case and thank the EC-funded MOSAIC-project (FP6-2003-IST-2 004341) and the SALTSA Mobility Group for their ongoing support in this project.

References

Kumar S, Zahn C (2003) Mobile communications: evolution and impact on business operations. Technovation 23(6):515–520

Perrow, C (1967) A framework for the comparative analysis of organizations. American Sociological Review 32(2):194–208

Lilischkis S (2003) More yo-yos, pendulums and nomads: trends of mobile and multi-location work in the information society. STAR issue report no. 36, Databank, Milano

Yin, R (1994) Case study research: design and methods. Sage Publications, London

Zilliox D (2002) Get-started guide to m-commerce and mobile technology. American Management Association, New York

Part 3

Organisational Strategies

13 Knowledge Sharing in Mobile Work

Mariano Corso[1], Antonella Martini[2], Luisa Pellegrini[2]

[1] Department of Management Engineering, Polytechnic University of Milano, Italy
[2] Faculty of Engineering, University of Pisa, Italy

13.1 The KMS challenge in mobile context

Leveraging on people's knowledge and creativity is a competitive must in today's business environment. The intensification of competition, however, forces companies to adopt new organisational models that seriously challenge traditional approaches to managing knowledge. Hence, this chapter answers the need of empirically grounded research to draw implications of the systems supporting Knowledge Management (KM) within such new organizational models.

When analyzed in terms of how people are integrated and relate to the rest of the organisation, many companies are characterized by two trends:

- *Mobility and distribution of workforce*: nowadays the concept itself of the workplace is changing. People spend an increasing amount of their working time outside the physical boundaries of their company, often in mobility and interacting with customers or people from partner organizations (Laubacher and Malone 2003). Also when working inside the company, people often change positions and work in multi-disciplinary virtual teams. As a consequence, individuals have fewer and fewer opportunities for face to face interaction with their colleagues and can hardly rely on their own experience
- *Turnover and loose contractual links*: provisional nature of employment, loose forms of contractual links to the company and high level of turnover (Drucker 2002), while in many cases considered competitive needs, make people's stay with organizations temporary and partial, thus creating barriers to the sharing of knowledge and expertise among individuals

These two factors converge in what we call "Mobile Virtual Work" (MVW). MVW is done by different people in ever changing situations who need to collaborate and to be connected to shared resources in order to achieve their common goals. Being a "mobile virtual" (MV) worker is in many cases a necessity rather than a choice that requires personal qualities such as independence and entrepreneurship that were far less fundamental in traditional organizations. As far as professional growth and access to knowledge is concerned, MV workers cannot simply trust their company HR development policies, but have to care, in first person, about creating growth opportunities and building a network of relations that, in many cases, transcend the boundaries of the company.

Nowadays, MV workers represent an increasingly more relevant share of the total workforce (Drucker 2002; Laubacher and Malone 2003). Traditional management systems are not adequate, simply because they were not designed to answer their needs. Many management systems should be reviewed including rewarding training, and carrier paths, but the real essence of the change is probably related to Knowledge Management: when dealing with MV workers, KM becomes a fundamental need rather than a wish, for two reasons:

- MV workers knowledge and experience are becoming a fundamental asset for the company: only with a proper management of this knowledge, in both tacit and explicit forms, the company can, at least partly, appropriate this knowledge
- A proper Knowledge Management System (KMS) can:
  - reconnect MV workers to the professional and social network of the company, preventing loss of knowledge
  - provide them with opportunities for interaction and learning, thus supporting their job and their professional growth, long term employability, ultimately improving job satisfaction and attractiveness

When dealing with this issue, the biggest opportunities, but at the same time the biggest competitive challenges, are represented today by the availability of new ICT-enabled services, and in particular web applications and mobile Value Added Services. At a rapidly decreasing cost, these technologies are making it possible to overcome geographical, time and organizational barriers to communication and knowledge transfer in dispersed networks.

Theory on how to successfully implement new ICTs to manage knowledge for MV workers, however, is still in its infancy, and only anecdotal evidence about best practices is available today. The challenge for management theory is therefore clear: to provide empirically grounded and actionable knowledge for companies to design and implement new ICT enabled KM Systems able to extend the boundaries of their knowledge creation to their MV workers. Based on comparison among three case studies, the chapter is a first attempt to draw implications on KMS requirements in mobile contexts.

The issue of managing knowledge of a dispersed workforce has already been covered in economics and management literature mainly in connection with the problems of preserving intellectual capital and competence from loss and spill over (Minkler 1993; Tsoukas 1996; Becker 2001; Cramton 2001; Maskell 2001).

For example, Minkler (1993) focuses on firms that tried to assess the importance of their dispersed knowledge; he emphasizes that some organizational innovations – employee participation, organization in cooperative teams, just-in-time stock management systems, forms of labour protection – are solutions that stem from firms' awareness of the dispersion of their knowledge assets.

The dispersion of knowledge exists in all organizations. However, in traditional companies workers interact within the organizational physical boundaries, thus facilitating exchanges. In fact, the level of knowledge dispersion has progressively increased over the past few years, exceeding previous boundaries. Various factors contribute to this trend: internalization of markets, companies are more widespread within areas and product and service customization. In many cases, these factors induce firms to decrease the physical distance that separates them from their customers/suppliers, having some employees temporarily located in the customers'/suppliers' offices. In this context, the main problem is to create a technological and social infrastructure that allows knowledge and information transfer.

Different authors have pointed out that there are many relevant organizational and managerial effects resulting from the level of knowledge dispersion. Becker (2001) indicates three factors as the cause of organizational problems: large numbers, asymmetries and uncertainty. He also identifies some strategies allowing a better use of dispersed knowledge:

- substitute knowledge with providing access to knowledge (individuals have to remember where it can be found), the recovery takes place only when it is necessary
- provide users with the capability of completing incomplete knowledge
- design institutions with appropriate coordination mechanisms
- decompose organizational units into smaller ones
- increase the information available to the decision-maker

Focusing on knowledge workers, Cramton (1997; 2001; 2002) identifies the problems that can occur when MV people communicate and collaborate: 1) failures to communicate and retain contextual information regarding different members; 2) interference between unevenly distributed information and team-level collaboration, 3) differences in evaluating the relevance of information, 4) differences in speed of access to information and 5) difficulties in interpreting the meaning of silence/lack of communication. The main problems that may arise are: i) the propensity to ascribe peoples' behaviour or results to members instead of to the situation, ii) the decrease in learning capacity, iii) the incapacity to reach other members' expectations, and the damage of interpersonal reliance.

Many authors have analysed and proposed possible solutions to facilitate cooperation between mobile or geographically scattered workers or virtual teams (Cramton 1997; 2001; Furst et al. 1999; Duarte and Snyder 1999; Lipnack and Stamps 1997).

Two aspects contribute to an effective management of distributed knowledge: an efficient communication/interaction structure (Cohen and Levinthal 1990) and a focused human resources management system (Tsoukas 1996).

Communication can be enabled by creating information channels, which are parts of the social capital and can have a technological or an organizational nature (Nahapiet and Ghoshal 1998; Gupta and Govindarajan 2000). The introduction of job rotation is an example of an organizational solution, while intranet and corporate portals are technological tools facilitating the interaction among experts.

Many authors have focused their attention on the impact of KMS on performances (Haanes and Lowendhal 1997; Petrash 1996; Roos et al. 1997; Schiuma and Marr 2001; Sveiby 1997). The impact on performances is strongly related to the approach adopted in the KMS (Davenport and Prusak 1998; Wiig 1997) and to the direct impacts on organizational behaviours in terms of knowledge creation, transfer and capitalization.

A fundamental assumption that is common to recent literature is that coordination and decision making do not require knowledge centralization, but rather should provide the access to knowledge (Nonaka 1990). Simple access to knowledge still requires users to have both competency and capacity for understanding, assimilating and using retrieved knowledge. In addition, users should also be able to correct possible mistakes (Collins and Kusch 1998), adapt knowledge to the specific problem and complete possible gaps (Nonaka and Takeuchi 1995).

More recently, the concept of communities of practice emerged as a key issue. Communities of practice consist of people with a joint interest, mutual engagement and a shared repertoire; they develop spontaneously outside the formal organization, can span organizational boundaries, create and are based on relationships (Wenger and Snyder 2000). The concept of community of practice has a strong potential when applied in the context of companies having MV workers: by facilitating interaction within communities, a company may reconnect its MV workers to its social and cognitive system. However, literature on development and management of communities of practice is still based on a few anecdotal contributions based on best practices.

Overall current literature seems to focus on the problem of coping with knowledge dispersion, rather than on the phenomenon of managing MV workers' dispersion: in particular, there is a lack of empirical research regarding its diffusion, characteristics and effects on Knowledge Management Systems.

The chapter is organized as follows: in the next paragraph a framework is introduced and the methodology for this research is described. Then results are presented and analyzed; limitation of this study and plan for further research are finally discussed.

13.2 Research framework and methodology

This contribution is based on the evidence from an empirical research project which started in 2002 (Corso et al. 2004) and aimed at exploring the issue of Knowledge Management in companies characterized by Mobile Virtual Work. Our aim is to answer the following research questions:

RQ1. Relevance and characteristics of MVW
1. What is the relevance of MVW in Italian companies?
2. What are the characteristics of MVW in Italy?

RQ2. What are the emerging approaches companies use to manage knowledge and their effects on performance in different MVW settings?

Funded by the Italian Ministry of Research, the project involved researchers from four universities and started with the development of six case studies that were used to explore the field and develop a framework for further explanatory research.

The lack of research and especially the lack of empirically grounded analyses on MVW in Italy meant that the investigation had to be divided into three major phases (Fig. 13.1):

• 1st research step. We conducted six explorative cases – not reported here - in order to identify the relevant variables of the phenomenon.

Such variables have been used to build the research protocol for the survey.

- 2nd research step. We developed a two-step survey. The first – phone survey – measured how relevant mobile work is in Italy (RQ1), while the second – paper/electronic survey – analyzes the MV workers' activities and the KM tools used in the firms, which declared to have Mobile workers (RQ2). The phone survey was based on a database of 1504 large and medium sized companies. Sampling was based on 2002 AIDA database (Bureau van Dijk): we were interested in large and medium sized enterprises in manufacturing industries. Out of the 1504 companies contacted 899 answered the survey (59.8% response rate), a sample that represents a 36% of the overall relevant population[1]. For the second step, the survey sample was made up of the people who declared to have Mobile workers in the first step.

- 3rd research step. On the basis of the survey results, we conducted three explicative case studies in order to explore the cause and effect links among the prominent variables in depth.

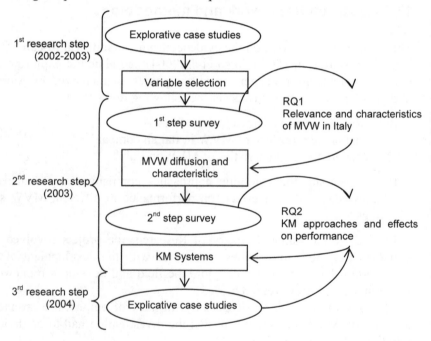

Fig. 13.1. Research methodology

---

[1] According to Mediobanca estimation of 2,500 large and medium sized companies operating in Italy.

The Investigation framework (Fig. 13.2) was developed starting from the analysis of management literature and available results of previous research projects. Six exploratory cases were conducted to identify the key variables that appear to be relevant to understand the phenomenon.

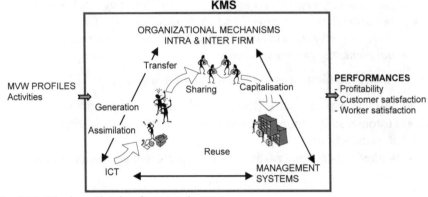

Fig. 13.2. The investigation framework

Following a contingent approach, the investigation framework assumes that performances are influenced by KMS, and that KMS effectiveness in terms of the ability to produce good performance depends on the internal coherence among choices (internal consistency) and on the adequacy with the contingent characteristics (Profiles) of MVW (external consistency).

Each group of variables has been analysed and described, based on the results of exploratory studies. For MV worker we referred to the worker who:

- is contractually linked to the firm and can be subjected to control by the firm and/or coordination
- mainly works outside the firm. Employees who are permanently assigned work outside the firm (such as, in some cases, the sales agents) and workers who, though having their own site in the firm, mainly work outside the firm (for example consultants and maintenance people)

MVW characteristics were analysed in terms of the type of activity that MV do, e.g. sales, maintenance, consulting.

We adopted the definition of KM and KMS by Corso et al. (2004):

Knowledge Management is about creating an environment that encourages people to learn and share knowledge by aligning goals, integrating bits and pieces of information within and across organizational boundaries, and producing new knowledge that is usable and useful to the organisation

The Knowledge Management System is the intended or emerging configuration of technical, organizational and managerial choices (KMS) with which the company influences people's behaviour in all phases of the knowledge lifecycle, including the acquisition, transfer and sharing, capitalisation and reuse of knowledge. KMS supporting knowledge processes (and their management, for that matter) therefore exist in, and must be designed to fit the internal and external context of the organisation

Finally, performances were analyzed in terms of:

- business performance (effects on costs and revenues, innovation)
- customer satisfaction (perceived quality of the product/service and overall satisfaction)
- worker satisfaction (quality of working life and professional growth)

13.3 Field research results

13.3.1 Mapping the MW phenomenon: the survey results

Research question 1: relevance and characteristics of MVW

Within the 899 firms which answered the survey, 410 stated that they have MV workers (45.6%) and provided information about the characteristics of these people and their activities. Three main Profiles of MV workers emerged:

- In 47% of the firms the most relevant group of MV workers are members of the sales force. In many cases these people, beside commercial competency, also need technical competency regarding products and are engaged in some form of customer service
- In 35% of the companies MV workers are mainly technicians, such as maintenance people or installers. Besides technical knowledge, in many cases, they also require complementary commercial competency
- In the remaining 18% of firms MV workers are managers: researchers, plant directors, inspectors or people responsible for affiliated units

Research question 2: KM approaches

This group of 410 companies was then contacted for the second step of the survey, through a questionnaire[2]. Eighty three companies answered with usable questionnaire data which accounts for a response rate of 20.2%.

In order to identify the emerging approaches used by companies to manage MVW knowledge, we used cluster analysis[3].

The most up-to-date literature as well as the explorative case studies provide evidence that the main problems connected with Knowledge Management for MVW are the following (Table 13.1):

- knowledge transfer
    - retrieval of knowledge from organizational knowledge storage banks, i. training on the job, ii. in case of problems, workers ii.1 use manuals, ii.2 contact experts, ii.3 use customer/supplier records, ii.4 use project database
    - feedback from MV workers to update knowledge domains, (sharing of knowledge, reports)
- planning and controlling MVW activities
    - MVW activity planning (autonomous vs. hierarchical planning)
    - MVW activity control (reports, performance measurement, results measurement)

These aspects were used to characterize four emerging Knowledge Management approaches (Table 13.1):

- *Products/services innovation orientation.* Tasks are partially repetitive: retrieval of knowledge is important and frequent, and hence supported by all the investigated tools. In particular, manuals and project databases allow recovery of explicit knowledge, while expert networks support the recovery of tacit knowledge. Feedback is important for updating knowl-

---

[2] The person in charge of answering the questions had the possibility of selecting the modality of transmission of the paper questionnaire between ordinary mail, e-mail or fax. Two-round reminders were organized in order to increase the returns

[3] In order to identify the most appropriate number of clusters, a series of hierarchical clusters were created. Because of the high number of isolated cases, four clusters were used to allow for differentiating behaviours and to provide a reasonable number of clusters. In the case where a lower number of clusters is chosen, most firms appear to be grouped together in only one cluster, while the other clusters are small and non- homogeneous. In the case where more than four clusters are chosen, smaller clusters are split, while bigger clusters, which are relatively homogeneous, are not influenced.

edge capital and achieved with reports. Workers are partially autonomous; therefore the adoption of a control and an incentive system, mostly based on performance measures and reports, is important.

- *Process standardization orientation*. Processes are easy to be analyzed and tasks repetitive. Therefore, retrieval of knowledge is not frequent and training is mainly on the job. New problems or exceptions are not frequent, but when they occur, MV workers examine manuals or contact experts; capitalization and sharing of knowledge generated when the rare exceptions take place, is strongly encouraged (reports). Activities are planned by the company and results can be easily controlled by means of reports.

- *Performance control orientation*. MV workers independently manage their non-repetitive activities. The retrieval mainly involves knowledge and information about customers and suppliers, which is useful to analyse the specific problem and to develop a customised solution and experts are the main source. For the characteristics of tasks, the company cannot fully plan MVW activities. Therefore, incentives are based on individual results. In these contexts, Knowledge Management is mainly focused on control by individual performance measures, but also supports informal networks.

- *Knowledge sharing orientation*. Context and problems are variable and the company cannot hierarchically plan MVW activities and use KMS in order to control MV workers and measure their results. Knowledge is mainly tacit: it cannot be memorized in manuals or other physical supports, because tasks are not repetitive, training on the job is not really useful. Experience is the most important requirement for MV workers, and for this reason expert networks are a fundamental resource in solving complex problems. The tacit form of knowledge inhibits adoption of formal incentive schemes for sharing of knowledge. Sharing is achieved in informal networks: systems are very important for identifying the right person to contact. Companies use their broad knowledge and customer and supplier records to analyze a specific problem and to develop a customised solution.

Table 13.1. Emergent KM approach in MVW

PROBLEMS	KM APPROACHES ORIENTED TO			
	PRODUCTS / SERVICES INNOVATION	PROCESSES STANDARDIZATION	PERFORMANCE CONTROL	KNOWLEDGE SHARING
Knowledge retrieval in case of exceptions	Exceptions are frequent: workers frequently use manuals, experts and records	Workers rarely face new problems. In these rare cases, they use manuals, experts and project databases Information concerning customers and suppliers is usually not useful	New problems are very frequent. Because of the nature of both knowledge and activities, workers get knowledge from experts. Customer and supplier records are also useful to analyze specific problems	Knowledge is complex and tacit knowledge and is capitalized by experts. Customers and suppliers records are important for customising solutions
Feedback for the company	Reports are used for creating an organizational memory about customers and suppliers, rather than for controlling purposes. This memory is useful for adapting solutions to customer specifications	Reports are useful for both control and identification of new problems and updating manuals and databases when MVW faces the rare exceptions	Tacit form of knowledge and the lack of task repetitiveness do not allow the creation of a company memory. Knowledge resides in individuals	Knowledge is shared spontaneously through informal networks of experts. Reports allow the identification of experts
Activity planning	As activities are only partly repetitive, MVW tasks are only partly planned by the company in a hierarchical way	Activities are repetitive so tasks are planned by the company	As activities are not repetitive, companies cannot plan tasks of MV workers who, indeed, are autonomous	MV workers are partially autonomous
Activity control	The control of partially autonomous workers is achieved with performance measures and reports	Tasks are hierarchically planned; therefore control can be achieved using only reports Result measures check only group activities and performance measures are not defined	Individual performance measures are used to control MV workers	MV workers are not controlled, although the submitting of reports is required

In order to understand whether the specific MVW profiles drive the selection of the KM approaches, an association analysis was carried out (Table 13.2).

Table 13.2. MVW profiles and KM approaches

		KM APPROACHES ORIENTED TO			
		PRODUCTS / SERVICES CUSTOMISATION	PROCESSES STANDARDIZATION	PERFORMANCE CONTROL	SHARING	TOTAL
MVW PROFILES	Sales force	19	4	8	2	33
	Technicians	6	11	-	4	21
	Manager	1	2	5	3	11
	Total	26	17	13	9	65

The analysis points out that:
- sales forces mainly use KM oriented to product/service innovation
- most technicians adopt KM oriented to process standardization
- managers are mainly associated with KM oriented to performance control

Based on these results, we can formulate the following hypothesis:

> *Hyp. 1: There is a relation between the characteristics of the task performed by MV workers, and the characteristics of the Knowledge Management System.*

In order to completely understand the survey results (Hypothesis 1), three explicative case studies were analyzed. The specific aims were to:

- underpin better the results of Table 13.1, trying to understand the association between the different MVW profiles and the four KM approaches (Table 13.2)
- explore the impact of different KM approaches on performance, and in particular on worker satisfaction

13.3.2 Cause and effect links: three explicative case studies

In order to analyze the two aspects mentioned above, Perrow's model of technology and structure (1967) was used (Corso et al. 2005). It highlights two key dimensions in order to describe a task: the existence (or otherwise) of well-established techniques for performing tasks i.e. task analyzability, and the degree of variety in the tasks encountered; number of exceptions. The two dimensions are commonly, and collectively, referred to as task uncertainty. Where established techniques for handling tasks do not exist i.e. low analyzability, or where substantial variety or novelty in the tasks encountered exists i.e. high number of exceptions, Perrow describes the task setting as "non-routine". Conversely, when tasks are analyzable with few exceptions, the task setting is "routine". Perrow proceeds to describe the structural arrangements necessary to achieve effective control and coordination for the different task environments faced by an organization.

Figure 13.3 presents a diagrammatic representation of Perrow's framework. Tasks in Cell 1 are repetitive and familiar i.e. few exceptions, with known routines for handling them (high analyzability). Perrow also argued that organizations facing such tasks would be able to rely on procedure guides, operating manuals, job codification and rigid lines of reporting and accountability for controlling employee behaviour.

In contrast, Cell 3 represents the "non-routine" situation, and it is here that Perrow expects that formal, bureaucratic controls will not be effective for controlling performance. Tasks cannot be "programmed" and thus behaviour cannot be controlled by implementing procedures which pre-specify desired actions or by monitoring individual actions through the use of supervisors. The remaining two situations depicted in Figure 15.3 (Cells 2 and 4) involve task settings where it is more difficult to predict which forms of control will prove most effective. Tasks may have little variety, yet exhibit uncertainty in the transformation process (Cell 2); others may have little uncertainty but a great deal of variety (Cell 4). They are in the middle of the routine/non-routine continuum, but they are not the same. Considering Cell 2, tasks here are low in variety suggesting the potential suitability of behaviour controls i.e. fine glassware. However, notwithstanding the lack of variety of tasks, little has been learned about the process by which inputs are transformed into outputs; programs for performing these tasks have not been established i.e. analyzability is low. It is, therefore, not possible to develop a set of manuals, guides or procedures, which can be drawn upon during task execution.

In Cell 4, much variety is encountered in tasks, but notwithstanding this variation, input-output relations can be readily specified, i.e. made-to-order machine, civil engineering. This enables the development and implementation of programmed controls, such as procedure guides and operating manuals, and/or the use of superior authority to ensure that behaviour is in accordance with what is known to achieve desired results.

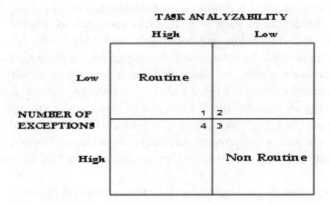

Fig. 13.3. Perrow model of technology and structure

Based on this classification and on existing literature on Knowledge Management, we can formulate more specific hypotheses about the characteristics of the Knowledge Management System that can better suit each specific situation.

We can use Perrow's model to classify the activities of the three main kinds of MV workers that emerged from the survey: managers, sales force and technicians.

The consulting process is characterized by low repetitiveness of activities, absence of standardized procedures and practices and unavailability of a clear body of knowledge, which can guide the work. According to Perrow's model the consultancy task represents the "non-routine" situation (Cell 3).

The sales task, on the other hand, in terms of the Perrow's model is characterized by little uncertainty but a great deal of variety.

Finally, if compared to the other tasks, the activities of field force technicians can be regarded as "routine" situations, characterized by little task variety and a clear view of input-output relations in task execution.

Table 13.3. Case settings

	A	B	C
Industry	Consultancy	Telecommunication	Multi-utilities
Core product	E- solutions	GSM communication system	Energy distribution and selling
Investigated process	Project management	Sales	Maintenance

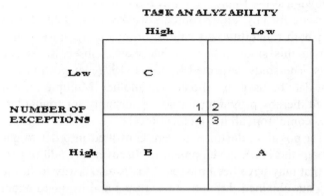

Fig. 13.4. Case position in Perrow model

In order to test and refine the research hypothesis three case studies have been developed:

- Case A is an Italian system integrator that recently developed a KMS to support its dispersed managers
- Case B is a Telecom Operator that developed a KMS supporting its indirect sales personnel
- Case C is a multi-utility, which produces, distributes and sells thermal and electric energy, manages the public lighting system, the traffic lights and the thermal and electrical systems

Table 13.3 compares the characteristics of the three case companies, while Figure 13.4 summarises the characteristics of their MV workers' activities in terms of the Perrow's model.

Data collection and analysis

Case studies were conducted in late 2003 and early 2004. During the site visit, impressions and informal observations were recorded too. Data were collected through semi-structured interviews with individual respondents and observations.

An interview guide and an open-ended questionnaire were used to conduct two-hour semi-structured interviews. The interview guide had four sections. The first part referred to general information about the firm; the second was focused on MVW profiles; the third investigated the KM tools and the fourth worker satisfaction about the KMS. Worker satisfaction was operationalized by means of a five point Likert scale, ranging from very low (=1) to very high (=5).

It is known that the triangulation of multi information sources, designed to compensate for any single-source's weaknesses, is an effective way of increasing both reliability and validity in qualitative research. Thus, data collection in this study relied on interviews, observations and archival documents. The study respected Kanter's (1977) suggestion that different sources of data be used to validate one another. Multiple informants were interviewed thereby providing further opportunity for triangulation. These informants come from all hierarchical levels.

Wherever possible, documents were consulted in order to gather information about the KMS development to discover any additional important elements that may have been missed. This is also a way to further confirm or refuse data obtained through other means and to guard against bias in informants' accounts (Leonard Barton 1990).

Data were analysed by first building individual case studies using the interviews and the record of impressions and then comparing cases to investigate the relationship between MVW activities and KM tools.

Empirical findings and test of hypothesis

Case A

Company A is a leading Italian system integrator company. It specializes in end-to-end financial solutions, e-security, intranet applications and web integration; everything from feasibility studies and the drawing up of an e-Business strategy, through the identification of business processes and the design of rich content, right up to the development and integration of software solutions.

A started its internal KM solution in 1998, and now it has become a standard model for its customers. The solution includes, in addition to the standard Intranet functionalities, specific tools to support communities online.

A employs 300 MV workers operating out of multiple locations and frequently on customer sites. The primary unit of work is a project that is carried out for one customer. Customers include private companies mainly banks and insurance companies and public service and local governments in Italy. Common projects include the design and development of Intranet/Extranet/Internet portal, content and Knowledge Management solutions, e-business integration, e-security, e-ERM/PRM/CRM (electronic employee/partnership/customer relationship management), e-learning and e-marketing applications. In order to completely satisfy the customers and to guarantee the full integration of the new solutions into existing systems, the company has to work closely with its customers. An important part of its business strategy is developing long-lasting customer relationships. In terms of task complexity, MV workers in *A* have to face a high variety of situations and exceptions that need customized and flexible solutions. Many customers need to be provided with a large portfolio of technologies and solutions, in a wide range of areas: from manufacturing to services, from the public to the private sector.

In 1998 the company started to design and develop a new organizational model in order to manage knowledge of its highly dispersed workers and pursue continuous improvement of internal processes and performances. Such a model, supported by the Intranet, is based on the creation of improvement groups, the "cubes", aiming at suggesting and implementing improvement and growth plans, in the company strategic areas, according to EFQM (European Foundation for Quality Management) that *A* joined in 1999. Each cube includes a limited number of employees, selected by the top management, headed by a chairman and a secretary. The chairman, directly chosen by the CEO who sponsored the project from the beginning, is responsible for the success of the cube: he coordinates activities, controls the newsgroup, approves the documentation and supervises the contents. The group interacts through both face-to-face and computer-mediated meetings. Each cube publishes the results of its activity (white papers, FAQ) on the intranet and interacts with all the employees through discussion newsgroups. Periodically the performances of each cube are evaluated by participation degree of the employees, work in progress and achieved result. In case they are not satisfactory, the cube may be closed.

The newsgroup management requires high investments both in terms of people, i.e. about one third of the MV workers is directly involved in the cubes, and of money, i.e. the system is constantly improved by a new release every 2 months. The company top management has been very satisfied with the results obtained till now by the cube model. Besides promoting the ongoing improvement, it also changed organizational relationships progressively, intensifying horizontal communication and making the vertical one easier.

The cube model is now well consolidated and *A* recently launched it on the market.

Job satisfaction concerning the cube model was assessed through a survey at the end of 2003. On a five-point Likert scale, the users expressed a satisfaction degree of 3.35 regarding the content management in the corporate portal; of 3.41 regarding the graphical interface and of 2.95 regarding the speed in content retrieval. Also according to the interviewees, user satisfaction seems to be medium level.

The KMS has a network structure that allows horizontal/vertical communication among participants, which suits the employee communication needs. As an interviewee underlines:

"The newsgroups are open to everyone and there are no barriers to communication: you can share knowledge/thoughts even with people you have never met and coming from all hierarchical levels".

According to the non-routine task type, the KMS in *A* does not provide a centralized knowledge storage-retrieval system. In fact, a company that sells customized services - that is, most of its work goes toward meeting particular customers' unique needs - takes limited advantage of codified knowledge.

Anyway, some criticisms emerge from specific aspects of the KMS, such as:

- Top-down development strategy. The evolution of the system is planned centrally by the Chief Knowledge Officer and the CEO that decide the requirements of the new releases. In fact, according to the worker satisfaction survey, 40% of the respondents complain about the usability of the KMS that does not care about the user needs, 29% about interactivity features, 19% about the content structure and 10% about graphics.
- Rigid hierarchical structures, task definition inside the cubes and formal performance measurement: a chairman and a secretary are nominated that coordinates a team of 8-9 people; the chairman is responsible for the success of the cube; formal document management; performance about the level of participation of the employees, work in progress, achieved results; in case performances are not satisfactory, the cube may be closed. As an interviewee says,

  "The formal control causes distortion in the use of cubes that tend to become self referential. The people that participate in the newsgroups are the same people that manage them".

- High specialization of cubes. Regarding this issue, an interviewee notes that:

  "Some cubes are too specialized, for example the IT one, and so hardly useful to me".

- According to the worker satisfaction survey, 54% of participants identify the contents as the most urgent issue to be improved and 27% asks for knowledge about processes and daily activities, overcoming functional boundaries. This point is connected to the knowledge needs of MV workers in *A*. In order to manage the consulting process in a system integrator company, a broad range of knowledge is required, and when specialized knowledge is needed, experts are contacted on-demand.

The criticisms expressed by the users give some indications that can be related to the appropriateness of the KM System to the task type. In fact in case A, criticisms are related to the aspects of the system that do not seem to follow Perrow's suggestions. Regarding non-routine situations, Perrow's model expects that formal bureaucratic systems will not be effective. Perrow argues that "collegial" structural arrangements are required in these settings. As regards contents, frequently cubes are perceived as too specialized and consequently not useful. This content structure seems to follow the bureaucratic model that establishes the high specialization of tasks inside the organization. Such a model seems to have been adopted by *A* also in the navigation path within the corporate intranet.

Thus, guidelines in case *A* could be summarized in shifting the architecture to a more informal one, avoiding a too strict and top-down control in favour of a self and peer group control process. Furthermore the company, by means of the KMS, should promote socialization processes that could lead to the emergence of spontaneous knowledge communities overcoming the boundaries between organizational functions.

Based on both positive and negative findings about the effectiveness of the KMS used by *A*, we can therefore confirm hypothesis 1 and refine it as follows:

> *Hyp. 1.1: in non-routine situations, KMS based on formal and bureaucratic controls (procedure guides and operating manuals) and/or the use of superior authority to monitor individual actions are expected not to be effective.*

Case B

Company *B* is the leading European operator in terms of GSM lines on a single network and leader in the domestic market with about 24.6 million lines. Due to its former monopolistic position, *B* played a trail-blazing role in the mobile telecommunication industry, both opening a mass market for the mobile business in Italy as well as making Italy itself one of the most advanced European markets in terms of penetration and supply of advanced services.

In order to keep the leadership in a market, in which the penetration level of the mobile voice services is already very high and competitors are more and more numerous, *B* competes on innovation both at the technological and the service level, consolidating its own leadership in the traditional voice business and concurrently becoming one of the fundamental players in the development of the whole telecommunication industry.

In the last years, *B* tried to enlarge its presence also outside Italy, particularly in Europe and in South America. In Italy, *B*'s sales force is divided into three groups: large firms are directly followed by dedicated account managers, final customers are contacted by means of shops and e-commerce, while for small and medium enterprises (SMEs), B adopts an indirect sales force, composed of approximately 150 agencies (Business Promoters), employing almost 1000 agents. The case focuses on B's indirect sales force.

At the end of 2000, the company was faced with the necessity to improve the poor knowledge and weak relationship with its agents, evidenced by their high turnover rate (greater than 50%), their unsatisfactory degree of qualification and their low commitment to the firm. In order to improve this situation, B introduced a web-based platform (B_plat) aimed at creating and developing a virtual community among the agents. The challenge was to make B_plat an environment where the agents could train, exchange experiences and acquire information regarding the company and its products. In other words, with B_plat the aim was to give sales agents the social dimension that the MVW conditions risked losing and to build direct communication with the agents, therefore avoiding the interface of the agency owners.

The use of the B_plat was encouraged by means of a game rewarding those users who proved to be more active in information sharing. The possibility of having a prize but, more importantly, the satisfaction the agents got in reaching the highest rank and boosting colleague esteem appeared to be the most stimulating factors in game participation.

Since its introduction, the platform received even more success than expected, as the rapid growth in the user number as well as usage during after work hours demonstrated. The forum, where the agents have the opportunity to ask questions/help and speak of their own experience, immediately became the heart of the system. Soon the agents became proactive in proposing and asking for changes to the platform. Among the most important changes, that make today B_plat a KMS, the following should be remembered: i) the introduction of a channel with up-to-date information on B products and services; ii) the setting up of a 'direct line' where B marketing people answer agents' questions such a 'direct line' was soon revealed as an important source of information and impressions regarding the market; iii) the introduction of a news channel for the publication of both information regarding industry and papers for stimulating dialogues with customers or colleagues and the enrichment of the training channel with programmes for the development of sales skills.

Nowadays, the platform is composed of five sections:

- News, where the most important information is classified and published
- Training, where courses, with asynchronous courses are provided

- Services-Products, containing information regarding *B's* portfolio and the benchmark with that of competitors
- Community, containing moderated forums, where agents can meet, discuss, ask questions and exchange experiences, as well as information
- Desktop with a schedule of interesting events and a selection of useful tools such as presentations, ideas for customers and a service offered by experts providing agents with support on commercial, fiscal and technological matters

According to the interviewees, worker satisfaction is very high. The KMS has a network structure that allows horizontal/vertical communication among participants, which suits the agents' communication needs. According to the interviewees, the system improved the feeling of belonging to a community as underlined in the words of the CEO:

"Since the introduction of the tool, in a six month time period, the agents' turnover rate reduced from over 50% to 29%"

The connection between the introduction of the tool and the turnover reduction is also proved by the enthusiastic feedback from agents. The turnover reduction together with knowledge sharing and training opportunities (e-learning) provided by the system, positively impacted on the agents' professional quality, which emerged from some interviews. The improvement of the agents' skills, enabling them to better cope with a high number of exceptions, is coherent with implications of Perrow's model. In fact, if task variety i.e. number of exceptions is very high, the number of procedures required to handle all the exceptions would be prohibitively costly to document. The organization, in order to achieve the coordination needed for task execution may need to resort to "personnel" controls (Perrow 1970).

Another aspect that suits well the implications of Perrow's model is the emergent feature of the KM solution. During the development of the system and successively, for the following releases, the feedback and suggestions from the field, were taken into high consideration. The involvement in the continuous improvement of the system was appreciated by the agents. As one of them reports:

"Our contributions proved to be determinant for the success of the tool. Now services and functionalities really fit our needs".

In fact, where tasks are highly analyzable and exceptions are many, "(…) it is more difficult to predict which configuration will prove most effective" (Perrow 1967). The system is dynamic, and thus new evolutions are going to be implemented. For example, one of the main concerns is decreasing the control of newsgroups and forums. At the moment, forums are supervised by a chairman that guarantees the reliability and privacy of published items. In the near future, this may not be necessary any more. According to Perrow, moving towards a less bureaucratic model fits with the characteristics of the task that is in the middle of a routine-/non-routine continuum: being high task analyzability procedure should be relevant, however high number of exceptions moves towards non-pre-determined procedures and information sharing.

Based on these findings we can therefore confirm hypothesis 1 and refine it as follows:

> *Hyp. 1.2: in situations characterized by high number of exceptions and high task analyzability, KMS based on non-pre-determined procedures, and person-to-person communication are expected to be effective.*

Case C

C is a multi-utility, which produces, distributes and sells thermal and electric energy, manages the public lighting system, the traffic lights and the thermal and electrical systems of Turin municipal buildings. C group extends to telecommunications and Global Service, but it also operates in complementary fields to core business, such as engineering services, consulting and reliability studies.

Because of the evolution of the competitive scenario, C is transforming into one of the main Italian multi-utilities, and it has been quoted on the telematic market since 2000. Group turnover achieved 458 million euro (+26%).

The case focuses on C mobile field force technicians in charge of maintenance, management and control of the energy network and on those who organize the activities of the field force. In both cases, their work is supported by a mobile device – MOB-I - for the daily activities of the field force technicians, the whole process of planning, management and reporting of the interventions and the access to the intranet, with the possibility of taking advantage of all the functionalities that were formerly obtainable only in the headquarters i.e. operating manuals, procedure guides.

MOB-I is a part of a wider plan sponsored by the general manager, which was started in 2000 with the introduction of SAP and allowed the creation of an information system that merges in only one workflow both the activities of maintenance and those typical of the customer relationship management. Besides, in 2000, C acquired the management of the electrical network of Turin from ENEL i.e. the main Italian generation company in the electricity industry, incorporating the connected company branch.

This event represented the transition from a maintenance management system, which was previously based on external staff coming from small companies, to a new system which mainly relies on the internal employees coming from ENEL. Concurrently, C created shower-equipped stores located all around Turin in order to facilitate intervention management: alerted technicians are able to collect the required tools in the most convenient store.

MOB-I project went through a 5 month definition phase (January-May 2004) and became operative in June 2004; a bottom-up solution development was developed, with involvement of the technicians. During the last phases of project definition till the first phases of operativeness, IT staff accompanied the field force technicians, while explaining how to use the new mobile device and indicating its functionalities and advantages.

Afterwards, during the pilot phase, the mobile device was tested by five selected teams, followed by another five teams and then by all the other teams. By the end of October, MOB-I will be used by 50 Mobile Worker teams out of 100; and also the field force technicians in charge of maintenance of the municipal plants systems and of the gas network will be equipped with the mobile device.

MOB-I introduced radical changes in the field force work and in the way interventions are carried out. More exactly, the process is articulated into:

- Intervention allocation: intervention planning is completely automated and submitted to the person responsible for the final approval. When approved, information regarding intervention allocation is directly shown on the mobile devices of the field force teams, with no paper to be printed
- Intervention arrangement: field force technicians have to collect the tools for carrying out the allocated interventions. After stores were set up, they have the possibility of retrieving material at the nearest store, so they can avoid going to the headquarters. Hence, technicians have the possibility of going directly to the place where they have to carry out the first intervention, in this case going to the store, which is nearest to their home, so it is not necessary to go to the headquarters at the beginning of the day
- Plant visit: the teams go to the plant where the breakdown occurred or wherever it is necessary to operate
- Intervention execution: the technicians carry out the required interventions
- Reporting: technicians are required to report the interventions directly on the mobile device, accounting for materials, operations, time

- Synchronization: reports are sent to the headquarters through Internet. Reports are stored automatically and data are immediately stored in the database

MOB-I introduction drove toward the intervention management in push modality: if a plant is out of order, the nearest technicians are directly alerted. All the above described changes – MOB-I with the connected possibility to access the Intranet and the stores – gave raise to a new figure, that of the single technician who is able to carry out interventions without colleagues.

MOB-I introduction lead to many benefits: a great saving of paper in supporting the activities, the simplification of the management of the maintenance process, a better control on the team activities and the possibility of dedicating the time, which was previously spent on bureaucratic activities to productive activities. The most outstanding example is the possibility to manage on SAP, through appropriate application, overtime work, retrieving data from team mobile devices. The intervention timeliness – and hence their increasing number – represents a great performance improvement for the customer.

High satisfaction by the mobile worker is a result of the optimization of the activities i.e. the possibility to take advantage of the stores, that allows them to leave home later and to waste little time in journeys, and of better motivation.

According to Perrow, where the task is highly analyzable and with few exceptions (routine), organization would be able to rely on procedure guides, operating manuals, job codification and rigid lines of reporting. The investments in the system have been high. The integration with the customer is the next step in order to improve the system as well as the functionality enlargement i.e. voice control.

Also in this case, the relation among the characteristics of the activity according to Perrow's model, and the KMS emerged quite clearly and allow us to confirm hypothesis 1 and refine it as follows:

> *Hyp. 1.3: in routine situations, KMS based on procedure guides, operation manuals, task codification and rigid lines of reporting for controlling employee behaviour are expected to be effective.*

13.4 Conclusions and implications

This chapter aimed at understanding the state of MVW in Italy and at exploring the relations between MV workers activities, KM tools and worker satisfaction. Using a representative survey, the main typologies of MV workers were identified and related to different KM approaches. A significant relation among MV workers typologies and KM approaches used emerged that was further analyzed by means of three explicative case studies. The characteristics of the activities performed by the three main types of MV workers that we find as relevant from a survey – namely managers, sales personnel and field force technicians – were classified using Perrow's model.

Results from the three case studies, summarised and compared in Table 13.4, confirmed the general hypothesis derived from the survey that there is a connection between the characteristics of the tasks and the characteristics that a KMS should have in order to contribute to business performance and workers satisfaction.

In particular we can expand our initial hypothesis as follows:

> *Hyp. 1.1: in non-routine situations, KMS based on formal and bureaucratic controls (procedure guides and operating manuals) and/or the use of superior authority to monitor individual actions are expected not to be effective.*
>
> *Hyp. 1.2: in situations characterized by high number of exceptions and high task analizability KMS based on non-predetermined procedures, and person-to-person communication are expected to be effective.*
>
> *Hyp. 1.3: in routine situations, KMS based on procedure guides, operation manuals, task codification and rigid lines of reporting for controlling employee behaviour are expected to be effective.*

When KMS is consistent with task characteristics, MV workers satisfaction, measured in terms of usefulness, appropriateness to the business and frequency of use, is high. Otherwise, worker satisfaction is low with the aspects of KMS that does not match with the organizational suggestions derived from Perrow model.

Table 13.4. Comparative case analysis

		A CONSULTING	B SALES	C MAINTENANCE
KMS MAIN EXPECTED RESULT		Improve efficiency and effectiveness	Enhance MVW social dimension	Improve efficiency and effectiveness
KMS ORGANIZATIONAL IMPACT		Impact on internal communication	Impact on power map	Impact on workload
MAIN SPONSOR		CEO	Sales executive	CEO
ICT CHOICES	ICT TOOLS	Intranet (Plumtree, Webcube™, Documentum, Cruisenet™, Digital Think, Applix, Eyenet™)	Internet (UNITIM, SimToolkit, WAP, GPRS)	Intranet (also via UMTS, Oracle mobile platform) Tablet pc
	ICT TOOL DEVELOPMENT	In-house Top-down High investment Dynamic (a new release every 2 months)	Outsourced Bottom-up High investment Dynamic	In-house Bottom-up High investment Dynamic
ORGANIZATIONAL CHOICES	INFORMATION FLOW	Network	Network	Network
	INTEGRATION WITH OTHER IS	No	Marketing IS	SAP IS
MANAGERIAL CHOICES	KMS ADOPTION	All the MV workers were forced to adopt the system	Adoption on voluntary basis, fostered by managerial levers (awards)	All the MV workers were forced to adopt the system
	CONTROL SYSTEM	On frequency of use and contents	No	On frequency of use
	FORMAL PERFORMANCE MEASUREMENT	Yes	Yes	No
WORKER SATISFACTION		Medium	Very high	Very high

We believe that this study can be a good starting point to develop future research with the aim of refining the concept of uncertainty and tailoring the guidelines for KMS design. More specifically, advances could be made by giving a specific theoretical meaning to the concept of uncertainty when applied to tasks characterized by knowledge intensity. Also guidelines could be more oriented to the definition of the KMS features that provide the best fit with the task characteristics.

In this study, we tried to attenuate many of the reliability problems by combining quantitative and qualitative research using multiple informants from different hierarchical levels, triangulation of different types of data sources and a systematic data analysis.

Generalization remains more of an issue. Further research is needed to prove whether this finding can be replicated in similar firms. But, although they must be treated with caution, the findings of this exploratory study are nonetheless suggestive.

Although the results suggest some general requirements for KMS design, it provides a first perspective on the theme with relevant managerial implications: the characteristics of the task performed by MV workers provide clear guidance for the design of the KMS in terms of degree of control and codification. The study of the three cases shows that the worker satisfaction for the KMS in terms of usefulness, appropriateness to the business and frequency of use seems to match the guidelines, which emerged from the analysis of the task type. In particular, worker satisfaction is low with the aspects of KMS that do not match with the organizational suggestions derived from Perrow.

References

Becker MC (2001) Managing dispersed knowledge: organizational problems, managerial strategies and their effectiveness. Journal of Management Studies 38(7): 1037–1051

Cohen WM, Levinthal DA (1990) Absorptive capacity: a new perspective on learning and innovation. Administrative Science Quarterly 35: 128–152

Collins H, Kusch M (1998) The shape of actions – what humans and machines can do. MIT Press, Cambridge

Corso M, Martini A, Paolucci E, Pellegrini L (2004) Knowledge management systems in continuous product innovation. In: Leondes CT (eds) Intelligent knowledge-based systems. Business and technology in the new millennium. vol 1: Knowledge-Based Systems, chapter 2, Kluwer Academic Press, pp 36–66

Corso M, Martini A, Massa S, Pellegrini L, Testa S (2005) Managing dispersed workers: the new challenge in knowledge management. Technovation, forthcoming

Cramton CD (1997) Information problems in dispersed teams. Academy of Management Proceedings: 298–302

Cramton CD (2001) The mutual knowledge problem and its consequences for dispersed collaboration. Organization Science 12: 346–371

Cramton CD (2002) Finding common ground in dispersed collaboration. Organizational Dynamics 30(4): 356–367

Drucker P (2002) They're not employees, they're people. Harvard Business Review, February: 70–77

Davenport T, Prusak L (1998) Working knowledge: how organizations manage what they know. HBS Press, Boston

Duarte DL, Snyder NT (1999) Mastering virtual teams. Jossey-Bass, San Francisco

Furst SR, Blackburn D, Rosen B (1999) Virtual teams: a proposed research agenda. Information Systems Journal 9(4): 249–269

Gupta AK, Govindarajan V (2000) Knowledge management's social dimension: lessons from Nucor steel. Sloan Management Review 42(1): 71–80

Haanes K, Lowendhal B (1997) The unit of activity: towards an alternative to the theories of the firm. Strategy, culture and style. John Wiley and Sons, London

Kanter RM (1977) Men and women of the corporation. New York: Basic Books

Lipnack J, Stamps J (1997) Virtual teams: working across space, time, and organizations. John Wiley & Sons, New York

Laubacher R, Malone TW (2003) Retreat of the firm and the rise of guilds: the employment relationship in an age of virtual business. In: Malone TW, Laubacher R, Scott-Morton MS (eds), Inventing the organization of the 21st century. MIT Press, Boston

Maskell P (2001) Knowledge creation and diffusion in geographic clusters. International Journal of Innovation Management 5(2): 213–237

Minkler AP (1993) The problem with dispersed knowledge: firms in theory and practice. Kyklos 46(4): 569–587

Nahapiet J, Ghoshal S (1998) Social capital, intellectual capital and the organizational advantage. The Academy of Management Review 23(2): 242–266

Nonaka I (1990) Redundant, overlapping organization: a Japanese approach to managing the innovation process. California Management Review 32(3): 27–38

Nonaka I, Takeuchi H (1995) The knowledge creating company. Oxford University Press, Oxford

Perrow C (1967) A framework for the comparative analysis of organizations. American Sociological Review 32(2): 194–208

Perrow C (1970) Departmental power and perspectives in industrial firms. In: Zald MN (ed) Power in organizations. Vanderbilt University Press, pp 59–89

Petrash G (1996) Dow's journey to a knowledge value management culture. European Management Journal 14: 365–373

Roos J, Roos G, Dragonetti N, Edvinsson L (1997) Intellectual capital: navigating in the new business landscape. Macmillan, London

Schiuma G, Marr B (2001) Measuring and managing intellectual capital and knowledge assets in new economy organizations. In: Bourne M (ed) Performance Measurement Handbook. GEE Publishing Ltd

Sveiby K (1997) The new organizational wealth: managing and measuring knowledge based assets. Barret-Kohler Publishers, San Francisco

Tsoukas H (1996) The firm as a distributed knowledge system: a constructionist approach. Strategic Management Journal 17: 11–15

Wenger EC, Snyder WM (2000) Communities of practice. The organizational frontier. Harvard Business Review January–February: 139–145

Wiig K (1997) Integrating intellectual capital and knowledge management. Long Range Planning 30: 399–405

14 Factors Influencing the Diffusion of New Mobile Services

Sven Lindmark[1], Mats Magnusson[1] and Filippo Renga[2]

[1]Department of Technology, Management and Economics
Chalmers University of Technology, Sweden
[2]Department of Management, Economics and Industrial Engineering
Politecnico di Milano, Italy

14.1 Mobile work and mobile services

Mobile work holds a potential to transform the way in which work is performed, as it creates opportunities to improve the quality of working life, increase efficiency, and allow for the development of new organisational forms. Although fruitful applications of mobile work are visible in some settings, there are also several examples of apparently slow adoption. This points to the need to understand more in detail what enables and disables innovation adoption and diffusion in the area of mobile work.

It is clear that a first prerequisite for effective mobile work is that a suitable technological infrastructure is in place, and much has been written on the development and use of new technological infrastructure solutions such as third generation (3G), radio frequency identification (RFID), and wireless LAN (WLAN). Less attention has been paid to the development and adoption of mobile services within these technology frameworks. Hence, there is a need to focus our attention on the apparent difficulties of developing and diffusing new mobile services, and in particular on the reasons behind these difficulties. This area of investigation is highly relevant not only for practice, but also for theory development. Generally, while the adoption and diffusion of new products have received much attention from researchers in marketing and innovation management, studies of the introduction of new services have been far less frequent and thus call for further input.

Based on the above, it is clear that there is a need for improved understanding of how services that allow for mobile work initiatives are developed and put into commercial use. This paper aims at investigating enablers and disablers of the development and diffusion of services for mobile work. Following case studies of companies developing services for mobile work, we primarily attempt to identify and analyze factors influencing the development and diffusion of such services. An attempt is also made to identify some of the practices utilized by companies to overcome the difficulties, in order to identify recommendations for how these processes can be accelerated. We will now turn to a theoretical exposition of issues concerning the development and diffusion of innovations. Given the composite nature of the phenomenon studied, the exposition draws upon studies from several fields, e.g. innovation management, entrepreneurship, marketing, and strategy.

14.2 Development and diffusion of innovations

The diffusion of innovations has been studied for a long time. The most influential work in this cross-disciplinary field is doubtless the innovation diffusion model of Rogers (1995, first published in 1962). The key components in this model are: (1) an innovation, i.e. an idea, practice or object that is perceived as new by someone; (2) communication channels allowing exchange of information; (3) time, in terms of the time until an innovation is adopted by someone; and (4) a social system, including the suppliers of the innovation, customers and users. By investigating these different dimensions, Rogers found that different individuals adopt innovations at various points in time, revealing consistently different behaviours. Based on this, he proposed a division into five categories of adopters: innovators, early adopters, early majority, late majority, and laggards. The very first individuals that adopt an innovation are the so-called innovators, who are then followed by the early adopters, and so forth. This categorization has gained notable appreciation and widespread use also outside the scientific community, as it has been made more popular by Moore (1991), who enriched the theory by adding empirical descriptions of how such diffusion takes place in the information technology (IT) industry.

Rogers' model is based upon the assumption that adoption of an innovation is normally distributed in a population. A later study by Mahajan et al. (1990) found this to be a fair approximation at an overall level, even though they stressed that the categorization of each single individual should not be determined only by when the individual in question adopts the innovation, but rather by what kind of information the individual depends upon in order to arrive at a decision, thereby underlining the need to move from mere descriptions of the adoption process to the factors influencing whether a customer will adopt a new product or service at a specific point in time.

A shortcoming of the predominant perspective on innovation diffusion is its tendency to focus on the adopters of new ideas, practices or products, and to overlook the influence of the suppliers of products and services (Frambach 1993). In an attempt to combine ideas from different streams of innovation diffusion studies, Frambach (1993) suggests that a more comprehensive model of innovation diffusion should comprise: (1) adopter characteristics, (2) information characteristics, (3) information processing characteristics, (4) innovation characteristics, (5) competitive environment, (6) innovation development, (7) network participation, and (8) marketing strategy used by the provider. This clearly highlights the need to consider factors related to the process of developing new products and services, and even more the need to consider marketing and competition characteristics. We will now turn to an exposition of some specific issues concerning the development and diffusion of new products and services that surface in different research streams.

14.2.1 Strategic issues related to resources and capabilities

A fundamental problem for innovation is the resources and capabilities that are held by the organisations involved. As Prahalad and Hamel (1990) pointed out, resources and capabilities are at the centre of innovation activities. Grant (1991) underlines this in his model on the formulation of resource-based strategies, regarding the existing resources of a firm as the starting point for the formulation of what offerings the firm should develop for its customers. Amit and Schoemaker (1993) present a more explicit connection between the resource side of the organisation and the competition in the marketplace. They argue that a key element of strategy is to match internal strategic assets with strategic industry factors. Taken together, these ideas indicate the potential problem of new actors not having the required internal resources to realize new services in the way they had initially intended to do. Yet another potential barrier is the perceived incompatibility between existing resources and the new ones required. Firms, in this case potentially both service providers and customers, often focus on business units instead of resources (Prahalad and Hamel 1990), or rely too much on the existing resource base (Leonard-Barton 1992), leading to inertia in the adoption of new innovations if new resources are needed.

A problem related to the resources and capabilities of firms is the need for absorptive capacity (Cohen and Levinthal 1990) of business partners, in order for them to be able to understand the advantages provided, and to make it possible to utilize their potential. When dealing with completely new products and services, it can be assumed that the need for absorptive capacity does not only apply to a set of collaborating companies on the supply side. Most likely, the need is also relevant for customers and users, as they normally require a certain level of relevant knowledge in order to understand the value of a new product or service and to use the innovation in the intended manner.

While received theory primarily deals with barriers to innovation, and has less to say about how to enable innovation, a few aspects of the latter should be brought up. On a general level, Rogers (1976) argues that the innovativeness of a system is positively related to the system's connectedness, as well as its openness, something that underlines the role of "weak ties" (Granovetter 1973). More specifically, as mentioned by Rogers (1976), these ties constitute a fruitful means to avoid exaggerated homophily and bring in new ideas. In systems where all parties resemble each other to a high degree, the requisite variety (Ashby 1956) is limited, and hence the potential for innovation to take place is limited (see e.g. Nonaka 1990). Turning back to the reasoning about absorptive capacity (Cohen and Levinthal 1990), it can be inferred that the relationship between the involved parties' knowledge bases is ambivalent. A shared basis is needed to facilitate communication and make common interpretation possible, yet significant diversity of knowledge ought to be fruitful for innovation.

As all the resources needed to realize a new product or service are rarely present within one single organisation, another factor that needs to be taken into consideration is the difficulties related to multi-organisational innovation. When innovations are the result of several actors, the coordination of these in order to generate a new product or service is often complex. First of all, the firms involved may have different goals, strategies and priorities, rendering the coordination of development activities far from trivial. One thing that may facilitate the necessary coordination is the existence of a strong lead firm. However, in new fields of business it is not always clear which firm should play this role, which is demanding but, from a business perspective, interesting and potentially rewarding.

Another key component for managing change and innovation, primarily relating to the discourse on resources and capabilities, is the existence of dynamic capabilities (Teece et al. 1997). Firms need to develop capabilities to transform and renew their resource-base over time, in terms of a particular set of managerial skills and organisational routines. In other words, firms need to become good at learning and unlearning (Hedberg 1981). This applies to both providers of services and their potential customers, as both parties probably have to change the way they do things in order to use new services in a fruitful manner.

14.2.2 Technological issues

A technology-related problem, which also refers to the organisational issues discussed earlier, was described by Christensen (1997) as the difficulty for incumbent firms in dealing with disruptive technologies. The main message here is that established organisations seem to be slow at adopting technologies that at the time of introduction do not have superior performance and are primarily desired by customers outside the traditional ones. As established firms focus their efforts on fulfilling the demands of their existing customers, they get locked into a specific value system and thereby often miss new opportunities. As a result of this tendency to overlook certain kinds of new technologies, it becomes important to find customers that are willing to try new products and services outside the intended main market (Moore 1991).

A more straightforward technological problem is the difficulty of obtaining adequate performance from the new technology. As is well known from theories of technology development patterns (cf. Sahal 1981; Foster 1986; Utterback 1994), the efforts needed to improve performance are far greater at the outset of a technology than later in its lifetime, when its key components are familiar and uncertainties about core design choices have been settled and thus allow for more focused improvement. The high degree of uncertainty in early-phase technology development makes it difficult to plan the process and foresee potential problems. Consequently, firms need to adopt an experimental approach and use contingency planning to be prepared for eventual changes (Bhidé 2000). The magnitude of this problem is such that Lester et al. (1998) actually point out exaggerated reliance on planning and execution, instead of experimentation and adaptation, as a key problem facing innovation in established firms.

Finally, technological complexity is known to raise barriers in both the innovation and diffusion processes. The more components are involved in a system and the more each of these components changes, the higher the complexity and the need for coordination (Teece 1986) and the more the resulting problems that may delay the innovation process or reduce reliability once the new product or service is in use.

14.2.3 Economic issues

One factor that obviously can constitute a major barrier to innovation is the need for investments in order to realize it. To raise the necessary financial resources for development is fundamental in order to realize a new product or service. While large firms can decide to go ahead with the development on their own, small firms characterizing new business areas must find the essential capital somewhere else. However, if the need for investments is substantial and the outcome uncertain, the possibility to attract investors will most likely be limited. An exception to this rule may occur if the area in question is considered to be a rapidly emerging one. In that case there may even be an abundance of available capital.

On the demand side there are problems if the commitment required to try out the innovation is high (Mansfield 1968). Another hindrance arises if potential customers need to share the risks involved. The benefits of the new solution must then be clear and communicable in order to get the customers solidly involved. As mentioned above, such clarity is unfortunately often lacking in business development processes, which are rather characterized by non-linearity and adaptation (e.g. Bhave 1994, Bhidé 2000). This underlines the need to win acceptance for an experimental development approach, frequently also requiring adaptation by the potential customers – something which normally calls for a high level of trust and a strong long-term relationship. If these prerequisites are not in place, the possibilities of motivating customers to accept the uncertainty and risk in innovative development processes are likely to be scarce.

14.2.4 Marketing issues

A more specific enabling factor than the ones mentioned above is the use of marketing in connection with the innovation process, a factor that wrongly often receives relatively little attention in high-tech firms. Rosen et al. (1998) address this explicitly and underline the widespread lack of customer focus in high-tech companies. Furthermore, they need to have a strict initial focus, and first thereafter broaden the span of offerings to customers. Moore (1991) points to the need for careful targeting of customers. Rosen et al. (1998) add that high-tech markets change rapidly, and consequently the targeting should be frequently monitored and, if necessary, revised.

Another important factor is that marketing in high-tech environments requires a different balance between demand- and supply-side marketing than is the case in more established settings (Rosen et al. 1998). While traditional marketing of established products and services deals primarily with getting information across to the customers, the information flow when dealing with marketing of completely new things needs to go primarily from the customers to the providers. As the market needs and requirements are rarely known in these settings, potential customers need to be involved in a co-creation process where they explicate their preferences and give rich feedback on suggested functionalities and features. Getting specific input regarding customer requirements, in order to be able to provide services that really solve the customers' perceived problems, appears decisive for the rapid development of the services. Apart from close collaboration with customers, one method for dealing with this problem is to use so-called concept testing, to get feedback from customers at a very early stage of development (Lodish et al. 2001).

14.2.5 Summary

The exposition above makes clear that the development and diffusion of new products and services are complex and challenging tasks, especially when taking place in a new field of business characterized by great uncertainty regarding both markets and technologies. Taken together, the factors promoting and opposing these processes can be summarized as in table 14.1.

Table 14.1. Summary of disablers and enablers

Disablers	Enablers
– Exaggerated use of existing resources and capabilities	– Learning, unlearning and changing capabilities
– Lack of absorptive capacity	– Experimental and adaptive development process
– Insufficient inter-organisational coordination	– Early customer feedback
– Unwillingness and capacity to change	– Use of standardized technology
– Immature technologies	– Access to venture capital
– Insufficient funding	– Customer financing
– Value network lock-in	– Long-term and trustful relationship with lead customers
– Lack of customer involvement	
– Focus on internal development	– Close collaboration with customers
– Unclear segmenting and market positioning	– Narrow and clear initial customer focus
	– Step-wise targeting of different customer groups
– Broad marketing approach	

While this list of general influencing factors is a wide-ranging one, it is probably far from complete. We should also keep in mind that most of the studies from which the above-mentioned theories have been derived concern products and not services, so there are still questions regarding the role of these factors for the development and diffusion of services. Furthermore, the specific area of mobile work may involve other factors, given the nature of change involved in the adoption of such services. Finally, what is seen from the list is that managerial implications hitherto have primarily been rather abstract, and there is a lack of descriptions of the actual practice involved in managing these processes. Before turning to an empirical investigation of what disablers and enablers can be found in the development and diffusion of new services for mobile work, and the operative approaches applied by firms to deal with these, we will next give a brief description of the research setting and methods used in the study.

14.3 Vehicle telematics in West Sweden

The empirical focus of this paper is on innovations for mobile work in the transportation sector, more specifically goods and public transportation industries in the Göteborg area, in West Sweden.[1] Such products and services are often labelled vehicle or mobile telematics, including e.g. dispatching and fleet management, remote vehicle diagnostics, navigation, positioning and messaging. They almost exclusively involve some interaction between the application itself and a mobile worker, i.e. a vehicle driver. The innovations are typically complex, involving a range of applications- and sometimes customer-specific hardware, e.g. terminal, network, server, and software, e.g. client, server, network, etc., components which have to be integrated.

Typical goods-transportation applications aim to control and manage fleets of road vehicles, e.g. road carriers keeping track of their trucks. Telematics can be used to facilitate this work by providing real-time information, such as vehicle location, the distance and time the driver has been driving, what and where the cargo is, and the planned route. These applications are used to increase operational efficiency, save costs, enhance safety and security, and monitor vehicle and driver performance. Public transportation telematics typically provides real-time traffic information resulting in better schedule time-keeping, planning support, driver support, and customer service in the form of better passenger information. By receiving real-time information on the location of buses and trams, the control centre can provide drivers with information and put in extra resources when needed. Positioning systems combined with real-time data-

---

[1] This section draws heavily on Gruvin & Karlsson (2001), Holmén (2001), Lindmark (2002) and www.telematicsvalley.org.

bases are often used to inform waiting passengers how many minutes there are until the next bus or tram arrives.

Göteborg, located on the west coast of Sweden, is particularly well placed to study innovation and diffusion processes of mobile telematics for transportation, since this region has a long history and strong presence of actors within this field. It started in the early 1980s when Televerket (the Swedish monopoly telecom operator at that time) developed a public packet-switched mobile data communications system – Mobitex. The development was further advanced by initiatives to improve the local and regional public transportation and by parallel developments in the strong regional vehicle manufacturing industry, Volvo in particular. While large software houses and equipment manufacturers were initially reluctant to enter the field, a few local start-ups, e.g. Thoreb and Hogia, took advantage of the business opportunities arising in developing transport applications. Eventually Ericsson also entered the field and localized a development centre for mobile data as well as the responsibility for Mobitex in Göteborg. The Göteborg region also attracted test Road Traffic Information projects, such as ARENA, financed by e.g. traffic authorities and conducted within the framework of the European Prometheus programme.

These were the beginnings of what has developed into a "cluster" for mobile telematics, now branded Telematics Valley.[2] In total, there are some 40 firms, with around 600 persons explicitly involved in mobile telematics in the region. These range from software firms to operators, service and content providers, terminal manufacturers, vehicle manufacturers, logistics and transport firms, to companies dedicated to developing applications for mobile telematics. Both Volvo and Saab have been appointed centres of excellence for telematics by Ford and GM respectively. Both of these are situated in the larger Göteborg area. To this can be added that Ericsson has also located a centre of excellence for Mobile Data Design here, and that some leading logistics companies have their head offices in Göteborg. Göteborg is also the largest air-freight and port city in Scandinavia. There are internationally known universities like Chalmers and Göteborg University in the region, both of which have substantial research and teaching activities in the fields of logistics and transportation.

However, although the region seems to have developed a strong technological competence base within mobile telematics, this competence has generated very little commercial value so far. At least partly, unexpectedly slow diffusion processes can explain this. To identify and attack barriers to

---

[2] Formally Telematics Valley is the name of the interest organisation formed to generate more business for the companies involved, e.g. through promoting networking.

diffusion is thus of crucial importance for the viability of this cluster. The present chapter aims to provide a first step in accomplishing exactly that.

14.4 Methods used

As mentioned above, the empirical focus is mobile work in freight and public transportation in Sweden. Initially, this issue will be investigated from the perspective of the firms trying to realize these new services. The deliberate choice to focus explicitly on the service developer has been made to facilitate the identification of problems regarding adoption and diffusion that emerge at very early stages of service development, and which are therefore difficult to observe if the focus is solely on the intended customers and users of the services, as has often been the case in earlier studies of diffusion. Admittedly, this method runs the risk of resulting in a biased technology- and supply-oriented view of the phenomenon at hand. Hence, we will later complement this initial study with data gathered from customers and, in addition, non-adopting customers.

Given the relative newness of the phenomena, and an apparent lack of earlier studies at the firm level of the development and diffusion of new services for mobile work, an explorative approach was chosen. Following this, a multiple case study of mobile telematics firms was conducted. A total of six firms involved in the development of new mobile telematics services were investigated by means of face-to-face interviews, which were all tape-recorded and summarized (Table 14.2). One of the authors (Renga) participated in all interviews. Some interviews were conducted by several of the authors. The interviews were semi-structured, with the interviewees being informed in advance of the purpose and structure of the interview. First, the interviewees were asked basic questions regarding the company, its history, products, services and customers. Main benefits as well as disutilities resulting from implementing their products were also investigated. The main focus of the interviews was to capture the innovators' perceptions of the barriers to, and enablers of, innovation and diffusion of their innovations. The barriers to diffusion were identified by asking both open questions, and specific questions relating to a checklist, which in turn was generated from a preliminary literature search and then successively refined. Finally, in regard to identifying barriers, the interviews addressed measures taken by the firms to overcome the barriers.

Mobile transportation telematics innovations were chosen for a number of reasons. First, these were among the first applications for mobile data communication, and this fact combined with their slow diffusion has the benefit of allowing us to observe and reflect on long and protracted diffusion processes. Second, these applications have the potential to yield very distinct and tangible benefits to customer organisations, while at the same time not providing equally tangible benefits, at least not initially, to the mobile workers. This creates an interesting tension, and our results could possibly be generalized to services with similar characteristics. Thirdly, identifying these barriers may give rise to a number of policy and managerial implications, of practical interest to stakeholders in the region. Finally, a convenience criterion applies as well.

14.5 Empirical observations

14.5.1 Overview

The case studies performed refer to two distinguishable application categories: (1) companies working on applications for private goods transportation, i.e. trucks, and (2) companies working specifically with public transportation, i.e. buses and trams. This categorization was made since some observations are common to both categories while others are applicable for only one category and, therefore, are seen as useful for further analysis. Table 14.2 summarizes the key characteristics of the investigated cases.

Table 14.2. Summary of cases

Company	Activity	Customer	Vehicle	Users
Vehco	Application installed in trucks; see case	Road carriers	Trucks	Truck drivers Fleet managers
Volvo Trucks	Transport information system (IS) for trucks	Road carriers Truck manufacturers	Trucks	Truck drivers Fleet managers
Transware	ERP for logistic companies with a mobile add-on	Postal companies Road carriers	Vans Trucks	Postal workers Van drivers Truck drivers Fleet managers

Table 14.2. (cont.)

Wireless Car	Management of telematics applications for vehicle manufacturers	Truck manufacturers Car manufacturers Yacht manufacturers	Trucks Cars Yachts	Truck drivers Boat drivers Boat owners Fleet managers
Thoreb	Real-time IS for traffic control etc. for public transportation	Transportation authority	Buses Trams	Bus and tram drivers Mobility managers
Volvo Mobility Systems	Ditto	Transportation authority	Buses	Bus drivers Mobility managers

14.5.2 Case illustration: Vehco and the Co-Driver

Vehco was founded in January 2001 with the support of Chalmers Invest and private investors. The company has nine employees and one product – the Co-driver – sold to a number of road carriers. The application is based on software that basically links the truck drivers and the truck company's back office. The truck driver has a personal digital assistant (PDA) on board, which communicates with the back office through general packet radio service (GPRS) network. The Vehco's application is embedded in a PDA on the truck (the client side) and hosted in Vehco's servers (the server side). The users of the application are thus a road carrier through its back-office and a truck driver. In addition a number of other stakeholders were identified, e.g. the company sending and receivers of transported goods, fuel suppliers, and truck manufacturers.

The Co-Driver has the following functionalities:

- Driving economy: real-time follow-up of each driver's and vehicle's fuel consumption and in addition supervised parameters (speed, idling) that affect the fuel consumption, helping the driver to improve driving economy
- Communication: messaging and positioning
- Administration functionalities: time reports and order handling in real time
- Truck drivers' satisfaction enhancement including Internet and intranet pages

These functionalities translate into the following customer benefits. First and foremost, the applications provide cost-savings in the form of reduced fuel consumption. The savings are substantial since fuel expenses are almost one third of road carriers' costs, and Co-driver has a claimed potential to reduce fuel consumption by 6-12 percent. The application also allows more efficient fleet management and control of other resources, e.g. drivers and administration. In addition, it allows for improved service through shorter response times and faster deliveries.

One of the most important problems for customer organisations has been to persuade the truck drivers to use the application. Moreover, the IT illiteracy of the drivers may reduce their willingness to use the application. With these usage-related barriers in mind, Vehco has improved the ease of use of the application, e.g. by providing larger buttons. It has also been important to design Co-driver with drivers' benefits in mind. These benefits are mainly: (1) more convenient communication with the company and (2) Internet capabilities for use during free time. In addition, through providing opportunities for observing other drivers' behaviour and performance, e.g. fuel consumption of colleagues, Co-driver has in some cases resulted in truck drivers competing with other drivers, thus creating a community.

Other problems, not directly related to drivers, were partly technology-related. For instance, systems' integration was perceived as a major problem. The application includes some 20 suppliers of components and subsystems, a number of which substantially increase the risks of system breakdowns, in addition to difficulties of integrating the different components. Another technology-related factor, adding to customers hesitating to adopt, is that adopting Co-driver is seen as limiting their range of choices when it comes to other IT investments.

14.5.3 Encountered benefits, problems and firm responses

In the following section, the main observations regarding benefits, problems and firm responses will be discussed thematically. The main observed benefits and problems are listed in table 14.3, while the main problems are listed in table 14.4.

Table 14.3. Main perceived benefits in the cases (add bullets for each item)

Company	Benefit for the customer	Benefit for the worker
Vehco	Lower fuel consumption More efficient fleet management Administrative improvements Better customer service	Easier-to-use communication Internet capabilities for spare time Performance competition with other drivers
Volvo Trucks	Fleet's active time is maximized Increase in efficiency, minimizing empty runs Improved follow-up Basis for regarding systems More efficient administration work	Higher quality of communication Reduced stress Feeling of more active decision-making
Transware	Increased goods volumes Real-time information to the customers Time saving in communication with drivers Increased information quality	Communication time and cost savings Reduction of phone calls (initially this was not perceived as positive) Task decentralized to the driver Fewer misunderstandings
Wireless Car	Lower fuel consumption Improved maintenance Increase in revenues Route optimization	n.a.
AB Thoreb	Revenue increase /better service Better service control Sometimes a decrease in costs (mainly fuel costs)	Support in keeping timetables, and informing passengers Better communication with the transport manager
Volvo Mobility Systems	Revenue increase /better service Reduced fuel consumption Reduced maintenance cost Less vulnerable transportation system	Less time spent in providing passenger information

Starting with benefits, these differ somewhat between the two application categories. Regarding truck applications, there are clear benefits for both the company and the drivers. For the companies, these relate primarily to cost reductions stemming from lower fuel consumption and, to some degree, lower maintenance costs. Lower fuel consumption can be obtained by using the information collected by the application in order to change the driving behaviour, and to indicate the most efficient shortest or fastest routes on electronic maps. The effects of the application on the maintenance costs are generated by better control of the mechanical and electronic apparatus of the truck, e.g. the tyre consumption, but are not as significant as the impact on fuel consumption. Less clear are the companies' benefits in terms of revenues. In some cases, the telematics applications can help the road carrier to provide better services to its customers so that it can charge a premium price, improving the fleet effectiveness by minimizing empty runs and optimizing the delivery paths through active scheduling. The driver can benefit from the application thanks to a communication tool that avoids misunderstandings in messaging and supports personal activities, such as Internet connections.

As for the applications developed in the public transportation area, their benefits are less clear both for the organisation managing the vehicles and for drivers. The main result for the company is a better passenger service, but often this benefit does not produce a direct and clear increase in revenues. The fuel consumption reduction can be obtained by using the application to reward the better drivers, but not by optimizing the routes (they are the same every day). The main benefit for drivers is generated by the automation of tasks such as stop announcements and other types of passenger information. Even though the drivers do not need a new schedule every day and do not need maps, benefits in terms of not having to communicate with the headquarters as often as before are also observed. Hence, the benefits for drivers do not appear to be decisive in these cases.

14.5.3.1 Encountered problems

A first set of disablers, related to *strategic issues* regarding resources and capabilities, concerns the absorptive capacity of customers and mobile workers (Table 14.4).

Table 14.4. Main problems encountered in the cases

Company	Problems/barriers
Vehco	Persuading truck driver to use the application
	Getting the first reference customers
	Complex system integration
	Investment priorities among customers
	Customers demanding additional functionalities
Volvo Trucks	Difficulties in understanding the value among customers
	Unnecessarily many functionalities in application, for many customers
	Complexity
	Volvo-specific
	Investment cost
	Operators pricing policies
Transwere	Investment cost
	Lack of confidence in and low acceptance of new technologies
	Complexity of the technological integration
Wireless Car	Customers' ability to exploit the potential of the application
	Small customers, lack of competence
	Investment costs
	Drivers' acceptance
	Complexity
	Value network coordination
AB Thoreb	Persuading drivers to use the application
	Competitors with poor products destroying market
	Lack of competence among customers
	High investment costs
	Complex technology
	Performance: delays and reliability of radio networks
	Managing all sub-suppliers in value network
Volvo Mobility Systems	Complex projects
	Adaptation cost to specific customers
	Investment size
	Maintenance
	Lack of standard interfaces

Especially the "IT illiteracy" of the employees was in all cases a barrier to the effective adoption of mobile telematics. Only if the truck, bus or tram driver accepts and uses the applications is it possible to exploit their related benefits. Therefore, it is very important to avoid the perception of the application as a "Big Brother". To further emphasize the importance of actually using the application, we can illustrate with tram and bus drivers who sometimes do not log into the system, thereby making the passenger information less relevant. In this light, the services must be developed to be as simple and usable as possible and sometimes specific functionalities or rewards must be developed to provide incentives to the drivers to use the application. Moreover, early adopters can be levers to spread the application's usage among colleagues. Often, the low acceptance is only transitory and is overcome once drivers start using the application.

The "IT illiteracy", or more generally absorptive capacity, was also a problem in other parts of customer organisations. Managers of the fleet companies are used to thinking of the trucks as a "hard product", but the service is very different from the truck, and consequently the competencies needed are also different. Often the fleet owner has difficulties in perceiving and understanding the overall benefits of the application, and his priorities are on other aspects that he knows better – the trucks, customers, fuel suppliers, etc. This often leads to unwillingness to experiment with new solutions, sometimes expressed as in the Vehco case: "Let someone else debug your product!" In the light of this, it appears to be important to have a consolidated number of customers, who trust the service developer and look for a long-term relationship making it worthwhile to use time for this kind of development work. Telematics applications do not automatically yield benefits, and in some cases the buying firms find it difficult to exploit their potential. Moreover, even if a company can detect that it is consuming too much fuel, it may be too concerned with other aspects of the business to do something about this.

Another issue related to the structure of the entire truck business is that most companies are small and have limited IT and management competences. It may even be that the owner of the fleet drives the truck himself and does not have the time to propose and implement changes. Finally, relating to value-chain coordination, there is no real support from the network operators with respect to pricing, marketing, technical support, etc.

The main *technological issue* seems to be the lack of standard interfaces among the different parts of the system. This increases the cost and the difficulties of the innovation and implementation projects. As one interviewee put it: "The system never functions as planned." In an evolving market with rapidly changing technology, it is difficult to integrate the large number of technologies and components necessary for the application, e.g. Java vs. C++, Personal Digital Assistants (PDAs) vs. Smartphone, Linux vs. Windows. Moreover, since all involved technologies and components have some probability of malfunctioning, the probability of failure increases exponentially with the number of components integrated. Some companies try to solve this problem by trying to use as much software as possible, resulting in increasing complexity and costs.

In truck applications developed by one vehicle manufacturer, it is difficult to adapt the application in competitors' vehicles, partly for competitive reasons, but also because of technical difficulties in installing sensors in competitors' vehicles – because of the different positions of electronics and mechanical parts in the truck. Such sensors are crucial to monitor the truck's parameters – like fuel consumption, engine performance, etc. The lack of standardization decreases the potential market of the application. This unwillingness to develop brand-independent solutions among the established firms opens up opportunities for new entrants to develop generic products and services that can be used by road carriers with vehicles of different brands in their fleets.

In the applications for public transportation, the most pertinent technological problems are the delays in data transmission, which reduce the "real-time" benefits of the application. Sometimes the delays are so long that the indication of a vehicle's position displayed at a certain place changes only when the vehicle has already passed that place. This in turn leads to passengers, buyers and drivers not trusting the system, and may even lead to vandalism. The reliability of the system is also very important, probably more so than the cost of the service. A particular problem in this case is that cellular networks do not provide enough reliability, and that is why public transportation authorities tend to use private networks, which are often more expensive.

Furthermore, the applications are not "plug and play", but complex, and this complexity decreases road carriers' willingness to adopt. Also, in order to make the applications as generic as possible, there are a lot of functionalities that most users do not need. The customers very often ask for a tailored application with a specific function. Therefore, often the applications have many technological features that customers do not understand, and either cannot or do not want to deal with, e.g. buying SIM cards, having antennas on the trucks, etc.

Economic issues relate primarily to the price and investment cost of the service, which becomes an issue in industries where the margins are thin. Often the owner of the fleet of trucks is not able to understand the overall value of the application and his priorities are on other aspects that he knows better than IT applications, i.e. the truck, the customers, the fuel suppliers, etc. In order to overcome this problem, new pricing models based on monthly fees have been developed, selling the system as a service. In this case, the company is in charge of maintaining the service. The price is then often considered to be low if compared to other costs that the customer has. In this light, it is important to have a consolidated number of customers to show the results obtained by someone else.

Marketing-related issues were not addressed systematically in the interviews. However, it is possible to distinguish between goods transportation and public transportation. While most goods-transportation applications were initially developed with a technology-push approach, public transportation applications were often developed in collaboration with, and initiated by, demanding customers.

14.6 Discussion

The empirical observations reveal a large number of issues related to strategic resources, technology economics and marketing. Some of these were more or less present across cases and will be further discussed here. First, however, it should be noted that all the studied innovations provide tangible and often measurable benefits to the customer organisations. These benefits relate to improved efficiency of operations, in particular cost-cutting and improved service to the end customers.

These potential benefits lead us to a first set of problems, regarding the capabilities of the customer organisations. To begin with, the benefits were difficult to absorb – at least initially – for the main user group, the drivers. In fact, for several users there were perceived disutilities, such as loss of personal freedom – the "Big Brother" effect. In addition, applications were often perceived as difficult to start using. Therefore, there was an initial resistance-to-use within the customer organisations. On the other hand, this resistance has been reduced as a result of learning within the organisations and of knowledge transfers among users and among application developers. Several of them have gradually improved usability, and added functionalities that enhance the mobile work experience for the users. Thus, these initial barriers are possible to overcome through learning.

Second, also relating to the absorptive capacity and capabilities, it was difficult to address the "right" persons in the customer organisations. Competence in mobile telematics has generally been low and, due to the size of investments, decisions have to be taken at high levels in the organisations. Often a fleet owner is not able to understand the overall value of the application and his priorities are elsewhere. More generally, due to the size, complexity, uncertainty and unfamiliarity of the investments, buying processes for mobile telematics applications were complicated, and purchasing as well as marketing competencies had to be developed. Analogously, marketing competencies had to be developed on the supply side. These factors are well known and investigated in the industrial marketing literature (Choffrey and Lilien 1980; Webster 1984) and also in the diffusion literature by Rogers. Finally, changing customers' processes is a well-known barrier when implementing IT-based business solutions. In this respect, the "old way to do the job" by using pen, paper and mobile phones is a strong substitute.

Another barrier that was repeatedly referred to was the complexity of the applications. A large number of software and hardware components had to be developed and integrated. This complexity has a number of implications. First, system integration becomes a time-consuming and costly process. Complexity also makes the applications difficult for customers to understand and relate to. In addition, technological complexity implies value-chain complexity. A large number of actors have to interact and make their products compatible. Their roles were in many cases unclear, and the business models were incompatible or unviable. Clearly, there seems to be a coordination problem.

This complexity and the resulting coordination problems may in fact be one key explanation for the perceived slow diffusion of mobile telematics services. As mentioned above and by Teece (1986), when innovations are systemic, i.e. when improvement in one component requires simultaneous improvements in other components or parts of the product, the need for coordination increases. Under such circumstances, integration under a single agent is likely to be the most efficient organisation, since this agent can more effectively redirect, coordinate and create the necessary capabilities, as well as destroying the unnecessary ones, to make the innovation work. Although the need for coordination can be expected to lessen in the long run, there may be room for e.g. the creation of modular standards to institutionalize some of the functions of coordination (Langlois and Robertson 1992). Thus, stimulation of standardized components and platforms seems to be a relevant policy issue.

A third set of factors relates to costs and pricing. Initially customers were reluctant to adopt, in spite of suppliers being able to show viable business cases for an investment. This reluctance partly stemmed from a large size of investments, which is a factor that is well known to slow down diffusion (e.g. Mansfield 1968). In order to overcome this barrier, new pricing models based on monthly fees have been developed.

Based on the empirical investigation, it can also be concluded that developing services for mobile work at least to some extent needs to be considered an experimental activity, as the infrastructure that they are to be based on is continuously evolving. Even more challenging, however, is the radical uncertainty concerning the demand side. Markets and customers are only known to a limited extent, turning the development of these services into qualified guesswork. Consequently, not only the development, but also the adoption and diffusion, of these services are uncertain and may either be slower or faster, or come to a quick end.

Summarizing the potential problems, we can conclude that these may be interdependent and thereby reinforce each other. For instance, targeting new customer groups sometimes implies that other performance criteria become important, which in turn may require new performance levels of the technology. If external parties develop this new technology, it is easily understood that the task of coordinating the development is not a simple one.

Addressing the question whether the observations apply more generally to mobile work we may, first, conclude that any mobile work application should be designed to lower the impact of the disablers. Applications need to be as simple as possible, easy-to-use and easy-to-understand, minimizing required changes in legacy systems and business processes, priced with low up-front costs, etc. Secondly, the case of mobile telematics shows the importance of adapting both technology and business models to better match customer and user needs. Thirdly, other applications with similar characteristics, i.e. complex technology, for different interest groups where the mobile workers' interests do not necessarily match those of the organisation or the customers' customers, etc., are likely to face similar barriers.

The investigated services have generated – or will, if the implemented ones generate – business value in terms of improved services and lower costs. They can form the basis for a work environment favourable to continuous improvement, and increase the efficiency of the whole system, which in the end may lead to making services for mobile work more widely adopted. Facilitating the implementation of such services should, therefore, be an important policy issue. Various measures can be taken in order to achieve this. For instance, knowledge transfer could be stimulated by providing arenas for sharing information on successful implementations etc. Coordinating and supporting development of generic platforms, e.g. test-beds, and standards is another measure. Further, many mobile work applications, not least telematics, have the potential to improve service and lower costs of the services of public authorities. Investments in these services can also create new opportunities for innovation upstream in the value chain.

Received policy implications from previous studies of the mobile telematics sector seem to focus on measures for strengthening competence and networks. This study instead emphasizes the diffusion of innovation as the weakest function in the innovation system. Thus, the over-riding policy target should focus on strengthening this system weakness, i.e. the weak market formation.

Problems that may be more specific to the particular area of telematics services, or at least to emerging industries and to innovations that are systemic, are that the general level of uncertainty regarding technologies and markets makes business forecasts quite precarious. It may be the case that the number of network components and actors, as well as network externalities, renders it more difficult to try new things out and create a more digital adoption process. Either all actors are in, or no sufficient critical mass can be generated. This suggests that some coordinating role has to be taken by strong actors.

Uncertainties concerning the distribution of created value make it too risky to experiment, and thus hamper the development work. One problem here is the lack of clarity concerning what each party needs to put into the development process and what can be expected in return. An important aspect of this issue is the lack of established business models that reduce such fundamental business uncertainty. Before these business models have been duly accepted, strong relationships with key collaborating partners appear to be the main way of overcoming this problem.

Looking at the barriers and the means used by the service providers to overcome them, we see that the service providers in this industry seem to suffer from some weaknesses that are typical for most high-tech companies. In several cases, there is a need for improved marketing of the new services, primarily in terms of clear targeting. Furthermore, few firms use collaborations with competitors in order to create critical mass, making it more difficult to find viable business models.

More generally these firms could improve their performance, not only by addressing the disablers, but by taking advantage of the enablers as identified above. Examples would be improving learning, unlearning and changing capabilities, using experimental and adaptive development processes in order to obtain early customer feedback, having an initially narrow and clear customer focus followed by step-wise targeting of different customer groups' use of standardized technology, developing long-term relationships and collaboration with – and possibly financing from – lead customers.

Finally, on the basis of the preliminary findings in this study, we suggest that barriers to, and enablers of, diffusion need to be studied also from the perspective of other actors in the value chain, particularly customers. Not only adopting but also non-adopting customers should be included in such a study. In addition, more services in more countries could be included, yielding a systematic study of barriers and drivers of diffusion.

Acknowledgements

We would like to acknowledge Erik Andriessen, Veli-Pekka Niitamo, Juhani Pekkola and Matti Vartiainen for comments on earlier drafts of this chapter

References

Amit R, Schoemaker PJ (1993) Strategic assets and organizational rent. Strategic Management Journal 14:33–46

Ashby WR (1956) An introduction to cybernetics. Champan & Hall, London

Bhave MP (1994) A process model of entrepreneurial venture creation. Journal of Business Venturing 9:223–242

Bhidé AV (2000) The origin and evolution of new business. Oxford University Press, New York

Choffray JM, Lilien GL (1980) Market planning for new industrial products. John Wiley & Sons, New York

Christensen CM (1997) The innovator's dilemma – When new technologies cause great firms to fail. Harvard Business School Press, Boston

David P, Steinmueller E (1994) Economics of compatibility standards and competition in telecommunication networks. Information Economics and Policy 6:217–241

Foster R (1986) Innovation: the attacker's advantage. Summit Books, New York

Frambach RT (1993) An integrated model of organizational adoption and diffusion of innovations. European Journal of Marketing 27:22–41

Granovetter MS (1973) The strength of weak ties. American Journal of Sociology 78:1360–1380

Grant RM (1991) A resource-based theory of competitive advantage: implications for strategy formulation. California Management Review 33:114–135

Gruvin S, Karlsson J (2001) The telematics industry in Göteborg. How to gain common advantages from co-localization of firms. Master thesis, Deptartment. of Industrial Dynamics, Chalmers University of Technology, Göteborg

Holmén M (2001) Emerging regional actor systems as regional industrial renewal? The case of software-based generic technologies. In: Holmén M. Emergence of regional actor systems – Generic technologies and the search for useful or saleable applications. Ph.D. thesis, Department of Industrial Dynamics, Chalmers University of Technology, Göteborg

Leonard-Barton D (1992) Core capabilities and core rigidities: A paradox in managing new product development. Strategic Management Journal 13:111–125

Lester RK, Piore MJ, Malek KM (1998) Interpretive management: What general managers can learn from design. Harvard Business Review, March–April: 86–96

Lindmark S (2002) Evolution of techno-economic systems – An investigation of the history of mobile communications. Ph.D. thesis, Department of Industrial Management and Economics, Chalmers University of Technology, Göteborg

Lodish L, Lee Morgan H, Kallimpur A (2001) Entrepreneurial marketing. John Wiley & Sons, New York

Mahajan V, Muller E, Srivastava RK (1990) Determination of adopter categories by using innovation diffusion models. Journal of Marketing Research 27:37–50

Mansfield E (1968) The economics of technological change. Norton and Co., New York

Moore G (1991) Crossing the chasm. Harper-Business, New York

Nonaka I (1990) Redundant, overlapping organization: A japanese approach to managing the innovation process. California Management Review Spring:27–38

Prahalad CK, Hamel G (1990) The core competence of the corporation. Harvard Business Review, May–June: 79–91

Rogers EM (1976) New product adoption and diffusion. Journal of Consumer Research 2: 290–301

Rogers, EM (1995) Diffusion of innovations. The Free Press, New York, 3rd edn

Rosen DE, Schroeder JE, Purinton EF (1998) Marketing high tech products: Lessons in customer focus from the marketplace. Academy of Marketing Science Review 6, found at http://www.amsreview.org/

Sahal D (1981) Patterns of technological innovation. Addison-Wesley, Reading

Teece D (1986) Profiting from technological innovation: Implications for integration, collaboration, licensing and public policy. Research Policy 15:285–305

Teece DJ, Pisano G, Shuen A (1997) Dynamic capabilities and strategic management. Strategic Management Journal 18:509–533

Utterback J (1994) Mastering the dynamics of innovation: How companies can seize opportunities in the face of technological change. Harvard Business School Press, Boston

Webster F (1984) Industrial marketing strategy, John Wiley & Sons, New York

15 Mobile Workplaces and Innovative Business Practice

Hans Schaffers[1], Liz Carver[2], Torsten Brodt[3], Terrence Fernando[4] and Robert Slagter[1]

[1]Telematica Instituut, The Netherlands
[2]BAE Systems, UK
[3]University of St. Gallen, Switzerland
[4]University of Salford, UK

15.1 The challenge of mobile workplaces

This chapter explores the potential and implications of new mobile and wireless technologies and applications for workplace innovation[1]. Driving forces for introducing new forms of mobile and context-aware work are both the business trends towards cost reduction and productivity increase, and the challenge of realizing more intuitive, user-oriented and 'human-centric' work environments where people are at the foreground. Technologies supporting mobility, context- and location-awareness, collaboration, networking and intelligent and unobtrusive interfaces will play an important role in implementing this challenge. However, the potential impacts of these technologies on the worker and business environment are not well understood. Therefore, workplace innovation and coping with social and behavioural issues in mobility, sustainability and quality of work should go hand in hand with innovations in mobile and wireless technologies and applications.

Making work environments less dependent from constraints for collaboration settings such as time and location, and increasing the creativity, effectiveness and efficiency of collaboration and communication, is an important driver for developing innovative mobile technologies and applications. Future scenarios for collaborative workplaces envisage an increasing flexibility of collaborative workplaces involving dimensions of workplace context and the realization of the "collaboration anytime any-

---

[1] Parts of this chapter are based on results of the MOSAIC project, 2004-2005, a specific support action under the Information Society Technologies priority within the 6th Framework programme of the European Commission. See: http://www.mosaic-network.org/

where" vision. Workplace context includes, besides location and time, other aspects such as task characteristics, market demands, organisational constraints, personal profiles, and team structure. Context awareness and adaptiveness is one of the key challenges. The 'mobile workplace' is not just focusing on enhancing the mobility of workers. Mobile work in a broader meaning includes the mobility and flexibility of the work, the workplace and the work organisation, increasingly adapting to the changing needs and opportunities of the mobile worker and team irrespective time, place and other context-related constraints. In this view, the network may become the working place. The mobile workplace thus evolves towards a scenario of work organisation, which is characterized by empowerment of workers being part of ad-hoc temporary project teams and networked organisations, and by a high level of awareness of and responsiveness to context.

This paper aims to explore current collaborative workplace practice and the perspectives for using mobile technologies for workplace innovation and innovation in business practice. We identify challenges and success factors for mobile workplace innovation and we discuss human, organisational and technical issues in the transformation to innovative mobile and networked workplace settings. As a starting point in section two the close relationship in workplaces between mobility and collaboration is discussed. Thereafter in section three we assess current practices and needs in different situations of mobile working to understand the mobile work business proposition. Section four then takes an industry perspective in describing developments in collaborative working in selected business areas in order to identify the business drivers and business demands in these areas and to see what the current and future prospects for deploying mobile technologies and applications are. Section five turns to the discussion of human and organisational factors in implementing mobile work in organisations. This leads us in section six to discuss plausible future scenarios of mobile collaborative working and to propose a roadmap for research and innovation. Finally, section seven completes the paper with discussion and conclusions.

15.2 Mobility and collaborative working

Our initial focus is on the role of mobility in collaborative workplaces. Collaboration is the key to most of current work practice. However, effective collaboration is difficult to achieve and success depends on a number of interdependent factors. Access to mobile technology is not enough on its own, and to be truly effective, organisational structure and support as well as effective collaborative behaviours are equally important. Partnership maturity can be measured and relationships evaluated but collaboration maturity is often measured just in terms of the frequency of usage and degree of uptake of the technology, not looking at the behavioural aspects at all. In particular communication strategy and knowledge sharing are key aspects, as well as the organisational context within which the work is carried out. Support is needed in the form of contact with peer groups and experts as well as provision of experimental training - not just to build competence with the technology but also to learn about the process of dispersed mobile working. Figure 15.1 gives an idea of some of the factors that will need to be considered to have a good chance of success.

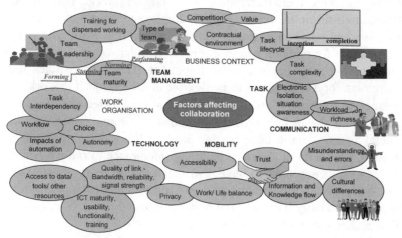

Fig. 15.1. Factors affecting collaboration in dispersed teams of mobile workers (Carver and Leggatt 2002a, 2002b)

As an example, in manufacturing engineering the commercial environment has changed the way business is carried out. Mergers and takeovers have built very large and globally dispersed companies. Risk sharing partnerships between organisations are now the norm, with supply chains that are required to work together to achieve the delivery of new products to the market in ever shorter timescales to ever more stringent cost constraints. To continue being innovative and producing world-class products in this environment requires new ways of working.

The new ways of working are within the context of virtual organisations. These organisations are often formed for the duration of projects and are then dismantled. Particular challenges for engineering are characterised by access to large databases such as product breakdown structures and geometries, product data management (PDM) systems and workflow, analysis and modelling tools.

This has driven the development of new collaborative and mobile technologies to allow work to be done in this way and to capitalize on the significant technological developments made in other domains - for example in mobile and wireless technology, Global Resource Information Database (GRID) computing, and HTML-based collaborative spaces. In summary the major driving forces towards new ways of working are:

- Changing work patterns and working groups: partnerships with other organisations, collaboration across discipline boundaries, organisational boundaries and national boundaries
- Changing project characteristics: very large projects, multi-organisations, multi-discipline teams, highly complex system development
- Mergers and takeovers: people increasingly need to work with others at other sites. As relocation is not always popular, options to work in a more mobile way become more important. This demonstrates the requirement for a willingness to be flexible in the approach to work
- 'Leaner' engineering – greater prevalence of knowledge workers
- Changes to the design process – modelling, digital mock-ups – less 'metal cutting' until later in the product lifecycle - different skills needed, people do not need to be in the same place to run mathematical models for example, or to have distributed design reviews using digital mock-ups where prime contractors and sub-system developers can work together on a daily basis without being co-located
- New technologies allow us to work in this way
- Requirement for better use of real estate
- Work life balance: there is a growing need to address the emerging risks with respect to mobile working such as increasing access hours where employees are always viewed as available, reduced individual autonomy and less freedom to plan tasks, pressure to work whilst travelling, multi tasking and regarding thinking time as 'non value-added' time. On the positive side, mobile working can allow some flexibility to redress the impact of travelling

The transition between traditional ways of working to mobile and multi-location ways of working presents risks and challenges as well as opportunities to do things that could not be done before. It is necessary to understand the requirements for working in a more traditional environment in order to understand what the impact will be when elements of the working environment are changed. The challenges of collaborating when co-located are still not fully addressed especially in a climate of competition. When teams become dispersed and /or mobile it is even more difficult. How can the technology replace the cues that are lost or how can new behaviours be trained, if important elements are lost?

We need to try to predict how to be successful and to mitigate against the emerging negative risks. One way to do this is to look at where the failure modes might be. For example there are many failure modes for e-mail, and e-mail is the most common form of communication for remote collaboration.

Currently there are technologies supporting collaboration to varying degrees: for example voice and video links, e-mail access and use, shared working spaces, conferencing tools, document repositories, tools for presence and situation awareness, calendaring tools. However, a holistic, integrative, approach to the impacts of mobile working is required, in order to:

- Understand the risks and failure modes of the new ways of working the communication strategy and aspects of accessibility and privacy protection
- Allow effective decision making and understand the requirements for collaboration, in a context of changing environments and informal networks, and understand to maintain situation awareness within the team and the project
- Broker access to tools ('analysis by the hour'), datasets, product breakdown structures, and control access to sensitive data
- Build membership within virtual teams and communities of practice

It is clear that further development is required for both the technology and for training behaviours to support aspects of mobile working in order to get the best out of the new ways of working. There is a significant challenge in managing the transition between static and mobile ways of working and the various hybrid working scenarios that are particularly prevalent at the early phases of new technologies.

15.3 Current perspectives in mobile collaborative work

With the advent of sophisticated end-to-end mobile solutions, the expectations for mobile applications for improved work environments began to grow. Mobile business applications range from, on the one end, straightforward extension of the connectivity to office software applications by replacing the wireline access with wireless access technology, and on the other end, to proprietary soft- and hardware applications for very specific work processes, utilizing various access technologies and realizing contextualized work support by using location and user specific information. In general, the application of mobile technology allows an elimination of the spatial dimension of business processes, which subsequently can lead to a flexible integration of connected business transactions between different business entities.

R&D forecasts mobile work environments to develop with disruptive change, generating significantly new ways in conducting work (Sousa and Garlan 2002; MIT 2004). Furthermore, experts in the field predict the number of mobile applications for business customers to be a dominant trend and even outnumber mobile consumer applications (Lehmann et al. 2004). Although business applications centred around voice, e-mail and SMS will remain the dominant share of applications, specific subgroups like mobile marketing and sales force applications or applications to remotely support maintenance, repair and field operations will evolve strongly (Lehmann and Lehner 2003). Also, the first evidence of increasing data traffic caused by mobile e-mail applications points in this direction (Swisscom 2005). However, first research results document that mobile work solutions rather increase operational efficiency than producing a long run, strategic competitive advantage. In other words, mobile work applications do seldom achieve a transformation of business processes, i.e. a fundamental degree of change in organisational processes using the mobile medium, nor do they generate unique benefits i.e. the capability to create entirely new service offerings or products with the wireless medium (Barnes 2004).

Prolonging the insight gained from mobile consumer research allows us to formulate two assumptions: Current examples of mobile work are characterised by (a) low adoption and (b) limited economic impact. Like the lack of attention paid to consumer requirements (Brodt and Heitmann 2004a), the development of mobile work solutions lacks an understanding "of the relationship between the context of work activities and mobile information usage. This means understanding how individuals center their job on mobile devices to communicate with the organisation" (Pica et al. 2004). Similar to the mistrust in technical performance of mobile applications on the consumer side (Brodt and Heitmann 2004b), management at present mistrusts the performance and cost efficiency of mobile work applications and therefore hesitates to infuse too much of mobile technology into their business processes (Frost & Sullivan 2004).

Consequently, the MOSAIC project has performed a number of business case studies in mobile working in order to understand the mobility needs of various mobile worker types and to understand the impact and benefits of mobile work in specific circumstances (sectors, functions). These case studies can be ordered in terms of a typology of mobile workplaces as shown in figure 15.2 The typology recognises four emerging forms of mobile and collaborative workplaces as currently found in practice, using the number of work locations and the frequency of changing worker locations as distinguishing characteristics[2]. The four forms comprise a variety of mobile and collaborative settings ranging from individual workplaces to co-located and distributed team and community workplaces.

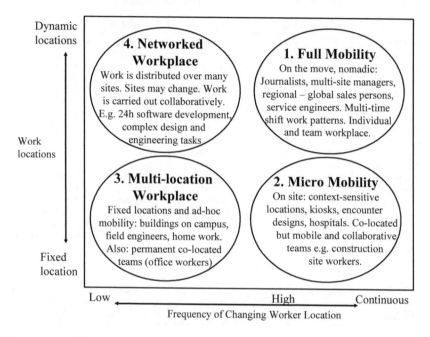

Fig. 15.2. Typology of mobile workplaces (adapted from Schaffers 2005)

The micro-mobility workplace is already emerging in hospitals or campus areas. The multi-location workplace, for example distributed design review in aerospace engineering, can be expected to grow in importance. The networked workplace is only rudimentary realized in practice and represents a situation where a collaborative workplace is truly networked and aware of all contextual variables, and goes through life-cycle stages of inception, operation and dissolution. The full mobility concept is realized for specific mobility-intensive jobs but its widespread introduction may be constrained by limits to physical infrastructure and also for work-life balance reasons.

---

[2] See (Lilischkis 2003) for a typology of mobile workplaces, including a set of criteria for distinguishing between various forms of mobile working. See also the chapters of Vartiainen and of Gareis in this volume.

As is shown in table 15.1, mobility needs are different according to functional requirements. The cases address individual work environments, but the individuals are collaborating with other workers at different locations. We are not discussing same-location same-time collaborative situations.

Table 15.1. Mobility needs of various mobile collaborative worker types

Personal assistant	CRM / Sales management	Operations manager	Maintenance man	Management consultant
Stationary data access at fixed work station Voice access in work location via DECT phones 24h mobile reachability for selected group (superiors) Automatic call forwarding from superiors Fixed line access to superior's databases and agendas, automatic synchronisation	Access to sales applications wherever she is Immediate access to updated work-critical information All information in small, easy-to-carry device: no more carrying heavy laptops and paperwork Rapid access to e-mails and PIM organiser	Manage time anywhere, anytime All information synchronised between devices Always on-line Simple access to all information at once without using laptop Rapid travel organisation Access to critical company information Small device	Constantly updated timetable Always on-line, always reachable Access to job-related information wherever he is Rapid way to report on task done All information in small, easy-to-carry device: no more carting heavy laptops	Simple and quick way of accessing all information Receive and answer e-mails anywhere Broadband download capacity to send/receive attachments Manage time anywhere, anytime Always on-line Rapid travel organisation International navigation support
=> Micro Mobility	=> Multi Mobility		=> Total Mobility	

Generating typical workdays of the worker types and identifying the typical use of mobile applications have accomplished the identification of mobility needs. As an example, a mobile collaborative workplace scenario for remote fieldwork is depicted in table 15.2. The remote field worker needs constantly updated schedules, permanent on-line access, and rapid back-reporting all information in a small and easy-to-carry device.

We have developed a benchmarking framework in order to reveal the particular strengths and weaknesses of the cases. As a very preliminary assessment, each of the cases is investigated in a number of assessment criteria, including criteria for mobile technology progressiveness, criteria for business model implications, and criteria indicating the implementation effort. The latter two sets of criteria indicate the mobile value proposition. The 'Business model implications' criterion investigates in how far the solution generates a competitive advantage, whereas the 'Implementation effort' criterion reveals the major obstacles in reaping the mobile solution benefits.

Table 15.2. A remote field worker scenario

Characteristics	Remote field work; a typical day	
• Home-based • Spends the day on the road • Has variable daily agenda • Has a laptop and mobile phone **Typical representative** • 28 years old, single • Technician for elevator repair company • Has a company mobile phone / company car • Lives in suburb but company based in large town • Has a company laptop and PDA	7:30 Wakes up, breakfast 8:15 Checks day's agenda on PDA 8:30 Looks up client details and address from company database. 9:30 First visit at building for maintenance check. Scans bar code on elevator to check history. Directly orders spare parts and warns the client that it will take 3 days to arrive 10:22 Checks agenda: urgent lift repair at Novotel – looks up task and location details 12:10 Sends in confirmation of repair and pick up afternoon details	13:00 Rapid lunch at Mac-Donald's. Checks cinema schedule on WAP phone and sends e-mail to girlfriend to organize cinema 13:45 Elevator repairs for multi-stores building. Looks up on-line manual with latest product specification of lift and main tasks to be done 14:30 1 hour drive to next visit. Sends in confirmation of elevator repair 17:00 Goes home, no need for reporting: all is up-dated and in order 19:00 Goes to cinema with girlfriend to see Matrix 2

A first conclusion is that the surveyed mobile technologies do support current working processes but do not yet achieve a mobile value proposition in terms of impact on the competitive position in the value chain. We observe that mobile work environments follow the trend towards increasing automation of current work processes and that changes in work environments are rather evolutionary than revolutionary. In order to gain wider scale business benefits it is required to apply a more radical restructuring of inter-organisational value systems and thus support innovations towards new ways of working.

A second, related, conclusion is that currently envisaged mobile workplaces are focusing primarily on the functional needs of individual workers. The potential of mobility in combination with new ways of collaboration in new forms of work organisation is not yet fulfilled. At the same time, forces of increasing globalization and competition in many industries lead to new business demands regarding collaboration. In the next section we explore the impacts of these forces.

15.4 Mobile work and new business practice

We address three key business sectors, automotive, aerospace and building and construction, in order to identify the critical driving forces in these industry sectors affecting mobile and collaborative workplace innovation[3].

15.4.1 Automotive industry

The automotive industry is one of the leading sectors in Europe, delivering products and services which are pervasive to everyday life as well as crucial in relation to other sectors, due to the necessity of moving goods and people for industrial, commercial, social and even leisure purposes. This causes a great deal of pressure on the product throughout its life from design through production, distribution, operation, to dismantling. The main economic pressure for this sector comes from the ongoing globalization of the markets, which has brought overseas manufacturers to take significant shares in the European markets. However, the globalization is also offering European manufacturers new opportunities of expanding their business in emerging countries and in advanced areas in which EU penetration was previously confined to specialities and niche products. This is causing the migration of significant research & development as well as production activities throughout the world, in order to optimize the logistic and supply chain, and to differentiate the product according to the needs and regulations of the particular market. Therefore, product standardization seems not to be the right choice: this situation holds also for the phenomenon of the so-called world cars, which major automotive manufacturers are producing and marketing in different and often distant markets. In this case, the car sold in central or southern Europe can present only a styling and equipment resemblance with the same produced and sold e.g. in Russia or in India, where the climatic and road conditions in fact require very different treatments of e.g. the engine or the climate system. An additional factor resides in the increasing role of the component and services suppliers who must, on the one hand, follow the vehicle manufacturer in its efforts to maintain or increase market presence and, on the other hand, see their responsibilities and roles in the value chain ever increasing due to the final

---

[3] Analyses presented here are mainly based on a MOSAIC Project Report on mobile working scenarios and business challenges in the automotive, aerospace and construction sectors (Fernando et al. 2005) and on results of the Future Workspaces project (Fernando et al. 2003).

product manufacturer's de-structuring and concentrating on core competencies.

Mobile technologies for the automotive industry

This situation has important implications for the automotive product design and engineering process. As product costs are incurred in all stages of the life cycle, including maintenance, product development must more and more be dealt with in terms of life cycle and total ownership cost. Time to market has become an important competitive factor. Overall, the complexity of the product and of its handling has enormously increased compared to a few years ago. To cope with this situation, the organisation of the product development process is changing. To be able to handle the holistic view of the product development process and the geographic dispersion of actors involved, companies are experimenting with distributed forms of the design and engineering process. This has various organisational implications. There is an increasing need to support ad-hoc collaboration processes such as unplanned meetings. Also, more robust control and supervision systems with corresponding workspaces will be necessary to coordinate multi-location working and to adapt assembly lines to changing customer needs and car usage information. Additionally, as innovation cuts across the product life cycle, adequate inter-related workspaces for each type of engineering activity are becoming a necessity.

As regards to mobile collaborative working, it can be foreseen that multi-location distributed forms of work organisation will be important to support collaborative product development tasks. Mobile technologies will allow the team members to join such collaborative product development activities at anytime from anywhere, offering greater work flexibility. Furthermore, organisations can improve the efficiency of their production processes by using smart electronic tags to support better logistics within the supply chain. Mobile technologies will be of high importance in supporting business processes such as remote field service e.g. remote car diagnosis, maintenance and repair, and road assistance, in relations management and sales, and in management and coordination.

15.4.2 Aerospace industry

The aerospace industry is under pressure from their customers to produce better quality, safer and cheaper products in ever-shorter periods. To meet these targets, similar to the automotive industry, the aerospace industry has embraced the concurrent engineering (CE) principles within their product life cycle. A CE approach encourages developers to consider all aspects of the product's life cycle from its conception through to disposal, including user requirements, cost, quality and maintenance. Parallel development of products may reduce considerably the time required for product development. CE promotes the introduction of specialist knowledge from the downstream product life cycle stages during design. By addressing issues such as manufacturing, assembly and maintenance in early stages, CE aims to reduce unforeseen problems creeping into the design as it progresses through its life cycle. Consequently, CE can save both time and money while improving product quality.

The aerospace industry consists of truly distributed virtual organisations that have complex characteristics compared to other sectors. Such characteristics include number of partners, i.e. the Airbus network, complexity of the product, i.e. number of components and related disciplines, size of the organisation including equipment manufacturers, risk-sharing partners, suppliers and sub-contractors, long lead times, and huge capital needs for developing products. For example, Airbus has about 150 sites throughout the world with distributed manufacturing facilities in France, Germany, UK and Spain. It works with an international network of about 1,500 suppliers in more than 30 countries. As a result, this sector needs efficient collaborative tools and processes to work as a distributed virtual organisation.

In the past years, the aerospace industry has moved from a discipline-based organisation (based on the different departments within a design office) to a process- or program-based organisation. As a result, people from several design office disciplines are gathered in co-located platforms (the product integrated teams) together with representatives from manufacturing and support engineering, during the product development phase. In the future, due to the need of higher responsiveness to market demands and to reach another significant step in term of costs, cycle time and quality, a more agile and adaptive organisation is expected. In this organisation the engineering process will be distributed among a variety of knowledge teams in a network or "mesh-like" structure.

Mobile technologies for the aerospace sector

The drive for concurrent engineering and reduced product lead times has lead to the development of secure shared working environments connecting the project partners, supply chain and the customer. The challenge is that it is still difficult to truly collaborate in a virtual environment and many design engineers still travel to take advantage of the rich communication environment offered by face-to-face meetings. This means the requirements for mobile working are even greater.

A significant step towards remote or mobile working has been the use of digital mock-ups (DMUs). This has made a dramatic difference to the ability of project stakeholders to have access to and visibility of the required data and information. DMUs allow sharing of, for example, product break down structures and visibility of conflicts highlighted by geometries. This has meant shared decision making, better impact assessment as well as more accurate design for assembly and maintenance. The next steps are to allow sharing and brokering of analysis tools, access to product data management systems, and the use of ontologies to allow the exchange of meaningful information from databases. As in the automotive industry, mobile technologies can be used to support the design phase and the production phase, allowing greater work flexibility and better logistics. Similarly, smart electronic devices can be used to monitor the performance of aero-engines and support predictive maintenance of aircrafts, saving millions of Euros for companies.

15.4.3 Building and construction industry

The building and construction industry is known to change at a very slow pace with little investment in ICT to enhance their work processes. In the building and construction process many partners play a role and it has a fragmented nature. The project organisation is created for each project. This means that in most cases different experts such as designers don't know each other and have not yet worked together when the project starts. The operating environment is a building site with no permanent infrastructure or factory-like services.

The traditional procurement mode is based on minimizing capital costs instead of optimizing performance. This gives little incentives for product or process innovation. There are some new contracting models in use extending the suppliers' responsibility and interest towards the long service life of buildings. Until now the main contractors have mainly been responsible to deliver the facility with a very short guarantee period, a year or two. In the future, if the main supplier e.g. contractor is ready to take the responsibility of operating and maintaining the building for the coming decades, it will certainly lead to organisational changes and new service concepts based on value networks.

Given the rapidly changing market environment, higher demands of asset managers and conscious users, single suppliers cannot provide the requested whole life performance and services alone in a sustainable way. The mistrust between client and supplier needs to be transformed into partnerships. The sub-optimized management of a changing chain of cheap subcontractors or suppliers and project based profit maximization must be developed to a value network providing sustainable business opportunities for those who are both willing and capable to improve their performance. In short, the transition from today's lose-lose business model to a win-win one is highly desirable.

The open market and the growth of the Community, combined with the unstable local markets, require the industry to seek international work and collaboration. Most of the key players in the national markets are already involved in international activities. These activities are either based on subsidiaries or strategic partnerships. Many of the companies are not trained in international collaboration and the management are neither structured nor complemented to address the challenges.

Mobile technologies for the building and construction industry

Similar to the automotive and the aerospace industries, the building and construction sector needs to bring together large number of geographically dispersed partners to design, construct and maintain a building. The use of mobile technology during the design phase could allow partners to interact with each other in a much more flexible way to work more efficiently. Some examples of the use of mobile technology during the construction phase include access to design data to clarify construction tasks, safety monitoring of workers and the use of smart electronic tags to support logistics and resource monitoring. The construction sector is also exploring the benefits of using mobile technology in the service phase of the building. Typical mobile force applications in the construction industry do equip the engineer with a mobile device, which is linked to the central dispatch and data system of the company. The mobile application can support the engineer in a multitude of processes which makes them independent from a physical office and offers the remote field worker total mobility. These applications are now in their initial stages in medium and large enterprises in the construction industry. The impact on costs becomes clearly visible, when we think of the number of remote engineers and the volume of the installed base, i.e. the number of sites to be served. For example, for a medium sized company in Switzerland, which was monitoring heating systems in 200.000 sites using more than 250 technicians, the introduction of such a solution decreased administration cost by 70%. In the future, services like elevators, heating systems and security systems can be equipped with mobile technologies for ongoing communication with central surveillance systems, ensuring continuous controlling and monitoring and data availability for maintenance and security. Although the industry has started in the mid nineties to centralize the development and standardization of e-

and m-technologies, the current state of the industry still needs to over-come structural challenges in order to allow stronger penetration of mobile technologies within its business processes.

15.4.4 Prospects for new ways of mobile working

From this overview of industry developments it can be concluded that industry drivers determining the potential of mobile workplaces are quite different in any of the sectors. In the automotive sector mobility seems to be primarily a competitive factor in support of processes like sales and relations management and to facilitate mobile access to data for engineering purposes. Multi-location work could be the primary direction of development. In the aerospace sector the situation is different as operations and maintenance are crucial business processes and mobility of airplanes is their natural characteristic. Mobile and collaborative working matches potentially very well with the underlying characteristics of the industry. In building and construction, the characteristic of complex projects and dispersed and temporary teams provide good opportunities for mobile workplace technologies. It is also clear that the benefits of mobile collaborative working cannot be realized without inter-organisational restructuring.

15.5 Introducing mobile collaborative work

What is a mobile organisation, and what are the key issues in introducing new mobile forms of working? A mobile organisation could be described as an organisation "...where people, processes, technology and management support work (are) done anyplace/anytime" (Neal 2003). This is a good description but does not indicate the variety of options that are possible particularly with respect to groups and teams of people who need to collaborate with each other and to access data, information and tools to support their activities.

The mobile organisation has to support not only individuals but also groups and teams who need to collaborate. In table 15.3, the true mobile organisation is described as highly collaborative, but acknowledges that co-located high performance teams are also important for success. A flexibility of approach is required that aims to support the collaboration process, to reduce unnecessary travel without creating further challenges for individuals, to enable people who are away from their 'home base' to carry on being effective and to allow individuals to make the best use of the time available to them to carry out both work and home commitments.

Table 15.3. Collaboration and mobility

Mobile	Collection of mobile individuals	The mobile organisation
Static	Collection of static individuals	A high performance team

Not collaborative   Highly
                         collaborative

Ideally, the mobile organisation from an ICT perspective can be seen to have the following attributes:

- *No fixed working space.* Working in the office is just another place for the worker to work and access to the network is available wherever he or she happens to be. Moreover, instead of the architect being in charge of creating a collaborative environment, the applications architect is now responsible. However, since 'office' spaces are now 'shared' spaces, and may be used for many different activities, considerable care still needs to be taken in designing workspaces in buildings. If the home becomes a workplace too, equal attention should be paid to the design of that environment. There may also be running cost implications for workers working in places other than the traditional 'office', for example Internet connections, dial-in facilities or additional printers.
- *Internet-based processes.* Processes are designed to be useful and accessible by both mobile workers and co-located workers, and administrative forms and procedures are available in electronic form, with applications using the HTML-based browser.
- *Mobile technology.* Technology is used seamlessly to enable any-place/anytime work. Different sorts of mobile devices can be used, and the choice of device is driven by user requirements rather than an organisation wide decision. All ICT devices are supported. Mobile devices are always on, are always connected, have rapid response rates and reliable connectivity, are light, small and non-intrusive, and most of all are not prohibitively expensive. Diversity of devices will incur costs – both in the hardware itself and in maintaining the skills and knowledge to support different systems and of course in the provision of 24hr support. The business plan needs to consider these elements and elaborate how the provision of technology will save costs and improve effectiveness.

The positive aspects include more effective use of time, reduced down time, high levels of availability and employee satisfaction if they can be in better control of the way in which they achieve their goals. It is also important to consider some of the potential negative aspects too – these might include time clock changes - for example the time taken to reach decisions or complete processes, there is additional pressure to ensure that contributions have been made and views considered, and not least the challenge of ensuring that there is understanding across the team, adequate situation awareness of the activities and requirements of the team, and no isolation of individuals.

- *Management of mobility and mobile working culture.* The organisation recognizes that mobile teams have different requirements and train their managers to motivate and manage mobile teams. Additionally, the organisation appreciates issues of privacy and accessibility and develops protocols to help workers maintain a work / life balance. One step further would be the acceptance of a mobility culture: mobility being the norm, not exception.

Many of the principles for a mobile organisation make sense for a more static or at least a mixed organisation too. But a mobile organisation is not just a collection of people with laptops, cell phones and pagers allowing people to take their office home after the "normal" working day. It is also not just a group of mobile workers bolted on to the standard organisation. However many organisations will not see a requirement to be entirely mobile and people may not work exclusively in one way all the time – this can be driven by individual preference, work life balance, or driven by project or task requirements. The role of the organisation and the type of work undertaken will also affect the type of choices of working environments open to an individual. The degree of choice is extremely variable across different industries, from engineering to telecommunications, and across domains from service industry e.g. health, consultancy, finance and insurance, to farming and other rural occupations.

Mobility leads to changes in working practices - as well as new terms and conditions. These might include expense account changes i.e. mobile phone charges, remote connection charges, teleconferencing costs, video conferencing costs, attribution of cost to project versus overhead, costs for IT support 24 hours per day, additional costs where IT devices are not all standardized, and potential health and safety considerations where employees are working outside the 'normal' working environment. In offering the flexibility to work at home or wherever is appropriate for the individual, the organisation also needs to address the risk of making team members feel isolated, unaware and not engaged in the process. Co-located team members may also exhibit virtual characteristics, for example, people using e-mail to talk to someone in the next room, or sending texts to someone in the same room.

One often cited business goal is to 'improve productivity by leveraging knowledge'. This is potentially even more difficult if the organisation is virtual and its employees mobile. However the challenge is realizing this and using the very mobility to create social networks and to build rich knowledge and information flows across the organisation. Leveraging knowledge across a dispersed organisation is often difficult if not impossible - not only because of the technical difficulties but also because of the politics and negative sharing ethos where knowledge still represents power rather than the other way round – i.e. sharing the knowledge creates the power.

Knowledge and information documentation always runs behind its acquisition, and furthermore all knowledge will not be captured or shared in formal ways. For this reason, organisations are reliant on informal ad hoc meetings to spread the knowledge and experience. This is a challenge that needs to be met within the virtual mobile organisation.

The socialization of knowledge, that is, the direct exchange of ideas in conversations and other interactions, both planned and unplanned, speeds up the exchange of knowledge allowing organisations to get more value from it. However, this takes place most readily when people are located in the same physical environment. With more mobile communities, it is still important to consider this requirement in the physical design of work spaces and to acknowledge different spaces are required for different types of work (Duffy 2000). Spontaneous interaction and ad-hoc meetings decrease as distance between people increases but these spontaneous meetings have significant value. It is often only when we perceive a colleague that we think of issues that they can help us to solve, or even help us to frame the right questions to ask. Ambient intelligent systems bringing computing power everywhere, but in the "background", may be one way of trying to support and facilitate these spontaneous interactions, but there may need to be cultural changes and training to enable individuals to succeed. Changes to the physical working environment and solutions linking the virtual world with the physical show promise but are as yet immature in their implementation. We need to think now about the impacts of these new environments and to consider how they might be integrated into new processes and organisational structures.

15.6 Towards a roadmap and innovation agenda

15.6.1 Future scenarios

What about the future forms of collaborative mobile workplaces? In order to stretch current thinking and to envisage and visualize more radical directions and discuss them with policy makers and industrial stakeholders for the purpose of building a roadmap for innovation, a framework for mobile and collaborative working scenarios is proposed in figure 15.3.

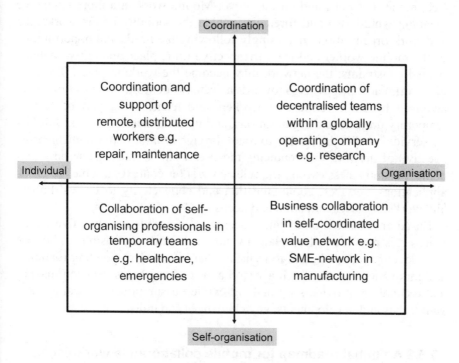

Fig. 15.3. MOSAIC mobile working scenarios (Schaffers et al. 2005)

Two key driving forces are recognized, the first is the focus of collaboration (individual versus organisational focus), and the second is the evolution of organisations (coordination versus self-organisation), resulting in four scenario types highlighting different directions of innovation and change as regards working, collaboration and mobility.

Such scenarios are not meant as forecasts or business cases but are developed primarily to highlight the underlying fundamental forces in innovation and change with respect to work environments, and to discuss their implementation requirements in terms of technologies, organisational variables, human behaviour, and policy conditions in order to build an innovation roadmap.

The scenarios also enable us to recognize that mobile work is to be considered at different levels: the worker, the workplace, the organisation and the organisational environment. Mobile work is a combination of technology, workplace organisation, (inter-) organisational procedures, and facilities and support systems allowing people to work at times and locations of choice. Mobile work involves not only a traditional meaning of 'worker mobility' focusing primarily on multiple work locations including the office, home, hotspots, and on the move. Mobile work in a more extensive meaning would also and foremost include the mobility of the workplace and work organisation, increasingly following the needs and opportunities of the mobile worker and team irrespective time, place and other context-related constraints: the network may become the working place. The mobile workplace thus evolves towards a scenario of work organisation characterised by empowerment of workers and teams being part of ad-hoc temporary projects and organisations, and by awareness of context. Mobility services enable the worker to roam through arbitrary environments irrespective of network environments the user is in. Context awareness and context adaptiveness exploit the relevant worker context variables to tailor applications, services, communication and connectivity to the workplace and workers' current situation and needs.

Based on a discussion of future scenarios of mobile collaborative workplaces it is possible to formulate a vision as regards a plausible and desirable development path, and to translate that into a corresponding roadmap and innovation agenda. Such a vision and roadmap helps decision makers and technology providers by making explicit assumptions regarding relevant trends and developments, key challenges and milestones.

15.6.2 An initial roadmap for mobile collaborative workplaces

The future of collaborative mobile workplaces will depend to a large extent on economical factors affecting mobility: transportation costs, computing technology costs, end-user equipment costs and telecommunication costs. Although the steady decrease of transportation costs has been a long-term trend, an increase in oil prices and costs associated with security measures may result in an increase in transportation costs. Moore's law, stating that the computing power available for a given price doubles every 18 months, is expected to hold at least for the next ten years. At the same time, battery life is expected to increase in a rapid pace. The telecommunication technologies that are expected to be dominant in the next ten years are mobile telephony – GPRS, UMTS – and various generations of WiFi. The existence of roaming contracts between many European mobile operators is an important enabler for mobile access to business services from anywhere in Europe. The various mobile access technologies will be available at competitive prices and offer the user an increasing amount of bandwidth and different Quality of Service levels. At the same time, the current heterogeneity of access technologies is likely to exist for the coming period of time as different access technologies have different advantages, such as high bandwidth or large coverage.

Another relevant trend is the migration towards all-IP networks: the current mix of Internet Protocol (IP) networks and circuit-switched networks, such as the current fixed telephone network, is likely to converge into multi-purpose all-IP networks. The availability of such networks facilitates the convergence of services, for instance allowing voice-over-IP calls to be placed to a mobile phone.

The following sections summarize the result of discussions and workshops with a large number of practitioners. We consider the following assumptions as being most relevant for mobile work in the short term 2005 – 2006, the medium term 2007 – 2008 and the long term 2009 – 2013.

Short-term scenario assumptions, 2005 – 2006

- The number of mobile workers will increase, while the types of mobile workers remain unchanged i.e. managers, sales, consultants, support technicians, scientists and academics
- Low costs associated with mobility i.e. travel cost
- Tele-maintenance, telemedicine, and all remote working activities call for wireless access by employees to report continuously on remote locations
- Connectivity and bandwidth allows for audio communication and image/document sharing
- Increasing globalization and decentralization of business require new modes of communication and coordination
- Mobile access takes place primarily through mobile phones and PDA's
- The individual with his requirements for usability and usefulness is a main driving factor in the design of mobile work

Medium-term scenario assumptions, 2007 – 2008

- The societal cost associated with mobility gradually increases

- Multi-cultural and multi-lingual support enables collaboration among foreign localized competencies
- Connectivity and bandwidth allow for rich multimedia sharing.
- Smart, agile business networks start to emerge, based on smart collaboration workspaces
- Mobile work is fully integrated into business processes
- Mobile devices seamlessly integrate with desktop-based systems
- In the design of mobile work, requirements of collaboration and coordination, as well as organisational requirements become more dominant

Long-term scenario assumptions, 2009 – 2013

- High cost mobility, leading to changes in the organisation of work: more mobile workers that mainly travel small distances
- Using mobile information technology is becoming an established cultural practice
- Independent experts form the flexible workforce any networked business organisation can recruit "on demand"
- Mobile workers have access to on-demand, service-based mobile cooperation support
- Computers disappear: interaction via non-intrusive, attentive interfaces
- There is a ubiquitous computing infrastructure, which is accessible anywhere, anytime

To structure our roadmap for collaborative mobile workplaces we have analyzed the scenarios based on the following six RTD / innovation areas: 1) Social and legal aspects; 2) Mobility and work settings e.g. work processes, business models and inter-organisational arrangements; 3) Implications for and developments in mobile applications; 4) Human interaction with mobile applications; 5) Mobile service platforms and context-awareness support; 6) Mobile access technology. Based on our holistic, integrated perspective, mobile workplace innovations are considered to cut across all of these layered areas. The initial roadmap, depicted in figure 15.4 at an aggregate level, shows the key challenges and milestones for mobile workplace innovation. We now discuss the roadmap in short, focusing primarily on the level of mobile applications.

In the short term from 2005 - 2006, it is expected an emerging demand for community services. Mobile workers will mainly use communication and presence services, and some special purpose mobile applications. Semantic-based information applications, to stimulate creating shared vision and understanding, are emerging. Basic life-cycle support of virtual teams is in rapid development. Web services allow mobile workers to access advanced functions and large databases whereas accessibility to mobile applications is improved.

For the medium term, 2007 - 2008, ad-hoc mobile workspaces are developing, supporting secure access to information archives and advanced cooperation e.g. via multimedia communication. Formats and techniques to deliver content to various platforms become more powerful and less expensive. Applications are allowing for tele-assistance and mobile learning. Support services are developing to set-up and develop remote businesses and to internationalize businesses.

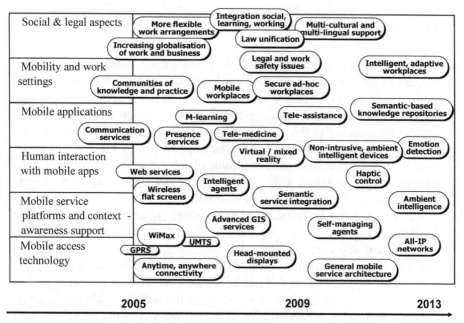

Fig. 15.4. Initial MOSAIC mobile work roadmap (Slagter and Schaffers (eds) 2005)

For the long term, 2009 - 2013, *work* would become more mobile with *less mobile workers*. Mobile workplaces have plug and play capabilities for flexible integration into a networked business organisation. We see a high level of adaptability of systems empowering users to shape the technology to their specific situational needs. Mobile workers will have access to semantic-based knowledge repositories.

As has been underlined, such development paths must not be seen in isolation and are combined with developments in societal and legal frameworks, changes in organisational structures and processes, and developments in key enabling technologies.

In the process of elaborating and refining the roadmap a concrete research and innovation agenda and strategy is being created. By discussing the roadmap with a large group of practitioners from industry and academia we aim to create a realistic and broadly supported innovation agenda that can help decision makers and technology providers throughout Europe in making strategic decisions for systemic innovation in mobile collaborative workplaces.

15.7 Final remarks

In this paper we have explored mobile workplace innovations and their success factors, focusing on different levels of innovation: human and organisational issues, industry drivers and underlying competitive forces, and technological trends and opportunities. We explored future scenarios for mobile working in the context of market and sector conditions and developed a strategic roadmap that can be used by policy makers and strategists to build a common understanding of joint innovation strategies and business implementation paths. We now conclude with some summarising observations and points for further elaboration.

We stressed the importance of supporting collaboration as a starting point for using mobile technologies. Mobility supports collaboration and collaboration supports mobility. In discussing the current practices and needs in different situations of mobile working to understand the mobile work business proposition and needs, we took an individual worker mobility perspective and raised the issue as when the mobile workplace innovation is a real value proposition in terms of improving the company business model and not just making individual work organisation more efficient. The benchmarking approach we are developing offers criteria that must be fulfilled in order to integrate mobile workplace facilities successfully into the company business model. To that end, the individual worker mobility approach can benefit from including more systematically team oriented and inter-organisational collaboration perspectives.

The driving factors for mobile collaborative workplaces in selected business areas were explored in order to identify prospects for innovation. As a general conclusion it can be stated that business drivers for mobile and collaborative work are very different across sectors. In all sectors, mobile work in its narrow sense of mobility enhancement of individual workers will be an important innovation in individual-oriented support services like sales, customer relations management (CRM), repair and maintenance. Mobile work in terms of virtual team collaboration will be important for sectors where work objects – like aeroplanes and cars - are mobile, and / or where the problem at hand requires individuals to intensively communicate with specialists at different locations and different time zones, like in R&D work and also in complex maintenance tasks.

We then turned to introduction issues and discussed human and organisational factors in implementing mobile work in organisations and provided a richer picture of success and failure factors in introducing mobile workplaces. This contributes to our understanding of the feasibility and realism of mobile technology deployment strategies in practice.

Finally, we explored a framework of future mobile workplace scenarios, in order to understand the underlying forces of innovation and to build a realistic vision as a basis for innovation strategy. On this basis a concrete roadmap of challenges and milestones in key areas of mobile working is proposed as a basis for an agenda for research and innovation that may enable business and policy stakeholders to structure their innovation agendas.

References

Barnes S (2004) Wireless support for mobile distributed work: a taxonomy and examples. Presented at 37th Hawaii International Conference on System Sciences, Hawaii

Brodt T, Heitmann M (2004a) Customer centric development of radically new products, a European case. Proceedings of the 10th Americas Conference on Information Systems New York, New York

Brodt T, Heitmann M (2004b) Customer needs in mobile rich media markets. In: P. Cunningham and M. Cunningham (eds.) eAdoption and the knowledge economy: Issues, applications, case studies. IOS Press, Amsterdam, pp 50–57

Carver E, Leggatt A (2002a) Using COSIGA to raise awareness of concurrent engineering in ENHANCE. (ENHANCE Project Report D7.2/3 – V4 Appendix 3)

Carver E, Leggatt A (2002b) Analysis of co-located and dispersed communication using the COSITE digital mock-up demonstrator. (ENHANCE Project Report D7.2/3 – V4 Appendix 2

Duffy F (1997) The new office. Conran Octopus Ltd, London

Fernando T, Wilson J, Dalton G, Dangelmaier M, Cros PH, Baudier Y, Skaerbaek J, Varalda G (2003) Business demands and visions. (Future Workspaces Project IST-2001–38346 Report)

Fernando T, L Carver, S Bowden, M Pallot, A Zarli, K Kristensen, J Counsell, M Puybaraud, P Huovila, Y Baudier, G Varalda, J Skaerbaek (2005) Report on scenarios for the life-cycle management sector for m-worker and m-workspaces. (MOSAIC Project FP6-2003-IST-2 Report D2.3a)

Frost & Sullivan (2004) Mobile Sales Force Automation (SFA) Markets, Report # F114-65, www.commapps.frost.com, retrieved August 2004

Lehmann H, Lehner F (2003) Is there a 'killer application' in mobile technology? A tailored research approach. FORWIN-Bericht-Nr. FWN-2003-004. Bamberg et al., Regensburg

Lehmann H, Kuhn J, Lehner F (2004) The future of mobile technology: findings from a European Delphi study. Presented at the 37th Hawaii International Conference on System Sciences, Hawaii

Lilischkis S (2003) More yo-yos, pendulums and nomads: trends of mobile and multi-location work in the information society'. (Empirica, STAR project issue report no 36)

MIT (2004) MIT Project Oxygen, http://oxygen.lcs.mit.edu/publications/ Oxygen.pdf, retrieved 2004

Neal D (2003) Collaboration – The key to getting value from new mobile technologies. CSC Research Services Web Conference, obtained from www.csc-researchservices.com

Pica D, Sørensen C, and Allen D (2004) On mobility and context of work: Exploring mobile police work. Proceedings of the 37th Hawaii International Conference on System Sciences, Hawaii

Porter M (1990) The competitive advantage of nations. The Free Press, New York.

Schaffers H (2004) Understanding mobile workplace innovation. In: Cunningham P and Cunningham M (Eds.) eAdoption and the knowledge economy: Issues, applications, case studies. IOS Press, Amsterdam, pp 1433–1440

Schaffers H (ed), Carver L, Fernando T, Hickey S, Hinrichs E, Martland D, Niitamo VP, Pallot M, Prinz W, Vollmer S (2005) Mobile working: vision, scenarios, challenges. (MOSAIC Project FP6-2003-IST-2 Report D1.1.1 (V1.3))

Schaffers H (2005) Innovation and systems change: the example of mobile collaborative work. Forthcoming in: AI & Society 19.4 Special Issue on Mobility, Technology and Development

Slagter R, Schaffers H (eds), Brugnoli C, Hickey S, Lorusso I, Niitamo VP, Pallot M, Prinz W, Rissanen M, Tarchalska A, Turowiec A (2005) Mobile workplaces roadmap report. (MOSAIC Project FP6-2003-IST-2 Report D1.2 (V1.14))

Sousa JP, Garlan D (2002) Aura: an architectural framework for user mobility in ubiquitous computing environments. In: Bosch G and Hofmeister K (eds) 3rd Working IEEE/IFIP Conference on Software Architecture. Kluwer Academic Publishers, pp 29–43

16 Mobile Virtual Work: What Have We Learned?

Matti Vartiainen[1] and Erik Andriessen[2]

[1]Laboratory of Work Psychology and Leadership, Helsinki University of Technology, Finland
[2]Faculty of Technology, Policy and Management, Delft University of Technology, The Netherlands

16.1 Introduction

The title of this book and the title of this chapter end with question marks. They are an indication of the fact that the subject of our study is novel, not yet clearly identified, rather fluid and ambiguous, and without common scientific concepts and models or clear guidelines for practitioners. Nevertheless the previous chapters have shown that mobile virtual work is among us, is increasing in its prevalence and can be expected to become a major phenomenon in the domain of work and organisations. Both for practitioners and for scientists it promises to be a fascinating challenge and a field of study. All the signs point in the direction of something that can be of real value for future organisational processes, although at the present it is sometimes not much more than making individual work organisation more efficient.

The novelty of the subject should prevent us from trying to define the phenomena too sharply. Better is the solution offered by Vartiainen (chapter 2) to identify certain dimensions that roughly constitute the domain where MVW phenomena can be found. The claim is that we should speak about mobile virtual work as a work system in its varied environments. As any system, it has many interrelated components. Each of them may have the quality of mobility and virtuality. A change in the task and in the environment, for example a need to carry out a global project instead of a local one, creates pressures to change all the other components and their internal relationship in order to optimise the system with its external requirements.

Why this change occurs? The authors of this book are quite unanimous and consistent. The driving forces form an interwoven system. Economical and business drivers are at the top. A driving force may be a *new business practice*, e.g. a globalised business is not possible with a local organisation. Customers of a product and creative employees, needed to create a product or a service, are globally dispersed. Because of the drive for competitive advantage, companies may want to operate near their customers, and therefore bring their production machinery and employees either permanently or on temporary basis there. This brings along moving and travelling people – but also raises the need to cooperate over distances and to develop new collaborative technologies. Another reason for mobilising work is to achieve cuttings in real estate costs. Companies and public sector as well are waiting for considerable savings by getting rid of under-utilised office spaces. On the other hand, work and workers are always somewhere doing their tasks, and somebody has to pay the premise bill there. A *new technology*, e.g. mobile and wireless information and communication technology (ICT) creates possibilities to work in any place and at any time. Technology has made it easier and more cost-effective to manage dispersed organisations. Although it is easy to pinpoint all the deficiencies in communication and collaboration technologies, the progress has been fast in the last ten years. The driving force may even be a *new strategic initiative*, e.g. the idea of developing a virtual community to increase mutual learning and creativity. This may start the design of new technology to support it and may later create new business opportunities.

16.2 MVW is among us

16.2.1 Mobile Virtual Work is strengthening

The contribution by Gareis and colleagues in this book (chapter 3) shows that mobile work in a broad sense is quite common in Europe and elsewhere. They distinguish *mobile workers* in general, including even employees working only a few hours away from the office and *high-intensity mobile workers*, who do so for 10 hours or more per week. *Mobile eWorkers* are those high-intensity mobile workers who use computer connections when travelling. They have also been defined as physically and virtually mobile in this book. Work commutes are not included in any category.

According to the data 28 per cent of EU15 workers in 2002 belonged to the category of mobile workers. In the USA the percentage is 32. The number of high-intensity mobile workers was roughly half of this, i.e. 15 per cent in Europe and 19 per cent in the USA. The share of mobile workers differs considerably between countries. In the EU15, the range is from 46 per cent in the Netherlands and 45 percent in Finland to 8 per cent in Portugal. In the ten New Member States and Acceding Countries, average shares of mobile workers are lower, although some of the smaller countries do have figures that are similar to the EU15 average.

Mobile eWork is found much less frequently: 4 percent of the EU15 work force belonged to the mobile eWorkers in 2002. In the USA the share of eWorkers was 6 per cent. Mobile eWorkers use online connections mainly for sending and reading e-mail (92%), but three quarters also browse the Internet and connect to their company's internal computer system.

The share of mobile eWorkers among overall EU15 employment has grown from 1.5 per cent to 4 per cent in the course of only three years (1999-2002). The share of home-based teleworkers has remained stagnant over that time period. This refers particularly to *permanent* teleworking at home, which remains an exotic phenomenon, and to *alternating* home-based telework. However, *supplementary* home-based telework, i.e. working for less than one full day per week at home, is on the rise. In 2002, there were more than two and a half times more supplementary teleworkers in the EU15 than three years before. These data suggest a shift among home-based teleworkers towards spending less time at home. This points towards a greater flexibility in the use of individual working locations, but at the possible expense of some of the traditional advantages ascribed to telecommuting such as savings on miles travelled. In fact, there are indications that whatever advantages the new developments may bring to stakeholders, mobile and virtual work, but perhaps even teleworking, may increase rather than decrease the assault on the environment.

Data were also collected on the extent to which the EU labour force is involved in distributed, i.e. virtual teamwork. For this, a very basic definition was used which included everybody who regularly uses e-mail or the Internet to communicate with work contacts located at other business sites, either in other organisations or at other sites of the same organisation. More than every third worker in the EU15 appears to be involved in regular tele-cooperation, if defined in that way - about three times as many as the number of teleworkers.

It has been suggested that to categorise teleworkers as either "home-based" or "mobile" distracts from the fact that many teleworkers spend their working time at a number of different locations, among which the home might be only one option. This trend has obviously been enabled by mobile office technology, which has liberated work from being bound to a particular space and time. For this phenomenon, the term "multi-locational telework" has been invented. It implies that persons work wherever it suits their work tasks, business schedule, and/or lifestyle.

16.2.2 A typology of MVW

The chapters in this book give a rich picture of various kinds of mobile virtual work settings, from a plumber using a mobile phone to keep into contact with his customers to a large network of customs agents using PDAs and notebooks to retrieve assignments and report back data about the work done. From a web-based home health care system to a system installed in trucks for informing the fleet manager about location of the truck and about fuel consumption (see Verburg et al. chapter 12).

Perry and Brodie (chapter 5) show the problems of individual workers like hairdresser and electric meter installer. Wilson's chapter 6 deals particularly with the issues of mobile collaborative work, such as in railway maintenance and design teams. Johansson and colleagues (chapter 8) and Wiethoff et al. (chapter 9) present several settings in the health care sector, where mobile medical professionals exchange patient data over the web. Corso (chapter 13) discusses the differences in knowledge exchange for settings that vary in the level of routinisation of the work: high routine heating and air conditioning maintenance men, medium routine salesmen, and low routine managers and system developers. Lindmark and colleagues (chapter 14) discuss the problems of the diffusion of various types of mobile systems for goods and public transportation.

The question arises whether these many examples and settings can somehow be clustered in a few categories to provide the reader and researcher with a more concise grip on the issues that are related to mobile work. Our analysis of the previous chapters suggests a typology that is based on three dimensions. The *first dimension* is the one presented in chapter 2, i.e. the typology developed by Empirica on the basis of the analysis of European workers' mobility: from the geographically and time wise very limited 'on-site movers', via 'pendulums', 'yo-yo's' and nomads to the 'carriers' who are almost permanently on the move (see Fig. 16.1). This typology can be described in terms of, on the one hand, the number of locations people work at and, on the other hand, the frequency of changing locations.

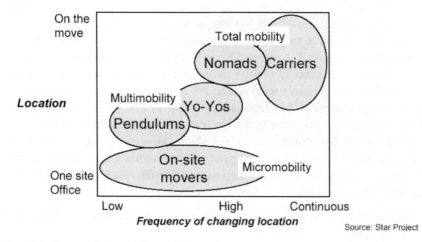

Fig. 16.1. Types of physically mobile workers

Niitamo (chapter 11) and Schaffers et al. (Chapter 15) use the same dimensions but prefer to categorise the potential combinations into three categories: desk-based or micromobility, campus or multi-location mobility and total or full mobility. In addition, Schaffers et al. present the networked workplace for a co-located and distributed team as the fourth type.

The *second dimension* is related to the issue whether MVW is focussing on the exchange of standard information such as patient records or maintenance forms, or on free person-to-person communication. This distinction is strongly related to Corso's distinction between routine and non-routine work settings. This dimension, i.e. type of work performed and data exchanged, needs some explanation. Standard data exchange takes place when, e.g. customs agents, maintenance men, ambulance workers or home nurses (see examples in chapters 8 and 12), retrieve their daily assignment, and possibly machine or patient specifications from their organisation's intranet, and report back the results in the same way. This information is generally in textual format, displayed on PDAs or tablets, but may in future also be visually displayed on a headset (= "augmented reality", see chapter 7). In this case, the *peripheral* mobile worker is the most active partner, who retrieves data from and sends data back to the *central* system. However, standard data exchange also takes place in cases where centrally located employees retrieve data from sensors attached in one way or the other to mobile people. Examples are the hospital personnel monitoring heart rate data from mobile patients, or fleet managers retrieving data concerning location and fuel consumption of their company's trucks.

A *third dimension* appears to be the level of cooperation: from purely individual mobile work, such as the work of salesmen, to collaborative teams. Here we have to present a remarkable finding: We have not found examples of *groups* of workers that perform their primary work task while 'on the move'. Obviously mobile interaction means generally the communication between a single worker and his or her home base. Some part of a team seems always to be stationary, staying in one place. It appears that the actual group work of, e.g. design teams or project teams, is rarely performed by totally mobile group members. However, many individually working mobile professionals appear to have contact now and then with colleagues to consult them on difficult problems. We can formulate here the following conclusions, or better hypotheses:

1. Mobile work is mainly done by individual workers, having contact with the head office or customers.
2. Virtual teamwork is mainly done by stationary or 'micro-mobile' workers, sitting behind their desks in different locations, which may be globally distributed.
3. Individual mobile workers do have remote (virtual) interaction, but that is mainly in the service of knowledge exchange and in the framework of *knowledge communities.*

We propose here a classification model of mobile work that combines the three dimensions, i.e. the *degree of physical mobility* of the people involved, the *level of routinisation of the type of work* and *type of data exchanged* and *degree of interaction* (Fig. 16.2). The value of a classification model depends on its objectives. In this case the objective is to find out to which extent different settings require different tools and organisational arrangements to succeed. This implies that we distinguish between work settings that differ both in technology required and in organisational issues involved, i.e. in issues such as managing, knowledge sharing and social identification.

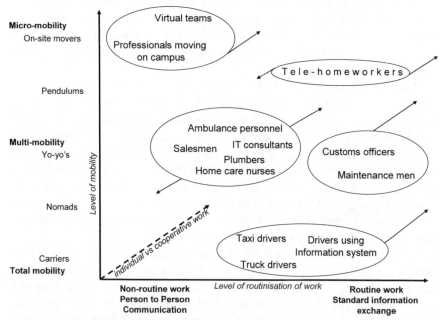

Fig. 16.2. Types of mobile work as combinations of the degree of physical mobility, the type of work, and the individual vs. cooperative nature of the work

According to the model in figure 16.1, there are about five types of MVW settings. This number is the same as in figure 16.2 but we consider this three-dimensional typology better suited to derive ideas about management and design of these groups.

16.3 Specific conclusions and implications

In this section, the main conclusions and implications of the separate chapters in this volume are summarised.

Part one of the book is a general introduction. It focuses on concepts, data about prevalence of the phenomena related with MVW, and the legal context of these developments.

Mobility as a feature of a work system, is the central issue of chapter two. Most often 'mobile work' is related to the possibility of a person to move and execute tasks anywhere and at any time with the help of wired and wireless technologies and in a flexible manner. However, studying and describing 'mobility' on the level of an individual is not enough: more levels, components, and viewpoints are needed to understand mobile work as a goal-oriented activity system and to describe it in a credible manner. Vartiainen provides a tripartite entity 'subject-tool-objective' as the basic functional unit of mobile work that performs actions in different working contexts or spaces.

'Mobility' is considered to be a feature of the system's parts. In a subject, it appears as its physical motion and virtual movement from place to place. Mobile technologies as tools allow communication and collaboration of subjects flexibly 'at any time and in any place'. Objects of work may be moved or transported from one place to another in physical (material) form or in electronic, digitalised form. Work is always carried out in some physical space, which is layered with virtual and social/mental spaces of a subject. This book is mainly about physically and virtually mobile individual subjects using distributed workplaces. To some extent, mobile virtual collaborative work is also discussed.

Because of the systemic nature of mobile work, challenges arise for the design, development and management of this work system. The system's parts are interrelated and very task- and context sensitive. Task complexity and contextual complexity have influence on the required regulation processes, which are related to both performance and well-being outcomes of the system. The relationships of features are very sensitive and fluid, and their balance unstable. For example, if a group and its members are physically mobile, the realisations of the other features are contingent on it; mobility indicates more locations, an increased number of people to meet, and a greater need to co-ordinate joint actions for collaboration.

Mobile e-Workforce in Europe. Traditional telework is very unlikely to achieve the significance for the labour market that was predicted only a few years ago. Instead networked work environments will play a key role for economic competitiveness. Gareis and colleagues show that the number of mobile e-workers, i.e. workers who are physically mobile and use ICT-support for communication and collaboration has strongly increased (see also section 16.2.1). For policy-making it will be essential to establish quantitative evidence about the effect of eWork on key variables of competitiveness such as productivity, innovativeness, and time-to-market. While recent research has provided insight into impacts of traditional telework on, for example, sustainable development, only little is known about the effects of mobile virtual work. In addition, policy-makers need more information about the barriers and facilitators of eWork applications. It is suggested that the take-up of eWork as well as tele-collaboration is negatively correlated with the degree of employment protection legislation, and also with an index of risk aversion at national level.

Mobile work legislation and agreements. Blurring of the borders between work and family or leisure time challenges the way working time legislation functions. Helle argues however in her chapter that new concepts to describe present and future phenomena in the field of organisational research and practice should not automatically be reflected in labour law, despite pressure to develop new legislation.

Major challenges are faced in legislation on working time and on health and safety, where there is an increasing need to tackle problems of stress. Distributed working locations do pose major challenges to personnel policy, which has to be even more transparent than before, and questions of equality between personnel in different locations will certainly arise. Challenges are also posed by the increase of cross-border working situations and the disappearance of the boundary between employment relationships and self-employed work. The position of many self-employed workers is precarious and unclear. The protection of the privacy of workers needs a European framework before monitoring practices become disproportionate for the purpose. Recently a European framework regulation has been developed concerning telehomework, and this covers quite some new work setting. It is therefore debatable whether separate new regulations should be developed for the case that a worker performs his or her job somewhere outside the employer's premises.

Part two, 'mobility at work', contains a series of chapters describing various cases of mobile and virtual work, analysing its functioning, its effects and testing new design strategies.

Conditions for mobilising individual work. Perry's and Brodie's chapter shows that mobile workers make ample use of the mobile tools, not for their primary work task, but for planning ahead, making use of travelling time, building and exploiting communities of practice, maintaining an awareness of colleagues and organisational changes, and managing and connecting their private and working lives. This is what is called 'mobilisation work activities', i.e. activities for organizing and coordinating the primary work activities.

By providing flexible opportunities for action and adaptable resources, users of mobile technology can be given access to a different and richer set of mechanisms for interaction. In this sense, a formal mobile information system that requires a particular form of engagement to perform mobile virtual work will probably fail because it does not support existing practices and contexts. The work itself is not virtual, but by making resources and technologies available, work can be conducted 'as if normally'.

A large part of the connectivity that is required and used by mobile workers is directed towards remote *people*, and not remote *things,* e.g. documents and remote devices. What is seen is a great deal of social interaction and community building, activities that cannot be reduced to simple goal driven action. The organisation then, as a closed commercial entity or open community of practice, is clearly a valuable informational resource for enabling the mobilisation of work. This aspect of connectivity is not, however, supported by most mobile technologies, apart from the mobile telephone, which appears to be the most common MVW device in use.

Enhancing collaboration within mobile virtual work. Wilson expresses the feeling that the push of technology development rather than the real pull of real users' need might be at work when speaking about new ambient collaborative technologies. He warns about 'developer euphoria' and about the ideas of self-appointed visionaries that the whole of Europe will be wired into a collaborative 'Grid', which is part of a knowledge economy with open knowledge availability and exchange, employing ambient intelligence.

Collaboration in its true sense has several critical components, and these must be supported by new systems of mobile virtual work, both organisational and technical systems. Good team working requires for instance that people can orient themselves, participate in team activities and apply distributed leadership. Collaborating teams must be supported in the handling of rich, high quality, open, flexible and yet disciplined communication, the latter requiring that messages are acknowledged and repeated where necessary, and that coordination underpins this communication such that appropriate information is passed on when required. Collaborators should be able to monitor and be aware of each other's activities, to give and receive feedback from colleagues, to fill in and back up team members who are unable to complete a particular task, to be sensitive to each other's workload and performance and to be able to adapt and reform as a team according to changes in the environment. These requirements have implications for tools and their functionality.

Wilson claims that collaboration within mobile virtual work will not always be carried out and supported remotely via ever more sophisticated ICT. Many mobile workers will continue to perform successfully using fairly traditional methods of communication, and others will carry out their activities through face-to-face contacts supported by technical tools when appropriate. It is the depth and quality of collaboration that is critical and it is this that we need to understand better.

Human-centred design and usability of mobile work systems. To create mobile work systems that enable efficient and effective work in a new way or to improve current work processes, it is necessary not only to focus on technology but also to look at the users, their qualifications and tasks, as well as to include aspects of work organisation in an integrative design approach.

Schmidt and Luczak provide a structured and model-based framework that includes a human-centred and task-oriented design approach. A two-dimensional design space is introduced. In the first dimension, five aspects of mobile work are differentiated, which are: (1) mobility of the individual, (2) mobility of work contents, (3) mobility of working tools, (4) mobility of work relations, and (5) virtual mobility. The second axis comprises aspects of technology, organisation and personnel (TOP). This framework can be used as a guideline to order and integrate the aspects of mobile work. The authors illustrate their approach with an example of the design of augmented equipment for mobile maintenance personnel.

According to *Johansson and colleagues,* in some occupations work is and has always been physically mobile, such as in home care and in technical maintenance fieldwork. For these jobs, technical support systems must of necessity be mobile, otherwise they cannot be used at all. In many such jobs there is, however, existing tools lack usability. The authors discuss various aspects of usability for mobile systems and argue that improvements in usability can result in new application areas and also promote the development of adequate work organisations and their efficiency.

They note, however, that conflicts arise between requirements for interface that support usability and what is technically possible in a mobile context. For example, the handling of large amounts of information requires a large screen, something, which generally is impossible in a mobile system. In many such situations a compromise must be found between what is useful, from an information retrieval point of view, and what is efficient to use in a mobile context.

The design process of usable support systems should be based on a detailed description and analysis of the work context, because usability criteria especially in a mobile environment are context dependent to a great extent. Moreover, it is also necessary to involve the potential end-users in the process since they have detailed knowledge about local needs and requirements. It is necessary to work according to an iterative development model, since the exact requirements are not known in advance. Design decisions can often be based on heuristic rules, but these must be formulated for a mobile situation and for the actual work context.

Wiethoff et al. use home health care as an example of a branch with important opportunities for developing mobile work arrangements that improve the quality of life and the quality of work. The reasons for the slow uptake of ICT in this branch are related to the limitations of the patients, and to the organisational limitations faced by health care workers. Wiethoff et al. applied a participative design method, combined with an ethnographic approach to design a socio-technical system for stakeholders with very diverse needs, and very limited acquaintance with new technologies. This approach was successful for translating requirements and needed functionalities into very clear ideas about the contents of the design.

Well-being and stress outcomes in mobile and virtual work. The increased degree of mobility and other factors of contextual and task complexity are supposed to be mental load factors from the viewpoints of well-being and stress. It is however not exactly known whether the consequences are principally positive, i.e. flow and motivation, or negative, i.e. fatigue and stress.

Richter, Meyer and Sommer refer to their own studies showing that work in virtual teams has more enriched job characteristics, such as variety of organisational tasks, learning requirements and level of participation, than traditional jobs. This could imply the potential of health and personality promotion. However, their results show that enriched job characteristics in the context of virtual teams are also associated with increased symptoms of job stress! There appears to be a curvilinear relation between enriched job demands and mental health. This 'over-enrichment' may cause excessive demands by requiring too many qualifications and skills and through informational and social overload. They underline, however, that job design should *not* try to decrease job demands and complexity in mobile virtual work. Rather employees' competence to cope with its precarious aspects should be improved. Moreover, the quality of teamwork has an important impact not only on performance, but also on job satisfaction in virtual mobile teams.

Mobile virtual work in practice. A case of a globally distributed corporation and four cases on team level in large enterprises show that mobile virtual work is already a reality in different business areas.

Niitamo describes how scenarios were built in Nokia corporation to mobilise its employees and to optimise the use of available competencies in different sites and time zones, in order to shorten the product creation process. Nokia's core competencies exist very much in its innovative capability to design and develop new products for the global market. One of the competitive advantages in this market is to provide solutions and products in a short time frame. Most product creation processes involve several partners, subcontractors and client sites, which should be orchestrated adequately.

The assumption behind the basic scenario was that managing a global product creation process will rapidly become the major competitive advantage to its holder. Success will depend on the ability to create and apply management tools as well as collaborative technologies. The scenario has the following elements: global talent and innovation capability distributed over many global locations, strong work mobility but limited labour mobility, utilization of the whole 24 hour cycle, new innovative ways of global partner collaboration, and new collaborative working environments. Through applying this scenario, Nokia has been able to develop successful mobile virtual work settings.

Verburg et al. present four case studies, dealing with customs agents, automation and support technicians, service engineers, and home care nurses. Overall the cases show a positive picture concerning the application of mobile solutions in practice. Employees stress the benefits of their mobile work. One of the possible barriers is the lack of user involvement as in the Swedish case, but as long as users are involved, mobile virtual work is perceived as a positive change. Potential barriers or possible downsides, such as limitations of decision capabilities, a lack of employee autonomy, and stronger propensity for control of employee behaviour, did not feature much in the cases. Since such factors have very negative impacts on employee motivation, they remain a point of concern for the deployment of future mobile virtual work settings.

Part 3, 'Organisational strategies', deals with the relations between MVW developments and organisational or sectoral characteristics.

Knowledge management in mobile work. Using data from three case studies, Corso argues that knowledge sharing by mobile employees requires new knowledge management strategies. These strategies, however, have to vary according to task complexity. In routine jobs, e.g. maintenance, knowledge management can effectively be done through operations guides, manuals, codification and reporting. In non-routine jobs like consulting and sales, knowledge management should focus on person-to-person communication. When the knowledge management strategy is consistent with task characteristics, mobile virtual workers' satisfaction appears to be highest.

Diffusion of mobile work and services. Lindmark and colleagues have observed that in spite of the availability of fruitful applications for mobile work, there appeared to be many examples of slow adoption. This was the more remarkable because the innovations provided tangible and often measurable benefits to the customer organisations, such as improved efficiency of operations, in particular cost-cutting and improved service to the end customers. They investigated, therefore, disablers and enablers of the development and diffusion of services for mobile work. Their empirical observations revealed several issues related to strategic resources, technology, economics and marketing.

The first set of disablers was related to the capabilities of the customer organisations. The benefits were difficult to absorb - at least initially - for the main user group, such as truck drivers. In fact, several users experienced disutilities, such as loss of personal freedom - the "Big Brother" effect. In addition, applications were often perceived as difficult to start using, because competences to use these systems were generally low. For the management of the companies, system integration appeared to be a time-consuming and costly process, because of the complexity of the applications. Complexity also made the applications difficult for customers to understand and to relate to. In addition, technological complexity implied value-chain complexity. A large number of actors had to interact and make their products compatible. In many cases their roles were unclear and the various business models were incompatible or unviable. Clearly, there seemed to be a coordination problem. A final set of factors related to costs and pricing. Because of this, customers were initially reluctant to adopt the new systems, despite the fact that suppliers could show viable business cases for an investment.

All in all, the study points at the diffusion of MVW systems as the weakest function in the innovation process.

Mobile work and new business practice. In the final and very thought provoking chapter Schaffers and colleagues explore mobile workplace innovations and their success factors, focusing on different levels of innovation: human and organisational issues, industry drivers and technological trends. Also different levels of analysis were taken into account, i.e. the individual, organisational and industry level, trying to identify criteria for the successful integration of MVW into company business models in various sectors. The driving factors for mobile collaborative workplaces in selected business areas - automotive, aerospace and construction - were explored in order to identify prospects for innovation. They conclude that business drivers for mobile and collaborative work are very different across sectors. In all sectors, mobile work in its narrow sense of mobility enhancement of individual workers will be an important innovation in individual-oriented support services like sales, customer relations management (CRM), repair and maintenance. Mobile work in terms of virtual team collaboration will be important for sectors where work objects - like aeroplanes and cars - are mobile, and / or where the problem at hand requires individuals to intensively communicate with specialists at different locations and different time zones, like in R&D work and also in complex maintenance tasks.

The authors then explore a framework of future mobile workplace scenarios, in order to understand the underlying forces of innovation and to build a realistic vision as a basis for innovation strategy, resulting in a concrete roadmap of challenges and milestones in key areas of mobile work (see next section).

16.4 Scenarios for the future

What can we expect concerning the further development of mobile and virtual work, of networked organisations and organisational networks? It is evident that we are on a threshold of something new, which is not yet fully recognised, understood and managed. Schaffers and colleagues present in chapter 15, the results of scenario development in the framework of the EU-Mosaic project. On the short term, it is expected that the number of mobile workers will increase, while the types of mobile workers remain unchanged, i.e. managers, sales, consultants, support technicians, scientists and academics. Tele-maintenance, telemedicine, and all remote working activities will call for wireless access by employees to report continuously on remote locations. The individual with his requirements for usability and usefulness will be the main driving force in the design of mobile work. Mobile access will take place primarily through mobile phones and PDAs, since bandwidth allows only for audio communication and image or document sharing.

It is expected that on the medium term, ca 2008, agile business networks start to emerge, based on smart collaborative workspaces. This implies that in the design of mobile work, requirements of collaboration and coordination, as well as organisational requirements become dominant. Mobile work will then be fully integrated into business processes and mobile devices seamlessly integrated with desktop-based systems. Connectivity and bandwidth will allow for rich multimedia sharing, but the implication of these developments are that the costs associated with mobility will gradually increase.

On the long term, e.g. 2010-13, major changes in the organisation of work are expected. The number of mobile workers will increase even more, also in the form of independent experts that can be recruited "on demand" by any networked business organisation. But this will also imply that the distances mobile workers travel will be or even become more limited, resulting in micro-mobility. Using mobile information technology will become an established cultural practice and mobile workers will have easy access to the on-demand, service-based mobile cooperation support. A ubiquitous computing infrastructure will be accessible anywhere, anytime and the present day computers are expected to be replaced by nonintrusive, attentive interfaces.

16.4.1 A European vision

For the European Union, the vision of mobile and virtual work should be to help in solving certain problems the EU is facing like low productivity, unbalanced development between European countries and dissatisfaction of Europeans with their working and living conditions. In the Lisbon declaration, the following objective was set for 2010: *"To become the most competitive and dynamic knowledge-based economy in the world, capable of sustainable economic growth with more and better jobs and greater social cohesion."* Whether this objective will be achieved or not within this period, Europe has to meet serious challenges in the time ahead. By itself Europe is a wide market area providing high demands of products and services and consequently bases to create jobs. On the other hand, there is the ongoing global relocation of mostly low quality standardized jobs to countries outside the EU resulting in job losses, while at the same time people from many regions and from rural areas need to be included in the workforce. The development of more efficient technologies, the shift from industrial to knowledge work and from traditional companies to flexible network organisations are in this context both a problem because of its job and skill losses, and an opportunity. The opportunity is provided by the fact that knowledge work can be done at a distance with the help of ICT and that networked companies of small and medium-sized firms and individual freelancers can find ample job opportunities. The EU is therefore, in its present and coming research programs, supporting many research projects concerning new infrastructures, new applications and services, and new organisational arrangements.

The EU-research program is driven by the vision that the economy should move from an organisation-centric to a human-centric perspective. This implies that new living and working environments for all have to be created, in which productivity and quality of life have to be combined. In this society, the emphasis is expected to fall more on (work) 'communities' and less on organisations. Technically speaking, human-centeredness implies independence from location, time and device, and therefore ambient intelligence that supports communication and collaboration anywhere, shared workspaces, enhanced social interaction, smart work environments and easy knowledge exchange and accumulation.

16.5 Conclusion

What have we learned about mobile virtual work? We have found answers for some of our research questions presented in chapter one. We now know what the building blocks of new work settings are. But we do not know much as yet concerning the social and human outcomes of mobile and virtual work, except for some suggestions and indications. One of the strong points of this book is the provision of many concrete case examples of mobile work practices, technologies and services. Through these examples the variety of MVW has been charted and a typology of MVW settings has been developed in this final chapter. The implication is, however, that effects differ and that development strategies should be differentiated.

Ergonomic requirements have been discovered, together with design methods that promise to lead to usable and useful systems if attention is paid to the contexts and the user needs. The relations between mobility and virtual cooperation has been analysed and some implications for managing MVW workers have been found. Finally, scenarios concerning expected future mobile virtual work settings have been formulated.

Concerning many questions the available data are, however, still very limited, partly because the developments are still in their infancy, partly because we have not covered all the available evidence. Not much can, therefore, be said about e.g. negative consequences for workers in terms of stress, labour conditions, employment or security. The cases discussed in this book do not point to severe problems is this respect, but these studies may be biased and not cover all relevant areas. Moreover, many western companies, in the IT industry as well in other sectors, are outsourcing activities such as call centres or software development to countries like India or China. There are indications that labour conditions in these places are quite different from what we have encountered in this volume.

Many questions we posed in the first chapter have not received full answers. We do not know much yet about required skills and competences, about how to coordinate and lead mobile virtual professionals, about knowledge exchange and organisational learning in an MVW environment? Which new business models should be developed to profit from the MVW developments, in terms of efficiency, innovation, effectiveness and sustainability? And how can remote areas benefit optimally from mobile systems and virtual work arrangements? In addition, we need insights into the technology and tools to support these aspects, and in the (social, organisational, economic) obstacles and conditions for introduction of MVW systems. The effects of MVW, but also the conditions have to be studied on the level of the individual and his/her task performance, at the group and cooperation level, at the level of the organisation and its strategies, and finally at sectoral and national level.

All these issues and questions are challenging, both for practitioners who should develop and experiment with new strategies in this area, and for researchers who want to analyse the phenomena systematically and test good practices. The real challenge, however, is for practioners and researchers to exchange their experiences and to cooperate in the development of viable and sustainable mobile virtual work systems.

Index

List of Contributors

Andriessen, J.H. Erik, Professor
Department of Work and Organisational Psychology, Delft University of Technology
Jaffalaan 5,
2628 BX Delft
The Netherlands

Brodie, Jackie, Dr.
Centre for Entrepreneurship, School of Management, Napier University,
Craiglockhart Campus,
Edinburgh, EH14 1DJ
UK

Brodt, Torsten, MSc.
Institute of Media and Communication Management,
University of St. Gallen
Blumenbergplatz 9,
9000 St. Gallen
Switzerland

Boxtel, Rogier van, MSc
TIBCO Software Inc.
Robijnstraat 76,
1812 RB Alkmaar
The Netherlands

Carver, Liz, Dr.
BAE Systems
P.O. Box 5 Filton,
Bristol BS34 7QW
United Kingdom

Corso, Mariano, Dr.
Department of Management Engineering (DIG), Polytechnic University of Milan
Piazza Leonardo da Vinci 32,
20133 Milano
Italy

Fernando, Terrence, Professor
Future Workspaces Research Centre, University of Salford
University Road, Salford M5 4WT
United Kingdom

Gareis, Karsten, Dr.
Empirica Gesellschaft für Kommunikations- und Technologieforschung GmbH
Oxfordstrasse. 2, 53111 Bonn
Germany

Helle, Minna, Master of Laws
AKAVA - The Confederation of Unions for Academic Professionals in Finland
Rautatieläisenkatu 6,
00520 Helsinki
Finland

Hyrkkänen, Ursula, MSc.
Turku Polytechnic
Kaskenkatu 5,
20700 Turku
Finland

Johansson, Niklas, MSc.
Department of Information
Technology, Human-Computer Interaction Uppsala University
Box 337, 75105 Uppsala
Sweden

Lilischkis, Stefan, Dr.
Empirica Gesellschaft für
Kommunikations- und Technologieforschung GmbH
Oxfordstrasse 2, 53111 Bonn
Germany

Luczak, Holger, Professor
Institute of Industrial Engineering and Ergonomics,
RWTH Aachen University
Bergdriesch 27, 52062 Aachen
Germany

Lind, Torbjörn, MSc.
UsersAward, Swedish Labour
Organization
105 53 Stockholm
Sweden

Lindmark, Sven, Dr.
Chalmers University of Technology
Vasa Building 2
412 96 Göteborg
Sweden

Magnusson, Mats, Professor
Department of Technology
Management and Economics,
Chalmers Univ.of Technology
Vera Sandbergs Allé 8, Vasa
Hus 2, 412 96 Göteborg
Sweden

Martini, Antonella, Dr.
Faculty of Engineering, University of Pisa
Via Diotisalvi, 2, 56126 Pisa
Italy

Meyer, Jelka, MSc.
Department of Psychology,
Dresden University of Technology
Zellescher Weg 17,
D-01062 Dresden
Germany

Meulenbroek, Thierry, MSc.
OPTA,
Postbus 90420,
2509 LK the Hague
The Netherlands

Mentrup, Alexander, MSc.
Empirica Gesellschaft für
Kommunikations- und Technologieforschung GmbH
Oxfordstrasse 2, 53111 Bonn
Germany

Niitamo, Veli-Pekka, MSc., MA.
Center for Knowledge and Innovation Research (CKIR)/
Nokia, Helsinki School of
Economics
PO Box 1210, 00101 Helsinki
Finland

Pellegrini, Luisa, Dr.
Faculty of Engineering, University of Pisa
Via Diotisalvi, 2,
56126 Pisa
Italy

Perry, Mark, Dr.
School of IS, Computing and Mathematics, Brunel University
Uxbridge
Middlesex, UB8 3PH
United Kingdom

Renga, Filippo, Dr.
Department of Management, Economics and Industrial Engineering Politec University of Milan
Piazza Leonardo da Vinci 32, 20133 Milano
Italy

Richter, Peter, Professor
Department of Psychology, Dresden University of Technology
Zellescher Weg 17,
D-01062 Dresden
Germany

Sandblad, Bengt, Professor
Department of Information Technology, Human-Computer Interaction
Uppsala University,
P.O.Box 337,
751 05 Uppsala
Sweden

Schaffers, Hans, Dr.
Telematica Instituut
P.O.Box 589,
7500 AN Enschede
The Netherlands

Slagter, Robert, Dr.
Telematica Instituut
P.O. Box 589,
7500 AN Enschede
The Netherlands

Stafleu, Hans, Dr.
TNO Information and Communication Technology
Brassersplein 2,
P.O. Box 5050,
2600 GB Delft
The Netherlands

Schmidt, Ludger, Dr.
Institute of Industrial Engineering and Ergonomics,
RWTH Aachen University
Bergdriesch 27,
52062 Aachen
Germany

Sommer, Fanny, MSc.
Department of Psychology, Dresden University of Technology
Zellescher Weg 17,
D-01062 Dresden
Germany

Testa, Stefania, Professor
Communication, Computer and System Sciences Department (DIST),
University of Genoa
Viale Causa 13,
16100 Genoa
Italy

Vartiainen, Matti, Professor
  Laboratory of Work Psychol-
  ogy and Leadership, Helsinki
  University of Technology
  P.O.Box 5500,
  02015 TKK Espoo
  Finland

Verburg, Robert M, Dr.
  Department of Work and Or-
  ganisational Psychology, Delft
  University of Technology
  Jaffalaan 5,
  2628 BX Delft
  The Netherlands

Wiethoff, Marion, Dr.
  Department of Work and Or-
  ganisational Psychology, Delft
  University of Technology
  Jaffalaan 5, 2628 Delft
  The Netherlands

Wilson, John R, Professor
  Institute for Occupational Er-
  gonomics, University of Not-
  tingham
  Nottingham NG7 2RD
  United Kingdom